WORLD BALLET AND DANCE
1992–93

WORLD BALLET AND DANCE
1992–93

An International Yearbook

under the auspices of
Conseil International de la Danse, UNESCO

Founder Editor
BENT SCHØNBERG

Associate Editors
ELIZABETH CHARMAN
SANJOY ROY
CRISTINA SCHØNBERG

DANCE BOOKS
Cecil Court London

Published in 1993 by Dance Books Ltd,
9 Cecil Court, London WC2N 4EZ

© 1993 Bent Schønberg

ISBN 1 85273 042 0

Printed and bound in Great Britain by
H. Charlesworth & Co. Ltd, Huddersfield

A CIP catalogue record for this book is available from the British Library

Contents

Illustrations

Bad Russian Companies and Swedish Legs

Bent Schønberg

There is a saying that it took the farmers of Bresse two hundred years to make the world's best chicken, and it took industry just ten years to destroy it.

It seems as if the Russians have been inspired by this. At least they try – and try hard – to throw away in the course of a few years what their forebears at the Maryinsky, Bolshoi and other fine theatres have spent generations building up in ballet, work and culture. Let's face it, it's natural, we would all do it. You can't get any food, booze, tulle, mascara – you name it, they don't have it – so they go West to earn money where the money is.

But, unfortunately, the good Russians have not yet fully understood what capitalism is. It is not only to do with earning money, as they seem to think, it also has something to do with selling a good product; and most of what we have been presented with in the West since the liberation of the former Soviet Union has not been worth many kopeks. Several of these strange companies, which have continually rolled over us in waves upon waves, have shown productions which just a few years ago would have earned those responsible several years stay in a Siberian salt-mine – and well would they have deserved it!

It is doubly tragic that this understandable but short-sighted policy should come at a time when ballet in the richer countries of the world is on the wane. It has now become very fashionable and chic to go and hear opera, but no longer that out-moded thing called ballet. Opera-goers will pay astronomical sums – compared with tickets for Terpsichore's humble servants' shows – to fulfil their pleasures. Not only that, they will happily sit through five hours of constant singing, whereas most people would scream at the mere thought of attending a ballet performance for more than three hours at the most (with Béjart's *Ring* as the only exception).

Another – not just a trend but an accepted fact – is that the audiences in many countries in Western Europe will only watch full-length ballets and shy away from triple bills. It seems that the Americans can again teach us a thing or two. They make their triple bills interchangeable, so that if you especially like three particular choreographic works and they don't all appear on the first night, then two of them may be danced the following

EN
O

Ballett der Deutschen Oper Berlin

BerlinBallet

Prof. Götz Friedrich

Peter Schaufuss

June 29-July 4

Giselle
The Rite of Spring
Swansong
The Opening
(British Premiere)

Box Office 071 836 3161
Credit Cards 071 240 5258

Presented by
English National Opera
at the London Coliseum
St Martin's Lane WC2

Poster for the Ballett der Deutsche Oper's production of *Giselle*.

night, and after about a week all three may appear together in the same programme. Here we have capitalism put into practice – it's as easy as that. It is strange that so many European companies have not yet learnt such plain and simple business sense; but necessity is the mother of invention, so I hope that the recession might bring about one good thing and teach the ballet managers to strike out in new directions.

A further question is: has time run out for the old classical ballets? Well, it has been proven that nothing – not even the greatest lack of talent – has been able to kill off *Lac* and that there will always be some dreadful children who can't get through the festivities in connection with the birthday of the little Jesus-child without a dose of even the worst *Nutcracker*.

But does *Sleeping Beauty* still have the same appeal for young people today as it did 25 years ago? Isn't the truth simply that the young ones – and it is they who count, not old fossils such as yours respectfully – are not interested in classical ballet and prefer modern dance? Is time and taste running out for big companies, with their same old five or ten ballets which they put on season after season? The Ballett der Deutsche Oper at least tried to be in the mould of the younger generations. The poster for *Giselle* during its London visit was clearly inspired by USA. It showed 'tits' on a – maybe ducal? – attractive torso, and that could, of course, have lured in some hussars. But it might be doubted whether they are going to be the balletophiles of the future, and one's imagination staggers at the thought of how a poster for *L'Après-midi d'un faune* would look in Berlin. However, if that is the direction ballet is going to take now, you can be sure that the Dutch and the Danes are going to be taking the lead.

In Sweden, Eva Ramel, a physiotherapist, decided to find out how well dancers were. The answer was: not well. Initially she wanted to examine how many were healthy and happy, and how they could be so with a job with such great physical and psychological demands. The poor lady was in for a shock. The 128 dancers from the three largest companies in the country had problems with the back (21%), problems with feet (65%) and problems with the neck (34%). But worse was to come; it was shown that during the last four years the number of registered injuries had quadrupled – and the true figures were far, far higher, but the dancers did not dare to talk about them, or seek professional help for these, feeling that they might put a performance in danger of being cancelled, or fearing that they might lose their job.

There did not seem to be any substantial difference in the number of casualties between men and women, but, surprisingly, there were just as many bad backs among female dancers as among male.

It is well known that one can manage a psychological load better if one can influence one's situation; but of all the dancers involved only three thought they were the deciding ones in any given situation. Fifty thought that they had a part in decision-making, but at least 75 felt that they had nothing to do or say concerning their work.

The investigation has horrified ballet people in Scandinavia. The first result is that very soon a medical centre for dance will be opened for the whole of Sweden, possibly at Karolinska Hospital in Stockholm. It will be partly sponsored by one of the country's big insurance companies and staffed by doctors, orthopaediatricians, physiotherapists and other experts, and the idea is that any dancer – from professional companies or private – from the whole country could be sent to this centre as necessary. The centre will not only draw on therapeutic experience from around the country's ballet companies, it will also do preventive work.

The discussion which has come about as a result of the survey showed that nobody wanted to attack or change the art itself, or to replace the existing repertory with other less demanding or risk-filled works. But a lot of people have been up in arms demanding better conditions and less stress for the dancers. For instance, someone has proposed that the ballet at the Royal Opera in Stockholm should be expanded to double the present number of dancers. What a sound and lovely idea – but try and tell that to Ministers of Finance or private sponsors!

Many of our American readers have complained that we have not written enough about USA. As you will see, this year we have expanded the American section rather heavily, so I hope everybody will be content now.

Another new item is an article about Estonia. We are happy to bid this country welcome, and in the years to come we will without doubt see reviews from other 'new' countries from the former Soviet Union.

We have again included South Africa. I wonder if we will next year?

And all is not bleak or black in the ballet world. Athens and Helsinki can be congratulated on new dance buildings, and if anyone thinks that the only interesting thing coming out of Sarasota, Florida, is an uncharming grunting genius from the tennis circuit, they are in for a surprise in the years to come if Eddy Toussaint's inspired and gifted company will continue to move up among the heavyweights.

As predicted, the sale of *World Ballet and Dance* went up with volume 3 – dramatically – we must say. This, combined with the even greater sale which we hope to achieve with volume 4, is the reason that for the fourth consecutive year we are able to keep the price of our book the same as when we started, a fact of which we are incredibly proud, as we are of the fact that the Conseil International de la Danse, UNESCO, and its dynamic president, M. Milorad Miskovitch, have graciously decided that this International Yearbook may come under the auspices of the Council, an honour for which we are heartily thankful. We shall try every year to live up to this confidence and we hope to continue to deliver a better and better product.

PART I

Two Appreciations

Sir Kenneth MacMillan

Rudolf Nureyev

Sir Kenneth MacMillan

Peter Brinson

On 29 October 1992, during a performance at the Royal Opera House, Covent Garden, of one of MacMillan's greatest works, British ballet - classical ballet throughout the world – lost its greatest living choreographic communicator. More than that. Kenneth MacMillan represented the most progressive trend in late twentieth-century classical choreography, on screen as well as on stage. He fought to maintain the integrity of his work against opposition at home and abroad, arguing his case in words as well as movement. He was - as Stendhal said of Vigano, and Garrick implied of Noverre - the glory of his profession, its champion and paragon.

Can so much be true, even of a world-class choreographer? MacMillan was a rebel. A product of the Royal Ballet, schooled in what is regarded everywhere as an establishment art, MacMillan nevertheless used his choreographic genius to illuminate through dance themes of great contemporary relevance - fear and oppression in *The Burrow*, sexual abuse in *The Invitation*, the waste of youth in war in *Gloria*, the imprisonment of individuals within social systems in *Romeo and Juliet* and *Mayerling* (the work being performed when he died). Through such works he exerted enormous influence upon younger choreographers and upon younger elements of audiences in Europe, the United Sates and Britain. Perhaps this is why his ideas excited so much resistance from bodies like the Board of Covent Garden and its ballet sub-committee, and from older members of audiences in Britain and the United States, bastions of establishment thinking.

The perception which lay behind his ideas developed out of personal struggles. Growing up in poverty in Scotland then in eastern England, he escaped this background only by secret lessons from a generous ballet teacher, by immersion in the programmes of a local cinema, then by guile through a letter to Ninette de Valois. He signed the letter as if from his father, seeking an audition at Sadler's Wells School. He was accepted, becoming one of the original members of Sadler's Wells Theatre Ballet when it was created in 1946. Thereby he absorbed the atmosphere of experiment, enthusiasm and audience contact which surrounded the Sadler's Wells companies in those days.

Two years later he moved to Sadler's Wells Ballet at Covent Garden but returned to the Theatre Ballet in 1952. I met him there through the Theatre Ballet director, Peggy van Praagh, who was the first to encourage his choreographic talent. My recollection is of a tall, obviously talented dancer with a terrific jump, who was notable also as a striking dancer-actor in John

Cranko's *The Lady and the Fool* and other ballets in the early 1950s. I remember, too, in the same period a set design he created for a ballet (I think by Peter Darrell) in a Sunday evening of new choreography for Ballet Workshop. Ballet Workshop was the first, and very fruitful, attempt by the Rambert family to create a platform for new choreography at their Mercury Theatre in Notting Hill Gate. In a sense, all professional choreographic workshops in Britain today descend from that idea.

MacMillan showed then the sensitivity of a visual artist; but the first indication of choreographic talent came through another workshop organized by David Poole and dancers of the Theatre Ballet at Sadler's Wells Theatre in 1953. His *Somnabulism* introduced a new choreographer, seemingly ready-formed without any long induction of trial and error. MacMillan's choreography was clear-cut, precise, highly original and very demanding of his dancers. Straight away he joined his friend John Cranko as a maker of ballet for Sadler's Wells Theatre Ballet and for Covent Garden. It seemed extraordinary that the comparatively young British ballet should produce within a short time two choreographers who would achieve international stature as major artists. Both choreographers ascribed their early development to the creative atmosphere and guidance established by Peggy van Praagh in the Theatre Ballet.

Quite soon the themes he pursued most often appeared in MacMillan's work: the outsider, the rebel, the down-trodden, the unhappy. His choice of jazz music by Stan Kenton for *Somnabulism*, unique at the time as music for ballet, indicated too that his creative practice would depart from accepted norms. So it turned out. *The Invitation* in 1960 was the first time sex and sexuality were treated so openly in classical ballet. His collaboration with Gillian Freeman as librettist for *Mayerling* in 19776 and *Isadora* in 1981 departed from the practice of most choreographers today, who insist on devising plot as well as choreography. Even his inheritance of Petipa's three- and four-act ballets of princes and princesses he translated into evening-long dramas of human conflict, like *Manon* and *Mayerling*, appropriate to today's postmodern world.

These departures went down well in Europe, though he hated his time directing the Deutsche Oper in Berlin from 1966–69. His ballets went down less well in the United States and were a source of argument and friction at Covent Garden. The frustration this caused him and the obvious establishment preference for Frederick Ashton's ballets, which he felt deeply, led for a time to a serious drink problem. It was dissipated as he achieved clearer recognition and the stability of a felicitous marriage in 1974 with the birth of a daughter.

Signs of success increased. He was director of the Royal Ballet from 1970-77, was awarded the honorary degree of Doctor of Music by Edinburgh University in 1975, became resident choreographer of the Royal Ballet in

1977, was knighted in 1983 and made Associate Director of American Ballet Theatre in 1984. When he died, on the night the Royal Ballet revived *Mayerling*, the finest example of achievement in his three-act genre, Birmingham Royal Ballet was presenting his *Romeo and Juliet*, and his ballets were appearing in other repertories in Britain and abroad. His reputation as the greatest living choreographic communicator was clearly established.

The humanism of his inspiration and emphasis on the human condition derived from personal experience. Often the zany, eccentric or fantastic were mingled to throw light on this condition. *Somnabulism*'s three characters apparently suffer from anxiety, monotony and premonition, but wake up to find they have been dreaming. Five years later *The Burrow* (also reproduced recently by the Birmingham Royal Ballet) explored the tension of persecuted people in a situation resembling the story of Anne Frank. Its many characters, refugees in one room from an outside terror, are defined precisely in the choreography, although the effect is one of improvisation. Their outbursts of fear, passion, temper arise from the threat of discovery.

MacMillan is, therefore, a poet of the oppressed. His exposé of polite society and establishment morals is presented in movements drawn from classical training, but with the clarity of early romantic artists. Sometimes the inner truthfulness of his choreography recalls for me the poetry of Shelley and Byron, or Géricault's *Raft of the Medusa* or, in a later period, Ibsen's plays.

The academic dance is his resource and inspiration so that, parallel with his social concern there runs a concern with the non-verbal communication of the human body. He explored all its movement possibilities. Early in his choreographic career, in *Agon* and *Le Baiser de la fée* to Stravinsky's music, the movements were angular, astringent, and abstract. Gradually, as his attitude matured, they acquired a more plastic quality. In *The Invitation* he said to me in 1960 'the movement is not nearly so broken, angular or sharp as it used to be, not sharp at all for the principal'. In *Romeo and Juliet*, in *Manon*, his great *Gloria* about the stupidities of war, in *Song of the Earth*, *Mayerling* and other later works, the line of the body became used more fully, running unbroken time and again through the whole length of stretched arms, legs and feet. The images flowed unhurriedly one from another. The vocabulary became economical and self-assured.

For me the change first became apparent in *The Rite of Spring* in 1962. The ballet had less of the sharpness and spikiness of his earlier work, however angular its sculptural effects remained. The assault was on the mind as much as on the heart, indicating an intellectual quality underpinning the emotion. In fact his creative process and assessment of the outside world seemed to combine intellect and emotion equally. 'There is a class system,' he said in an interview on BBC2 in April 1990, 'an old boy network to which I have never belonged and I never will . . . I am very interested in people . . .

in portraying the dilemma of people living and working with each other. That was not a very popular approach to ballet in the 1950s.'

It remains unpopular in some circles. The same BBC programme included an attack by the Anglo-American critic Clive Barnes on MacMillan's directorship of the Royal Ballet, another manifestation of Ashton nostalgia. When MacMillan succeeded Ashton as director of the Royal Ballet in 1970, he found his ideas resisted not only within the Royal Ballet and by some British audiences, but also by audiences in the United States, influenced by Barnes as much as anyone. Barnes failed to understand the British scene, where the problem lay not with MacMillan but with the Board of Covent Garden, fixed, like Barnes, in its worship of Ashton. The nature of the problem had already been demonstrated by the Board's reception of MacMillan's idea for a ballet to Mahler's *Das Lied von der Erde* in 1964. It was rejected. He took the idea to John Cranko in Stuttgart, where there emerged on 6 November 1965 *Song of the Earth*, one of MacMillan's finest works, now in the repertory of the Royal Ballet. It is a ballet which caught the changing mood of post-war Europe particularly clearly. If there was a decline in the Royal Ballet, as Barnes alleged, it derived from decisions of this kind by the Board.

'I prefer to explore the human psyche,' MacMillan continued to the BBC, 'I try to make people sometimes feel uncomfortable in the theatre . . . I have always been drawn to the narrative, to real people, and what they feel.' This implied addressing reality head-on, and may have been the nub of the problem for the Board. Ashton's concern, as he told me once, was for 'beauty'. Pursued with unfailing good taste, 'beauty' was unlikely to ruffle the social surface. Rather it could confirm the sweetness and stability of the world. MacMillan by contrast saw his work as a synthesis of life, with particular concern for the underdogs and, as he said, 'people at odds with world'. This for certain would make people (perhaps the Board and Clive Barnes?) 'sometimes feel uncomfortable in the theatre'.

Such attitudes and such toughness were not immediately apparent when you met MacMillan. The tall, shy figure, with prematurely grey hair and a fey voice, did not suggest the artist who could be brutal, when necessary, with dancers who did not measure up to his own professional standards. I worked with him at the beginning of the 1970s when I was directing the Royal Ballet's Ballet for All group. I saw and learned from the way he handled dancers. I noted also the strain of having to direct a large company as well as be its principal choreographer. He made the right decision to return to full-time choreography in 1976.

Almost always in creating a new ballet he started with the principal *pas de deux*. This would set the tone of what he planned and provide the emotional climax. It influenced what came before and would come after. Always he was inspired by dancers' bodies as well as by the music, by what

5

dancers themselves could contribute. 'I like my artists to find themselves in their role.' Early on in rehearsal he rarely dictated to his dancers. Lynn Seymour, his muse and the dancer he worked with most closely, contributed greatly to the creation of her roles. So, too, did Christopher Gable, with Seymour in *Romeo and Juliet,* and David Wall in *Mayerling*. A similar relationship was developing with Irek Mukhamedov, Darcey Bussell, and other dancers, who are losers like the rest of us from his passing.

It was the same with collaborators back-stage - Nicholas Georgiadis especially for design, and Richard Rodney Bennett for the music of *Isadora*. He drew on their ideas and shared his own ideas. Ideas came from other sources too: not only music, but also reading and films and pictures and just talking to friends. He never lost his early fascination with the cinema, and developed it in translating his ballet for television. Because of this, part of his legacy of ballet is preserved on film - the beautiful *Winter Dreams, Isadora*, substantial parts of *Mayerling*, other ballets.

Fundamentally, though, what counted were dancers and their bodies. 'As a choreographer', he said once to Clement Crisp and Mary Clarke, 'I look in the main for musicality and expressiveness of the body rather than a great technique, though I am grateful if it is there of course.' Attitudes of this kind, manifest in the rehearsal studio, were replicated outside in his concern for dancers and their work. 'He used to come out to see us on tour,' said Werdon Anglin, general manager of Ballet for All. 'He would ask me always how things were with our dancers. And he was generous in letting us use his work "if the dancers can do it".' As always, standards came first.

People say he was a master of *pas de deux* and of dances for small numbers of artists, less good at orchestrating larger numbers of *corps de ballet*. To a point this is true. I was never impressed by the street scenes of his *Romeo and Juliet*. Then I think of the crowd scenes, the *corps* in *Mayerling*, his extraordinary portrait of the corrupt Austrian court around Emperor Franz Josef and Crown Prince Rudolf. On a smaller scale, I think of *The Burrow*, also a remarkable orchestration of group movement. It was not true he could not orchestrate a *corps* - provided the idea moved him.

The idea, the importance of content and its communication, dominated his creative process. Either he started with the music, which suggested an idea, or, as in *The Invitation, Solitaire* and *Anastasia*, he found the music to realise the idea. He might draw from any source, including popular culture, as he did in *Elite Syncopations* to Scott Joplin's music. In this way he was classical ballet's effective answer to those trends in postmodern dance which emphasize movement over content.

One can be moved greatly, for certain, by an evening of works by Merce Cunningham, the leading exponent of postmodern trends. Such works, though, rarely illuminate the human condition, move the soul, or inflame the mind. MacMillan's mastery of movement and penetration of human emotion does just that. He pours his feeling for humanity and his own emotion into his *pas de deux*, strengthened by his own experience and the blessing of his marriage. Therefore his revelation of those areas of human communication which cannot be expressed in words extended the boundaries of dance art, and strengthened its place in contemporary society. In doing so he challenged and changed the established forms and ideology of classical ballet, especially in his last ballet, *The Judas Tree*, created in 1992. Set in a building site, its many layers of meaning, its mystery and images of contemporary life, above all its continuation of his concern for people, show a creativity in full flood, now forever lost. His legacy of humanity expressed through the beauty of human movement is his lasting memorial. That, and all his ballets. It was right that Westminster Abbey should be the place of his commemoration in February 1993. The huge Abbey was full.

This appreciation is based on an obituary by Peter Brinson which appeared in The Independent *on 31 October 1992.*

Rudolf Nureyev

Jann Parry

R udolf Nureyev defined himself by dancing. He knew from the moment he first saw ballet as a boy of seven that he had been born to dance. 'It was love at first sight', he said in his autobiography, 'but only through housebreaking'. His mother had managed to smuggle all four of her children into the Ufa Opera House for a New Year's Eve ballet performance.

He had to fight to achieve his ambition, defying his father, who beat him, and the Vaganova Ballet Academy authorities who tried to tame his rebellious spirit. 'All my life I had to gatecrash', he said, using another vivid and violent image. He gatecrashed his way into the Vaganova School in Leningrad at the late age of 17, insisted on being allowed to join the Kirov (instead of being sent back to Ufa) and then defected to the West at 23.

Photographs of him them show the same defiant expression he wore in the last tragic photographs on stage at the Paris Opéra, shortly before his death. The imperiously tilted head and flaring nostrils mask the panic of a wild creature refusing to surrender. A mocking, confident version of the same stare was caught on newsreel footage of his brief arrest in San Francisco, with Margot Fonteyn, on drugs charges: refusing to speak, he turned and winked at the camera.

He fought the debilitating effects of AIDS as fiercely as he resisted the onset of age. He hung on as long as he could to his hard-won classical technique, continuing to dance demanding roles into his fifties. He had known that he was HIV positive since 1984: to give up a role must have seemed an admission of weakness rather than a concession to ageing. He was aware that although his reputation may have suffered in the short term, his achievements would survive him.

He needed the challenge of performing. He kept going during his punishing tours of Mexico, the United States, Britain and Australia on massages, tea and soup. He never complained of pain or exhaustion, believing, like Fonteyn, that the public should never know the physical price a dancer pays for success. In his last years, he turned to conducting, calling it his 'third time to Golgotha to be crucified' (having been there already as a dancer and choreographer).

Studying scores and playing the piano or a portable electronic keyboard kept him stimulated – and conducting was another way of performing. He pulled himself round after a severe cardiac illness to conduct Prokofiev's *Romeo and Juliet* for a performance by American Ballet Theatre in New York and Mahler's *Song of a Wayfarer* for Patrick Dupond and Peter Schaufuss in Berlin.

The conductor' baton was for him like Prospero's magic wand, the last symbol of his art and power to enchant. His own ballet, *The Tempest*, made for The Royal Ballet in 1982, now seems an allegory of his career. In Shakespeare's play, Prospero renounces his power by breaking his staff; in Nureyev's ballet, Prospero (danced by Nureyev himself) was dragged reluctantly from his island, his wand snatched from him by Ariel. Caliban and Ariel were perhaps two halves of his own nature, dark and mercurial, atavistic and sophisticated. He was capable of terrible rages and of great sweetness. He had many loyal friends and fans, yet he was slow to trust. He held up the example of the much-loved dog which bit him when he was young, leaving a life-long scar on his lip.

Stories of his volatile temper and colourful language are legion. Yet dancers all over the world pay tribute to the encouragement he gave them, both in terms of advice and through the inspiration of his dancing. He appeared with countless companies, absorbing what they had to offer and giving them the benefit of his experience. He organized seasons in Paris, New York and London of 'Nureyev and Friends', appearing annually at the London Coliseum for ten years with different companies. Although some dancers may have resented being regarded as 'rent-a-corps', his presence gave them international exposure and the excitement of being on stage with one of the most magnetic personalities in the history of dance.

It sounds an easy cliché to say that he has taken his place alongside Nijinsky as the male dancer whose name is synonymous with ballet. But his legend is made of the same stuff. Like Nijinsky, he revolutionized the West's idea of the male dancer. He was admired as an athlete as well as an artist, idolized as a sexual icon as well as a fantastic, romantic spirit. Perhaps his greatest achievement is to have touched the lives of so many people, whether or not they were able to see him perform.

PART II

Music and dance

The musician's view

Insights into music and musicality at the Royal Ballet

Howard Friend and Stephanie Jordan in interview with
Barry Wordsworth, Philip Gammon and Anthony Twiner.

Much has been written about the role of music and musicians in the ballet, about the importance of music, the tensions between the demands of dance and music, even the subservience of music in ballet. But the picture remains incomplete. In interviews with the Royal Ballet's music director Barry Wordsworth and the two conductor/rehearsal pianists Philip Gammon and Anthony Twiner, we tried to find out more about how different choreographers have approached music, how they, as musicians themselves, work with different dancers, and about the ballet world's conception and understanding of their collaborative art.

Here is the musician's view, couched in musician's terms (terms, incidentally, that are often more precise than those of dancers and choreographers). The interviews raise the issue that, too often, time and money work against musicality and musical growth: pressured rehearsal time for dancers, shortage of time for orchestral rehearsal, lack of money for commissions – there is not one new score on the books of the Royal Ballet companies for the foreseeable future. But the interviews also suggest that the rapport between musician and choreographer/dancer can be extraordinarily valuable, a crucial factor indeed in determining the particulars of style.

Perhaps more questions are raised than answered, but these are crucial, central to the business of creating, reviving and performing ballets. How much detail of choreographic style is bound up with a choreographer's own ideas about musical performance – which emerge subtly during the creative process and can so easily be forgotten during later revivals? When dancers really listen, what happens to their performance? Can the 'authentic' musical interpretation be less lively than one newly thought through in response to a new dancer, or a new era? If dancers feel that the right musical tempo matters more than anything else, doesn't the audience have a broader set of values?

Gammon and Twiner both joined the Royal Ballet in the early 1990s, gained experience in class as well as rehearsal accompaniment, in improvising as well as playing from scores, developing a broad knowledge of the dance vocabulary and of the needs and whims of dancers. After a while, they began to take on conducting work – Twiner now spends an increasing amount of his time on the rostrum. The two pianists stress the importance of linking studio musicality with stage performance, insisting that what is practised in rehearsal, what is established during the creative process – of which they have precious, first-hand experience – should be transferred sensitively to the stage.

Wordsworth joined the Sadler's Wells Royal Ballet as conductor in 1973 after having made his debut as soloist in Frank Martin's Harpsichord Concerto (for MacMillan's *Las Hermañas*). Developing a conducting career with both Royal companies (and with several ballet companies abroad), he was appointed music director in 1991. He has an important musical life outside the ballet as principal conductor of the BBC Concert Orchestra and Brighton Philharmonic Society. Wordsworth establishes himself as a 'new generation' Royal Ballet conductor who has stepped aside from the tradition of former music directors Constant Lambert and John Lanchbery.

The interviews took place on 17 July 1992 at Covent Garden.

BW: Unfortunately I didn't work with Sir Fred on anything new. By the time I came to the Royal Ballet we were mostly doing revivals. So the people that I've really worked with more closely on the creation of ballets are Kenneth MacMillan, Glen Tetley and David Bintley. Probably I'm more attuned to Sir Kenneth than to Sir Fred: Sir Kenneth's idea is to try and broaden the horizons of ballet. There are very few people who have really tried to push the world of ballet into more than a divertissement, and Kenneth is definitely one of those. He has been bold enough to commission quite a few scores, like *The Judas Tree*, which we did recently – he had such a good time with Brian Elias, even if he's been nervous of commissions in the past. David Bintley as well has commissioned a lot. He's very good, very adventurous. And I really think that that's the best way forward: commissions. I'm not particularly keen on people using concert music. There's always a problem, always a few bars too many, or it doesn't fit the plan.

SJ: Ashton preferred to have existing scores arranged rather than to commission from scratch. He wanted to know what he was going to get.

BW: A pity. But I suppose also he preferred music that wasn't quite so contemporary, and he also had a very good collaboration with Jack [John Lanchbery], and once you've hit on a formula like that which works, then the temptation is to go along with that.

HF: Do you arrange for ballet at all?

BW: No. I did one arrangement, but I haven't the time; there are other people around who do it better and, in any case, I wouldn't do it as a matter of principle, because I think that that's not the way forward for ballet anyway. I'm not in favour of pastiche or accessible, pretty-pretty music. I think it is time that the ballet grew out of all that; the whole idea is something that I find distasteful. I really think that the only way is to have composers writing specifically for the ballet.

HF: Apart from affording them, what problems are raised by commissioned scores?

BW: You have to plan so far in advance, two or three years ahead. The choreographer has to say what he is going to work on in three years' time, and choreographers are very nervous about doing that. They tend to work in shorter spans than that. The other reason that people are nervous about commissioning scores is that, with contemporary music, it's very difficult to get an idea of what the score is going to sound like on the orchestra early enough to be certain about it. And that's why with *The Judas Tree*, we were lucky enough to be able to get the Friends of Covent Garden to pay for two recording sessions with the orchestra, about a year and a half before the first performance happened, and almost six months before Sir Kenneth started work on the piece. It's the only occasion when we've been able to do that. Contemporary music, if it's at all adventurous, is really not presentable on the piano in a way which gives the choreographer an idea of what the orchestra is going to sound like.

SJ: *The Judas Tree* recording was made largely so that MacMillan himself would be able to have a safer idea of what it was going to sound like. The dancers would have had to use piano in rehearsal, wouldn't they, for Musicians' Union reasons?

BW: There are rules and regulations that the Musicians' Union has. It's also true that the Royal Ballet is a live music company, and that applies to its rehearsals as well as to its performances, although we do have works that have been created to tape music, like electronic music, or, for instance, the William Forsythe ballet *In the middle, somewhat elevated*, that we did this season. For the sort of ballet that the Royal specializes in, there is a partnership between dance and music, which needs that live music element to get it off the ground. This was always foremost in de Valois' thinking. You also find that, if dancers get used to a tape, they get used to one way of dancing a piece, and that can become terribly mechanical, and you don't have that excitement of responding to the little nuances and differences that inevitably occur with live music. And I think it's rather sterile, dance to tape – it doesn't excite me at all, even the pieces that are specially written with that in mind.

You also find that if you're in a theatre which has a pit and the pit is blacked out, there's this great chasm between the stage and the audience, and the ballet seems to recede somehow. That wouldn't be true in a theatre where you could get rid of the pit, but in a house like Covent Garden it's very difficult, if the pit is empty, to get the same kind of contact with the audience.

HF: Is that always a problem?

14

BW: In MacMillan's *Winter Dreams* [1991], a particularly intimate piece, the music is on stage, and in that case, it works in the ballet's favour. Somehow the focus of attention is drawn to the dancers, despite the fact that the pit is blacked out. That's a special case.

SJ: The blackened pit reinforces the intimacy; it distances the audience to make them feel that they think they are looking in on something very personal.

Different choreographers have different methods of approaching their music when they choreograph. Can you comment on that from your experience?

AT: Ashton viewed the music in phrases – in other words, he rarely counted. He'd say 'Play me the next section', or 'Play me the next phrase'. Mind you, I think all choreographers come to the studio knowing their music very well, but you sometimes get the impression that they don't because they'll say 'What's the next phrase?' or 'How long is the next phrase?' They know the music, but they want a musician's guidance as to the actual phrasing of each section. Sir Kenneth MacMillan is completely different. He won't say 'Play me the next phrase.' He'll say 'What is the next count?' It is up to you, the pianist, to look at the phrase and then tell him the number of beats within that phrase. But Ashton never did that. He's say 'Just play me it' and in his own mind, he would judge the length of the phrase.

SJ: So he'd be thinking much more about the sweep of the phrase.

AT: And MacMillan is very aware of how many beats there are: he does all his choreography to counts. Now that may sound very pedantic, but in the end it works. Rather than be unaware of where he is in the phrase, he'll know it by the number of the beat.

SJ: Will he have known that himself, having listened to the music?

AT: Not the counts, no.

PG: Neither of those two choreographers could actually read music, to any degree.

SJ: But you could work out the counts, just by listening.

AT: MacMillan probably could, but he doesn't want to waste time doing it. That's what he has a musician there to do for him. And then he can't go wrong. Now Hans van Manen did a ballet to the Adagio of Beethoven's 'Hammerklavier' Sonata [*Adagio Hammerklavier*, 1973]. He heard Christoph von Eschenbach play that music and was completely bowled over by it, but he choreographed it to the record. He didn't know anything about counts. He just listened to it and choreographed it. But when it came to be notated, so many problems became evident, because he had listened to one man's interpretation of it, and you know how a pianist can be very flexible. Van Manen would think that one note was worth two of the last one – not being able to read music – and, on paper, it isn't.

15

PG: And that's also very difficult for the pianist following the record.

AT: Yes, I had to play his interpretation.

SJ: Did you go back to the recording?

AT: Indeed. Van Manen said it can't be done. The management said, 'If you want your ballet performed here, you've got to have it done live.' So I took the record home, and I listened to it, and I played along with it, memorized it, and marked my own copy as to how long this or that note was held by this man. In the end, Van Manen said, 'I never would have believed it'. I said, 'Well, it's not impossible. It may not be my personal interpretation but if that's the way you want it played, it can be done.'

HF: Have there been any other instances of that, where somebody has worked very closely with a record?

PG: Not that I can think of. But when MacMillan did *Concerto* [1966], he rehearsed it and created it in Berlin, the pianist found it a bit much playing the outer quick movements, or maybe the process of the choreography slowed the pianist down, because it was so cut up in short phrases. Consequently, in the final product, all the tempos are way way under what they should be. That's a problem. Because it was created like that, we have to carry on in that vein, keep that same tempo. All three movements are slower than they should be.

AT: The first movement particularly.

HF: Can you think of any very disturbing examples when you as musicians felt you had to compromise?

AT: In particular when Nureyev came to do his production of *The Nutcracker* [1968]. His choreography was so very way out, so very slow and deliberate, and had no relation to Tchaikovsky's markings.

SJ: I hear that David Bintley reads music. How does he approach a new score?

BW: David would make sure that he studied the precise musical structure of the score for himself, as indeed Balanchine would have done, whereas other choreographers would ask for much more guidance. But we would still talk about the structure. When David recently choreographed *Job* in San Francisco, he was very interested to see the score that I gave him, littered with my markings and structural comments. He's now doing a new ballet for us later on this season and I said to him, 'Would you like to look at my score for that?' (Walton's *Variation on a Theme by Hindemith*). He said, 'Well, I've already got one and I've marked it up rather along the way you do . . .' That's a delight for a musician, that a choreographer can suss out the structure of a score in as much detail as a musician would, before he's even started choreographing.

SJ (*to the pianists*): Can you say whether some choreographers whom you've worked with have been much more precise than others about exactly how they wanted you to play a piece, apart from the van Manen example, which is extreme. Sir Fred, for instance? Was there rubato of his making, and then you responded to that, and felt that you must keep relatively close to what he did?

AT: Yes, we're essentially compromisers. This business about music having to be played in a certain manner is absolute rubbish. Listen to two or three recordings of a Beethoven symphony: all are different. So if the choreographer does do the sort of rubato that you think is acceptable, I would go along with it, and then it stays. When other people come to conduct a piece, they often ask 'Why is that suddenly slower?' And you think 'Well, it's just an interpretation.'

SJ: You've been involved so much at the beginning of the creative process, and so sensitive to nuances right through a ballet. Subtle as those may be, they must make such a difference to the style of a piece. I'm thinking of the difference for someone coming along ten years later who didn't go through that process. Mr Twiner, you played for *Symphonic Variations* [1946] under Ashton's guidance. Can you say anything about Ashton's particular view of that music?

AT: I can't be specific, but there was a time when we had a very distinguished lady pianist come to play it as a guest. She played it beautifully, much better than I could, but Ashton said to me, 'I don't like the way she plays it'. She was just sitting there playing it straight, as she had learnt it, like a concert piece: she didn't know what was going on on stage. But you can't always do that, because there are certain nuances – he wants the music to bend slightly or to relax, which is perfectly legitimate.

SJ: She wasn't given any directives?

PG: Unless you've had years playing for ballet, you can't instil what is needed.

AT: No. Sitting there playing for rehearsal, you learn where the choreographer and dancers would like a little bit of time or something, and providing what they want is legitimate, you accept it. You say 'I could play it like that myself, quite naturally'.

HF: You must feel a strong link between your work as a pianist and conductor.

AT: When I'm conducting for principal dancers, I prefer to play my own rehearsal. I have something in my hands which transfers to my body, the speeds which they would like and which they can dance to. When I pick up the stick, there is something already in my body.

But conducting a rehearsal, if you feel that the pianist can't respond to you – there are quite a lot of pianists who can't follow a beat – you think 'Go away! Let me play myself!'

PG: Not only following the beat, but a lot of the time they don't have the right feel, atmosphere.

AT: Yes, the right expression that you want to convey. That, I suppose,

17

is one of the disadvantages of being a pianist. You know how you would play the music yourself, and you desperately want it played the way you would play it. When it doesn't happen, it's frustrating.

But to return to conducting: if we have a guest conductor who comes to do a standard work, and he hears it played a certain way in rehearsal, he might well question it and say 'I don't want to do it that way'. And then he either has to accept it or the dancers will have to rethink it.

PG: And very often there's not time to rethink. But this does show the terrific responsibility for the pianist playing for a choreographer who's creating a completely new ballet. Because, very often, the person who's conducting the first performance doesn't come to watch rehearsal until a week before. And then if he wants to change anything, it's too late.

SJ: The choreographer at that stage might be very firm about how he wants the music. Is that correct?

AT: I think he's entitled to be, providing that what he wants is not 'unmusical'. There is a line which you can't go over. For example, that Nureyev *Nutcracker*. That was pretty tense.

HF: Mr Wordsworth, have you ever been called upon to conduct according to somebody else's particular interpretation, like Mr Twiner was asked to play the Beethoven for Hans van Manen according to an existing recording?

BW: All the choreographers I've worked with have listened to as many recordings as have been available, but where a choreographer has been particularly inspired by a certain performance, I've always listened to the recording in question, and if I've had any problems with it, or any different ideas, then I've discussed them, and again, either persuaded the choreographer or been persuaded by him about, for instance, a particular tempo.

You don't try to recreate somebody else's performance, because that is a very boring and sterile thing for a musician to do, and in any case, over a series of performances, the dancers' own feelings about a piece tend to mature. Things are constantly evolving.

The most important thing is that, by listening to the recording – and bear in mind also that the choreographer will have spent hours listening to it and absorbing the music – at least you have a common experience to start from. You have a foundation which is the same. You may then, after that, decide to go in a different direction, or to modify something slightly. As performances go on, they evolve.

HF: But has the fact that a particular recording has been inspiring in the creative process ever posed problems?

BW: I had an experience recently when Sylvie Guillem was dancing a solo [*La Luna* by Béjart], to the slow movement of the Bach E major Violin Concerto, which had been choreographed to a recording which I had not heard – the piece was put in rather at the last minute [in 1991]. That was very difficult because one tends to have very strong ideas about Baroque music and, with the change of fashion that we've had recently in how Baroque music ought to be played, this created a big problem for me. It was choreographed to a recording which is frankly out of fashion now, and it was absolutely essential that one took the tempo that Béjart had choreographed to in order to keep the whole essence of the piece. It was a very interesting exercise to try and sink one's imagination into how a particular interpreter felt about the piece of Bach. And I also had to persuade the musicians that we were going to play it in a way which they probably would not have wished to on the concert platform.

SJ: Are there choreographers you have worked with whom you felt particularly positive about – their handling of music, their flexibility with you as the pianists and conductors?

BW: For totally different reasons, Tetley, MacMillan and Bintley. They're all very strong musical personalities in different ways. MacMillan's *Gloria* [1980] to the Poulenc, for instance: the ballet adds up to more than a sum of its parts. He can find things to do, even with concert pieces, which shed new light on the work. Tetley too. I did *Tagore* with him in Toronto (to Zemlinsky's *Lyric Symphony*) and I adore *Voluntaries* (to Poulenc's *Organ Concerto*) – there again the choreography is saying something that is not just a mirror of the music. Glen is not of the Balanchine school where the choreography is very closely allied to the musical structure. Some people would say that Balanchine doesn't tell you any more about the music than the music could have told you. I'm not saying that's true. Balanchine at his best is first rate, but for certain of his pieces (which I haven't conducted), I've felt that it wasn't necessary to have choreographed the music. That's always the danger when you use concert music, which is why I believe that the only way forward for ballet is to commission scores, Diaghilev's idea after all. If I was really pressed for a personal viewpoint, I would say that I am more interested in working with somebody like Kenneth MacMillan.

PG *(to AT)*: Wasn't Jerome Robbins terrifically precise about what he wanted?

SJ: That can be irritating surely?

AT: It can be, especially if it's piano music. He does a lot of Chopin. Having learned all those pieces when you were young as a student and got some idea about how to play them . . . the choreographer says 'I want you to play it like this,' you might think 'Where did you get that idea from?' But Robbins is a very musical man. He's a joy to work with, a perfectionist. Very tiring to work with, but in the end you think that it was worth it.

SJ: But then there must be choreographers who are more flexible, and you've found them good to work with as well.

AT: Glen Tetley. He's very flexible, quite different from Robbins. As he was creating *Dances of Albion* [1980] to Britten, he was open to suggestions.

PG: That's one thing I liked particularly about Ashton: he would welcome any comment I would like to make about the musicality of the choreography, the look of the step in relation to the music, whereas with MacMillan, he tends not to want to hear a thing, except his counts. I must tell you: I have contributed to the choreography of *A Month in the Country* [1976]! It actually says in the score: 'Gammon *port de bras*'. Ashton got me to play the end of the Polacca over and over again, and I got so fed up, just the last eight or so bars. At the end, I did a huge gesture (flings his arms up and outwards). He doesn't miss a thing. He got all the dancers on stage do exactly what I did.

AT: On the other hand, I remember Ashton was creating *The Dream* [1964] and we had a lady pianist who complained about a certain thing that we were doing. He just looked at her and said 'Don't be such a purist!' Incidentally, both Ashton and MacMillan are constantly saying 'How much more is there? How many more pages are there? How far have we got?'

PG: Sometimes it seems that that is all they're concerned with! They are so anxious to finish.

AT: And you say 'We've got another three pages'. Horror!

PG: Then they are thinking of cuts.

AT: And that's when the trouble starts. When Kenneth was working on *Isadora* [1981], with a specially written score by Richard Rodney Bennett, he couldn't believe that there was so much music. Rodney Bennett was composing it and sending it bit by bit, and he would say, 'I don't want all that music. Can't we cut it?' Then one had to look at the music and say 'All I can suggest is this, but you must check with Rodney Bennett that he accepts it.' There was a lot of telephoning.

PG: The same thing now with *Prince of the Pagodas* [1989]. We had to go through a lot of bother getting it sanctioned from the Britten Estate in the first place, there were a lot of cuts, and the order of Act III was completely changed from what Britten originally wrote. But since then, for the next revival, it's going to be changed yet again, to make it shorter, especially Acts II and III. But also to change the order yet again of Act III. We need permission for that, too.

SJ: Do you object to some of these cuts on musical grounds?

PG: Sometimes. But the changes to Act III of *Pagodas* are not so bad because of the pauses after a lot of the pieces, like Act III of *Sleeping Beauty*, so it doesn't matter so much. MacMillan doesn't want to cut bars, usually sections.

SJ: Which choreographers have needed most help with finding music?

AT: Choreographers are listening all the time. And they have their own ideas, especially the younger choreographers like Hindle and Bintley.

SJ: Do you think there is an older generation of choreographers who were more likely to ask for advice? I gather, for instance, that Mr Gammon, you helped choose the Tchaikovsky pieces for MacMillan's *Winter Dreams* [1991].

AT: And I remember asking MacMillan once, when some project had to be abandoned, 'Have you ever done a ballet to Bartók's Two Piano Sonata and Percussion?' He asked what it was like and then thought it was a good idea to use it. That was *Rituals* [1975].

SJ: Constant Lambert musically educated Ashton, but it is partly because choreographers now have much better access to musical recordings than they did then.

PG: In those days they didn't have any way of listening to music, except for going to concerts.

BW: It was necessary at that time for Lambert to bring scores to the attention of would-be choreographers in the company. A lot of people have said – one hears this the whole time, it gets so boring – how wonderful Lambert was in being such a musical guidance for the company. Well, he had to be, because there was no choice! It's really not necessary for people like myself to do that any more. Bintley, for instance, has a far bigger and more interesting record collection than I have.

SJ: It's really easy to forget that point about availability of recordings. But then Balanchine the pianist had a tremendous advantage over all the other choreographers whom we have discussed because he could try things out on the piano and even make his own orchestral reductions.

SJ: How do you respond to different situations, conducting the same piece for live ballet, concert hall and for recordings?

BW: A lot of people haven't taken on board the issues here. In ballet, the audience has the stimulation of watching. In the concert hall, you also do, to a lesser extent. When you listen to a record, there's none of that at all – the entire stimulation has to be aural, and that makes a difference to the way that you conduct something.

HF: You apply different criteria for different situations?

BW: By and large, without the visual aspect, you tend to go faster. What is an exciting tempo musically with only musical considerations is not necessarily an exciting tempo for dance. It may be that if you're pushing the dancers too hard and therefore a lot of detail of the choreography is getting lost in their effort to keep up, the overall effect is actually rather more boring. But it also depends on the dancer. If the dancer has a quality where every detail is sharp, clear and precise, he or she needs more time in order to achieve that. Then you might do a passage rather differently for that dancer than you would do it for another.

SJ *(to the pianists)*: Have there been any pieces that you've played here for the ballet that you also played outside on the concert platform?

AT: Apart from the Chopin used in Robbins' *Dances at a Gathering* [1969] and *In the Night* [1970], no.

SJ: And you perform these differently as a concert pianist?

AT: Oh yes.

PG: Usually I find that things I play here I play faster in concert.

SJ: Do you find that pieces get slower as they get older?

AT: Yes they do. For example, *Romeo and Juliet* [1965]. If you see the film that we did and you compare the speeds on that film with what we do now, you think to yourself, 'What's happened to it?'

SJ: Is this well known?

AT: In musical circles, yes.

SJ: Does MacMillan know and find the tempo slow now?

AT: I think probably as they grow older, both people's bodies and their actual works, they assume a slightly more ponderous air.

HF: Do you think that this is possibly a modern tendency generally: tempos seem to be slacker than they were say 30 years ago? Thomas Beecham's recordings seem very up-tempo now, don't they?

AT: It's strange. Take for example, Bintley's *Cyrano* [1991]. They did it on tour in Birmingham and I was allotted the task of doing all the performances, and Bintley came to Birmingham and said 'That's really good, terrific!' When I came to do it here, a few months later, he came up to me and said 'All I can say is that it was rather careful'. Perhaps something had happened to me. In other words he was saying that I wasn't pushing it as much as I could. And I thought 'Well, I'm only doing what I think I did before'. But we're only human, like a dancer one day dances at a different speed because of the way she feels.

SJ: I think Balanchine would have probably been very aware of that sort of change going on, and he was always excited by speed anyway. *Agon* [1957], for instance: Stravinsky had to tell him to slow it down at one point! But you haven't come across any choreographers who wanted to whip things up?

PG: I wish they would!

AT: It would make a change! Balanchine is an exception. He was a musician. Now, not everything that Balanchine did was, as far as I'm concerned, very musical. For instance, he sanctioned (very short) cuts. You think, 'Why did he do that, just for the sake of about four bars?' So many say how musical Balanchine is, and I think to myself, 'Well, why did he even contemplate allowing that?'

SJ: *Ballet Imperial* [1941]. You play that, don't you?

AT: Yes, there are cuts in that, in the cadenza particularly. The cuts aren't that long, and that makes you think: 'Just for the sake of how many seconds, why did he do that? Why couldn't he have invented a few more steps?'

SJ: Did you ever have a chance to work with Balanchine?

AT: Only when he came to put on his ballets here, not when he was creating anything, just reviving or to see what was happening to a ballet.

PG: One of the first things that I ever did here was *The Four Temperaments* [1946]. And I'll never forget, he came to a rehearsal once and he got me to stand up and showed me how to play it! I was flabbergasted!

SJ: Coming back to Nureyev – do you think that the peculiarities of his *Nutcracker* arose partly because he is from the Russian tradition where dancers are much freer about messing about with tempos? Makarova, for instance, slows things down and changes phrasing.

AT: Yes, absolutely.

PG: We'd never played the *Lac* solo as slowly as when she did it. It was painfully slow. It distorted the music.

SJ: You lose all sense of the sweep of the musical phrase.

HF: Mr Wordsworth, have there been times when your musical interpretation has been at odds with that of the dancers or choreographer?

BW: Yes, frequently. And then it's a question of discussion, and some sort of compromise or indeed, in some cases, a dancer will say 'Oh, I'd never thought of it like that. Yes, let's do it this way'. You also have the problem of second casts or revivals where perhaps the choreographer isn't present, and the piece is being mounted by somebody else. Or a principal dancer will think quite differently about a role and that has to be ironed out – we have to come to agreement about how he or she feels about certain passages.

SJ: What kinds of musical discussion about interpretation do you have with dancers?

BW: There are two kinds, and they're quite different. There is the kind when you're talking on a very high level about what the impact of a certain passage would be if it was taken at a slightly different tempo, or if there was more or less rubato. That's a very interesting discussion. The other discussion is when somebody is having a technical problem and you have to change the music in order to help the dancer to get through the passage. That's less interesting, but nevertheless very important. After all, more even than the voice, a dancer's body is very individual, and you have to be mindful of that in your approach to the music, at the same time making sure that the integrity of the music isn't threatened. Problems of integrity and difference between dancers and conductor happen far less than you would think.

SJ: Can you give an example of differences of interpretation that have affected a particular piece that you've conducted?

BW: There's an example with *Romeo and Juliet* (which we're rehearsing right now), which is in the repertoire of both Birmingham and London companies. There's no doubt that the two companies approach the work in a different way, to my mind equally successfully. When Kenneth was working in Birmingham, he had a very open mind to what the company and I felt about things.

HF: Are you conducting two separate interpretations of *Romeo and Juliet*? Do you have one annotated score for Birmingham and another for London?

BW: I think that they are sufficiently different that, if a new conductor were coming in and having to follow me, he would need to have two separate versions. But, especially when I know the dancers and the piece very well, I get into the pit and just try and go with what's happening. And I'm almost unaware of the differences. There are one or two places where there are obvious tempi differences, which are partly due to the size of the *corps de ballet* – it's smaller in Birmingham. As it's not quite so complicated on stage, you can go faster.

SJ: Can you give me an example?

BW: The middle of *Romeo and Juliet* Act II, a particularly fast section, which has to be a little slower here in London – a *corps de ballet* piece which we call the 'tun-up', during the crowd scenes – because the *corps de ballet* is larger, and so is the stage (size of stage affects the time it takes to get from one side to the other). There's also a slightly different emphasis, in terms of what is the most important element in the choreography. It seems to me that at that particular point in Birmingham the idea is to go for quite a light-hearted romp, because of the drama that's about to happen. It's felt that the maximum contrast is called for. At the Garden, there tends to be more of a lead up to the drama. Those differences emerged for all sorts of reasons, because of the dancers involved, the character of the company, rather than a conscious effort on anybody's part to say 'Right, we're going to do it this way'. These things just develop over a period of time.

HF: In terms of interpretation, can working as a ballet conductor some-times seem like a drudge, a major impediment to your musicality?

BW: It can be very tiresome when you're having to compromise because of technical deficiencies from bad casting. Of course, ballet conducting is hard. To be a success at it, you have to absorb both disciplines. It was very interesting: Bernard Haitink, who has conducted for ballet here, said to me the other day, 'You know it's not so different, working with singers and working with dancers'. Or indeed conducting a concerto in a concert hall. The soloist is going to have very definite ideas about what he or she wants to do, and your role is to accommodate that if you possibly can. I think the reason that a lot of conductors find accompanying concertos less interest-ing and harder than symphonies is exactly the same reason that a lot of conductors find working in opera and ballet difficult. It's because they can't put their egos in place, work with other people and take on board other ideas.

SJ *(to the pianists)*: Do you make any comments to the dancers about their musical approach?

AT: The ballet pianist who is not a conductor will not feel that he is qualified, or perhaps it would be impolite to suggest to people that what they were doing was wrong. But we also conduct and a conductor is somebody different. I think that the conductor should suggest to dancers sometimes that they are thinking a passage the wrong way round or that it could be adjusted slightly.

SJ: Can you give me an example of when you've done that, and you feel usefully, and your advice was taken?

AT: It often happens, sometimes in silly things, unimportant things to other people. For instance, like pauses. In *The Sleeping Beauty* duet, there are slight pauses in the steps and if a pianist plays the music one way, the dancers will do it that way. They'll think that's the way it's right. The conductor asks 'Why are you performing it with so many pauses?' and the dancer will answer 'that's the way we've rehearsed it'. Then the conductor will say, 'Can you not do that a little bit quicker, with less pause, to keep the rhythm going?' and they'll say, 'Fine'. But, unless you actually approach them, they'll think that the way they've been doing the steps is right. Because they themselves don't read music. They can only listen. So therefore the conductor must, I think, point out new possibilities. It's worth doing.

PG: The most essential thing for a conductor to do is to go to the rehearsals. All the preparation is the most important thing.

SJ: But dancers rehearsing with different pianists must get used to some range of interpretation?

AT: Indeed, which is good, because then they have to respond to what they hear, which is what they have to do in performance.

PG: Another problem with pianists playing for rehearsals is that dancers don't think of the music orchestrally. You've got to point out things in the orchestration as well, make them aware of what instruments will be playing.

SJ: But when you're playing for a rehearsal, you'll do that, won't you? You'll take on board that other dimension because you're also likely to be conducting.

PG: Particularly in new ballets like *Judas Tree* and *Prince of the Pagodas*.

SJ: There must be enormous problems sometimes for dancers when they first encounter the orchestration of a new score.

HF: Have you heard of a recent example at English National Ballet where the composer, Gerard McBurney, sent a tape of himself playing the piano reduction of his score to the ballet *White Nights*, and when the dancers came to the orchestral performance, nobody could actually recognize the music. So the dancers were completely lost.

AT: Yes, it's very difficult with a modern work. The sounds are so complex.

HF: Do you ever use an orchestral recording to ease this problem?

PG: No. We're not allowed to use recorded sound in the studio, and to dance to it [Musicians' Union regulations]. But the dancers are allowed to stand and listen to it, and to hear what it sounds like. We did this for *Judas Tree*, because it's such a complex score.

SJ: Which dancers in the company have you found exceptionally musical?

AT: There are many ways of defining 'musical'. Merle Park, in one way, was very musical in that she danced to the phrase, not on the beat. She had an overall idea to the end of the phrase so that therefore what you thought was not on the music, was on the music at the end. She had an interpretation of the phrase rather than of the beats. Now that's one of the many ways of being musical. But you'll find quite a few musical dancers here – Deborah Bull is very musical.

SJ: She's interesting. She told me that she passed Grade VIII piano.

AT: The other day she was rehearsing and the music wasn't quite as she would have liked it to have been. But she said at the end 'Oh, I don't like to say anything unless it's absolutely impossible'. In other words, she will take what comes, providing it's not impossible. She's willing to go along with somebody else. That's another way of being musical, in responding in that way.

PG: There's one person I miss very much who took rehearsals latterly. And that's Michael Somes. He could sing anything, accurately, from the ballets.

AT: He again was conscious of the phrase. He used to tell the dancers 'I don't want to see you dancing on every beat. It's boring. But I think of the beginning and the end of the phrase.' Also Brian Shaw. When he took rehearsals, he'd say 'Listen to the music!' He was absolutely adamant about it, saying 'You're not responding to the music'. And I thought 'What a joy for someone to keep on saying that'.

BW: The dancers that I get most pleasure from are the ones that have a real sense of rubato, and know how to play around the music. The first person who showed me what that really was about was Brenda Last. I found that she had a wonderful musical sense which meant that she didn't always dance bang on every note, but that she would linger and then catch me up. We used to play terrific games with one another, because after a time, we got to trust each other. In the middle of a performance she would suddenly rush for four bars and then wait for me, or I would do the same back to her. It would be terrific fun. And that was only possible because she was so assured with what she was doing – she was so on top of everything technically that you could really relax and make a performance.

SJ: Have you any ideas about the relative virtues of approaching music using counts or not?

AT: Quite often people say that it destroys the music if you count it, but you know musicians themselves count. There's an element of that for musicians. And *Agon*, for instance, like the dance, there the musician has to count like blazes – blow the phrases!

SJ: But with musicians, it's not taken to such a degree as with dancers.

AT: No, I quite agree. But dancers feel that counts give them something solid.

PG: Yes, I think it's an extra form of security. I've found that working so long with ballet, the count business has helped me in my own preparation of solo piano pieces. I adopted their way of counting. It's very beneficial: especially for learning things from memory.

BW: Counting is a short cut: it provides you with a skeleton framework on which you can hang the choreography and therefore remember it more easily. But counting also gives you an idea of phrases, and in that way, very often a dancer's intuitive response to music is keener than that of musicians, which is governed largely by the bar line. It has been said that the bar line is the most unmusical thing that was ever devised – it's because it makes people think in terms of very short moments rather than the long phrase.

SJ: I've heard that English and American dancers tend to count much more than French dancers, who sing internally.

PG: Yes, that's true. And Irek Mukhamedov never counts. He knows the music so thoroughly, he doesn't count at all, not even *Judas Tree*. Everybody else counted that one.

SJ: Do you think that it's better to learn the music by singing it and learning it without counts?

AT: I would think so, yes.

PG: What I can't understand is that dancers hear their music so much, yet very few of them can actually sing bits when they're trying to tell you something about a specific step. They can rarely sing the actual tune that fits that step.

AT: But it's the way one learns. There are dancing teachers who are themselves musically ignorant and, if they aren't, they can't convey that musicality to their pupils. If you're taught musically, that's always an important aspect in your dancing.

SJ: Do you think over the years dancing to the beat and the fixation with counts has grown? In the early days when you were here, was there more concentration on musicality?

PG: The repertoire has developed so much and we're using such complex music that you really have to count.

AT: I think that the *corps de ballet* doesn't dance together now – for

27

example in *Les Sylphides*. I'm very much aware when I look up that they're not doing this thing together. There's a jarring aspect to it. You see something which isn't quite right.

SJ: Is that because they're not listening?

AT: Now that I don't know. I think it is, personally. You immediately think that some people are responding to the music and some are in another world; whether that comes from discipline in rehearsal, I don't know. It worries me! Now, there was a time when the *corps* was absolutely perfect.

SJ: For the Kirov *Sylphide* the tempos are faster than they are over here, which is much better musically.

AT: Yes indeed.

SJ: But furthermore, the *corps* breathed together. There was a tremendous sense of the dancers not jamming on the count, but breathing, and there were the effects of rubato which they all had. It was beautiful.

AT: I'm sure that was painstaking rehearsal. In the West, so many things are thrown on the stage, you know.

SJ: Staging dances quickly on a company, in order to get the information across quickly, you'll teach by counts. And there's no time to think about listening.

AT: You're absolutely right. The problem is time.

Music and dance in our time

Alastair Macaulay

We can see now that the first half of the twentieth century was a rich period for music written for dance. Will we be able to say the same for the second half? It seems mighty unlikely. The years 1900-1950 contained several extraordinary figures – Serge Diaghilev above all; Ida Rubinstein and Elizabeth Sprague Coolidge also – who commissioned numerous great scores, many of them for dance, from a wide range of composers. (Diaghilev's scores spanned from Stravinsky's *Firebird* and Ravel's *Daphnis and Chloë* to Sauguet's *La Chatte* and Prokofiev's *The Prodigal Son*; Rubinstein's included Ravel's *Bolero* and *La Valse* and Stravinsky's *Le Baiser de la fée*; Coolidge's ranged from Stravinsky's *Apollo* to Copland's *Appalachian Spring*.) Thanks largely to the influence of these remarkable people, the new ballet companies in England and America, the remoulded ballet companies of Soviet Russia and the young, fast-growing genre of modern dance all acquired important music direction and an impressive supply of new music. More vital yet, there was a lively connection between Western ballet and popular music, as the work of George Balanchine, Frederick Ashton, and their composers demonstrated. There is jazz in most of Stravinsky's music from *Apollo* on, and in much of Constant Lambert's. There is jazz in the way Balanchine choreographed to Bach in *Concerto Barocco* and the way Ashton choreographed to Auber in *Les Rendezvous*; the influence of Fred Astaire can be discerned in the work of both choreographers; both men did plenty of work in popular revues and new musicals. Much of the essence of jazz was perpetuated through the age of swing.

Then along came rock. People dance to it, people choreograph to it, people have been suffused by it since the 1950s. But it has been a fell influence on dance. Rock has beefed up people's rhythmic sense only by rendering it crude and simple. Some of the world's leading choreographers have tried to use it; but they have also fled, with much better result, to jazz. There have been rock ballets, rock modern dances, and rock postmodern dances; and there have even been attempts, in both music and dance, to construct a rock classicism. The results have often been popular and have sometimes been critically acclaimed. I don't, however, think they bear serious scrutiny: for rhythmic reasons, they just don't have enough inner life.

It would be wrong, however, to propose that our century began with a golden age of music for dance. What may be nearer the truth is that the jazz age was simply the tail end of a great tradition in which dance rhythms enriched musical composition. Though much of the classical music written in the eighteenth and nineteenth centuries was not written to be danced to, much of it was informed by dance (Bach's suites are a perfect example). The diminution of the dance element can be felt, however, in the nineteenth-century German symphonic tradition: and in the non-dance music of Wagner it is absent. Nietzsche levelled the charge at Wagner that his music 'had lost contact with the body', that one could not dance to it as one could to Mozart.[1] By the start of our century, the separation of new dance and new music became marked. Whereas, before 1900, almost all new choreography had employed new or newish music, usually music conceived as dance music, now choreographers started to reject (a) new music (b) dance music. Isadora Duncan's taste was largely for concert-hall music: she even took on Beethoven's Seventh Symphony and Tchaikovsky's *Marche Slave*. That Mikhail Fokine worked with Stravinsky, Ravel and Richard Strauss was thanks to Diaghilev. Left to his own devices, Fokine's musical instincts were Duncanist. He, like Duncan, turned to the old music of Chopin; he also choreographed to concert-hall music by Saint-Saëns, Schumann, Rimsky-Korsakov, Weber, Liszt, Tchaikovsky, Beethoven and Rachmaninov. It is to the influence of Duncan and Fokine that our century owes many of its choreography's musical tendencies: 'music visualization', 'the symphonic ballet', and their progeny. To Duncan and Fokine the rhythms of the jazz era were not the rhythms of serious choreography. Balanchine and Ashton taught us otherwise, but even they did not want to concentrate on new music. Despite the work of Stravinsky, Gershwin, Lambert, Prokofiev and others, it grew harder to hear the dance element in new music. Naturally, choreographers turned to old music.

This peculiarly twentieth-century preoccupation with old music extends beyond dance, of course. Think of opera, where singers up to the generation of Caruso performed a repertory consisting largely of new or recent music, but where fewer and fewer singers after 1920 were able to work with living composers. Think of popular music, where, in the 1930s, singers like Lee Wiley started to turn back the clock and record old favourites and not only the latest hits. Think of recording itself, which gave the public evergrowing access to music of the past. There is also the fact that modernism, the dominant artistic climate of the century's first seven decades, was often far distant from popular culture. Today we hear of the chasm between high art and low art; in dance we can see it. Formal stage choreography (high art) is often miles apart from popular music (low art). There are exceptions to this, but it's only too plain that that's what they are – exceptions. A chasm like this is a tragedy in our culture.

Live music or taped?

It is startling to realize how much dance today does not have music as an important ingredient. Some dance is founded on the principle of independence from music, in particular choreography by Merce Cunningham and others. Then there is dance to which music is merely incidental: after all, no one goes to the dance theatre of Pina Bausch for its music or its musicality.

And it is startling how much musical dance today is not accompanied by live music. Or maybe not so startling. At parties and clubs everywhere, people dance to recordings, don't they? Naturally then, choreographers have been using recordings too. Numerous new works have been made to commissioned but taped scores – such as the music by David Byrne and Talking Heads for Twyla Tharp's *The Catherine Wheel* (1981), by David van Tieghem for *Fait Accompli* (1983) and by Philip Glass for *In the Upper Room* (1987). Or, in England, John Marc Gowans' scores for Richard Alston's *Strong Language* (1987) and Siobhan Davies's *Wyoming* (1988). Needless to say, taped music also avoids the considerable expense of live musicians.

Then there's another genre, which has sprung up in recent decades – the ballet choreographed to a group of records by the same artist or artists. The genre has produced several of the biggest dance hits in our time. Its greatest expert is, perhaps, Twyla Tharp: she has made individual works to groups of records by Jelly Roll Morton and his Red Hot Peppers (*Eight Jelly Rolls*,

1971), the Beach Boys (*Deuce Coupe*, 1973), Fats Waller (*Sue's Leg*, 1974), Chuck Berry (*Ocean's Motion*, 1975), Willie 'the Lion' Smith (*Baker's Dozen*, 1979), Bruce Springsteen and Supertramp (*Short Stories*, 1980) and Frank Sinatra (several – in particular *Nine Sinatra Songs*, 1984). Mark Morris has made pieces to the Louvin Brothers (*Songs that Tell a Story*, 1984), Yoko Ono (*Dogtown*, 1985), the Violent Femmes (*Lovey*, 1985), Bob Wills and His Texas Playboys (*Going Away Party*, 1990). In this country, Richard Alston has used the Inkspots (*Java Jive*, 1983 and 1985). Recently, Paul Taylor has joined this number, with his 1991 Andrews Sisters hit, *Company B*. On one level, these works mean to capture something of the way we feel in listening to an LP or CD; and on another they tease us by showing us interpretations of the music we hadn't expected.

But there are quite a few choreographers and dancers who've never had the chance to work with live music; and quite a few viewers who haven't had the chance to find out the difference that live music can make between one performance and the next – how it can stimulate dancers. Though Alston has used his share of taped sound, he has often said that the best thing that Ballet Rambert (now Rambert Dance Company) had to offer him, when he moved there in 1980 as resident choreographer, was the opportunity to employ live music. Mark Morris sometimes presents programmes of all-taped music and others of all-live – as in April 1992, when his New York season featured one week of live music, superbly played, and another week of works made to specific recordings or to silence. The danger of taped music – that it encourages taped performances – does not become important where the standards of a company's live music is high; and where the musical style of a company's own dancing is keen. There are, however, dance companies whose standards of live music and of musical responsiveness are in decline; and in these cases the infiltration of taped music gives cause for concern.

Musical policies in ballet

'I do not believe that any ballet company can have roots or a policy of lasting value, or hold the prolonged interest of the public, if it lacks first-class musical leadership,' wrote Ninette de Valois in 1951.[2] Today, it is worth questioning whether there is even one major ballet company which has musical leadership of that first-class level. There are a few good ballet conductors; and a number of composers who are prepared to write for ballet; but that does not add up to much.

It is particularly interesting to examine the musical tendencies of New York City Ballet in recent years. George Balanchine, its founding ballet-master, made dancing to music the centre of his kind of dance theatre. Scenery, costumes, acting, narrative, story, were only of secondary or occasional importance. The standards of musicality in dancing, and of conducting, were exceptionally high. Among the wide range of music to which the company danced, whole festivals were devoted to the works of specific composers (Stravinsky, Ravel, Tchaikovsky); and a number of works were danced to commissioned or recent scores by leading composers (Stravinsky, Gershwin, Rodgers, Hindemith, Bernstein).

Since Balanchine's death in 1983, the company's priorities have not officially changed. In 1988, the company held a three-week American Music Festival, presenting choreography to American composers, from Charles Ives to Ray Charles. The festival included existing choreography by Balanchine, Jerome Robbins and the company's current ballet-master-in-chief Peter Martins, but mainly presented new choreography by a wide selection of choreographers from within NYCB (especially Martins himself), from other ballet companies and from modern and postmodern dance. Five of the scores were commissioned. The festival's determined pursuit of the new, however, emerged more as a PR exercise in demonstrating Life After Balanchine than as a serious celebration of whatever constitutes American music. (With the exceptions of Lukas Foss and Balanchine himself – two songs by whom were employed – the definition of an American composer was that he/she had to be American-born. The 'American' Stravinsky of *Jeu de cartes*, *Danses concertantes*, *Orpheus* and *Agon* was omitted.) The loudest applause went to *Behind the China Dogs*, made by William Forsythe (of the Frankfurt Ballet), to a commissioned taped rock-based score by Leslie Stuck. Several of the guest choreographers attended more to costumes, sets, themes than to either dance or music; the festival began and ended with works in which women danced without pointe shoes. The festival obtained the worst reviews of NYCB's history to date.

In May 1992, NYCB launched a Diamond Project, an array of new choreography specifically focused on dancing (*ballet* dancing) to music. Eleven ballets, made by choreographers from inside and outside the company, were presented within four days. This time, Martins himself attended to the American Stravinsky, with a new version of *Jeu de cartes* in which the original scenario had been 'discarded' or abstracted. Forsythe returned to NYCB and again choreographed to a commissioned taped rock-based score, this one by his regular collaborator Thom Willems. Robert La Fosse used a commissioned jazz-meets-rock-meets-classical score by Eve Begiarian – part for electronic 'cello, part taped. Other choices of music included Haydn, Mozart, Dvorák, Respighi, Debussy, Bloch, and Kamran Ince. But several of these scores were weakly conducted and poorly played; NYCB's orchestral standards and musical direction have declined considerably in recent years, especially the last two.

Not that NYCB is directionless in its musical taste. Martins has worked several times now to music by the young American composer Michael

Torke, who appears to take ideas in roughly equal proportions from rock, minimalism, and post-1930 Stravinsky; Martins has also used music by the post-minimalist John Adams and, earlier this year, commissioned from Charles Wuorinen a postmodern post-Mozart composition. Slick, modish, clever scores, these have brought out the same qualities in Martins. They haven't brought out, however, the most remarkable features of NYCB dance musicality or technique. After the premiere of Martin's 1989 *Echo*, Arlene Croce declared: 'Torke, Martins' Stravinsky, writes bad music. His music for *Echo* repeats a short-phrase pattern obsessively in a kind of hiccupping rhythm for about eight minutes; then, with minor differences, it repeats that three times. Music like this strikes NYCB at its very heart.'

Britain's Royal Ballet, whose musical direction had wobbled in the '70s and plummeted in the '80s, has recently recovered much lost ground in terms of sheer orchestral quality. Some guest conductors – in particular, Gennady Rozhdestvensky and Bernard Haitink – have produced accounts of their scores (Tchaikovsky, Stravinsky, Prokofiev) of the highest standards; and the permanent team of conductors – though over-parted by such scores as Stravinsky's *Agon* – work at a level generally competent and sometimes more than that. But first-rate playing and conducting do not guarantee a brilliant dance musicality: see the Paris Opéra, where scores are often given superb renderings but accorded merely superficial courtesy by the Opéra dancers. Royal dancers may have slightly improved their timing in recent sessions, but they have not regained the lucidity of musical phrasing that once distinguished their dancing.

The company's resident choreographer, David Bintley, has created ballets to a number of commissioned scores; but there is little remarkable to say here except to note that, like Martins, Bintley shares the self-conscious, precedent-conscious and craft-conscious qualities of his several composers. The company's resident choreographer, Kenneth MacMillan, who has generally concentrated on twentieth-century music throughout his career, created *The Judas Tree* in March 1992 to a commissioned score by Brian Elias. It was a perfect collaboration of its kind. Elias's music was strong, atmospheric, finely orchestrated, theatrically effective and ambiguous, very much as MacMillan's choreography was. If it was only fleetingly concerned with dancing, there too it was at one with MacMillan. It seems symptomatic of the whole scene that, when Harrison Birtwistle began his magnum opus *Earth Dances* in the mid-1980s, he did some planning of the work with choreographer Ashley Page, who hoped to stage his choreography to the score soon after the work's orchestral premiere; and that this scheme fell through. Despite the second half of its title, Birtwistle's composition became too important and heavyweight to succeed alongside mere dance.

Twyla Tharp

Few choreographers have been more concerned with bridging high and low art than Twyla Tharp, and this is reflected in her musical practice. In the '60s she was a post-Cunningham dancemaker, who worked without music. In the '70s she began employing music and musical rhythm; and made a series of great jazz and pop dances throughout the decade, as well as looking back to the Baroque. In the '80s she also moved into rock or rock-based music, musical (post-)minimalism, narrative and expressionist concerns; and became a choreographer who made classical ballets not only for some of the world's leading ballet troupes (she was attached for three seasons to American Ballet Theatre) but also for her own company. She mastered all this with immense proficiency. Few if any choreographers work better to rock than she. In *The Catherine Wheel* (1981), she elicited real rhythmic vitality from David Byrne and, in the work's final 'Golden Section', she showed how well she could catch its overall wave-like impetus while varying the infrastructure of her own rhythmic response. Still, it may well have been her new emphasis on rock that eliminated the extraordinary spontaneity (the appearance, though not the act, of improvisation) that had made her dances to jazz music so exceptionally vivid. It was apparent that she continued to grow ever smarter in choreographic accomplishment. It was also apparent that she no longer made her scores get under your skin, as they had in the '70s.

Tharp today is the Queen of Crossover. She mixes ballet, rock, modern, and plenty of other movement forms; it shows in her choice of music. In 1992, she presented a fortnight season with her own pick-up dance company in New York. There were four new works, all to new music. One of them, *Men's Piece*, involved Tharp herself 'rehearsing' with some male dancers to a medley of songs; it was the most 'old-Twyla' and least balletic work of the season. Another, *Octet*, was to new music by Edgar Meyer; it was perhaps Tharp's most considerable success to date in fusing ballet and rock. *Grand Pas: Rhythm of the Saints*, a gala *pas de deux* for two Paris Opéra dancers, was to out-takes from Paul Simon music that Tharp and Simon had selected together. As for *Sextet*, its commissioned score, by Bob Telson, prompted Tharp to a bright ballet-Latin carnival; she caught the brisk pulse of this score, though without much by way of solid phrases. None of these pieces proved a great breakthrough on Tharp's part, but *Octet* and *Sextet* go further than anything before towards breaking down barriers between officially recognized genres. Likewise, no one has done more to bring the dance element of ballet into line with this era of recorded sound, with modern life, and with music high and low.

Minimalism

During the 1960s and 1970s, late modernist and early postmodern tenden-

cies in music and dance led to the emergence of the form we call minimalism. There are, of course, earlier examples of minimalist choreography
– the repetitions and multiplications of the same step in the entrance of the
corps of Shades in *La Bayadère*, the highly restricted vocabulary of Nijinsky's
L'Après-midi d'un faune. But now it became a school, with small patterns of
music being repeated. This minimalist music had a heavy beat. Usually so
regular that it showed a subcutaneous relation to rock; and it had an
accompanying atmosphere that was often quasi-religious – gushing and
ecstatic, or incantatory, echo-laden and full of mystique. Philip Glass, Steve
Reich and other composers became gurus to a number of dancemakers,
who included Meredith Monk, Lucinda Childs, and Laura Dean. John
Adams and Michael Nyman joined the ranks of minimalist musicians.
Numerous choreographers found that they simply had to try a Glass work:
Jerome Robbins, Twyla Tharp, Lar Lubovitch, David Gordon were the
most eminent of those who did. Even those choreographers who are far
from minimalism were challenged by this music to reduce their vocabulary
to less than a handful of movements, and to recycle them in loop patterns.
The loops might keep gradually changing or they might stay more or less
fixed – usually the former. The effect could be hypnotic and trance-like.

But if minimalism became a school in the '70s, what was there to learn in
it? Not a lot. Some of the composers began to diversify – Steve Reich
towards jazz, Philip Glass towards pop and exotic mystique, John Adams
towards Lisztian sub-Romanticism, Michael Nyman towards Hollywood.
The dance companies which most specialized in dance minimalism – Laura
Dean's and Lucinda Childs' – made increasingly less impact from the mid-
'80s on. (In 1988, Childs had to close her troupe for some time). We can feel,
however, the general effect of minimalism easily today. It's there in several
works by Siobhan Davies, especially those to music by Michael Nyman.
(*and do they do*, 1986), John Adams (*New Galileo*, 1984 and *Dancing Ledge*,
1990), Steve Reich (*Embarque*, 1988 and *Different Trains*, 1990). The cycles of
movement build and gather excitement. Or, in the dances or Ian Spink and
the music of (among others) Orlando Gough for Second Stride's works –
most notably *Further and Further into Night*, (1984) – the cycles serve
a deconstructionist purpose. They turn a movement ritual into a dance
rhythm; and they make us find increasing irony about the meanings of the
movements that are being repeated. The repetitions in Gough's music, with
its element of jazz and its surprisingly beautiful sonorities, heighten this
effect.

Multiculturalism

Multiculturalism is not something new in our culture or our music or our
dance – it has always been more or less present – but in recent years it has
attracted a new emphasis (distinguishing it in particular from the cultural

imperialism whereby Western culture has absorbed features from the cultures of conquered or occupied lands).

Multiculturalism has much to do with race relations within polytechnic urban Western culture; and something to do with post-imperialist white guilt. Among the composers who have embraced it, one is the British Nigel Osborne – who, for several years during the '80s, enjoyed a collaboration with the choreographer Richard Alston. His music has consciously imbibed the multiple layerings of rhythm from African music and also its sonorities. (It has, of course, many other fine features, and it is absurd that I place him under the 'multiculturalism' label as if he belonged nowhere else.) To Osborne's music, Alston made *Apollo Distraught* (1982), *Wildlife* (commissioned score, 1984), *Mythologies* (1985 and, rechoreographed, 1989) and *Zansa* (1986). Together, the two have also presented lecture-demonstrations and open discussions. In both body-shapes and rhythms, this music has extended Alston's dance language. (His own dance multiculturalism has been apparent in other works too, such as the 'Balinese' *Pulau Dewata* (1989), to luminous music by the Canadian Claude Vivier.)

One can find such examples of multiculturalism in numerous other dance works and their scores. It was a strong influence on the primitivism of Louis Horst and Martha Graham, and on the unorthodox quest for a wider conception of rhythm and movement in the work of John Cage and Merce Cunningham. We may, I believe, feel its liberating influence on the vocalizations of the postmodern performance artist Meredith Monk. And we can see it prominent in two dances Mark Morris has made to music by Lou Harrison – whose American Indian choral chants inform the imagery and fluent course of *Strict Songs* (1988) and whose Grand Duo for Piano and Violin supplies the urgent primitivist/modernist rhythms and language of *Polka* (1992).

Like jazz or rock, multiculturalism becomes a sensibility that suffuses some choreographers' oeuvre. Thus, for example, Morris's dance rendition of Purcell's *Dido and Aeneas* (1989) has Dido and her court as Eastern, formal and ancient (in contrast to the western slangy and modern sorceress and her coven). In the hands of some choreographers, music and dance are juxtaposed in a deliberate exercise of East meets West. The most prominent example of this in Britain is the highly conceptual work of Shobana Jeyasingh, who now applies western choreographic structures to her inherited Indian dance language, and who collaborates with western composers in providing them with an accompaniment.

The school of Cage

I write this just two days after the news of John Cage's death. Even now, the principles lying behind the famous Cage-Cunningham concept – that dance and music should be independent from each other – are often misunderstood. Cage, as his great 1944 essay 'Grace and Clarity' makes clear,[3] urged the importance of a firm rhythmic structure in a score; and the form of dance theatre that Cage and Cunningham developed succeeds best where there is a broad understanding of rhythm – French rhythm, in fact, as Virgil Thomson had defined it – between score and choreography.[4] As already stated, there is also a multiculturalism in much work by Cage and/or Cunningham that has seldom been discussed. I mention it here because it is abundantly evident in a score composed for Cunningham in 1989, 'Peace Talks' by Michael Pugliese – an enthralling score that, like several by Cage and other Cunningham composers, is a collage of tapes of percussion music. (Percussiveness is generally a characteristic of Cage-Cunningham rhythm.) Pugliese's tapes – recorded in various parts of Africa, India, the Far East and perhaps elsewhere – are of great beauty. In 1991, he composed a quite different score, the peaceful and pastoral 'Mixed Signals', to accompany (most effectively) Cunningham's *Loosestrife*. In the same year, for another of Cunningham's nature studies, *Beachbirds*, Cage himself provided *Four*[3], an idyllic and exceptionally quiet overlaying of three types of sound – single piano notes; some long mechanical bleeps like bird-calls; the rustling made by a rainstick (sounding like a wave retreating over a beach) – all set against silence. I single these out; much of what has been provided to accompany Cunningham in recent years is far less distinguished.

This survey of dance and music is, of course, woefully incomplete and extremely partial. I have isolated certain figures and trends because they reveal larger tendencies. Much work has been overlooked, and much has not been given due justice. 'But', as Bernard Shaw wrote in 1895, 'my criticism has not, I think, any other fault than the inevitable fault of extreme unfairness.'

1. Ronald Gray, 'The German Intellectual Background', p. 55 of *The Wagner Companion*, ed. Peter Burbidge and Richard Sutton, Faber, 1979.
2. Quoted in Mary Clarke, *The Sadler's Wells Ballet*, p. 11, A & C Black, 1955.
3. Originally published in *Dance Observer*, 11 November 1944, pp. 108–9. Reprinted in Cage's *Silence*, Calder & Boyars, 1968.
4. Virgil Thomson, 'French Rhythm', *New York Herald Tribune*, 14 November 1943, reprinted in *A Virgil Thomson Reader*, pp. 241ff., Dutton Obelisk, 1984. Also Alastair Macaulay, 'Happy Hooligan', *The New Yorker*, 28 April 1992.

Dance and music:
a north and south view

Rachel Richardson

L iving in the north of England and working in the south can sometimes be exasperating – one can often seem to be at the wrong end of the country for especially interesting dance events. The reverse can also be true, of course, and over the last season or two there have been highlights for me in both north and south, on stage and small screen, in dance works new and old; with sound accompaniment including minimal and electronic music, full-scale orchestral works and small-scale piano pieces.

In Rambert Dance Company's second programme at the Royalty Theatre in June 1992 there was the chance to see Merce Cunningham's first work choreographed for a British company: *Touchbase*, with music by Michael Pugliese (*Icebreeze*). Also on the programme were two new works by company members: Mark Baldwin's *Island to Island* with sound by Ben Craft, and Paul Old's *Still Dance*, performed in silence. To end the programme, there was one of the most popular of Richard Alston's recent works, *Roughcut*, to a score by Steve Reich.

In *Touchbase*, dance and music each maintain individual identities; they are independent of each other, but at the same time complementary in the sense that each allows the other space to be itself. The music's intriguing whirrings and whinings, with patches of rhythmic impulse and melodic fragments, are sufficiently spacious to 'set off' the dance's own varied rhythms, phrasing, dynamic shape, its relationships of dancers to each other, to the space around them and to the set. In comparison with some of the harsh cacophony in Cage's music for Cunningham's dances, where there may be a feeling that the two elements are forcing a relationship by inhabiting the same time span, it seems that, in *Touchbase*, these two are inhabitants of the same environment; different species, but in harmony with each other and that environment. This is partly because of the spaciousness of the music, its mellow, if unfamiliar timbres, its fragments of melody and rhythmic shape all coming together into an interesting whole structure. Combined with that, the dance's clarity of image and structuring device, its sense of unhurried but positive momentum, create a satisfying feeling of completeness as the work unfolds.

Performance on the small screen inevitably loses the immediacy of live performance, but some of the works shown in the BBC's 'Dance House' season demonstrate clearly the different possibilities offered by the medium. Close-up shots of dancers' faces, hands or feet, can create an intimacy not possible on the large stage. At the same time, the use of film techniques – such as cutting from one dancer to another, from one angle to another, repeating phrases in slow motion, and so on – has the effect of distancing the dance from its sound accompaniment. The sound, usually, is constant, heard as emanating from one place throughout, whereas we are shown the dance from different standpoints and even in different time scales, and as happening in different environments. This creates a sense of dislocation between dance and music, even if the two share structural, rhythmic or dynamic aspects; and that, in turn, affects the way we perceive and 'read' the dance.

In Nahid Siddiqui's solo, to music by John Marc Gowans, there is a clear sense of the choreographer understanding the rich possibilities offered by minimalist music for choreography. The dance can be complex without losing clarity because of the constant underlying pulse and stability of the music, which provides a floor for the dance without necessarily imposing a structure. Having said that, there is a clear link between dance and music structures especially in the first part of the solo, with the dance phrase coinciding with the music phrase, both stopping, dead, together. But there are also several occasions when dance phrases are shown in slow motion – an action-replay effect which draws attention to specific features of the dance while the music continues in its rhythmic minimalism (usually the last movement of a phrase is repeated immediately after the whole phrase has been seen in normal time). Throughout this solo the dance rhythms are more complex than the music rhythms, with wide variations in speed and dynamic, sometimes between feet and arms and hands, creating contrapuntal layers of movement and sound. The dance phrasing itself becomes more complex in relation to music as the piece progresses, coming together with the music again only for the perfectly synchronized ending.

Sometimes, as in Carolyn Choa's *Go*, to a score by Orlando Gough, the music provides atmosphere in a relatively conventional way, suggesting undercurrents of feeling and relationships. In this case, the music and dance are structured to fit each other as well, in terms of the overall shape of the piece. There are three sections: the first beginning slowly and with gentle dynamic in both dance and music; a sudden climactic silence following ominous drumbeats as the dancers confront each other in brief stillness before the second section; punctuating chords and silence again as the woman breaks away from her partner to move into the slow final section. However, there is still a sense of distance between the two elements, not only because the details of dance and music material do not relate closely (the music is built up of rhythmic patterns gradually superimposed on each other, while the dance maintains a fluid, sustained quality, moving independently of these rhythms) but also because the dance is filmed on the

39

seashore. No sounds of that environment or the dancers' movement within it are heard, only the music, underlining the dislocation between the two.

Jonathan Lunn's *Mosaic* to a monologue by Anthony Minghella, performed by Juliet Stevenson and Lauren Potter, uses television's own strengths – the intimacy of the monologue spoken by one character, the two characters moving in an economical but not bare set. Dance images seem to pick up on certain words or phrases, but not necessarily in an immediately literal sense, so that other connections are suggested, other levels of meaning hinted at. Particular words or phrases, such as 'crying', 'arms', 'ran away' are given pictorial image in the dance; elsewhere the movement is more abstract, although the two performers, actress and dancer, stay close to one another and frequently relate to each other in different ways – through touch, focus, or movement together in the same direction but with different speeds and dynamic levels. The provocative final sentence – 'I, for some reason, have never seen a pattern in these things' – challenges the spectator to find a pattern in what has passed before in movement and words and in the rhythms of both.

Many dance works are inspired by literary or dramatic sources, and one of these, in a traditional theatrical form, is Northern Ballet Theatre's new version of *Romeo and Juliet*, choreographed by Massimo Moricone to Prokofiev's score, which had its premiere in Blackpool in February 1991. Artistic director Christopher Gable's commitment to the theatrical dimension of ballet is clearly demonstrated in this production in which dance, drama, music and design all contribute significantly to the total effect. However, it is the imaginative relationship of dance and music in many scenes which make the ballet truly memorable.

Prokofiev's gloriously lyrical aspect is fully exploited by Moricone in the various *pas de deux* of *Romeo and Juliet*, in which the expansive flow of dance is interwoven with small, evocative gestures such as the hand of one tracing over the face of the other, or their sudden clutching embrace. These dances do not make symbols of the two lovers, but allow them to appear both spontaneous and sometimes even awkward, as befits their youth and inexperience, so that the passages of uninterrupted, soaring lyricism have a more poignant aspect. In the Balcony *pas de deux*, the broad sweep of melody in ecstatic mood is echoed in the overall quality of movement, but phrasing and rhythmic patterning coincide only occasionally. For example, the opening phrase of this *pas de deux* is rich and sensuous, in contracting and unfolding movements, matching quite closely the music's rise and fall, but, immediately, the dance begins to move much faster and with a lighter dynamic colouring as Romeo lifts Juliet and turns with her. This lighter quality is typical of most of the *pas de deux*; the many lifts tend to be low and often almost childlike, for example the lift in which Juliet's knees are bent up to her chest and she clings closely to Romeo as he spins her round. At these moments one is perhaps most aware of the youth and inexperience of the pair through the choreography, while the music's richness suggests the maturity towards which the lovers are growing.

Having suggested that the major strength of Moricone's *Romeo and Juliet* is its musicality, there are times when this is certainly not the case. In the ballroom scene, when Romeo and Juliet meet for the first time, the music cuts from the stately court dance to the gentle intimate music of the lovers' meeting and back again, not once but several times, in an attempt to convey the double layers of action and meaning. This is clumsily done. There are other, more subtle ways of suggesting different layers of experience at the same time, and dance and music together present many possibilities for interaction and complementing each other.

Another jarring note is created by the introduction of the sound of thunder before each act. Again, Prokofiev has already written into the score the sense of foreboding which underlies the drama, and 'realistic' thunder is superfluous. However, as pointed out above, this is to highlight two areas of contention; those aside, the ballet is compelling and convincing in many ways.

Music is an important source of inspiration in Alvin Ailey's *Revelations* (1960), which was performed by the Alvin Ailey American Dance Theater at Bradford's Alhambra Theatre in October 1991. Langston Hughes wrote in the programme note: 'This suite explores motivations and emotions of African-American religious music. . .'

Revelations has taken on something of the quality of a legend since its first performance in 1960. Set to a selection of spirituals both traditional and new, it explores aspects of black American heritage and religious faith through a choreographic style which embraces the intensely physical expressive potential of Martha Graham's technique and the light-hearted *joie de vivre* of American social dance.

The opening section of the ballet, 'I been 'buked', is structured in five verses. Ailey uses the structure of the spiritual by giving each verse its own identity, while using repeated imagery to link them all together.

The first serves as introduction: the dancers are motionless and the unaccompanied vocal harmony is hummed. The dancers only begin to move as the last note dies away, so that the transition into the next verse is smooth. The first verse proper is sung slowly, legato, and the movement quality is sustained almost throughout, also matching the musical phrasing to a large extent. This is achieved, not by having the dancers arrive in a position or a tableau on the last melody note and holding it through the note's duration, but, more interestingly, by having the dancers gradually complete the formation or tableau only at the last moment – sometimes the last dancers have to move very fast to reach their positions in time, while the first dancers move slowly, extending arms and body into the image they are creating. This is a subtle point, but one which gives the dance a kind of elastic tension which is never fully relaxed – there are no 'dead' moments.

Dancers continue to move in the silences, too – after the very striking group image suggesting a bird in flight with focus to the earth – one of the images that are completed gradually – the rear central dancer suddenly straightens his arms out of the inward-rotated curve. This is a surprising moment, especially as it happens as the sound is dying away, without the support of music.

The two central verses are both taken at a faster speed and with a generally stronger dynamic level in music and dance. The group, which had been very close for much of the time in the first verse, now begins to split and reform, split and reform. The result of this is a picture of individuality within community, and the relationship of dance and music is clear in that the more powerful dynamic and faster tempo of the music are reflected in the quality and speed of movement, with lunges, turns and leaps prevalent, although the dance structure is different from that of the music.

There are phrases of unison for small groups, occasional passages of unison for the whole group – coinciding with a climactic moment in the music – and much individual choreography in which dancers move at different speeds. Again, they reach the group unison moments only gradually, so that a few dancers will still be leaping and turning as the music slows towards the end of the phrase. Each verse ends in a different group formation, underlining the sense of community. The final verse is a repeat of the first, except for the end. After the slow lift of hands in an asymmetric prayer-like gesture, the dancers open their arms out sideways with staccato-like movements which are unsynchronized with either each other or the music. The music is dying slowly into silence, so that, as in the moment at the end of the first verse, it provides no rhythmic support for this movement. The tension created in the contrast between movement and dance suggests further layers of possible meaning in the dance. The other sections of the work show similar instances of dance-music relationships to a greater or lesser extent, but in few is there the strength of independent dance imagery evident in the opening.

Many choreographers choose to use 'concert' music for ballets which may have no obvious or intended link with dance but which offers various possibilities to the choreographer in terms of structure, rhythmic and dynamic phrasing, melodic shape, mood or drama, and so on. Romantic or late-Romantic music is attractive to some choreographers because of the long melodic lines which lend themselves to dance of a lyrical aspect; also the rich variety of mood and atmosphere can be exploited by being given more specific meaning in dance with a dramatic theme, or by being allowed to give emotional colouring to dance of a more abstract nature.

Massine's *Choreartium*, revived by the Birmingham Royal Ballet in 1991, falls into the last category. Brahms' Fourth Symphony has a rich orchestral texture, a broad sweep of melodic invention, and an intensity of drama inherent in the large-scale development of musical ideas.

Massine balances the considerable orchestral resources with a large cast which, for much of the ballet, functions as a complex group within its own choreographic structure. The accomplished and imaginative manipulation of group patterns, shapes and movement through space, with the *corps de ballet* working sometimes as a movement choir, sometimes in kaleidoscopic patterns which form, re-form, and dissolve, appear and disappear, presents a compelling counterpart to the symphony.

The imagery in the ballet is original, and the sometimes surprising quirky rhythms of steps and gestures – the use of the body with sudden, percussive contracting movements of the arms into the body, for example – add a piquant contrast to the broad sweep of melody, while at the same time responding obliquely to the inner complexity of rhythm and orchestration in the score. Characteristic also of the movement style are the low sweeps towards the floor, the angled wrists with palms uppermost and soft elbows, arms lifted and body tilting. The dappled light on the backdrop, the gentle or pulsating colours of the costumes, complement the musical and choreographic evocation of shifting moods.

Another colourful, late-Romantic work is used by Ben Stevenson for his ballet *Four Last Songs* (1980) to a song cycle of the same title by Richard Strauss, and performed by English National Ballet. Again, the music employs considerable orchestral resources with the addition this time of the solo voice, which brings a more specific emotional colouring to the whole.

In contrast to Massine, Stevenson uses only eight dancers, dressed in white unitards, with white hanging drapes which are lifted and lowered at different times during the piece, and finally lowered onto the recumbent figures of the dancers at the end. The preponderance of white, and the intimately scaled structure – *pas de deux* with three couples, trio, *pas de deux*, solo with ensemble – balance the richness of the musical score in a quite different way from Massine's approach. Here, the relative starkness of the visual image presented in the choreography complements the aural complexity of the music. At the same time, Stevenson does pick up on the mood of the music, and its almost decadent aspect, by creating a mood of general nostalgia at the beginning ('Spring'), with a hinted-at dramatic theme developed throughout. Swirling shapes and patterns in lifts or canon movements of the arms are redolent of some indefinable mood. In the trio ('September'), the changing relationship between the three dancers is slightly ambiguous and seems unresolved – as indeed is the shifting, chromatic tonality of the music, although the latter's long postlude does resolve these ambiguities at the end, and this evokes further subtleties of meaning in the dance as a whole. In the *pas de deux* ('Going to sleep'), beginning before the music with a diagonal pathway, the woman is supported in swooning walks as if mortally sick. The music itself seems to creep in gradually, low and quiet, and the dance's beginning foreshadows the music. There are poignant images of suffering, longing, searching for each other and finding each other, during the long, elegiac solo violin passage between verses. Two other men enter and lift the woman who is carried off, lifted high, horizontally, as the music ends with a long, slow descending arpeggio in the horn. Her partner follows, extending an arm in a reaching gesture towards her, suggesting that it is perhaps death, rather than sleep, which has claimed her. The long female solo ('At gloaming') is different, with more percussive, angular, awkward movements, swooping low on pointe to the floor, pulling in to the body, contrasting with the sustained sweeps of richly orchestrated melody. Towards the end, the other dancers now on stage, little woodwind flurries gently punctuate the stream of sound as it fades very, very gradually, and all the dancers are lowered by one woman to the floor for the end. The final words of the song are 'How tired we are of travelling – is this perchance death?' and it is only really at the end of the ballet that the meaning becomes clear, so subtle and gradual is the unfolding of the theme in relationship to the music.

Stanton Welch's *Of Blessed Memory (Beata Memoriae)*, for the Australian Ballet, is a work in some ways similar to Stevenson's, in that it is set to a cycle of songs ('Songs from the Auvergne' by Joseph Canteloube), and the dancers are costumed in white. However, despite references to both Kylián and Tudor in the choreography, the ballet quickly lapses into sugary sentimentality because of a failure to look any deeper than the surface melodies of the score. A reliance on repetition of imagery which is rarely subtle tends to make the music itself seem shallow and lacking in interest.

Each of the above programmes brought the possibility of seeing older works, some to commissioned scores, some to existing concert music. Birmingham Royal Ballet's programme included *Petrushka*, Fokine's 1911 masterpiece of collaboration with Stravinsky, and Balanchine's *Divertimento No. 15* (1956, Mozart). English National Ballet presented Act II of Petipa's *La Bayadère* (1877, Minkus), and Lichine's *Graduation Ball* (1940, Johann Strauss). The Australian Ballet brought two English ballets from the 1930s: Antony Tudor's *Gala Performance* (1938, Prokofiev) and Ninette de Valois' *Checkmate* (1937, Arthur Bliss).

Music at quite the opposite end of the spectrum in terms of scale was used throughout the programme presented by Irek Mukhamedov and Company. Two pianos comprised the instrumental resources, and often only one was used. Of the five new creations for the company, one had a commissioned score: *Portrait*, by Matthew Hart, to music by Augustin Fernandez. The second half of the programme began with the Nocturne *pas de deux* from Frederick Ashton's *The Dream*. The choreography illuminates detail by bringing out different layers of Mendelssohn's music – small instrumental ornamentation as in Oberon's 'scattering' shake of the hand over Titania, or broader melodic sweep as in the unison phrase of leaps and turns round the stage – at different times in the dance. This is evident just as strongly in the two-piano arrangement as in the original orchestral scoring.

One of the new creations was a solo by David Bintley, made for Deborah Bull. Entitled *Undine*, it is set to the 'Ondine' section from Ravel's major piano work *Gaspard de la Nuit*. This is piano writing of considerable complexity and magical atmosphere and, while Bintley sometimes seems to capture something of the latter, he never comes near the former. Individual images of water and supernatural existence appear, in response to the shimmering piano music, but, in the end, the Bintley symmetry and tendency to overwork good ideas without developing them, results in a shallow and unsatisfying work. By contrast, the duet by William Tuckett, *The Unobtrusive Detail* set to Chopin's Nocturne No. 8 in D Flat, was the highlight of the evening. Danced by Larissa Bamber and Michael Nunn, both dressed in black shirts and trousers against a black floor and backcloth, and lit with soft spotlights, it is a duet that is both tender and passionate, with an intensity of feeling which is at times contained, at times uninhibited. Its unison, understated movements close together, keep with the underlying pulse, but create contrapuntal rhythms with the melody – not complex, but matching the quiet clarity of the music. Its gentle lifts, not virtuosic but close, sometimes fluid, sometimes with a sharper dynamic, lead into an intimate, introverted shape – the intimacy of the music is echoed in the intimacy of the dancing.

Antony Tudor, a master of musical choreography, has been represented in this country more often during the last year or two than is usually the case, and other works of his seen, in addition to the Australian Ballet's production of *Gala Performance* (1938), were *Pillar of Fire*, *The Leaves are Fading*, *Jardin aux lilas* and *Dark Elegies*; also *Echoing of Trumpets* in a revival after nearly twenty years by English National Ballet, and *Dark Elegies* performed by the Ballet du Rhin in June 1992. All of these, except the last two, were performed by American Ballet Theatre, either at the London Coliseum, or on BBC television as part of the 'Dance Makers' series on BBC2 in August 1992.

The Australian Ballet was coached in Tudor's *Gala Performance* by Maude Lloyd, Tudor's leading ballerina in most of his works made during the 1930s, but the dancers still fell into the trap of overplaying their parts. The choreography is itself satirical, and the music aptly chosen. Prokofiev had a gift for humour both rollicking and ironic, and it is the latter variety which is present, albeit understated, in the third Piano Concerto and the 'Classical' Symphony. This is made to work with the choreography to convey the sense of satire by colouring the dance movement – which is clearly classi- cally based but gently manipulated through the subtle exaggeration of individual mannerisms in the styles of the three ballerinas – to provide ironic comment on the traditions of nineteenth-century ballet.

Tudor only once made a ballet to a commissioned score, and his frequent preference was for music of the late nineteenth or early twentieth century. He once commented that audiences probably didn't realize that if a ballet particularly moved them, it was very likely due to the effect of the music, rather than anything happening on stage. However, perhaps no other choreographer has so successfully harnessed the emotive power of music in his work. Tudor's musicality as a choreographer is evident on several different levels: in the overall structure of ballets, their beginnings and endings, the use of leitmotif and of rhythmic patterns and, through all of this, the balancing of much of his chosen music's emotional intensity with a choreographic vocabulary which is tightly controlled. In *Dark Elegies*, for example, Mahler's song-cycle 'Kindertotenlieder', provides a clear struc- ture for the ballet, which Tudor uses to explore individual and communal responses to grief and bereavement through solos, a duet, and ensemble work. Within this structure, he manipulates rhythm and dynamic elements with flexibility, and the choreography responds more often to the underly- ing mood of individual songs than to specific imagery in the poems. This approach to structure – using the large-scale form as a basis, and working out a complementary dance structure within it – is evident in his other ballets, too, such as *Jardin aux lilas* and *Pillar of Fire*. *The Leaves are Fading* (1975) is different in that Tudor compiled the music score himself, from a selection of chamber works for strings by Dvořák, and it is interesting, but perhaps not surprising, that the impression of overall structure in this ballet is of something much more open-ended, less tightly contained. One might say that this is appropriate, since the theme of the ballet – elusive as it certainly is – is much less concerned with the changing experiences of a group of people over a period of time.

An interesting feature of Tudor's choreography in terms of rhythm is the fact that he has several different approaches. Sometimes the dancers move in close synchronization with the melodic line, as in the first duet for Caroline and her Lover in *Jardin*, or the beginning of the first solo in *Dark Elegies*. At other times, the discrepancy between music and dance rhythms is extreme; for example, the two dancing girls in *Jardin*, who waltz off-stage to an inaudible rhythm, while Caroline struggles to regain her self-control; also, the ending of the second song in *Dark Elegies*, where the woman runs swiftly round the stage and into the wings, against a slowly dying musical line. In each case (and there are many others) the image presented is complex: one is aware of different layers of experience at the same time.

In *Jardin*, central musical themes are used in different ways; not always associated with a particular character (although the solo violin is frequently associated with Caroline), but, rather, with moods and feelings, and always given different treatment. The most famous of these is the 'frozen tableau' near the end of the ballet, when the theme is played fortissimo by full orchestra, and the full cast is motionless on stage, the focus of the main characters on Caroline. The disparity between music and dance here is extreme, and Tudor has made use of this idea in different ways in several of his ballets, to create a particular kind of tension which draws the focus in to the central character at a critical moment in her experience. The extreme contrast between richly romantic sweeps of melody and disciplined movement vocabulary is especially evident in *Dark Elegies* because of the starkness of the movement vocabulary, with its angular gestures, use of parallel placement of the legs, very little pointework, and sense of being weighted into the ground.

But it is also the case in *Jardin*, where the basis of *danse d'école* is allowed to suggest the gentility of the characters, their social values and manners. The music, with its relatively uninhibited lyrical flow can speak of inner experience, augmented by the subtle detail of the choreography, movements derived from life which delineate character and states of mind – for example, Caroline's sudden dropping of her face into her hands, and the sympathetic comforting gesture of her friend who encourages her to keep up appearances.

The music colours the mood of the whole in *Pillar* in a similar way. For example, the very different movement styles of the various characters are set against the continuous forward momentum of the music – the upright, stilted movements of the Old Maids, the pedestrian, 'ordinariness' of the Friend, and the changing style of Hagar herself: from the extreme tension of reserve and frustration, through desperation and shame, to hope, acceptance and love.

It is interesting to compare the endings of these ballets. In each, there is a long cadential passage in the music which is used by the choreographer to draw threads together and resolve tensions. In *Jardin*, the final resolution of tonality in the music, after the shifting ambiguities of the rest, is given to the long process of farewells to guests, and to Caroline's efforts to face up to the bleak future mapped out for her. However, her Lover, left alone on stage, introduces the notion of something still unresolved.

Resignation is also the mood of the ending of *Dark Elegies* although this time a more hopeful resignation, which is not only expressed in the calm after the storm in the music, but also in the formal, ritualistic movements of the dancers round the stage. They seem to be drawing strength from each other, and the ability to move forward into the future, as the music slowly fades. In *Pillar of Fire*, the long cadential ending focuses on the new-found trust and hope experienced by Hagar, as she and the Friend also move on into a hopeful future. In the case of both these ballets, the dying away of the music does not suggest the end of the story, but the release of the particular complex web of tension which has been in focus during the ballet. This effect is achieved because, although the music is certainly dying away into silence, the dance is never seen to end – the dancers continue to move as the curtain falls.

PART III

The Dancing World

Australia

Jill Sykes

What is Australian dance? It's a question often asked in this part of the world, and the answers are so diverse that they are best summed up as 'dance that is done in Australia'. In the past year, this has ranged from a *Nutcracker* relocated to an Australian setting, the launch of a second Aboriginal contemporary dance company, and an Asian coproduction based on the Ramayana, to small works in the international idiom of postmodernism.

If it is possible to pin down an Australian style of dancing, it would probably be characterized across the spectrum by a generosity of movement, a bold use of space and the confidence of creative freedom – qualities that could be said to reflect Australia's size, isolation and relatively recent white settlement.

They are all to be found in abundance in the **Australian Ballet**'s major new production for 1992, a *Nutcracker* choreographed by Graeme Murphy and designed by Kristian Fredrikson on a scenario they developed.

The story begins in the southern hemisphere's hot Christmas, with a former Diaghilev dancer preparing celebrations for her emigré friends in the 1950s. She had settled in Australia at the outbreak of World War II, when stranded on a tour with the de Basil Ballets Russes, and the unfolding of her memories brings together past and present, tradition and the ways of a new world.

The concept echoes reality, illustrating the nation's migrant history and cultural foundations. The people who dance it, young and old, represent several generations of classical ballet with links back over a century.

Murphy and Fredrikson have retained elements such as the Christmas gift of a nutcracker doll, Clara's nightmare of terrifying fighting rats, a journey through exotic cultures, the Sugar Plum Fairy, waltzing flowers and swirling snowflakes. But they have substituted a genuine, dramatic storyline for the usual divertissements of the second act.

At the premiere in March 1992, the elderly Clara was danced by 69-year-old Margaret Scott, who alternated with former de Basil dancer Valrene Tweedie in contrasting but equally vivid and poignant interpretations. Miranda Coney, as Clara at the height of her career, looked and danced as though she were born for the role, in an eloquent performance. Steven Heathcote as her lover and Greg Horsman as her partner danced with ardour and bravura finesse, respectively.

This new *Nutcracker* is a handsome addition to the Australian Ballet's

Sydney Dance Company's *Some Rooms*, choreographed by Graeme Murphy to music by Poulenc. Dancers: Janet Vernon and Ross Philip.　PHOTO: BRANCO GAICA

repertoire, a major work which the nation's dancegoers can call their own and proudly hope to share worldwide through touring and video recording.

A short work premiered in 1991 by the national ballet company, in an unusually good period for local creative opportunities, has already been seen overseas during the Australian Ballet's 1992 tour to Italy and England.

Of Blessed Memory, Stanton Welch's tribute and star vehicle for his mother, former Australian Ballet principal Marilyn Jones, is a promising choreographic start for this young company member.

Besides the new works, the Australian Ballet revived a variety of ballets for its thirtieth anniversary year, including Ninette de Valois' *Checkmate*, Jerome Robbins' *The Concert*, John Cranko's *Romeo and Juliet*, Stephen Baynes' *Catalyst* and Maina Gielgud's production of *Giselle*, providing a diverse selection of roles for its accomplished and versatile dancers.

Aboriginal dance is expanding from its traditional base in staged performance to take advantage of the breadth of dance expertise which has been emerging from the five-year course offered by the **Aboriginal Islander Dance Theatre** (AIDT).

AIDT – the company – has sprung directly from the course, presenting its first season in 1991. Led by artistic director Raymond Blanco with Paul Saliba as chief choreographer, it is a development of the annual student presentations which combine staged recreations of traditional Aboriginal and Islander styles with new choreography. This draws on the gamut of the performers' experience, from their heritage dance to Graham technique.

Bangarra Dance Theatre, established in 1989 by former AIDT staff and students, was revitalized in 1991 with the appointment of Stephen Page as artistic director and chief choreographer. In his first full-length work, *Praying Mantis Dreaming*, he explored counterpoint themes of urban and outback Aboriginal lifestyles with great sensitivity and convincing theatricality.

Both companies have already performed outside Australia, and have plans for more overseas tours. They have added an interesting creative dimension to the more conventional programmes of traditional Aboriginal groups – ironically, in both cases, more in demand abroad than at home.

The influence of Asia is becoming more prominent in dance, as in other areas of the arts, business and daily life in Australia. The most exciting example of Asian-Australian fusion so far has been **One Extra Company**'s *Dancing Demons*, directed by the group's founder, Kai Tai Chan, before he handed over artistic direction to Graeme Watson at the end of 1991. *Dancing Demons*, with a cast of Australian and Indonesian performers, was developed in workshop style by the dancers in Bali. Using the Ramayana as a thematic foundation, and winding Balinese dance and music traditions through a generally international vocabulary, they explored the effects of mass tourism on the island's culture. Performed first in Indonesia and then in Sydney, *Dancing Demons* was typical of One Extra's ability to create dance theatre which is notable for its relevance, vitality and rich theatricality.

Around Australia, the State companies have experienced the extremes of low key continuity and traumatic upheaval. In Adelaide, the **Australian**

Dance Theatre's artistic director, Leigh Warren, was told at the end of 1991 that his contract would be shortened by a year. Meryl Tankard, who has been earning considerable acclaim as director and choreographer of Canberra's resident professional dance company, bearing her name, was appointed to succeed him in 1993.

The circumstances of this 'sacking' sparked controversy amongst company members and the local community, with Warren responding by making a new version of *Petrouchka* in which all the characters were pointedly portrayed as puppets of the system. He expects to launch a new group, **Leigh Warren and Dancers**, to give Adelaide two dance companies – though how funding can be expanded to accommodate them both is an unanswered question.

In Perth, the **West Australian Ballet** under the direction of Barry Moreland maintains its pattern of upbeat contemporary classicism. After the international flourish of Moreland's *A Midsummer Night's Dream* touring to Melbourne and the Philippines in mid-1991, the October season featured four new short works, two by company members Edmund Stripe and Elizabeth Hill and the others by Chrissie Parrott and Moreland.

In May 1992, Moreland's *Lady of the Camellias* was revived, with the first night performance declared a testimonial to Ronnie Van den Bergh, the stylish company stalwart who created the role of Armand Duval in this charming evocation of the tragic romance.

Meanwhile the **Chrissie Parrott Dance Collective** has taken off in a more exploratory style, mostly showing Parrott's own freshly individual choreography. This included *Terra*, her first full-length work, a witty piece of theatrical dance premiered in June 1991, and the abrasive *Factory*, an edgy examination of angst and alienation in a desensitized industrial society.

Factory was choreographed for the Festival of Perth in February 1992 as the major piece on the group's programme, which included the Australian debut of choreography by Stephen Petronio: the brief but tumultuous duet, *Surrender II*, which was given a slick staging by Rebecca Hilton, an Australian in Petronio's company and a former member of Sydney's Dance Exchange.

The Queensland Ballet, directed by Harold Collins, continued its policy of translating familiar stories to classically-based dance by remaking Shakespeare's *Taming of the Shrew* and Euripedes' *Medea*, in which the title roles were vehicles for the particular grace, musicality and theatrical talents of the company's leading dancer, Rosetta Cook.

But the company also turned away from narrative, taking on less specific themes in Graeme Watson's *Intersections*, a pacey abstraction on the possibilities of relationships, and Jacqui Carroll's *Transfigured Night*, inspired by the breaking down of the Berlin Wall.

Elsewhere in Brisbane, **Expressions Dance Company** pursued its mis-

Dianne Reid and Brett Daffy in Danceworks' *Human to Human*, choreographed by Helen Herbertson.   PHOTO: DAVID B. SIMMONDS

sion of developing a contemporary dance repertoire under the leadership of Maggi Sietsma. And 1000 kilometres away in Townsville, **Dance North** continued its twenty-first anniversary celebrations with a typically eclectic and accessible touring programme devised, and in some cases choreographed, by artistic director Cheryl Stock.

At the **Sydney Dance Company**, Graeme Murphy celebrated fifteen years as artistic director in 1992 with a combined season of revivals and three new works. They were *Edgeing*, a moody encounter between dance and rollerskating by former SDC dancer and star of the film *Strictly Ballroom*, Paul Mercurio; Kim Walker's politically inspired and atmospheric *Monkey See*; and Murphy's own *Piano Sonata*, an essay in scintillating movement to a commissioned score by Carl Vine.

Earlier, the SDC brought back Murphy's first full-length work, *Poppy*, in its best-ever production, and presented a programme of diverse new pieces by company members under the thematic title of the *Shakespeare Dances*, one of the programmes it took overseas in 1992 on a tour of France, Colombia and Venezuela.

Around the country, dozens of small, struggling, adventurous groups and individuals enrich the dance and movement landscape with regular or intermittent appearances and original choreography. Among them are **Danceworks**, freelance choreographer **Nanette Hassall**, Russell Dumas' **Dance Exchange**, **Tasdance**, **2 Dance Plus**, **Diana Reyes Flamenco**, the **Bharatam Dance Company**, **Danza Viva Spanish Dance Company**, **Entr'acte Theatre** and **David Atkins'** tap dance productions.

A National Dance Summit, convened in 1991, highlighted the diversity of dance in Australia and sparked fresh attempts to bring together its disparate forms in a loose coalition which would raise the profile of the art form and its lobbying strength in these tough economic times.

Obituaries

Margaret Barr, died in Sydney on 29 May, 1991, aged 86. As a teacher, choreographer and director, her influence on dance and theatre in Australia was widespread and unique. Born in India, she studied with Martha Graham and then taught for her in the 1920s. After working at Dartington Hall, she went to New Zealand at the outbreak of World War II, moving to Australia in the 1950s. In a style that never changed, she choreographed her social concerns on Australian and international themes as dance drama of the most direct and accessible kind, giving annual seasons in Sydney from 1953 to 1990.

Kelvin Coe, died in Melbourne on 9 July 1992, aged 45. Probably the greatest male classical dancer Australia has produced, he was a foundation member of the Australian Ballet in 1962 and danced with the national company for most of his career until he resigned on principle after the dancers' strike in 1981. Thereafter he danced with State companies, creating new roles in ballets such as Graeme Murphy's *Homelands* for the Sydney Dance Company. But he returned as a guest artist to the Australian Ballet to revive *Beyond Twelve*, which Murphy created for him, and danced it in the company's 1988 season at Covent Garden. As a young dancer, Coe looked to Erik Bruhn as his example, and the influence of this *danseur noble* was always evident in his buoyant, elegant style. In a wide range of roles, Coe's sensitivity and intelligent, analytical approach brought an emotional depth to the electricity of his dancing. Remembered for so much as a performer – most indelibly for *Beyond Twelve* and his Albrecht in *Giselle* – he also contributed to the enrichment of a new generation of dancers through teaching at the Australian Ballet School from 1986 and directing the Dancers Company for three years.

Gary Hill, died in Perth on 17 April 1992, aged 47. Having danced with the Australian Ballet since 1965, he moved to Ballet Victoria in 1974 and the Sydney Dance Company in 1977 before going to the West Australian Ballet as dancer, choreographer and ballet master, becoming assistant artistic director. He was appointed artistic director of the North Queensland Ballet Company, now Dance North, in 1983, and later managed the Perth company Still Moves.

Peter Lucas, died in Queensland on 27 May 1992, aged 46. Starting his performing career with Phyllis Danaher's Queensland Ballet Theatre, he worked for J. C. Williamson on tour with Joan Sutherland and Luciano Pavarotti before joining the Australian Dance Theatre under the direction of Jaap Flier, moving with him to the Dance Company (NSW). He was a founding member and the pivotal force behind the Contemporary Dance Theatre in Brisbane, an important focus for new choreography in the 1970s. Taking his practical knowledge and quiet integrity into arts administration, he was administrator of Dance Exchange from 1981 to 1985 before joining the Australia Council as a project officer.

Joan Potter, died in Melbourne on 8 June 1991. With her husband Vassilie Trunoff, she danced with the Borovansky Ballet in the late 1940s before joining London Festival Ballet, first as performers then ballet master and ballet mistress. In 1980 they reproduced *Schéhérazade* and *Graduation Ball* for the Australian Ballet's 'Tribute to Borovansky' programme.

Frank Salter, died in Sydney on 25 July 1992, aged 71. Best known for his association with the Borovansky Ballet, first as a dancer, then as stage manager over an eventful decade for dance in Australia, he has left a lasting memory in his vivid biography of Edouard Borovansky. He also worked for Sol Hurok in London, for Orson Welles, as stage manager at the National Theatre under the direction of Laurence Olivier, and for 12 years with the BBC as a scriptwriter, interviewer and radio producer before returning to Australia.

Austria

Edith M. Wolf Perez

When Elena Tchernichova took over as the director of the **Vienna Staatsoper** in autumn 1991 the company got a lot of publicity. The press was divided into two camps: some critics feared that the dancers she brought from the USA would finally put an end to the 'Viennese' ballet. Others hoped that Tchernichova would succeed in what she had set out to do – to improve the quality of dancing.

There is no question that Tchernichova succeeded in the latter respect. When she presented the company in *Don Quixote*, the only premiere of the season, it was not only the soloists Svetlana Kuznetsova and Kenneth Greeve who gave an impressive example of brilliant dancing – the whole company radiated high spirits. Considering the mere five months that Tchernichova had spent working with them, it was a fine achievement. This was not the case, however, with the choreography. The ballet, to the music of Ludwig Minkus, consisted of a number of *divertissements* which were loosely strung together. The showy effect was emphasized by the choice of very colourful stage sets (by Ray Hecht and Dimitri Strizhov) and costumes (by Eduard Erlikh). Tchernichova explained her choice: 'When you cannot provide a high quality [of dancing] you put on a lot of colour and costumes. You cover.'

The new dynamism of the company was fully expressed in the revival of John Cranko's *Romeo and Juliet*. The guest star on the opening night was the young Russian Vladimir Malakhov as Romeo, who will join the company as a principal dancer this autumn. With the principal dancers Katherine Healy, Svetlana Kuznetsova, Alexej Lapschin, and Michael Shannon who have come to the company with Tchernichova, plus the principals from the 'old' company, Marialuise Jaska, Brigitte Stadler and Karl Ludwig and now Malakhov, and a strong body of soloists (among them Christian Musil, Christian Rovny, Christine Gaugusch, Roswitha Over, Greet Vinckier) and a much-improved *corps de ballet*, the company has the best possible base for further development.

However, Tchernichova seems to be tilting at windmills. When she saw the ballet before signing her contract, she called it 'an adopted child' – the opera house had an excellent opera, but the ballet was second-rate both in quality and status. According to her, she was appointed to change this situation and develop the ballet to match the quality of the opera. However, the help she is getting from the director of the house tells a different story. The number of performances this year was 37 instead of the agreed 45. Next year there will not be 60 but 42; in the third year not 80, but 50. The second promise to the ballet company – performances of modern choreography and one-act ballets – is nowhere in sight. There is also no support for touring, which Tchernichova considers vital for building up an international reputation. 'In this case', she says, 'you can see that actually nobody needs our international reputation, except us.' When the director of the Staatsoper, Eberhard Waechter, died in March this year, his former co-director Ioan Holender was appointed as his successor. While, according to Tchernichova, Waechter was supportive of the ballet company, this support is not so unequivocal in the case of Holender.

All this makes it quite difficult, if not impossible, to develop the attractive and fresh repertoire that the company urgently needs. The only premiere of the 1992/93 season will be *Giselle* choreographed by Tchernichova (all in black and white, by the way). The Strauss evening with Rudi van Dantzig's *Letzte Lieder* and John Neumeier's *Josephs Legende* will be revived. The rest of the repertoire will be the same as last year's. Apart from the ballets mentioned above this includes *The Nutcracker*, *La Fille mal gardée* and *A Midsummer Night's Dream*.

Beside the problems of working within an opera house which maintains a huge ballet company without appropriately supporting it, Tchernichova herself, though excellent in developing the technical standard of dancing, does not provide the artistic vision one would like to see for the repertoire. This is a considerable deficit in view of the fact that the Viennese audience is well informed about choreographic developments through the biannual festival 'Tanz 92', which this year presented, amongst others Johann Kresnik's **Bremer Theater**, **Garth Fagan Dance**, **Le Ballet National de Marseille** and the **Cullberg Ballet** with Mats Ek's *Swan Lake*.

In **Salzburg** the ballet company, now reduced to half its former size, and directed by Peter Breuer, re-emerged strongly with Breuer's choreography to Gluck's *Orpheus and Eurydike*. In **Graz** the ballet company premiered Heinz Spoerli's *Romeo and Juliet* with the touching Linda Papworth in the leading role. The second premiere of the season was an evening with van Manen's *5 Tangos*, a new work by the Czechoslovakian choreographer Pavel Smok, and *Shakers Loops* by Rami Be'er. The plan to have Be'er's solo *Dreamwings* performed by a dancer from Graz had to be abandoned because none could achieve the quality of the Israeli dancer Nitza Gambo for whom it was originally choreographed.

There is also movement on the fringe dance scene. Apart from the regular productions of Austrian dance groups, some new initiatives have been started to support their development. Organizational changes are under way in the Szene Salzburg which has earned a high reputation over the last few years for its summer festivals, which present some of the most interesting choreographers from Europe, the USA and Canada. Now the Szene is offering its premises to young dancers to develop their work. The first artists in residence have been **Editta Braun and Company** and **Hubert Lepka**, both from Salzburg, and **Esther Linley** from Vienna. Editta Braun made a real breakthrough this season, touring her work around Europe. Her choreography, is full of high energy and humour, and has become an international success.

Other new inititiatives included the founding of the Austria Dances festival at the Minoritentheater in Graz, where approximately ten companies from Vienna and Graz showed their work; and Vienna.Acts, an organization to promote Austrian dance and theatre abroad, which started an exchange of productions with Munich and Moscow.

At the Kornmarkttheater in Bregenz the second of a series of choreographic meetings took place in August 1992, in which a group of choreographers from Austria, Switzerland and Slovenia worked together for a week. Another coproduction was initiated by the choreographer Sebastian Prantl in St Pölten, the new capital of Lower Austria, where 14 international choreographers/dancers came together to work on a piece. John Cage's philosophy of artistic creation was the key element of the choreographic process, which was filmed over a period of several months. Several working sessions were open to the public, but the final product will be the film, to be released in 1993. Initiatives like these might well contribute to a positive development of dance 'made in Austria'.

Belgium

Luisa Moffett

Y ou can't please everyone, and the shift towards postmodernism that has characterized the Belgian dance scene ever since Maurice Béjart left Brussels for Lausanne in 1987 has continued its inexorable course, leaving the Royal Ballet of Flanders as the only classical company in the country.

Many Belgian balletomanes are still inconsolable over the loss of the Ballet of the 20th Century, the only company whose popularity had managed to cross the invisible cultural frontier that divides this small kingdom (about the size of Wales) into the prosperous Dutch-speaking north and the economically depressed French-speaking south.

Now that even the Ballet de Wallonie in Charleroi has been disbanded following the death of its artistic director, Jorge Lefebre, in 1990, many bemoan the fact that the would-be capital of Europe has no ballet company of its own. But the move away from traditional towards contemporary forms of dance has gained strength and is clearly here to stay.

Call it 'la vague belge' or 'the Belgian phenomenon', there is no doubt that the unprecedented surge of choreographic activity is something to be reckoned with. This, at least, is the message that has finally reached the ears of the indifferent regional authorities when they decided to appoint Frédéric Flamand as artistic director of the group that was to replace the Ballet de Wallonie.

With the general economic recession prowling outside one door while the young dancemakers were knocking at another in the hope of receiving badly needed funding, the authorities' decision was undeniably shrewd, if almost inevitable: the 80 million Belgian francs that for ten years had financed a one-choreographer ballet company would be used for a much smaller contemporary dance group that, with simpler productions, would consume a fraction of the sum spent on the lavish theatrical ballets of Jorge Lefebre. This would leave a substantial amount to be earmarked for other activities, such as inviting young choreographers to perform with their groups in Charleroi, commissioning new works from them, or co-producing them.

Frédéric Flamand's experience in the field of dance is limited to his concern with movement, a concern that for ten years has been evident in the productions of the Plan K theatre company which he founded and continues to direct. He has proven his uncommon talent as a catalyst in different artistic media, as well as his commitment to experimentation. All of which would hold precious little interest for budget-conscious politicians if it were not for his organizing skills and his wide-ranging connections – more than likely the factors that led to his appointment.

He lost no time. The number of dancers was drastically reduced (the Ballet de Wallonie had 35, the new company has 14), most of them recruited from abroad since only three from the former company decided to venture into what for them was the uncharted territory of postmodern dance. He gave the group the simple if somewhat unglamorous name of **Charleroi/Danses**, a conscious choice and a clear signal to one and all: he would refuse to hide the fact that the group was rooted in the heart of the Pays Noir, the Black Country, the economically depressed region whose landscape, marked with slagheaps, is a sobering reminder of the once-glorious if grim industrial past of coal mining and steel-making.

It is this vision that prompted Flamand to organize and launch an international festival, the Biennale de Charleroi/Danses which took place in March 1992 – an ambitious project, not to say Utopian. Even with the participation of companies from several countries, there was no guarantee

Compagnie Michèle Anne De Mey in *Châteaux en Espagne*.   PHOTO: JORGE LEON

that the Charleroi public would have cared for a genre so different from what they had been used to during Lefebre's tenure, namely a mix of classical vocabulary, rock and Béjart-influenced theatricality. In fact, a capacity audience had already given a clear indication of their preference when a selection of Lefebre's works was performed for the last time in a posthumous homage: their long emotional standing ovation could be interpreted as an unambiguous message for Lefebre's successor, their attachment to the past and wariness of change.

Even more unlikely was the hope that people from other parts of Belgium would make the trip to Charleroi. As a setting for the festival, Charleroi is not exactly Glyndebourne. But the sceptics, including me, were proven wrong. Promoted jointly with the already established contemporary music festival in Brussels, Ars Musica, the Biennale turned out to be a resounding success, with 36 performances given in five different venues almost invariably sold out.

Trisha Brown's company opened the festival with a splendid programme and a well-deserved triumph in the large theatre of the Palais des Beaux-Arts. For his own Plan K production of *Titanic*, Flamand chose an unorthodox site, a huge space that used to be a steel mill and now houses the Museum of Industrial Archaeology. Usually filled with the kind of giant obsolete machinery that could have inspired Chaplin's *Modern Times* (40 tonnes of it had to be moved out to make room for the stage), it proved to be a spectacular setting for his highly successful work based on the historical tragedy of the sinking ship and the fifteenth-century allegory of the Ship of Fools. The visual impact of the decor created by the Italian video installation artist, Fabrizio Plessi, was powerfully effective, while the interplay of movement, music and visual art was more subtly balanced than in Flamand's previous works.

The museum turned out to be the perfect framework, too, for the young **Claudio Bernardo**'s *Sodoma* inspired by the story of the exploited gold miners in his native Brazil, and for **Susanne Linke**'s *Ruhrort Tanz*, a scorching denunciation of the brutal toil of workers in another industrial region, the Ruhr in Germany, performed with a stark, angry force by Linke's group of six outstanding dancer-actors.

In addition to a number of other foreign companies from France, Great Britain, Italy and Japan, all the Belgian groups were present (with the exception of Anne Teresa De Keersmaeker), some, like Michèle Anne De Mey and José Besprosvany, with works in progress; others, like Wim Vandekeybus, with major productions. Vandekeybus's *Immer das Selbe Gelogen* had received its Belgian premiere in Antwerp some months before, but the presence of a Flemish choreographer in Wallonia is an event whose significance understandably escapes anyone who is not familiar with the vehement absurdities of the politico-cultural divisions in this country. A performance by a Fleming in the French-speaking part of Belgium (or vice versa) is virtually unheard of. The success of this important breakthrough may signal the beginning of further interregional cultural exchanges to come.

The festival provided Flamand with the opportunity to give much-needed exposure to his young company. Its first performance in December had revealed more earnestness than mastery of the subtleties of Paul Taylor and Merce Cunningham, hardly surprising considering its brief existence and the individual dancers' varied backgrounds. They had followed up Taylor's *Mercuric Tidings* and Cunningham's *Inlets II* with Karole Armitage's *Overboard*, a work especially commissioned for the company. They danced *Overboard* with an enthusiasm that seemed wasted on the aggressive goings-on so similar to most **Armitage** ballets.

Flamand had asked Lucinda Childs to choreograph a new work, and *Naama* showed that the time Childs spent working with the dancers had been extremely valuable, helping them to acquire a much greater stylistic awareness. But with its unfocused look, it is not a work that will add greatly to her glory.

In addition to the 36 performances, a workshop and two exhibitions – one of original documents of choreographic notation by Nijinsky, Nikolais, Cunningham and others, the other of photographs of dancers and companies – helped to make this first Biennale of Charleroi/Danses a distinctly satisfying experience for dance-goers. Flamand is already working on the second Biennale for the spring of 1994.

In Brussels on 1 January 1992, Anne Teresa De Keersmaeker's group, **Rosas**, became the company in residence at the Théâtre Royale de la Monnaie, home of the National Opera, at the same time as director Bernard Foccroulle took over the post from the outgoing Gérard Mortier. In these troubled times of dwindling subsidies many choreographers will envy De Keersmaeker her newly found financial security. Jean-Yves Langlais, who was appointed dance director at the Monnaie at the same time, is and always has been a fervent admirer of her work which he had followed when he was still in Grenoble as codirector of the Groupe Emile Dubois, Jean-Claude Gallotta's company. She will be able to count on his uncondi-tional support, besides having the use of the Opera facilities and orchestra. For anyone as deeply musical as De Keersmaeker, being able to work directly with musicians and singers counts much more than the luxury of the red velvet seats, crystal chandeliers and gilt boxes in the lovely eight-eenth-century opera house that is now her home.

Erts, the first work she choreographed after taking up her new post, was seen in February. The word means 'ore' in Dutch, which turned out to be more appropriate than she knew, with its unsifted material that seemed almost randomly assembled, lost among such distracting visual ploys as giant television screens. These effects were in startling contrast to the lucid vision and stark intensity of most of her past works. The revival of her admirable *Rosas Danst Rosas*, seen shortly before, could only emphasize the distance between the corruscating rigour of the one and the odd looseness of the other.

Mozart/Concert Arias. Un moto di gioia, premiered in July at the Festival d'Avignon (which coproduced it with the Monnaie, Expo 92 in Seville and the Octobre en Normandie festival), is a fresh, personal and deliciously impertinent interpretation for seven girls and six boys of some of the arias for soprano that Mozart wrote when the same age as De Keersmaeker. Visually enchanting, with a stunning marquetry floor (brought to Avignon from Brussels) and exquisite eighteenth-century costumes, it has humour, verve and grace. Greeted in Avignon by an intense crossfire of applause and boos, it scored a triumph in Seville and Brussels a month later. Her fans waited eagerly for the November revival of her first work, *Fase*, where she returned to dancing after having devoted herself exclusively to choreogra-phy over the past few years.

The fire last spring that destroyed the building that had originally been the home of Béjart's Ballet of the 20th Century and his school Mudra, has meant the postponement of Jean-Yves Langlais' plan to use the space as a centre for contemporary dance and choreographic activity. Bricks are read-ily replaceable and a modern building will be built on the site of the old warehouse. But what has been irretrievably lost are the archives, films and other records of 28 years of the work of Béjart's company, as well as those of the three years between 1988 and 1991 that Mark Morris spent here.

That other great name in Belgian (or does one have to say Flemish?) dance, **Wim Vandekeybus**, had reserved the Belgian premiere in January 1992 of his latest work, *Immer das Selbe Gelogen* for De Singel, the Antwerp theatre that for years has offered the most consistently intelligent and qualitatively reliable calendar of contemporary dance in the whole of Belgium. It's another work where Vandekeybus's physicality and danger-skirting feats of virtuosity vie for attention with the imaginative visual props: the immense patchwork cloth on the floor that is then raised to become a backdrop and, finally, lit from behind, a cathedral-like stained glass window; the dangling ropes that turn into violently swinging hammocks for the women. A few touches of Pina Bausch here and there seemed dispensable, but on the whole *Immer* is another success.

Michèle Anne De Mey's gently subdued *Châteaux en Espagne* seemed bland after her previous *Sinfonia Eroica*, and **Nicole Mossoux**'s *The Hallucinations of Lucas Cranach the Elder*, a visually arresting but utterly static work, represents yet another step in the direction of mime and away from dance – regrettable when one thinks of Mossoux's promise with the marvellous *Juste Ciel* of some years ago.

In Antwerp, American choreographer Peter Anastos was asked by the artistic director of the **Royal Ballet of Flanders**, Robert Denvers, to choreograph a new version of *Cinderella* for the company. Anastos will go down in dance history as the co-choreographer with Baryshnikov of a *Cinderella* that turned out to be the American Ballet Theatre's most expensive production to date. The Flemish version, premiered in February 1992, though not choreographically inventive and marred by serious aesthetic lapses in the decor and costumes, has the advantage of showing off the entire company. At the premiere, the radiant Dawn Fay was partnered by the Cuban Julio Arozarena, a strong, elegant dancer; the two other casts were admirable as well.

The Flemish company is truly brimming with talent which can be better appreciated by balletomanes in the classics (like their exquisite production of *Sylphide*) and in the repertory of Balanchine works that Denvers is intent on building up. The latest acquisition is *Concerto Barocco*, to be seen during the Festival of Flanders in September with *Carnaval*, a commissioned work by Ib Andersen, and *Spent Passions* by the talented house choreographer Daniel Rosseel. Many countries would be happy to have these dancers as their national company. But as long as Belgium is Belgium, Flanders will have it all to itself.

Canada

Michael Crabb

I t's standard procedure in bad weather to reef the sails, batten down the hatches and wait for the storm to pass. The arts in Canada have been battling their own particular storm for more than two years now – an economically-generated storm characterized by declining government grants, corporate donations and box-office returns.

Major orchestras and theatre companies across the country teeter on the brink of bankruptcy and while no dance company seems in imminent danger of closing its doors, a number of them are having to weather heavy seas – from the august National Ballet of Canada to the less established Vancouver troupe, Ballet British Columbia, and the struggling Ottawa Ballet.

Unfortunately, artistic organizations cannot simply batten the hatches and wait the storm out. Somehow they have to keep bravely steering a course towards what they trust will be calmer waters. In practical terms, this means playing safe, not upsetting audiences or sponsors, yet at the same time generating enough creative fodder to keep the crew and ever-demanding critics in good spirits. It takes a very skilled navigator to chart such dangerous waters.

By and large, the directors of Canada's dance companies have shown themselves to be able captains, offering programmes designed to have strong audience appeal while not forgetting the need to remain artistically vital.

In Montreal, for example, **Les Grands Ballets Canadiens**, under the direction of Lawrence Rhodes, countered the audience-pandering idiocy of Peter Anastos's parodic *The Gilded Bat* with respectable if flawed revivals of Massine's *Le Tricorne* and Tudor's *Gala Performance* and *Lilac Garden*, together with a vibrant new ballet, *Paukenschlag*, commissioned from the fertile imagination of American choreographer Mark Morris.

Anastos's 1989 *The Gilded Bat*, borrowed from America's Ballet West, might have sat well on the hairy-chested primas of Les Ballets Trockadéro de Monte-Carlo (the travesty company Anastos cofounded), but this silly attempt to blend plot elements of *The Red Shoes* with a general send-up of classical ballet had all the buoyancy of a lead balloon.

While Les Grands Ballets' Tudor revivals received a generally favourable reception, its painstaking efforts to reproduce Massine's 1919 classic were less successful. Under the aegis of its former administrator, Colin McIntyre, Les Grands Ballets has slowly been assembling a repertoire of works from the Diaghilev era: Balanchine's *The Prodigal Son* and *La Chatte*, Fokine's *Petrushka*, Nijinsky's *L'Après-midi d'un faune* and Nijinska's *Les Noces*. In each case the careful research lavished on choreography and decor has been undermined by the dancers' general inability to grasp the required refinements of style and dramatic motivation.

However, given work tailor-made for their particular gifts, the dancers of Les Grands Ballets Canadiens shine radiantly. Such was the case with Morris's *Paukenschlag*, his first work for a Canadian company. It's a humane, joyful and witty work, set to Haydn's 'Surprise' Symphony No. 94 in G major: humane, because it presents not just a company of dancers executing some very sophisticated choreography, but implies a whole society with its own history, dynamic and harmony; joyful, because Morris uses Haydn's music as the springboard for a celebration of life; and witty, because he manages to deconstruct the conventions of academic classical ballet in unexpected and revealing ways, confusing gender roles and playing with structure. Morris's stance is thoroughly respectful without being reverential. He achieves the kind of pure physical excitement of William Forsythe without the dark overcoat of what American critic Tobi Tobias has aptly dubbed, 'chic menace'.

Like Lawrence Rhodes in Montreal, **The Royal Winnipeg Ballet**'s John Meehan also offered his audiences a balance of old and new work. Meehan, rather than digging in the store cupboard for possible revivals, decided to bolster the company's repertoire with a stroll through the international supermarket of twentieth-century masterworks, and added productions of Ashton's *The Dream* and Tudor's *Lilac Garden*, the latter with evocative new sets and costumes by Desmond Heeley.

The Royal Winnipeg Ballet has a more deeply-rooted dramatic tradition than Les Grands Ballets, which may account for the generally more vivid characterizations offered in both works. Even so, neither production quite managed to capture the subtle essences that transform *Lilac Garden* from melodrama to poignant tragedy, and *The Dream* from pantomimic comedy to poetic romance.

It was unfortunate for the Royal Winnipeg Ballet that Evelyn Hart, who now splits her time between Winnipeg and the Bavarian State Opera Ballet in Munich, was unavailable for both productions. Hart has the kind of extraordinary dramatic instincts that can galvanize and focus a whole production. Tudor's Caroline and Ashton's Titania are natural roles for Hart, and her absence was keenly felt.

The Dream, of course, also depends very much on the presence of an imperious Oberon who must also be able to dance like a demon. Meehan brought in Anthony Dowell, the original Oberon, to supervise final preparation of the production, and it was apparent that Stephen Hyde, the Royal Winnipeg's fairy king, had been an attentive student. What he could not muster, however, was the combination of mystery and pure malice which made Dowell a truly unforgettable Oberon. Nor did Hyde manage to establish the kind of intense dramatic rapport with his Titanias, Laura Graham and Suzanne Rubio, which makes the final, sizzling reconciliation *pas de deux* believable. Instead of a love poem, all we got were steps.

In contrast, *Angels in the Architecture*, by the Royal Winnipeg Ballet's resident choreographer Mark Godden, showed just how much inner focus and conviction the company can muster for a created work. Godden's reading of Aaron Copland's *Appalachian Spring* is bold and arresting. Instead of Martha Graham's 1944 celebration of the pioneer spirit, Godden extends Copland's inclusion of the Shaker hymn, 'Tis a gift to be simple', to make the whole ballet a reflection on the communal life of an often misunderstood and now almost extinct American fundamentalist sect. In formal terms, Godden presents the Shaker's tightly regimented way of life through equally regimented and symmetrical choreography. However, instead of evoking a society that has achieved spiritual harmony through the subjection of individual will, Godden's ballet heaves with repressed anger and sexual longing. The distinctive, free-standing Shaker brooms, with their unavoidably phallic symbolism, shout defiance at the sect's much-vaunted triumph over the flesh. Sudden violent breaks from the regimentation of the choreography suggest a society rife with potential for disorder and fragmentation. Godden seems to draw back from conveying a specific message. He's certainly not out to trash the memory of the Shaker movement. Yet throughout *Angels in the Architecture* it is clear that he views utopian attempts to create an ordered, egalitarian and self-sufficient society as carrying a heavy human cost.

In Toronto, Reid Anderson of the **National Ballet of Canada**, had been relying on Glen Tetley to provide the kind of high-profile creativity needed to balance the company's popular image as a custodian of the nineteenth-century classics and purveyor of opulent costume parades. Unfortunately, Tetley, who has had a decade-long association with the Canadian company, was unable to produce a new work because of ill health. Instead, the National Ballet mounted Tetley's mildly controversial 1974, male-focused staging of *The Rite of Spring*, which proved a magnificent vehicle for the impassioned dancing of Rex Harrington.

Other additions from the international ballet supermarket were more questionable. Toronto's dance community was rife with gossip about how much the dancers hated learning John Cranko's 1966 *Concerto for Flute and Harp*, and its premiere more than confirmed these grim forebodings. One local critic's dismissal of this dismal work as a 'rather negligible *ballet blanc*' aptly summed up the general reaction. The National Ballet's men looked miserable, as did the ballerinas they were lifting. If this minor Cranko throwaway ever had musical values they were lost years ago.

The company premiere of Cranko's *The Taming of the Shrew* fared better with audiences; understandably, perhaps, in a country where madmen bearing grudges and high-powered weapons gun down women in university cafeterias, anti-feminist slogans are daubed on campus walls and wife-beating, if one is to believe statistics, is apparently as popular a pastime as clear-cutting primal forest. What more could an audience ask for than a burlesque version of Shakespeare's problematic comedy in which the heroine is beaten, starved and generally abused into submission? Just the ticket for a night out on the town.

Ironically, *The Taming of the Shrew* did serve to reveal what a depth of dramatic talent resides within the National Ballet. Harrington, the best of the Petruchios, evoked memories of Richard Cragun in his prime, while Jeremy Ransom and Robert Tewsley in turn made unforgettably lovable yet pathetic Hortensios. Gizella Witkowsky was the only Katherina to emerge from this miscreant work with a shred of dignity.

It was left to the National Ballet's resident choreographer, John Alleyne, to provide lovers of actual dancing with enough nourishment to preserve their health and sanity. Alleyne has generally been cast as a slavish devotee of William Forsythe's slick, hyperphysical style; yet Alleyne's most recent works have underlined important differences. There's a more obvious refinement and appreciation of form-as-metaphor in Alleyne's ballets, and a subtle emotional patina of human warmth. There were hints of this in Alleyne's autumn premiere of *Interrogating Slam*, set to an exhilarating Morton Subotnik score, and even stronger emotional chords in a trimmed-down version of *Split House Geometric*, originally created for the National Ballet's small touring Concert Group in 1990 and given its mainstage premiere in May, 1992.

Apart from these endeavours, Alleyne, a former company soloist who has now completely retired from dancing, also found time to contribute an excellent work called *Bet Ann's Dance* to the New York City Ballet's Diamond Project of new choreography, and presented a similarly titled though different ballet, *The Real Bet Ann's Dance*, at the Canada Dance Festival in July. This work was set on the dancers of the Vancouver-based Ballet British Columbia, where Alleyne was named artistic director in the spring following the death of Barry Ingham. The move left the National Ballet without a resident choreographer for the first time in many years, a situation shrewdly remedied a few months later by the appointment of James Kudelka as artist-in-residence. Kudelka has the National Ballet in his blood. He was trained at the National Ballet School, became one of the company's most gifted soloists, and began his choreographic career there. In 1981 Kudelka left Toronto to join Montreal's Les Grands Ballets Canadiens, a company that has traditionally given higher priority to the creation of new work and which during Kudelka's stay seemed even more willing

Karen Kain, in the National Ballet of Canada's production of *Elite Syncopations*, choreographed by Kenneth MacMillan.   PHOTO: ANDREW OXENHAM

to experiment with a range of choreographic styles both modern and classical. Kudelka thrived in this environment, producing some of his most interesting work, expanding his choreographic range and winning the attention of companies in the United States. Although he has been back to the National Ballet since 1981, most significantly to create a highly imaginative interpretation of Beethoven's 'Pastoral' Symphony, Kudelka's new position with the company represents an important homecoming. His

69

initial contract is for two seasons, during which he will continue to accept certain commissions outside the National Ballet (notably one from the Martha Graham company in 1993).

Meanwhile, Alleyne's move to Vancouver provides the chronically debt-ridden **Ballet British Columbia** with the chance to develop a truly distinctive artistic personality under the guidance of a director with a real choreographic vision and an enlightened perception of where the art form itself must move in the late twentieth century. Alleyne is a thinking choreographer who is not afraid to grapple with troubling philosophical ideas or the most taxing of contemporary music. His challenge is to win audiences to his progressive point of view.

Ballet British Columbia was not the only company to get a new director during the season. After twenty years, Geneviève Salbaing, the French-born co-founder and artistic director of **Les Ballets Jazz de Montreal** for much of its life, passed her company over to William Whitener, a man widely and affectionately remembered as one of the most jelly-boned dancers in the old Twyla Tharp company.

Les Ballets Jazz is Canada's most travelled dance troupe, but also one of its most reviled. Big-city critics have routinely decried its eager-to-please, hip-gyrating style, forgetting the company's ability, through its very accessibility, to win new audiences for dance, and overlooking the fact that while its choreographic offerings have varied widely in quality, its dancers always perform as if there were no tomorrow. Whitener's challenge now is to win Les Ballets Jazz the kind of artistic respectability which it has always craved but never secured, while not losing the popular appeal that has made the troupe a valuable ambassador for dance.

There was another important change-over, this time in Winnipeg, following the stormy conclusion of the short-lived directorship of American choreographer-director Charles Moulton at **Contemporary Dancers**. The company, battling with dire money problems, moved swiftly to anoint Tom Stroud as the person charged with healing wounds so deep that they threatened the very survival of the country's oldest modern-dance troupe.

Although Contemporary Dancers is still struggling to re-establish a secure foothold on the prairies, Stroud's first project, the hour-long *Songs*, made a strong impression in its home city and on tour. *Songs'* six moveable stairways provided a flexible architectural environment that both predicted and echoed the emotional dynamics of Stroud's choreography. It was a hard, driving, intensely-felt work that in many was seemed closer to the European/tanztheater leanings of Montreal-based choreographers than to the more traditional dance values found in most of English-Canada.

The European focus of Montreal dance, something vigorously denied by its practitioners, is best observed in what has now become the French-Canadian city's annual Festival of New Dance. Its programmers largely ignore English Canada and the United States in favour of what choreographer Mark Morris has brightly dubbed the 'high heels and red lipstick' school of European dance angst.

This is not, however, to suggest that Montreal choreographers ape the Europeans. Their work, even if it seems aimed to attract programmers on the European festival circuit, has strong individuality, notably demonstrated by two contrasting works at the 1991 festival in September.

Paul André Fortier's *La Tentation de la transparence*, with its small, sloping platform stage, at first promised a return to 1970s minimalism, but in fact blossomed into a rich spiritual journey as Fortier, so close to his audience he could have reached out and touched them, found physical gestures to express deep longings, fears and joys.

One left Fortier's tiny performing space feeling somehow cleansed. Leaving the 3000-seat Salle Wilfrid Pelletier of Montreal's Place des Arts after the premiere of Edouard Lock's *Destroy*, there was a far stronger inclination to slit one's wrists and end the whole nasty business once and for all.

Lock and his company, **La La La Human Steps**, have become media darlings incapable of doing wrong. Lock's amoral presentation of human existence seems to strike a sympathetic chord among those who have given up any hope of forging a better world. Lock's violent bursts of dance crackle with a kind of fashionable disdain for human values. In *Destroy* he presents the androgynous Louise Lacavalier, his most bankable star turn, as a kind of symbol of late twentieth-century ennui. Her naked body-spasms on stage are overlaid with huge and intimate projections of her anatomy that verge on the pornographic as they mix with images of fierce dogs, imprisoning chains and flesh-piercing swords. And to think I was momentarily puzzled as to why the woman next to me was in tears.

Lock's seemingly grim, misogynistic and apocalyptic vision could easily have been countered by the presence of **Peggy Baker**, except that her deeply humane choreography and dancing has no doubt escaped the attention of the Montreal festival programmers.

Baker was a relatively late starter in dance, who quickly transformed her tall, long-limbed body into a wonderfully expressive human form. This season, after a lengthy sojourn in the United States, principally with Lar Lubovitch, Baker resettled in Canada and took her new solo show across the country to rapturous response from audiences and critics alike.

Baker is one of those glorious dancers who is incapable of making an empty move. She can ennoble indifferent choreography and enrich worthy pieces with an approach that mixes personal modesty and physical boldness. There are few dancers I have seen who can present dance with such selfless simplicity that you believe you have partaken in a sacred act. If this is the future of Canadian dance it is worth sticking around to see.

71

Obituaries

Barry Ingham, British-born dancer, choreographer and director, died of complications arising from AIDS in Vancouver, British Columbia, 31 January 1992. Ingham, who was born in Manchester, 19 June 1950, moved to Germany in 1986, first dancing for the Heidelberg Ballet, and then with the Stuttgart Ballet, 1970–81, where he became a principal. Ingham then joined the Frankfurt Ballet, where, after a brief interlude in Zurich, he became ballet master in 1988, staging the works of William Forsythe and beginning to choreograph. He became artistic director of Vancouver's Ballet British Columbia, following the stormy departure of Patricia Neary. He is credited with restoring the company's morale and leading it on successful tours in Canada and Asia.

   Alan Lund died of cancer on 1 July 1992, age 67. He was respected throughout Canada as a choreographer and director of enormous ingenuity. Often working with limited resources and inexperienced casts, Lund staged spectacular revues for many Canadian theatre companies and for television. He was considered particularly adept at choreography for large ensembles. He will perhaps be best remembered as artistic director of the Charlottetown Festival in Prince Edward Island, 1966–86. Lund was born in Toronto in 1925, and established himself as a dancer in musical theatre during World War II. He choreographed frequently for CBC-TV in its early days, as well as for popular revues and musicals. He leaves his former dancing partner and wife Blanche Lund, and their four sons.

Chile

Hans Ehrmann

After a normal 1991 season, this year started with a bang. An absolutely unprecedented grassroots rebellion at the **Ballet de Santiago** made headlines in the local press when the dancers, ranging all the way from the *corps de ballet* to the soloists and ballerina, unanimously called a press conference to announce its rejection of company director Luz Lorca because of 'her erratic artistic judgement and the dissociative relationships she creates within the company'. The dancers pointed out that they had more than once brought these matters to the attention of Santiago's Cultural Corporation, whose lack of response had forced them to go public. The authorities refused to act under pressure, but are expected to proceed when Lorca's contract runs out in November.

Georgette Farias and Patricio Melo of the Ballet de Santiago in *Los Fuegos del Hielo*, choreographed by Jaime Pinto.

A couple of months later the head of the University of Chile's Extension Centre announced that she had accepted the resignation of the National Ballet's director, Maritza Parada, only to be overruled a few days later by the University's vice-president who decided to maintain Parada at the head of the company.

Both episodes point towards a malaise that inevitably affects artistic results.

The Ballet de Santiago's 1991 season (March to December), was to a large extent programmed by Imre Dosza, whose tenure as company director had lasted until the end of 1990. Trumpeted as a world premiere, André Prokovsky's *Macbeth* (music by David Earl; scenery and costumes, Robin Cameron Don) began with a scene reminiscent of a battle of toy soldiers, followed by some rather limp witches. Worse, Macbeth's combination of ambition and weakness and Lady Macbeth's part in the proceedings were hardly expressed in the choreography, in spite of Rolando Candia and Sara Nieto's efforts in the leading roles.

This was followed in the next programme by *Tiempo de Percusión*, an interesting but minor work by Hilda Riveros, and a revival of Ivan Nagy and Marilyn Burr's elegant version of *La Sylphide*. After that, the season provided three full-evening classics which, for better and sometimes for worse, predominate in the company's repertoire. A more balanced combination between these and contemporary works is definitely needed.

Don Quixote had been staged a decade earlier by the Koslovs, and the new version by Jaime Pinto was a considerable improvement, partly due no doubt to a much higher standard in the company. The choreography flowed naturally and even made the tenuous plot seem more consistent than usual, conditions that were also met, though to a lesser extent, in Ben Stevenson's *The Snow Maiden*. On the other hand, the revival of the latter's Christmas *Nutcracker*, which closed the season, was as successful as ever.

The company's 1992 season consisted of four revivals of previously staged full-evening works (*La Fille mal gardée, Don Quixote, Cinderella, Rosalind*) and only one programme with new works. This was obviously a testimonial to unimaginative artistic direction.

First came *Fille* staged by Marilyn Burr who, in view of the company's problems, had been brought in as assistant artistic director. Her version was satisfactory, although an attempt to 'chileanize' the ballet by dressing the peasants in local *huaso* costumes failed to work.

In July 1992 this was at last followed by three works new to the company. Balanchine's *The Four Temperaments* was staged by Melissa Hayden but, beyond one's pro or con feelings about Hindemith's score, dancing was imprecise and sometimes lacking in musicality.

Los Fuegos del Hielo ('Fires of the Ice') had choreography by Jaime Pinto to music by Sergio González, played by Congreso, a Latin fusion jazz group. Although potentially exciting, this evocation of the Tierra del Fuego Indians (from the southern tip of South America) at the turn of last century, with interesting although at times monotonous music, the dramatic outline drowned in excessive and not always clear symbolism. Pinto's choreography was of little help: it failed to develop a style to blend with the subject, and instead leaned too heavily on the classics he usually deals with. This work was scheduled for a tour to Expo 92 at Seville.

The programme's third item saved the day. Marcia Haydée's version of *The Firebird*, enhanced by Pablo Nuñez's imaginative scenery and costumes, provided both an enchanting fairytale and the year's best dancing by the company's soloists – especially ballerina Sara Nieto (Firebird) and Marcela Goicoechea (Tsarevna). The principal male roles were guested by the Stuttgart Ballet's excellent Jean-Christophe Blavier (Kastchei) and Wolfgang Stollwitzer (Tsarevitch).

Basically it was another year in which the company performed as they went along, but lacked a sense of direction and failed to fulfil the dancers' potential.

The National Ballet is perhaps less vulnerable in this respect, but disadvantaged by being chronically strapped for money and also by the near failure of the university's dance school to provide it with a new generation of dancers. The National aims at a clear differentiation from the Ballet de Santiago (not always the case in the past). The general policy is to move within the modern dance field, only natural for a company founded half a century ago by members of the Ballets Jooss, but far removed from the outright rejection of classical dancing of its beginnings.

The implicit eclecticism manifested itself in a programme of works by Michael Uthoff, son of the company's founder, and for many years director of the Hartford Ballet in the US, and also in *Cantares* by Argentine choreographer Oscar Araíz.

Another Argentine, Mauricio Wainrot, gave the National, whose audiences have been eroding for several years, a much needed popular success with *Anne Frank*. While Bartók's *Music for strings, percussion and celesta* alternates with *Lili Marlene*, the Frank and Van Daan families live and bicker in their hiding place. Anne, despite everything, lives, learns and even enjoys her limited life, but periodically the Gestapo, like hovering angels of death, pass on the outside, creating a threatening framework of inevitable doom.

Although, given the book, play and film, novelty is hardly an ingredient, the ballet succeeds in creating an emotionally powerful atmosphere. Two other Wainrot works, *Symphony of Psalms* and the lyrical *Ecos*, were also interesting, although they did not create a similar impact.

When Patricio Bunster's *Calaucán* was created some three decades ago, it was very successful both in Chile and on several of the National Ballet's Latin-American tours. On its revival, Mexican composer Carlos Chávez's *Toccata for Percussion Instruments* is as powerful as ever and the subject of the Spanish conquest of America and oppression of the native Indians could not have been more timely amid the celebrations of the fifth centennial of the discovery of America. But the choreography not only lost its punch and felt dated, but the dancers themselves were substandard, performing in the Jooss idiom used by Bunster as if they no longer believed in it.

Small modern dance groups work hard and perform occasionally, but no breakthrough is in sight. Audiences are very small, press coverage is minimal and, it must be admitted, their actual work is not yet of particular interest.

Back in the 1950s and 1960s there were frequent tours by foreign soloists and companies. After the 1973 coup and during the seventeen years of military government visitors were far and in between, a situation that has now changed for the better.

Visitors ranged all the way from the **Siobhan Davies Dance Company** and **Pilobolus**, to the **Hartford Ballet**, the **Stuttgart Ballet** with *Eugene Onegin*, the **Ballet Nacional de España** (including José Antonio's version of *The Three-Cornered Hat*) and **Yunost** from the Ukraine, a folk dance ensemble whose amateur status certainly did not show in their performance.

The **Bolshoi** arrived with a rather mixed bag: *Sleeping Beauty* (Act II), *La Bayadère* (Act II) and *Raymonda* (Act III) and a cast that was largely a sort of second eleven. On the other hand the **Kirov**, although only represented by a small group of soloists, brought some of their top dancers (Asylmuratova, Chenchikova, Lezhnina, Makhalina, Kurkov, Vaziev, Zaklinsky and Zelensky) and, in a stunning exhibition of classical dancing, gave the standard *pas de deux* a new lease of life.

Of special interest to local audiences was the **Ballet Nacional de Cuba** which had previously danced at Santiago's Teatro Municipal in 1949, 1954, and 1959. Since then Alicia Alonso has become a living legend, although it was certainly difficult to evaluate her performance in *La Diva*, which was the closing item in all performances. Unfortunately, cruel though it may sound, her dancing may have been impressive for a seventy-year-old ballerina, but hardly justifiable from any other point of view. It was a particularly sad occasion for those who had had the privilege of seeing her in her prime. The company itself shone in Alonso's version of *Giselle* (Act II) with a beautiful *corps de ballet*, and also did well in shorter works.

China

Ou Jian-ping

The past seasons in China have been very varied and exciting indeed – the first Chinese professional modern dance company was officially born of both Chinese and foreign parents. Video dance made a poetic and academic appearance in the TV film 'Calligraphy and Dancing'. Folk dance theatre developed folklorically, theatrically and aesthetically, in the northeastern city of Shenyang. Beijing Dance Academy launched three surprises for the audience; the army dance took in fresh forces; Central Ballet premiered a new production on the Chinese revolutionary theme and restaged *The Red Detachment of Women*. The Third China Art Festival in the southernmost city, Kinmung, broke records in Chinese dance history.

The first Chinese professional modern dance company, **Guangdong Modern Dance Company** was officially established on 6 June 1992 in Guangzhou City (Canton) with a gala performance at the local Friendship Theatre, after four and a half years cooperation between Guangdong Dance School headed by Yang Mei-qi, the American Dance Festival (ADF) directed by Charles Reinhart, and the Asian Cultural Council (ACC) led by Richard Lanier and Ralph Samuelson. The company was a great success at

ADF in July 1991 with seven self-choreographed dances, which Anna Kisselgoff, senior dance critic of *The New York Times*, recorded as 'so remarkable in general and so clearly heartfelt', and 'executed with such polish' that the company 'closed its performance with a cheering audience on its feet at Page Auditorium at Duke University'. So, we are confident of the company's success under the leadership of its first officially appointed managing director Yang Mei-qi, who first conceived and created the company, and its first officially appointed artistic director Willy Tsao, who has generously helped the company in many ways all these years, and still heads City Contemporary Dance Company in Hong Kong. The fact that he has been allowed to lead this first Chinese modern dance company is the fruit of the 'Reform and Open' policy of the Chinese government.

Video dance is still a young form of visual art in this country, and last summer CCTV (China Central TV) broadcast a four-part TV film 'Calligraphy and Dancing', which aroused great interest from both amateurs and professionals in calligraphy, painting, sculpture, philology, poetry, music, dance and video techniques, as it was inspired by the traditionally-based but innovative calligraphy of the Chinese-American calligrapher and linguist, Professor Wang Fang-yu. It was full of ancient Chinese philology and poetry, but was also very amusing and educating, with its vivid and animated images of Chinese characters in different styles of calligraphy and dance. It gave precise step-by-step descriptions of how 'pictographing' (the first of the six ways of structuring Chinese characters), worked historically, and was closely associated with human figures (both Yin and Yang, or female and male), human relationships, developing senses of beauty and movement, and creations of calligraphy and dance. The director, Madam Yü Lin, originally a dancer and now a director at CCTV, had worked on this experimental production for five years after the pilot had been shown at CCTV in 1986. The choreographers were Zhao Wan-hua, Zhou Bin, Wang Lian-cheng, Chen Guo and Zhang Man-yin.

In Shenyang and Beijing, the **Shenyang Song and Dance Ensemble** presented a dance-drama about north-eastern Chinese peasants' daily life, *The Five Watches Under the Crescent Moon* (a watch is one of the five two-hour periods into which the night was divided in the old Chinese custom). The evening-length production consisted of a prologue, and five acts – 'Longing for Love' (a boy and a girl's first awakening of love); 'Husband' (beautiful blind young woman and a charmingly naive carter); 'Son' (a group of would-be fathers looking forward to having healthy sons); 'Wife' (a poor bachelor's pillow turns first into an ugly girl, then a pretty one); 'Good Luck' (a wedding ceremony) – and an epilogue. This work explored the folkloric root of north-eastern Chinese psychology and tried to establish authentic images of the local ordinary people, particularly the peasants. It purposely used a kind of collage to juxtapose all these details and images in the same theatrical time and space, which not only enriched the stage content, but also condensed the stage time. It showed on stage what is traditionally considered 'ugly' by both Chinese dance and Western ballet, such as a sturdy middle-aged man with brawny arms and thick waist, standing heroically on a high platform, triumphantly waving a heavy hammer; a group of pregnant women proudly walking across the stage with their big bellies sticking out – but it was all done in a natural way, thereby pleasing all kinds and levels of audiences.

Beijing Dance Academy has been the cradle of Chinese theatre dance since its foundation in 1954. The last few seasons saw innovations in both its folk and ballet departments. Last summer, Zhang Ji-gang, a graduate of the choreography department and later a teacher there, created an evening -length concert of theatre folk dances, *Dedicated to my Father and Mother*, on the graduates of the folk dance department, which began a resurgence of 'Yellow River' dance culture started a few years ago by two programmes by the Shanxi Song and Dance Theatre: *The Affections of the Yellow River's Sons and Daughters* and *The Earth Along the Yellow River*. Three pieces were striking among the nine shown. *We're Coming From the Yellow River* began with a man posed with a bent back, seemingly carrying a heavy load, while a woman stood quietly with a drooping head. Those two postures were duplicated by an ensemble of men and women, who then progressed to a kind of variation, as the men straightened their backs and opened their arms, symbolizing their open minds. The whole team moved slowly but steadily towards a red sun. *A Yangge Dancer* depicted a spell-bound peasant who was 'married' to the Yangge Dance (the most typical folk dance of the Chinese majority, the Han nationality) and breathed his last breath in his dancing, wearing a satisfied smile. The young male star Yü Xiao-xue imbued the peasant character with mature subtleties: he was shrewd, as an experienced man; charmingly feminine as a man occasionally dancing a woman's role; rough, as a rustic farmer; and vulgar, as a peasant. Yü's flexibility, as well as his natural and unrestrained beauty as a dancer who was 'on' every minute, helped him win the first prize in the folk dance division at the Third Peach and Plum Cup Dance Competition, the national contest for all Chinese dance schools and academies held from 25 August to 4 September 1991 in Beijing. Together with Yellow River, the term 'Yellow Earth' has been regarded as the essential symbol of ancient Chinese culture in recent years, and *Yellow Earth Yellow* was a symbolic ensemble dance performed by more than forty young men and women beating drums hanging on their chests. What was most exciting about this performance was that they were really good drummers, and their shouts at the climax evoked earth-shaking heroism.

The second breakthrough was that the Academy introduced jazz repertoire into its ballet department – *The Young Sky*, choreographed by Willy

Guangdong Modern Dance Company in *Flat Bottom Basket and Bamboo* at the 1991 American Dance Festival.

Tsao to the popular songs of Cui Jian, the hottest rock 'n' roll star in mainland China. Obviously, the success of the choreography had much to do with Tsao's penetrating insight, and a well-muscled young man named Huang Qi-cheng, who had seemed very awkward in the first two ballet works on the programme, but shone in this jazz piece which made good use of his more mature body that seemed to express more inner conflict and outer force than the younger dancers did. Tsao's mastery of all kinds of movement was also very impressive, particularly at the songs' electrifying climaxes.

The third innovation was that the Academy invited **Le Jeune Ballet de France** from Paris for a one-month residency, and to join its ballet department in presenting a full-length performance of a range of Western dance from folk, court, waltz, and square dances to ballet classics; from Duncan to Fokine; from can-can and tap to charleston and tango; from *Grand Pas Classique* by Victor Gsovsky to the finale of *A Chorus Line* and several stimulating contemporary pieces including two premieres, *La Fête des roses* and *Le Chant des singes*, choreographed respectively by French choreographer Bertrand D'At and Chinese choreographer Chen Wei-ya. The Chinese young dancers looked much stronger in the classic works yet far weaker in the modern and contemporary than their French counterparts, as the Academy has only just begun to establish a modern dance major, and had never taken it as a regular course in its thirty-eight year history.

The **Song and Dance Ensemble of the Chinese People's Liberation Army General Political Department** has always been famous for its handsome uniform and strong training of the large team of dancers, particularly the males. The programme *The Soul of the Army*, premiered last May, showed that fresh forces – not only a large group of boys and girls in their teens, but also the talented young choreographer Zhang Ji-gang, originally from Beijing Dance Academy – had joined its dance team. Nevertheless, the weak point in Zhang's choreography was immediately obvious: his country folk dance movement language did not work well in its new surroundings – a more city-orientated contemporary soldier's world. Of course it will take him some time to find a new language for this environment.

Last June, the **PLA Arts Institute** also gave a song and dance concert with six ensemble dances, in which the beautifully trained dancers shone, yet the hard-working teachers and choreographers were belittled. Of course, all these ensemble dances gave equal chances to all the student dancers, but without hope of nurturing future stars. Frankly, as far as the choreography was concerned there was hardly anything new or creative. The running and chasing dancers, in simple floor patterns, the luxurious and exaggerated costumes of silk and gauze and overdecorated fans of silk and feathers, the shining and colourful lights (including spotlights and UV light), the magnificent movable backcloth of mountains, rivers and cave dwellings – all these non-dance elements wasted a large amount of money and submerged the dance, although they did fill the gaps in the weak and old-fashioned choreography.

Central Ballet staged another revolutionary ballet named *The Wild Goose Flies Southwards* in June 1991, fifteen years after last performing *The Red Detachment of Women*. And, interestingly, in May 1992, at the request of the audience, the company successfully restaged this internationally famous revolutionary ballet. The enthusiasm from the audience for this full-length work was not only because of interest in the past when every professional (and some amateur) company was staging it, when it was a training piece for all the dancers now in their thirties and early forties, but also because of its dramatic structure, highly-refined choreography and performance, realistic scenery and soul-stirring music. Most of the audience, particularly those outside Beijing where Central Ballet is located, had only been able to see the work on film. So for the first time in twenty years they were able to see this well-known Chinese ballet.

Another important event in Chinese dance history was the Third China Art Festival which took place in Kunming City, Yunnan Province where 25 of the country's 56 nationalities live together. At a cost of 300 million Chinese Yuan (US$50 million) and with nearly 12,000 performers, the festival created many records. First, all 56 nationalities were brought together on the same stage for the first time; second, all the nationalities selected and sent dancers from remote countryside and mountainous areas for the first time, and the number of amateur (mainly peasant) dancers proved the biggest; third, the Chinese artists from the mainland, Hong Kong and Taiwan joined hands in the dances or the artistic discussions at this festival for the first time. Last, the grand parade of all the folk dancers passed through the city centre at the opening ceremony, and the four magnificent dance shows in the local gymnasium gave a most comprehensive and compact picture of Chinese dance culture. Furthermore, the Western ballet classic *Swan Lake* by China's own Central Ballet was a great success as it was a sharp contrast to all the Chinese folk dances. A newly created legendary work, *Ashima*, by the local **Yunnan Provincial Song and Dance Ensemble** proved that the movement vocabulary of a single minority, if used properly, is more than enough to fill a full-length dance drama. Additionally, a modern dance drama, *The Snow is Red*, by the Hong Kong Dance Company, headed for years by the Shanghai choreographer Shu Qiao, provoked a heated discussion over the evaluation of old dance traditions and their significance to today's creativity.

Cuba

Jane King

As Cuba's blockaded economy battles for survival, dancers are in the front line. The dance companies are among the most valuable of the country's exports and tourist attractions, earning hard currency for the import of essential foods, petrol, paper and medical supplies. To a visitor aware of the acute shortages experienced in almost every aspect of Cuban life at this time it is impressive to find the theatres still functioning with such commitment. Today a printed programme is a luxury only the **National Ballet** can afford (on brown, recycled paper). Lights are dimmer, taped music is scarce and well-worn, bus and taxi services are minimal; yet standards remain high, ticket prices low, and seats are filled. Audiences cheer as enthusiastically as ever each time Rosario Suarez, as Aurora, dives faultlessly into Lienz Chang's chivalrously extended arms, or Yat Sen Chang hurls himself skywards in Brian Macdonald's *Tempo Fuera de la Memoria*. (The two remarkable Chang brothers are, despite their names, Cuban born, and trained at the National Ballet School.)

Regla Salvent in *Fausto,* choreographed by Victor Cuellar for Danza Contemporánea de Cuba.

1992, the five-hundredth anniversary of the 'Encounter of Two Worlds', is of very special significance throughout Latin-America and the Caribbean, and Cuban artists played a prominent part in the important cultural events marking this historic year on both sides of the Atlantic. More Cuban dance groups, choreographers, teachers and dancers have been working abroad than ever before. The Cuban National Ballet, the **Conjunto Folklorico Nacional**, and the **Cutumba**, were all in Spain for the anniversary festivities. Alicia Alonso, *prima ballerina assoluta*, designed the gala for the Madrid summit, to show 'the variety of Latin-American culture and the influence Spanish dance has upon it'. Alonso herself danced, with Orlando Salgado, a *pas de deux* from Alberto Alonso's *Carmen*. The company then left on its first ever visit to Australia and the Melbourne Arts Festival, followed by an extensive tour of Europe.

In Havana, meanwhile, plans went ahead for the 13th International Ballet Festival (28 October–8 November) to open with a gala 'Lo Español en los Clasicos'. The Spanish choreographer Goyo Montero is rehearsing a new work with the company, based on García Lorca's *Mariana Piñera*. Mendez, Tenorio and Herrera are contributing new works, and there is to be a new production of *Swan Lake*. Guest artists and whole companies from Latin-America will bring works celebrating the Spanish-American influence in the art of ballet.

The National Ballet School this year achieved, for the first time, parity of the sexes: 30 boys and 30 girls. A group of handsome, finely-tuned young performers distinguished themselves at the student graduation in June and afterwards went with their teacher, Ramona de Sáa, to win still further distinctions in Italy at the Vignales Festival. Announcements are soon expected of promotions within the company, the result of a recent evaluation, and recognition of the very high quality of the talent emerging from the school in recent years.

The **Ballet de Camagüey** suffered a serious blow last year when one of their principal choreographers, Francisco Lang, was killed in a car accident. Their sixth Latin-American Dance Festival, postponed in 1991, took place instead in June this year and produced some pleasant surprises. The most surprising and pleasant of these was the reappearance, after a long absence abroad, of Jorge Esquivel, dancing in the Ravel/Béjart *Bolero*. With Menia Martínez, another long-absent Cuban étoile, Esquivel also danced a *pas de deux*, choreographed for the occasion by the ballerina herself. Immediately after the Festival, the company, under their new director Jorge Vede, set off on a tour of Martinique. Fernando Alonso, Camgüey's former director, is now living and working in Mexico.

Yet another company on the move this summer was Laura Alonso's **La Joven Guardia**, which took its first trip to Europe to participate, at the invitation of Robert Bertier (director of the Jeune Ballet de France), in the

Encuentro de la Danza de la Baule. The Joven Guardia and members of the ProDanza organization give frequent performances on Sunday mornings at the García Lorca theatre. Among the most interesting are the 'New Choreographers' programmes where there may be as many as twelve new works, ranging in length from two to fifteen minutes, and in music and style from Afro-Caribbean to Vivaldi to Jean-Michel Jarre. It is on these occasions that one is most aware of the limited availability of taped music, but the range of ideas is unlimited.

Another of Laura Alonso's enterprises still extending its range and influence, the **Cuballet** international courses, took place last year in Argentina and Mexico, and in 1992 in Argentina and Brazil (where Alicia Alonso gave master classes), Mexico and Sweden.

Cuba's **Danza Contemporánea**, large and particularly impressive for its strong male dancers, has in the last two years produced eleven new works while undertaking twenty overseas visits. In addition, three interesting young choreographers have emerged from the company and formed small groups, to whom the parent company lends dancers, rehearsal space, and items of essential equipment.

Gestos Transitorios is one of these groups. The director, Narciso Medina, is a tall, compelling dancer with Afro-Hispanic roots, whose work is clearly influenced by Latin-American magic realism. His *Metamórfosis, Caverna Mágica,* and *Espacio-Hombre-Solo* are already included in the repertoire of several companies. Gestos Transitorios is currently working on a new piece with the US choreographer Suki John, who describes herself as 'eclectic with a bias toward Limón'.

Rosario Cárdenas, another Danza Contemporánea member, has recently reformed her small group, **Danza Combinatoria**, and is initiating her dancers into her own imaginative training methods and choreographic theory. She was recently commissioned to design the movement for Raquel Revuelta's production of the play *Concerto Barroco,* based on Alejo Carpentier's novel, which transferred from Havana to Cadiz, Seville and Madrid.

Marianela Boán's **Danza Abierta**, originally also an offshoot of Danza Contemporánea, drew full houses at the Mella Theatre partly, one suspects, for the novelty of 21-year-old José Hevia's *Desnudo* for two naked women, but more, one hopes, for the fascinating *Godot* (also for two women) by Victor Varela, based on Beckett's famous play. Boán's latest work, *Retorna,* asks the interesting question, for a postmodernist committed to 'provocation and aggression', how much space in art and life do we really give to our genuinely Cuban cultural traditions?

Santiago at festival time is the city of dance. The Festival de Fuego bursts into flame every morning at ten o'clock, when every park and square begins to throb with drums and blaze with movement and colour. Only when the music stops and the lights go out over the platform in Céspedes

Park, in front of the cathedral, do the Santiaguerans go home to bed – in the small hours of the next morning. **Tumba Francesa, Bantú Yoruba, Sarabanda, Mayombe, Renacer Haitiano, Danza Caribe** (from the University), **3 de Diciembre** (from the Medical School), among a hundred others, dance, sing and play their way round the city for four hot, brilliant days and nights.

The new 2500-seater Heredia Theatre was filled for the performance of *El Aguaro del Roko*, a lavish dance spectacle telling a tale familiar in Yoruba folklore, with a fine score mixing traditional percussion, electronic and orchestral music. Antonio Pérez Martínez, the director of **Ballet Folklórico de Oriente**, is seeking to make the work of his company more relevant to the problems of the twentieth century by mixing Afro-Cuban ballet and contemporary dance. He is particularly interested in making contact with companies in other countries who may be tackling problems of content and choreography similar to his own.

The performances at the Teatro Oriente by the **Compañia Teatro de la Danza del Caribe** gave a vivid illustration of the aims of their director, Eduardo Rivero, a pioneer of Cuban modern dance, to show 'la fuerza, vitalidad y alegría de los hombres y mujeres de nuestros pueblos' ('the strength, vitality and gaiety of our people'). This very young and athletic company is building a repertoire of works, old and new, by Rivero himself (from *Okántomi* to *Mandela*) and short pieces by young choreographers, some of them dancers in the company. Rivero's classes in England at the Birmingham international summer school this year created a genuine enthusiasm among the students for the technique and the expressive qualities of Cuban modern dance.

Santiago's classical ballet company has made its home in the Heredia Theatre, giving its first performance there to a conference of 2500 construction workers! The eleven young women and nine young men, between the ages of 18 and 20, all graduates of the national ballet schools, have given 50 performances in their first two years of existence, including two in Havana's Gran Teatro; and progress has been spectacular. At their first evaluation (a biannual event for all companies) three dancers attained the rank of soloist, and two of *coryphée*. María Elena Martínez, an inspiring director, teaches, assisted by visiting teachers from Havana and Camagüey, and also choreographs. Her *Para ti Argentina*, a ballet-tango both sophisticated and exuberant, was received with delight by the Festival audience at the Heredia.

The **Conjunto de Danzas de Guantánamo** was given a rousing reception when it appeared in the Teatro Oriente in a new programme of contemporary and folkloric choreography, and each time they danced, between two and three in the morning, on the platform in Céspedes Park. Two new pieces by company members, Tomás Guilarte and Alfredo Velasquez, are based on the work of the philosophers, Nietzsche and Thomas Aquinas! Despite their abstract concepts, these pieces go down well at the Saturday night concerts (admission free) held in the Conjunto's Guantánamo studios. Director Elfrida Mahler is preparing a major new work, *Tiempo Muerto, Tiempo Vivo*, inspired by *Elogía a Jésus Menendez* by Cuba's national poet Nicolás Guillen. There are also plans to revive *Suite Yoruba*, a classic of Cuba's modern dance by its founder, Ramiro Guerra.

Despite every frustration and difficulty, the dancing goes enthusiastically on. The absence of Cuba's one dance magazine and the shortage of newspapers, reviews and advertising, make news of companies' activities difficult to obtain. Materials for pointe shoes are in short supply; power cuts interrupt rehearsals; scarcity of petrol restricts travel. The Conjunto Folklórico Nacional reluctantly had to cancel the International Festival planned this summer to celebrate their thirtieth anniversary. Postpone, but not abandon.

Miguel Iglesias, director of the Contemporánea, commenting on his own company's limited resources, spoke for them all when he said: 'Milk for the children? Or money for dance? There is no choice'. The dance in Cuba is bravely determined to survive.

Denmark

The Royal Danish Ballet
Bent Schønberg

The greatest event in the season was the Royal Danish Ballet's new production of Bournonville's *A Folk Tale*, directed by the company's artistic director Frank Andersen, and Anne Marie Vessel Schlüter, an expert on the old master. That in itself would have been beguiling, but the main topic of interest was, for obvious reasons, the design by Queen Margrethe II, which further cemented the close connection between the Royal family and the Royal Ballet – which, incidentally was the company's original title. We Danes actually had a Royal Ballet almost 200 years before the English suddenly took our name – after which, good people that we are, we called our company the Royal Danish Ballet, for foreign use.

When she is not governing, and has the time for it, Queen Margrethe is a most gifted artist. She has designed bishop's ornaments, a Christmas stamp, and the Georg Jensen Christmas spoon (in 1984), completed a myriad of paintings, translated books, and lately began a series of paintings on Christian subjects for a calendar.

From the rehearsals of the Royal Danish Ballet's *A Folk Tale*. Front row: Michael Bastian and Sorella Englund as Diderik and Viderik. Back row: Queen Margrethe II (the designer of the ballet), Mette Buchwald (Muri), and Silja Schandorff (Hilda).

PHOTO: RIGMOR MYDTSKOV

A Folk Tale is the most Danish of Bournonville's ballets. And who better to support and bring that out than the Queen of Denmark? It was a master stroke by Frank Andersen to talk Her Majesty into undertaking this assignment.

Inevitably there was criticism of this daring initiative. It was pointed out that as so many Danish designers needed a job it was neither here nor there to ask the Crown to compete with them – a strange point of view in a country where sex and race discrimination are forbidden by law, that, so it seems, Queen-discrimination should be allowed. (Quite apart from the fact that if the theatre should pass out jobs according to social criteria, the results could be astonishing.) And it will come as no surprise to anybody in the know that Queen Margrethe gave her fee to a project inside the ballet world.

Alexander Kølpin, principal dancer of the Royal Danish Ballet, on stage at the Bolshoi to receive a prize from Yuri Grigorovich as the best male dancer in the world.

The really interesting thing was that the experiment worked. The front curtain in a modernized Biedermeier-style was lovely in its naivety, the decor – especially that for the well scene, a typical Danish hilly landscape on a summer morning – was taken straight out of a fairy tale, and all the dangerous, alarming and funny participants at the Troll ball were charming and delightful.

It is said that the Queen was surprised at how big a job it was, and that she would not have the time to do such a task again. Quite apart from the enormous tourist appeal, artistically it would be annoying if the audience did not get a second chance to see a new work from the successful debutante. Maybe the intelligent Lisa la Cour could persuade the royal artist to lend a helping hand with her next Hans Christian Andersen ballet for children.

There were things in *A Folk Tale* which Bournonville would not have liked – especially the swing, which allowed the audience to have several good looks at Birthe's legs. The old choreographer would have left Denmark had he lived to see that. Why the missing painting in the dream scene, and why change the mirror's position, as it didn't achieve any artistic results?

Silja Schandorff was as pretty and blonde a Hilde as could ever be, and Peter Bo Bendixen as her Squire Ove – who (together with the spectators) profited with a new little solo put in for the occasion – was as noble as one could wish. Lis Jeppesen was funny as Birthe, but not as evil and dangerous as the role implies. Sorella Englund was a lively, nervous, ever-moving Viderik, a more comic figure than we are used to seeing, but always at the centre of our attention. Michael Bastian as brother Diderik was not as wicked as his predecessors, whilst Jette Buchwald's acting as Muri was demonic and wilful.

The ballet was one of the high points of the Second Bournonville Festival in April, given thirteen years after the first festival – and, says the theatre, thirteen years before the next – a decision which ought to be changed to not more than seven or eight years, in view of the festival's enormous success.

138 foreign ballet critics participated in the festival, together with hundreds and hundreds of guests from all over the world – including a prominent bunch of ballet lovers from England, who came across in an arrangement with *World Ballet and Dance, Dancing Times,* and Dance Books. The Queen attended every night, except when she was in France and Germany, and on that occasion the Queen Mother, Queen Ingrid, an ardent ballet lover herself, was at the theatre.

The other big event was the staging of *Napoli,* where Andersen and Henning Kronstam had directed Acts I and III, and Dinna Bjørn, daughter of the famous mime artist Niels Bjørn Larsen, and now artistic director of

the Norwegian Ballet in Oslo, had taken Act II back to the original as far as possible.

At the Royal Theatre this poor act has been cut and cut over decades until it was finally down from 30 to 13 minutes. Elsa Marianne von Rosen expanded the act for her productions in Leningrad and Sweden, and Dinna Bjørn had found all the original music and brought it back. Therefore this previously crippled act again stood out as the dramatic and – rare for Bournonville – highly charged erotic feature that it was meant to be.

This was best demonstrated by the first cast, Lis Jeppesen and Nikolaj Hübbe as Teresina and Gennaro, he with formidable attack, a firework of *grand jetés*, an explosion of pace, and she with a fine sensitive understanding of the role. In the second act, where she leaves the grotto and bids farewell to that dangerous and impressive Golfo, to which Arne Willumsen lent his extremely well-built body, she seemed to say 'I am going home to where I belong with the man I love, and so everything is as it should be. But brother, this *has* been fun!' Not since the divine – yes, she was – Margot Lander has it been done in this way, and one fears that poor Gennaro is in for the surprise of his life on the wedding night.

Søren Frandsen's designs had fortunately not changed, and in the second act only expanded the bridge to two arches as in the original production. It was done with fine taste and a feeling for style – which he unfortunately lacked when it came to the costumes of the naiads and their male followers in the second act.

The second cast had Heidi Ryom and Lloyd Riggins as the loving couple. She was the most charming and disarming Italian girl, and he a sensitive and sympathetic fisher-boy, who in Peter Bo Bendixen as the sea spirit, found a rival of the same standing. And in that gripping enthusiastic tarantella, which was performed no less than four times during the festival, all the company dancers shone in their own right on their home ground.

Napoli celebrated its 150th birthday at the festival, and the last deferential compliment to the laurel-wreathed bust of August on the stage was given to him by the company, followed in his honour by a fanfare from the orchestra and a standing ovation from the packed theatre led by the royal family. Imagine that – and Bournonville thought his works would die with him!

Conservatoriet is – apart from the mirror dance in *La Ventana* – technically the most difficult piece of Bournonville danced today. Here the original French school is danced at its purest; here you have living threads back to Vestris and Gardel – and it is extremely difficult to perform. Normally the audience likes this dancing school for the first act of the ballet – the company still owes the second act it promised for the festival – but nothing more. Small wonder when there are usually only ten or fifteen in the theatre who can evaluate the terrifying, demanding technique which is being demonstrated on stage. But during the festival, where 70–80% of the spectators were skilled experts, the applause was at the deserved, but normally never registered, height; this time especially addressed to that delightful dancer, Christina Olsson, with Riggins and Caroline Cavallo of the second cast, the theatre's two ballerinas Jeppesen and Ryom, together with Hübbe, a discerning first.

The Flower Festival in Genzano was beautifully performed by Victor Alvarez and Petrusjka Broholm (whom the theatre has temporarily lost to the Schaufuss company in Berlin), alternating with Henriette Muus and Johan Kobborg, the new international team which has sparkled around the world in the last seasons.

Far from Denmark was the weakest card the Danes played. There is not much dance in it; it is rather boring. Worst of all, however, are the parodic black people – this might have gone down well with the audience in 1860; today it just won't do. The foreign guests in particular seemed to dislike it – with good reason – and it is a pertinent question whether this ballet shouldn't be packed away with mothballs for a decade or two.

Abdallah is a fine and gentle reconstruction, talentfully made by Toni Lander, Bruce Marks and Flemming Ryberg. Jens-Jacob Worsaae's design is as much a shining pearl of the harem as is Silja Schandorff in her glittering beauty. Riggins is a most disarming shoemaker, and Christina Olsson captivates as the forgiving Irma. Everybody dances finely, but nothing can hide the lightness of the ballet.,

Henning Kronstam had restaged *La Sylphide* with a gentle hand – apart from having cut the scene with the nest, immortalized by the etchings of Marie Taglioni, and clearly specified by Bournonville in his libretto. It seemed to be the main topic for discussion during the festival, and the foreign spectators were simply nonplussed. I think it was simply a gaffe by that thoughtful and caring director – an experiment which flopped. I predict that it will be back very soon.

It was something of a gamble to put Rose Gad in the title role. Her talent is a stroke of genius, her technique impeccable, and she has a terrifying erotic undercurrent, but at the first performance she lacked that touch of poetry which is so important for this, the most intriguing and bewildering of all the choreographer's female characters. The two men were set out more clearly: Hübbe, unsurpassed in his sweeping *grands jetés*, and finishing in positions as clear cut as could be wished; and Michael Weidinger as Gurn was a dangerous and well-matched adversary. But the evening belonged to Sorella Englund, who was a most formidable Madge, a lightning column of wickedness and hate – a feat which burned in the mind of the spectator.

The King's Volunteers on Amager – a vaudeville ballet (with stress on the 'vaudeville') belongs to the national repertory, and could be taken out and dusted down every fifteen years – I thought. But it seemed as if the balleto-philes from other countries disagreed. They were knocked out by this lightest of feathers, and thoroughly impressed by Villumsen's ever-flirting lieutenant and his alarmingly pretty, disarming and charming wife, Eva Cloborg – so what do you know?

Anne Marie Vessel Schlüter got the best out of the company's mime resources in *The Kermesse in Bruges*. Moving in her youthful innocence, Henriette Muus charmed her way into the hearts of the audience. The three adventurous brothers, Villumsen, Johan Kobborg, and Morten Munksdorf, were virile and charming. Lis Jeppesen and Lise Stripp were funny as the flirtatious sisters; and, sparkling with strong stage personality, Kjeld Noack as the alchemist said goodbye to the theatre he has served for more than fifty years. To top it all, Kirsten Simone as the rich van Everdingen and her stylish butler Flemming Ryberg were luxurious.

Fortunately the Royal Ballet can do more that its Bournonville. Kenneth MacMillan's *Concerto* was beautifully danced in Jürgen Rose's strongly coloured costumes and showed how well the Royal Ballet can dance it, just as inspired as its British counterpart. Heidi Ryom and Lloyd Riggins, a breath of youth and happiness, were only surpassed by Silja Schandorff's majestic appearance, playing up to Bo Bendixen's elegance, to end happily with the sexy Christina Olsson sparkling in the third movement. In another cast, Lis Jeppesen, with her raving beauty, seemed far away from her powerful partner Michael Weidinger, until her last glance at him suddenly changed the mood between them.

Patricia Neary staged *Allegro Brillante*, Balanchine's demanding and brilliant Tchaikovsky *pas de deux* for Heidi Ryom and Lloyd Riggins later in the season. It had to be Ms Ryom who got the part in this work, so characteristic of its creator. She leads the other dancers majestically and with bravura, exploding from one set of steps into the next – a myriad of intricate *pas*, each becoming more difficult – beautifully supported by her American-Danish partner, who seems to surpass himself with every new role.

There can be no doubt that Anna Lærkersen is the most talented chore-ographer the Royal Ballet has fostered in the last decades. It is daring to dance 55 minutes to Chopin, and it has not been done since Robbins' *Dances at a Gathering*. It was a bold but interesting idea to let every second piece of music in *Polacca* be played by two gifted young musicians on marimba, which broke the monotony of the piano. Still, the thirteen pieces are a bit too long – a cut of 10 minutes will do wonders with this work, which is still one of the most promising new ballets the company has shown for years.

Lærkesen reveals a lot about the six young dancers she works with: Rose Gad, Silja Schandorff, Christina Olsson, Victor Alvarez, Nikolaj Hübbe and Michael Weidinger. A tiny bit of humour, and some delicate dancing are sidelights from this choreographer who – in contrast with Robbins – let a moodily elegiac atmosphere fill the work. Each role is tailor-made for the specific dancer's forte, and usually the mood is in the minor.

It seems that Lærkesen has even more to tell us. I hope her next work – and no theatre would dare refuse a new opus from this incredibly gifted artist – will be built upon a story. Lærkesen has shown us that she can master the technique of staging *pas*, feelings, hopes – now she must take the final step.

To celebrate the silver wedding of Queen Margrethe and Prince Henrik, a ballet was made in Aarhus by Flemming Flindt to music by Carl Nielsen. The subject was inspired by another Great Dane, Baroness Karen Blixen, though the ballet put less emphasis on the author's turbulent life and more on her artistic side – her struggle within herself, her pact with Lucifer, her cacophony of feelings, talent and unhappiness. Considering the work was made in honour of the nice Danish Queen, who is a first class artist in her own right, and has had a most harmonious childhood and an extremely happy marriage, the chosen subject might not be the first that comes to

The great mime, seventy-nine-year-old Niels Bjørn Larsen, on the Royal Danish Ballet's tour of America. Here he is being honoured with the Philip Morris dance prize, presented at the Royal Danish Embassy in Washington by Neel Resling Halpern, vice-president of the American-Scandinavian Foundation. Taken together, the photographs shown in this chapter indicate the extraordinary scope of this company from one of the world's tiniest nations.

mind. The suicide of Blixen's father is strongly dramatic. The eternal un-faithfulness of Bror – danced with wonderfully convincing unreliability by Peter Schaufuss, who made one of his career's most dangerous roles – was just as moving as the Baroness's amorous *pas de deux* with Denys, starting to the noise of streaming rain, for which Flindt has made a fine piece of choreography – not the strongest point of this clever theatre man, who is usually better at plotting a convincing story than making steps for it. But the end doesn't make sense. If you must suffer all imaginable dreadful things in order to be an artist, you don't suddenly end up, as Flindt does, by letting everybody live happily ever after, as happens in the banal finale. So although attention is held the whole way though, you are not moved – and in the end, you don't know what to believe.

Still, Vivi Flindt, an international sensuous beauty, ignited the theatre; Schaufuss – a sleek, cheap hero of the housemaids – has seldom created a stronger character; Peter Bo Bendixen was a romantic if unattainable lover if ever the was one; and Jacob Sparso, impressive as Lucifer – all were excellent.

The combination of Blixen and Nielsen is exciting. I hope Flindt can work on the idea and one day give us a more logical and convincing ballet.

New Dance
Erik Aschengreen
Modern dance, new dance, contemporary dance, or whatever you call it, came late to Denmark. In the 1970s small groups emerged and disap-peared. In the 1980s they became more stable, but it was not until the beginning of the 1990s that some of them established their artistic profile, and all with a budget economy (though four of them are more regularly subsidized now).

The strongest company is **Nyt Dansk Danseteater** (New Danish Dance Theatre). The artistic directors Anette Abildgaard and Warren Spears are also the chief choreographers. Last season they produced *Men Dansen, den går* ('And the dance goes on'), inspired by three medieval folk ballads. Most convincing was Abildgaard's *Elverskud*, built upon the spleen and dishar-mony which also fascinated choreographers in the romantic period. They toured with big performances from previous seasons *Skagen* ('Spears') and Abildgaard's *Morels Opfindelse* ('Morel's Invention'), the latter performed when the company guested at the Royal Theatre, and the subject of a fascinating video by Torben Skljødt Jensen. When invited to the Royal Theatre they also performed Abildgaard's version of *Qarrtsiluni*, once a famous ballet by Harald Lander and Knudåge Riisager.

Uppercut Danseteater has always done a lot to introduce new dance to a young and unfamiliar audience. This year they did this with *Parat Start Dans* ('Ready Start Dance'). They work with foreign choreographers like

In step with the needs of the international traveller

Gill Clarke, Janet Smith and Holly Cavrell, and they invited the English composer Christopher Benstead for their work *Henriettes Ord* ('Henriette's Words'), a dance about a retarded girl, her thoughts, her hopes and her fears. It was choreographed by the two artistic directors Sheila de Val and Cher Geurtze.

Together with the two previously mentioned companies **Corona** forms the Travelling Dancetheatre, a new institution subsidized by state money from this season. Corona, directed by Jørgen Carlslund and James McBride, has been successful with children's performances. For the grown-ups they did *Human Tangos in a Zoo*, inspired by and dedicated to the homosexuals who, having just escaped the Nazi concentration camps of the war, were convicted for their sexuality and sent to prison.

For more than ten years the Swedish Nanna Nilson has contributed energy and vitality to the Danish dance community. Her company anniversary was celebrated with *Stop*, danced by her **New Now Dancers**. Originally a strict Cunningham performer, Nanna Nilson has moved on to become a personal choreographer, open to humour and humanity. Her *Stop* was about all the situations in life where we wait.

Jorge Holguin Dansteater is now directed by Kathryn Ricketts, who was codirector with Holguin. He came from Colombia and settled in Denmark, where he died in 1989. Kathryn Ricketts' style is both physical and highly theatrical. Sometimes she uses actors and text (*Family I* and *II*) sometimes she relies on pure movements, as in *Blomster* ('Flowers'). Her company is known for using unconventional performing spaces, and for its bittersweet humour.

Unconventional also is Rhea Leman and her **Teater Tango**, specializing in blending film, dance, text and song. Her company had two productions last season: *Fodgængerfryd* ('Pedestrian Delight'), which was a charming outdoor performance in the harbour, and *Sovevognens Madonna* ('The Madonna of the Sleeper'), where Rhea performed with one of Denmark's well-known actresses, Anne Marie Helger.

Copenhagen also has the dance company **Micado**, directed by Mikala Bjarnov Lage, who choreographed *Pandoras Æske* ('Pandora's Box') and Charlotte Rindom, who created the strongly dramatic *Bare et par små stik* ('Only a few small stings') about a woman's journey to harmony through different and difficult love relationships. The company **Kompagni** is directed by Christine Meldal and Susanne Frederiksen, both graduates from London Contemporary Dance School. Their performance this year was a sophisticated mixture of song and dance called *Dagenes Skum* ('The Foam of Everyday'), created with texts by Boris Vian. In Århus the Swedish **Marie Borlin-Tani** has had a great success with her **Dance Theatre**. In 1992 it became a regional dance institution. She is a strong choreographer with a good way of telling a story, for instance in *Woyzzek* or *Picasso*. Her latest work was *Dans til livet* ('Dance for Life'), in a programme in which she also invited Norwegian choreographer Kjersti Ålveberg, who did *Rav* ('Amber'), and the Swedish Jessica Iwanson, who did *Ansigter* ('Faces'). In the margins of the dance world is the fantastic performance artist **Kirsten Dehlholm**, who with her group **Hotel Pro Forma**, in the city hall of Gentofte, created *Skyggens Kvadrat* ('The Square of the Shadow'), a strange and wonderful world about memories and silence.

The yearly New Dance Festival, where almost all the aforementioned groups were performing, and the big event Dancin' City created by the energetic Trevor Davies, were important for the profile of new dance in Denmark. In June and July we saw more than twenty groups coming from all over the country. The standard was very high. Perhaps the Danish dance community will climb the international ladder – especially now the first state-subsidized dance education for modern dance in Denmark is to begin in September 1992, directed by the Swede Christel Wallin.

Obituaries

Allan Fridericia, the Danish ballet historian, writer, designer and promoter, died just after his seventieth birthday on New Year's Eve 1991. After studying theatre history in Stockholm and Copenhagen, Fridericia began working as a writer on ballet history, becoming an outstanding author in the international art world. He wrote many books, including the first biography of August Bournonville, considered a definitive work. It was later translated into Russian, where 50,000 copies were sold in two days. After directing at provincial Danish theatres, he founded the Scandinavian Ballet (1960–66) with his wife, the Swedish ballerina and choreographer Elsa Marianne von Rosen. Besides arranging ballet exhibitions around the world, he directed many television programmes, notably the series on the Bournonville school, made in collaboration with the late Hans Brenaa. He was enormously knowledgeable, a sharp and feared critic on several papers in Denmark, and a contributor to a great number of international ballet magazines. He was an honourable member of the Critics Circle in London, a member of countless juries at ballet competitions around the world, and a contributor to *World Ballet and Dance*. He reconstructed several Bournonville ballets for his Scandinavian company, in collaboration with his wife. The first was *The Feast in Albano*. Thereafter he directed *La Sylphide*, which he gave in its original version. He also designed *Napoli* for several companies in the West, and for the Kirov Ballet. His last staging was *The Lay of Thrym* for the Royal Theatre in Copenhagen.

Estonia

Heili Einasto

From the beginning of the twentieth century, which marks the starting point of professional dance in Estonia, the art has stood on two bases: Estonia Theatre in Tallinn and Vanemuine Theatre in Tartu. Both house an opera, and Vanemuine also has a theatre company, which has a strong impact on ballet there.

The season of 1991/92 saw the birth of a new dance company – **Nordic Star Dance Theatre**, which was formed on 3 May 1991, but had its first performance on 24 September 1991. The artistic director of the Σcompany – Saima Kranig – is a former ballerina of the Estonia Theatre, and the members of the company have a mainly ballet background, though three of them do not hold a diploma from the Ballet School. 'Nordic Star sees its aim in cultivating various styles and techniques, in inviting different and interesting choreographers', says Saima Kranig, who studied Limón technique in Finland, and puts an emphasis on modern dance. The first programme showed three postmodern pieces by American choreographers: Barbara Hofrenning's *One Hand Takes from the Other*, Tamar Rogoff's *The Case* and Bonnie Sue Stein's *The Journey*. The company's ability to feel free in this new, unfamiliar approach was a pleasant surprise, and the burst of energy and creative activity this unfamiliar style unleashed, a wonderful experience.

The company's second programme was premiered at the Kaunas International Dance Festival (Lithuania) in October 1991. It consisted of two revivals by Mai Murdmaa: *Farewell* and *Woman*, which use ballet vocabulary in a modern way; Jeanne Yasko's *Quiet Chaos* in a Limón style, originally created for the Estonia Theatre two years previously on the initiative of Saima Kranig; *Piet* by Lithuanian Jurius Smoriginas, an expressionistic, classical ballet duet; and *Kisses of the Wind* by the same choreographer, specially created for the company using a modern idiom. Nordic Star is facing severe financial problems, as the economic situation in Estonia is far from favourable to the arts. But they are very dedicated, and Saima Kranig and René Nommik are attending the International Choreographers Workshop at the American Dance Festival in summer 1992.

The **Estonia Theatre** ballet company had its greatest success in November 1991, when Mai Murdmaa's *Crime and Punishment* was premiered. This two-act ballet is based on Dostoyevsky's famous novel; the music is compiled from different pieces by Arvo Pärt. Murdmaa's works could be called modern ballets – though she uses classical ballet vocabulary, her approach is modern. In this piece she used everyday movements (like washing) for

Estonia Theatre Ballet in the second act of Mai Murdmaa's *Crime and Punishment*, based on Dostoyevsky's novel.   PHOTO: G. VAIDLA

the first time, and large pantomime sections. The piece won the best production award in Estonia. Excerpts from the ballet were performed in New York in March 1992.

The second programme in February consisted of three revivals. The divertissement from *Paquita* was followed by two Murdmaa pieces: *Little Symphony*, an abstract music visualization, and *Miraculous Mandarin* which gave an opportunity for Kaie Korb and Tatjana Kilgas to demonstrate their dramatic skills. All these pieces, with the exception of *Little Symphony*, were performed at the Karlsruhe Culture Days festival in Germany, which this year was dedicated to Estonia, independent again after fifty years of Soviet occupation.

The latest premiere of the company was Murdmaa's *Carmina Burana* on 13 June 1992, which was performed in the open air on Virumaa Day of Culture in front of the Palmse mansion. This was the first open-air ballet performance in Estonia.

One of the problems of the Estonia Theatre is how to keep their dancers. Many younger ones have found better hunting grounds abroad: Toomas Edur and Age Oks (Agnes Oaks) are dancing with English National Ballet for the second season; Inna and Meelis Pakri are in Denver. Prima ballerina Kaie Korb is mainly touring with her partner Viesturs Jansons from Latvia.

In late summer 1991, these two were filmed for Swedish TV in Birgit Cullberg's *The Winds of Love*, a 17-minute ballet specially created for them.

Vanemuine ballet company has always had difficulties with the physical form of their dancers. Being considered the second, and thus less significant company, there have sometimes been moods of laxity. At the same time this company has been more open to innovations and experiments than the Estonia Theatre, which has looked down on this kind of 'dilettantism'. The 199/92 season perhaps belongs to Mare Tommingas as she choreographed all new works. Ballet-trained, she began choreographing a couple of years ago; her greatest success being Orff's *Carmina Burana*. This season she has formed her own studio where the main participants are students of Tartu University. Her *Little Prince*, based on Saint-Exupéry's story, demonstrated her independent thinking and original ideas, but was often fettered by her ballet training. *African Sanctus*, premiered in April 1992, was more free, and had stunning mass-scenes, the movement indicating African traditional and Indian classical dance influence. *Barcelona* used ballet vocabulary, and was a cut above *Little Prince*.

The latest premiere this season in Estonia was by **GOH Productions** from New York which has close ties with Estonia. *Emapolv* was inspired by the holistic principles of prehistoric matrilineal society, where the mother spirit harmoniously encompassed all aspects of the life cycle. The piece was choreographed and performed by Marika Blossfeldt, an Estonian dancer living in New York, and during the performance a snake is painted by Epp-Maria Kokamägi. The Estonian Philharmonic Chamber Choir also play a significant role, singing Lisa Karrer's music, and participating in the movement. This piece was performed at the Esto Days Festival – for Estonians living abroad – in New York in July 1992.

Finland

Rebecca Libermann

Three events dominated the Finnish ballet world in the past season – the deep recession in the country, the seventieth anniversary of the Finnish National Ballet, and the changes in directorship at this company and the City Theatre Dance Group. The economic crisis was putting on pressure, particularly for small dance groups – fewer state subsidies and private funding were available – yet creativity and skills, as well as variety and numbers of performances, have not yet suffered.

The first new production in October for the **Finnish National Ballet,** by Californian dance pedagogue, choreographer and dancer Carolyn Carlson, was a good example of these innovations. *Maa – Land, Crossing The Great Waters*, set to music by the Finn Kaija Saariaho, brought a sequence of images on stage called 'The Trip', 'The Portal', 'The Door', 'The Forest', 'The Window', 'The Fall' and 'The Phoenix'. The production was created around Carlson's idea of a mythological world, more precisely of a hero who travels to a mythological underworld. Basically the performance revolved around doors which opened, and windows through which new vistas were seen – an easy trip through life and death, the beyond and back. The dancing itself was based on improvisation, a quite new experience for the company dancers, who took a while to get used to it.

A journey of a different nature was undertaken in January, a trip through both classical and contemporary dance pieces – the seventieth anniversary of the National Ballet was celebrated in grand style with the first ballet ever staged by Finns – namely *Swan Lake*. The week of celebration also featured *Giselle*, Marjo Kuusela's *Seven Brothers*, Tommi Kitti's *Loviisa*, Carolyn Carlson's *Maa*, Balanchine's *Divertimento No. 15*, and van Dantzig's *Four Last Songs*. Last but not least came scenes from *Aurora's Wedding*, choreographed by Doris Laine, director of the ballet since 1984, who at the gala evening handed her leadership of the Finnish National Ballet over to Jorma Uotinen, till then director of the City Theatre Dance Group.

With the departure of Doris Laine, now head of the ballet of the Komische Oper in Berlin, a new era dawns for the company. Doris Laine's reign might be missed by some lovers of pure classical ballets – it solidified the company, particularly with regard to technique, though it did not lead to any great number of performances that were contemporary in terms of either content and aesthetics. But it will be up to Uotinen now to lead the company to new horizons and to a new century, a task which is not so easy to fulfil, even for Uotinen, with his visions of total ballet theatre. His plans are many – more individual training, modern or new interpretations of classical ballets, contemporary choreographers, more discussion, more responsibility intellectually and otherwise for the dancers, and so forth. Which of his goals he will be able to fulfil remains to be seen – the mills of an old institution like the Finnish National Ballet grind slowly.

But back to the 1991/92 season. March saw a first night of John Neumeier's *As You Like It*, a new experience for the company, who worked for the first time with this gifted choreographer. After extensive rehearsals both sides were satisfied with the outcome, which was appreciated by critics and public alike. Also in the repertory were Marjo Kuusela's *Ronja, The Robber's Daughter* (for which a TV version was made this season), Jorma Uotinen's *Faun*, Nils Christe's *Pulcinella*, Domy Reiter-Soffer's *Lady of the Camellias*, as well as Spoerli's *La Belle Vie* and *La Fille mal gardée*.

Some of these pieces were shown in China, where a part of the company toured.

For the 1992/93 season, the last season in the current theatre, a mix of the old and new is planned: there will be first nights for *Stelle* by Oscar Araíz, who is quite unknown in Finland, followed by Balanchine's *Rubies* and, also for the first time, a piece by William Forsythe – *Steptext*. Jorma Uotinen will premiere his as yet untitled new work – not on the opera stage but in an abandoned cable factory. And finally Uotinen will give the Finnish dancers Tero Saarinen and Arja Raatikain each a chance to show off their new choreography. Also planned are tours to Rome and Amsterdam with *Maa*, and new Sunday matinées. Then in autumn 1993, the whole company will move to a newly built venue, with two stages and far more possibilities for expression and creativity. The new house is to be inaugurated with *Swan Lake* on 1 December 1993.

During the past season the **City Theatre Ballet Group** also got a new leader, Carolyn Carlson, who has in past years kept close contact with the group (she and Jorma Uotinen are friends who have worked together in Paris and Helsinki for years). For the City Theatre last season she staged her solo *Blue Lady*, the dreams and recollections of a woman, and *Who Took the August*, based on paintings by Hopper, portraying the American mid-West

Susanna Vironmäki and Sampo Kivelä of the Finnish National Ballet in John Neumeier's *Mozart, and Themes from 'As You Like It'*.   PHOTO: KARI HAKLI

Marja Korhola's *The Mummy Ballet*, for her company Tanssiteatteri Raatikko. The dancers are Paula Tuovinen and Marja Korhola. PHOTO: SAKARI VIIKA

in the 1940s as tableaux of emotions. This piece was also shown at the International Dance Festival in Copenhagen.

Also new was an evening entitled 'Devil's Field' with two works – one by Tommi Kitti and another by his wife Marjo Kuusela. *Kilimancharo* was about cultural developments and differences, with music by Miles Davies. The second ballet, *Runar* was a wild and melancholic ballad about a poor devil who could not rebel. Both were noteworthy. Also in the repertory was the tragic-comic *Pathetique* by Jorma Uotinen, with which he went on tour to the Art Festival in Iceland and to the Kuopio International Dance Festival. The latter also presented *Cold Star* the newest work by **Ulla Koivisto** (a former student of Merce Cunningham), as well as Raija Lehmussaari's *Carmen* with the **Sun Ballet**; a solo piece by the expressive **Tero Saarinen**; and a premiere by the **Dance Theatre Raatikko**, *The Mummy Ballet*, absurd and comical, as is the company's new style since the satirist choreographer Marja Korhola took over from the founder Marjo Kuusela. Also at the festival were **Dance Theatre Hurjaruuth,** performing *1001* by Arja Pettersson, and **Tuomo Railo** with his work *Khora*, clearly influenced by Japanese Butoh. **Dance Theatre Eri** ('Different Dance Theatre') joined with a bandola orchestra and a singer in *Tango Remembrance*, a tango cabaret (tango being almost like folk music in Finland) and also staged Stravinsky's *Soldier's Tale* choreographed by Tiina Lindfors.

This festival to which groups and dancers from abroad were also invited (for instance from Sweden, Spain, China, the United States) marked with this display of Finnish dance not only the seventy-fifth anniversary of Finland's independence, but also the coming of a new age of gifted, unique and exciting Finnish choreographers and expressively rich and versatile Finnish dancers. Let us only hope that the recession does not sweep them away.

France

Simone Dupuis

The most significant event of the Parisian season was undoubtedly the addition of *Dances at a Gathering* to the repertoire of the **Ballet de l'Opéra** in November – doubly so, given that in the previous season Robbins had voiced dissatisfaction with the amount of rehearsals scheduled. Filled with subtlety, nostalgia, tender and vagrant humour, this absolute work of art was interpreted with fervour by the top dancers of the

Opéra, particularly Manuel Legris, Monique Loudières and Marie Claude Pietragalla.

The season opened at Théâtre de Ville with two American companies. **Merce Cunningham** was unequalled with *Loosestrife*, dedicated to the recently deceased Michel Guy, who was responsible for Cunningham's early success in France. The other company was **Lucinda Childs and Dancers** in *Rhythm Plus*, followed by *Dance*, in which the dancers appeared live on stage and also in a film by Sol de Witt, which played simultaneously.

As usual, the Ballet de l'Opéra opened in October with *Giselle*, this time restaged in black and white designs by the minimalist painter Loic Le Groumellec. Deliberately anti-romantic, this version aroused no interest. Once more the dancers – rigged in hideous costumes – saved the day through their excellent dancing.

Luckily, in December at the **Ballet de Nancy**, Pierre Lacotte (who had just been appointed director) revived a *Giselle* which was hyper-romantic and thus, closer to the original version. The reintroduction of the Act I *grand pas de deux*, rebalanced the ballet, since both Albrecht and Giselle take equal part in the action. In the title role (which was created for Carlotta Grisi when she was twenty-two years old) the sixteen-year-old Spaniard Amaya Iglesias demonstrated a bravura dance technique, full of spontaneity. Next to her, Laurent Hilaire interpreted a prince full of nobility and thus provided an attentive partner. However, the use of a tape recording, rather than an orchestra was deplorable.

Once again, choreographers were inspired by ancient myths. This year Expo 92 in Seville and the Olympic Games in Barcelona placed Spain at the centre of focus, and we witnessed the rebirths of two *Carmen*s. At the Opéra in Paris, Roland Petit's version returned, having lost none of its daring modernity. Marie Claude Pietragalla, who has the right physique for the role, has yet to cast off the shadow of Zizi Jeanmaire. In an different category, the passionate games played by Alessandra Ferri, making a guest appearance, caused a sensation. At the Théâtre de Ville in June, the **Cullberg Ballet** presented the long-awaited version by Mats Ek. Ana Laguna appeared to have sprung out of a grim story book. Free from all aesthetic binds, she smoked a cigar, adopted a macho stance and teased the fragile Don José, played by Marc Hwang.

In the same theatre, only a month earlier, the *Carmen* by **Karine Saporta** developed as a narcissistic ritual, at times exasperating and at times fascinating. Saporta exploited the fetishistic qualities of the fan, hair, and red roses, with Carmen, both yielding and refusing, questioning the nature of desire. In September, the Biennale de la Danse at Lyon offered a *Carmen Suite* by Alberto Alonso, danced by Alicia, as well as another more eccentric version by Dominique Boivin, considered the Pierrot Lunaire of the young, new French dance. In Grenoble, Jean-Claude Gallotta, often considered the

Deborah Salmirs and Eric Alfieri of Jean-Claude Gallotta's Groupe Emile Dubois in his *Docteur Labus*.   PHOTO: DELAHAYE

leader of the **Groupe Emile Dubois**, directed *The Legend of Don Juan*, in which he transformed the seducer into a rock star. Overlong, monotonous and repetitive, it was burdened by a text that lacked interest. The whole enterprise was received coolly, as had been its predecessor, *The Legend of Romeo and Juliet*, a total flop, falsely intellectual and naively provocative, as banal as the most conventional of productions. *Romeo and Juliet* was also given at the Paris Opéra in Nureyev's monumental version – again terribly long. Sylvie Guillem appeared as a guest, and created a Juliet of full of wisdom, next to an inspired performance by Laurent Hilaire. A young choreographer of Albanian origin, Angelin Preljocaj directed for the **Lyon Opera Ballet** an astonishing and strong *Romeo and Juliet*, set in an oppressive totalitarian state where love is a crime punishable by death. At the Opéra Garnier, Petit's iconoclastic version of the *Sleeping Beauty* (with Zizi Jeanmaire in a vampish portrayal of Carabosse) left its public indifferent. John Neumeier did not fare any better. His *Eugene Onegin* seemed too long, and his *Streetcar Named Desire* was both grandiloquent and outmoded.

In March, however, the programme 'Picasso and the Dance' piqued the audience's curiosity. In spite of the magnificent scene painting and Chanel's amusing costumes, *Le Train bleu* never rose beyond a cute *divertissement*. Massine's *Le Tricorne* was not a revelation either, and curiously enough the first cast (Monique Loudières and Patrick Dupond) was eclipsed by the second (Clotilde Vayer and José Martinez, medal winner at Varna). The surprise of the evening was *Le Rendezvous* by Roland Petit. First created in 1945, this short ballet conserved its original mystery intact.

In February the **Ballet du Rhin**, rejuvenated by Jean Paul Gravier's efforts to open out its repertoire, which now includes Tudor and Jooss, caused a stir with *Jason and Medea*, after the original by Noverre. Ivo Cramer, inspired by his research at the Royal Library in Stockholm, created an interpretation with his own artistic signature. The dance, which favours *ballon* and elegance, nonetheless managed to express the psychology of the characters and thus aided in the development of the action.

In March the **Frankfurt Ballet** presented *Artifact* by William Forsythe. This work, one of the most explosive from the buoyant Billy, appeared to have provisionally reconciled the classicists and the modernists. At the Théâtre de Champs d'Elysée, the audience, lured by the presence of Baryshnikov, crowded the two programmes of his **White Oak Dance Project**. The disappointment was felt as much by those nostalgic for the star of the Kirov as those who had applauded Misha's conversion to modernism. The exception was in Martha Graham's *El Penitente*, where Baryshnikov excelled with force and superb conviction. Mark Morris' pieces – *Canonic 3/4 Studies*, *A Lake*, and *Ten Thousand Suggestions* – did not generate any interest, but the worst piece was *Oz* by Paul Taylor, a little ballet which succeeded in emptying a good percentage of the house. At the Maison des Arts de Creteil, the **Sydney Dance Company** baffled the audience with *Some Rooms* in which modern dance, ghosts and psychoanalysis were used to create the phantasmagorical universe of choreographer Graeme Murphy.

Patrick Dupond's determination to modernize the repertoire of the Ballet de l'Opéra is well known. This is why he invited Daniel Larrieu (already remarked upon by William Forsythe) and Odile Duboc. Unfortunately, *Attentat poétique* by Larrieu came through as a disaster, an amateur and inconsistent piece, incapable of using the full potential of dancers of professional stature. Odile Duboc had better luck with *Retours de scène*, though it did not prove indispensable for the company's repertoire.

June was a real marathon for the balletomanes. Apart from the ballets already discussed, we should mention 'Mouv' Dance' at the Opéra Comique. This was a hip-hop festival where young immigrant dancers gave testimony of their vitality and professionalism. At the Théâtre de Ville, two enigmatic pieces by Mats Ek captured everyone's attention. *Vieux enfants* developed within a nightmare atmosphere where primitive instincts were symbolized by an obscene monkey (the extraordinary Yvan Auzely). With *Etres lumineux*, amidst sinister candelabra resembling serpents, Ana Laguna, seemed to invent with total abandonment, a dance as never seen before: in defiance of its hermeticism, this strange ballet proved totally passionate from beginning to end. At the Théâtre de la Bastille

Compagnie Bagouet in *Necesito, Pièce pour Grenade*, choreographed by Dominique Bagouet.   PHOTO: MARC GINOT

DV8 Physical Theatre presented *Strange Fish*, a disturbing piece whose main theme was desire; it was original, with remarkable dancers, a mixture of violence and humour. In one evening Lloyd Newson became an important choreographer in the eyes of the French.

The season finished with **Pina Bausch**'s annual visit to the Théâtre de la Ville with her new piece *Tanzabend II*. In a forest of hanging birches (through which from time to time a white polar bear was seen ambling), the lady from Wuppertal retold her favourite themes of the cruelties of life (not unlike life in dance) and her anguish concerning the fate of the planet.

The Ballet de l'Opéra moved to the Opéra Bastille (Parisians' most hated building) to present the ancient version of *Swan Lake* by Bourmeister. The new, grotesque costumes by the Japanese Tomito Mohri transformed the characters into Samurai (why?) and did nothing but disfigure Act I (especially tasteless) and Act III. The acts in white, danced to the hilt by the company, kept all their original magic. All the performers were dominated by Sylvie Guillem. From the moment she appeared it was as if a real swan had come on stage. As the solitary Prince Siegfried, Laurent Hilaire showed the same magnificence as her partner.

The summer festivals have been announced with *La Peu du monde* by Angelin Preljocaj at Chateauvallon, and *Le Rêve d'Esther* by Karine Saporta at Montpellier. These two pieces, created in Paris and touring in 1992/93, stave off a sense of despair about the state of young French choreographers.

Germany

Ballet

Horst Koegler

The German 1991/92 ballet season has seen a remarkable process of recovery and strengthening of some of the big opera-house companies, which in recent years have gone through a period of stagnation, with little creative activity. The cities which have most profited from this encouraging trend are Berlin, Düsseldorf, Leipzig and Munich (in strictly alphabetical order), while Hamburg and Stuttgart continue to compete for the pre-eminent position among Germany's classically orientated companies. Frankfurt, of course, is a case on its own – determinedly following its highly idiosyncratic course set by the American William Forsythe, considered by more and more people not only here, but obviously in Paris too, as the legitimate heir to Balanchine, destined to steer ballet into the twenty-first century (and in doing so paying back to Europe what Europe had generously lent America in the person of Balanchine).

Peter Schaufuss at the **West Berlin German Opera** successfully continued his two-track repertory policy – with himself in charge of the classics, not only of the Bournonville school, but branching out for the first time on French territory and staging *Giselle* (too conventional for German tastes, at least those of the majority of critics) – while inviting other choreographers to take care of the contemporary wing of the repertory: Christopher Bruce, for instance, (with *Cruel Garden*), Michael Clark (*BOG.3.0.*), Stephen Petronio (*Laytext*) and Bill T. Jones (*The Opening*). Another of his highly welcome initiatives is his encouragement of young dancers to try their hand at choreography. This is still the strongest among Berlin's companies, with the most interesting repertory and dancers, and the two other companies in the Eastern part of the city, much poorer in every respect, very much appreciate Schaufuss's unconventional open-mindedness and willingness to cooperate with them – not only in joint venture programmes, but also in the search for talented young choreographers.

At the two other opera houses, situated in the eastern part of the city, stabilization needs more time. Egon Bischoff and Martin Puttke still continue to head the company at the **German State Opera**, but their days are obviously approaching an end. The only substantial contribution to the repertory during the 1991/92 season was another staging of Nureyev's *Sleeping Beauty*, which went rather well – with the master himself letting his hair down as Carabosse. A new hope at the house is Michael Denard, who will join the company as artistic advisor for the 1992/93 season (and has immediately won over Maurice Béjart to stage new versions of Schönberg's *Transfigured Night* and Bartók's *The Miraculous Mandarin* – the other big event will be Nureyev's *Don Quixote*). Everybody expects him to be appointed artistic director, starting with the 1993/94 season, and hopes to see a permanent working relationship with Béjart, who from his earliest days has always enjoyed an especially heartwarming relationship with the Berlin public.

Whether Doris Laine, the new artistic director of the ballet company at the **Komische Oper**, will be able to settle the unrest among the dancers and the loss of orientation in artistic policy, remains to be seen. One has the impression that she is only an emergency stand-by. The chief choreographer is still Tom Schilling, but so far he has only revived some of his former pieces and is clearly waiting for his contract to expire at the end of the 1992/93 season. The big event of the 1991/92 season was Arila Siegert's staging of Hans Werner Henze's *Ondine* – according to trustworthy reports a rather forced attempt at modernizing and psychologizing the romantic plot, and not very convincing.

The big success story of the season is undoubtedly the progress of the

The third-act *pas de cinq* of Nureyev's version of *The Sleeping Beauty*, performed by Victoria Lahigura and Mario Perricone of the Ballett der Deutsche Staatsoper Berlin.   PHOTO: CHRISTINE GRUCHOT

Ballet of the German Opera on the Rhine at Düsseldorf-Duisburg under the energetic leadership of Heinz Spoerli: a dramaturgically plausible re-telling of *Swan Lake* within the traditional confines (set in a ballet studio), where the two ballerinas are competing not only as Odile and Odette but also privately for the favours of the *danseur noble* – with the ballet master himself intervening as Rothbart) – the second programme ingeniously double-billing *Transfigured Night* and Strauss's highly problematic *Legend of Joseph*. The company looks reborn after the Bortoluzzi fatigue, with many new, young and promising dancers, the best of them hailing from Russia and Romania, already now astonishingly integrated. There are more performances then ever before, most of them sold out, and the audience fully participates in the spring-like optimism which so strongly sweeps the auditorium. One would never have thought that so much could be achieved during just ten months of hard work!

In **Frankfurt**, William Forsythe continued along the deconstructionist road; hardly anyone understands what it means or knows where it leads – one even doubts whether Forsythe himself knows. The latest products of his incessantly working brain were *The Loss of Small Detail, Snap, Woven Effort*, and *As Garden in this Setting*. All have at least some textual passages, and computerized sounds and noises by Thom Willems, and all have one or other sculptural object, to which the dancers more or less relate. It is almost impossible to tell what these pieces are about apart from such commonplace subjects as loneliness and the impossibility of lasting relationships. Yet they are gripping to watch, as they slowly progress. And they have dance at their base, even classic-academic dance, though this is often distorted and dissected to the point of unrecognizability.

Other contributions to the repertory were Balanchine's *Agon* (smartly costumed by Gianni Versace and not at all to the detriment of the choreography), some pieces by Amanda Miller, Ohad Naharin's *Arbos* and Alonzo King's *Without Wax*. There can be no doubt that the dancers have made great strides in developing a corporate identity, and their technique looks much more polished now, though I still find it difficult to attest homogeneity to a company which cultivates the principle of selecting dancers for their different, even contrasting physiques and odd shapes. But that is obviously what the young audience is looking for, being bored to death by a uniformly classical *corps de ballet*. I must say that I watch most of these Forsythe ballets with a sort of horrid awe, but cannot imagine them to last (there are some exceptions, though, among them the mesmerizing *In the middle, somewhat elevated*).

At **Hamburg** John Neumeier continues to challenge the critics (so successfully that the *Frankfurter Allgemeine*, Germany's number one national paper, has stopped reporting on the company's performances – a case of inverted censorship, it seems), while the public adores its 'American in

Hamburg'. At the end of the 1990/91 season he presented his full-length *Window for Mozart*, a biographical survey of the life of the composer, set within an allegorical frame, which has him born from music as his parents, follows him through his various periods of life (in which Mozart is represented by five different dancers) to arrive at the apotheosis of the 'Jupiter Symphony'. It was certainly one of the intellectually more ambitious contributions to the Mozart year, worked at least in parts, and never insulted one's mind. I must admit, though, that I found his following *Requiem*, which he first staged at the Salzburg Festival, a rather long-winded and laborious undertaking, especially as it was interspersed with Gregorian chant by monks who had their dancing counterpart in a group of modern dancers who repeatedly intruded upon the sepulchral rites of their classically manipulated colleagues – 'metaphysical soul jogging', it was termed by one of the critics, and I couldn't have agreed more wholeheartedly. Next came his staging of Bernstein's *On the Town* – the musical, not the ballet inspired by it. This again was a rather mixed experience, as his handling of the dialogues was very poor, although the majority of the musical numbers and dances went with fizz and panache. But his best ballet for a long time is certainly *A Cinderella Story* based upon the familiar Prokofiev score, which has been somewhat revised. It's a wonderfully modern retelling of the old fairy-tale, in which some of the missing elements (the sorting out of peas, the testing of shoes) are compensated for by shedding new light on the characters and the psychological relationship between the roles. It's Neumeier's richest choreography for many years, looks gorgeous in the most simple setting Jürgen Rose has ever created, and is danced with wonderful involvement by Bettina Beckmann in the title role, Manuel Legris as the Prince, and Ivan Liska in the here crucially dominating role of the Father (the step-sisters are, thank goodness, not danced *en travestie*, but by Stefanie Arndt and Emmanuelle Broncin, one more beautiful than the other). It embodies a very modern, deeply gripping fairy-tale.

Leipzig fell an easy prey to the charms of the still rather boyish Uwe Scholz when he revived his Zurich hit production of Haydn's *The Seasons* and Delibes' *Coppélia* – while people who had followed his work at Zurich found him just stewing in his own juice. Much more interesting were Arila Siegert's full-length *Medea Landscapes*, set to music by Sofia Gubaidulina, with a stark primaeval quality, a strong contrast against Scholz's more frivolous and superficial undertakings. That Scholz is undoubtedly a highly gifted choreographer he had proved at Stuttgart just before taking up his new job in Leipzig, where he staged a staggering Beethoven *Seventh Symphony* for Stuttgart's younger soloists, full of zest and drive, which reminded me a bit of the young Robbins and the Feld of the 1960s.

The Munich-based **Bavarian State Ballet** scored a hit with its new production of *Don Quixote* – if not exactly with the critics, at least with audiences. It is by Ray Barra, who has lately worked in Spain, but his boast of folkloric authenticity is sheer fiddlesticks – it's really Petipa in the wake of Beriozoff. But it's a feast for the dancers, who made a jolly job of it, headed by Kiki Lammersen (Kitri), Oliver Matz (Basilio), Tomasz Kajdanski (Sancho Panza), Christina McDermott (Dulcinea), Oliver Wehe (Matador) and Judith Turos (Mercedes). It's second premiere was given over to contemporary choreographers and brought together Balanchine's *Symphony in C*, Nils Christe's *Before Nightfall* and Jirí Kylián's *Svadebka* – a mouth-watering triple-bill, attractively danced. The company now has a house of its own, with splendid new studio facilities, and under Konstanze Vernon's direction it is going from strength to strength. For the first time she too, has introduced a 'forum for young choreographers', where the dancers of the company can test their talents.

Nothing new from the ballet company of the **State Theatre at the Gaertnerplatz** (Munich's second opera-house of Opéra Comique size), where Günter Pick offered plain cooking with Birgit Cullberg's *Miss Julie* and his own *Pelleas and Melisande* as his most recent double bill.

Stuttgart has a very mixed record for the period covered in this report (the last months of the 1990/91 season through to 1991/92). It started with Marcia Haydée's absolute nadir, when she was, for the first time ever, heavily booed at the premiere of her incredibly pretentious and rather kitschy *The Planets*, in which almost the whole company was involved. Her defeat was all the more resounding for being double-billed with Scholz's pristine *Seventh Symphony*. Next came the inevitable 'Hommage à Mozart' programme with new ballets by Egon Madsen and Renato Zanella plus Hans van Manen's *Kwintett* – the only work of the triple bill which approached the quality of the music (three adagios for brass and winds). This was followed by some Stravinskian *petit fours*, served by Zanella, Marco Santi and Daniela Kurz – none of real importance. Kurz was much better in her new *Bourgeois gentilhomme* (not the familiar Strauss score, but music by Lully and Charpentier), with splendid *travestie* roles for Haydée and Richard Cragun, very witty and beautifully designed by Katrin Scholz, but not much liked by the audience. Anyway it had to compete with Kylián's *Stepping Stones*, his creation for four couples of the company, set to pieces by Webern and Cage and undoubtedly one of the masterworks of the season. It was a piece of shifting relationships with some almost hallucinatory echoes from the past, and in its enigmatic beauty occasionally reminded me of the lone and distanced statues and groups of Henry Moore. There was definitely no lack of activity and soon we were invited back for a new full-length ballet by Zanella, *Man in the Shadow*, based upon a specially commissioned score by Israeli composer Richard Farber – eclectic work with interesting roles for Cragun and Christoph Lechner. But the new darling choreographer, especially with Stuttgart's younger audiences, is clearly Marco Santi, who produces ballets by the dozen – he is of the flippant Michael Clark school and his ballets are one-way products only, to be forgotten as soon as they are over (*Holding Your Own*, *The Door is Ajar*).

As far as dancers are concerned, the one most talked about in Stuttgart was Vladimir Malakhov, who guested in a variety of roles like Prince Desiré and Blue Bird, *Spectre de la rose*, excerpts from *Les Sylphides*, and even a school staging of the second act of *La Bayadère* – but revealed his true nature probably best in the *Narcisse* solo which Goleizovsky created originally for Baryshnikov. Hailed by some – though not by me – as the legitimate heir to Nijinsky, with the most beautiful legs of the world next to Marlene Dietrich's, he is definitely a charismatic dancer, with prodigious technical gifts and highly expressive face and eyes, but at the tender age of twenty-four he still has to travel far to perfect his technique and achieve full maturity.

What worries me about the Stuttgart Ballet at present is Haydée's lack of perspective concerning the future of the company, her living from hand to mouth, exposing her dancers too often to second and third rate choreographers (she herself definitely belonging in the latter group).

It's impossible to list all the balletic activities in Germany, but it's also unnecessary as much of it is of local interest only. One of these cases, for instance, is the ballet company of the **Hanover State Opera**, headed for years by Lothar Höfgen (who some may remember as a member of Béjart's Ballet of the 20th Century in its infancy) and offering all sorts of works from full-length classics through pop and rock ballets. But it's so commonplace that nobody outside Hanover cares to notice what is going on there. Then there are those mixed companies, which are hard to categorize: the **Cologne Dance Forum** under Jochen Ulrich, Krisztina Horvath at **Cassel**, Pavel Mikulastik at **Freiburg**, Joachim Schlömer at **Ulm** and the newly installed Johannes Bönig at the **Dresden State Opera** – choreographers with strong modern leanings who would abhor the label 'classical', and yet one hesitates to reckon them among the representatives of the contemporary school. But perhaps it's just this mixture which lets the German dance scene of the beginning 1990s appear so vibrantly alive.

Tanztheater

Hedwig Muller

In terms of audience attendance, the last dance season in Germany was as much a success as the previous one. However, not one piece could be singled out as providing a new impulse or direction to the current tanztheater scene. Tanztheater has indeed developed as a stable art form, founded on the belief that combining elements of dance with those of theatre can produce a new form of dramaturgy which pushes forward the boundaries of the performing arts.

116

If one were to sum up in a single word the character of the year's events, it would have to be 'retrospective'. Pina Bausch presented a double bill, first, a new piece in the winter season, and second the revival of an earlier work. Susanne Linke restaged a ballet first produced ten years ago. In Bremen, Johann Kresnick staged one of his early works from his directorship at Heidelberg. The season was not only retrospective, but introspective, as the audience was able to reflect on past works which are still both remarkable and novel in their approach to dance-making – an approach which has established tanztheater as one of the strongest dance movements today.

Pina Bausch presented a new work, with the functional title of *Tanzabend II*. It was reminiscent of many previous works, and gave a constant sense of déjà-vu. The piece was both new and old, not an uncommon characteristic of post-war tanztheater.

Pina Bausch offered the audience a three-hour piece: one could identify many aspects of past pieces. From the very first viewing the elements of Bausch's theatrical style were there: trees hanging from the ceiling, an ambling animal (this time a polar bear), a drinking fountain, the dancers' interacting with the audience (asking them for money), the display of bodily faults, the agonizing nature of the dance world, the absurdity of man's everyday rituals. The action on stage was also familiar: the recurring front line across the stage apron, the synchronized, rhythmic movement on the diagonals, the characteristic crossed-arm gestures, the detailed use of the hand, the use of whole body movements, the stillness counterpointed against sudden bursts of motion, and the loud hustle and bustle of the ensemble.

At times one had the sensation of reviewing the catalogue of questions and answers that Bausch and her dancers use in rehearsal, through which the pieces are developed. Although we saw a new set of questions and answers, the effect was weaker than in previous works. White snow descended from the theatre's heavens; the birch trees created a forest which was slowly lowered; screen projections turned the theatre and its audience into a strange landscape of desert, beaches and mountains. All the stage elements were rife with symbolic meaning, creating a world where humans and objects inhabit a space in which their individual identities are lost. However, the connections between the scenes were not as tight as in previous works.

The aforementioned retrospective was the restaging of Bausch's 1975 version of *Orpheus and Eurydike*. When it was first performed seventeen years ago it put forth a concept of 'dance' as had never been seen before. Based on the opera by Gluck, the dancers do not dance in any traditional sense. Moreover, the singing parts of Orpheus and Eurydike are doubled up by a male and female dancer respectively, and more often than not, the four performers are treated as a single ensemble for a heightened expressive effect. The performance deals sensitively with the connections between song and dance. The dance movement and the choral dramaturgy relate perfectly to the spatial arrangements and the total theatre picture. Once again Bausch proved her mastery of both theatrical direction and choreography. She developed the emotional aspects of the characters through their physicality. This performance was a reminder of Bausch's first works with the Wuppertal Tanztheater which in later years took tanztheater to international acclaim.

Susanne Linke's new work this season was an evening-length piece entitled *Ruhr-Ort*, inspired by the industrial world of the Ruhr. Six performers recreated the world of work around a gloomy steel and iron construction which evoked images of charcoal, mines, and physical enslavement. From this machine roared the constant noise of industry – stomping, hammering, punching – noises made as the dancer's bodies came in contact with it. To create the piece, Susanne Linke and her dance partner Urs Dietrich had visited many pubs in the area. The piece was very naturalistic, although the artistic use of their experience provided a certain aesthetic distance. One could see the perspiration on the dancers' faces as they used the sledgehammers – everyday reality was transported on the stage. But the theatre is not the place for such realism, which at times gave the piece a sense of implausibility. However, this piece marked a radical change in Linke's work, since she is better known for more intimate solo dances. Linke's strength is not in large narrative forms, but in smaller emotional and intimate themes.

Her virtuosity was witnessed in the restaging of *Frauenballets* ('Women's Ballet'). This piece was first produced in 1981 for the Folkwang Tanzstudio, the dance company affiliated to the Folkwang Schule in Essen under the direction of Pina Bausch. It was Linke's first attempt at a group choreography, and is now considered one of her masterpieces. In successive scenes Linke depicts women going to work in the morning; during the day their work consists of folding, gathering, rolling a line of fabric; in the evening they return to their homes. The dullness of their work serves to bring out their individual temperaments and passions; their longing is made visible. The tedium of the work, day in and day out, creates a monotony within which the meaning of their lives is lost. Two men are also present, discussing their sociably accepted work. The women toil around them, but neither man takes any notice. With minimum means, depending mostly on a physical language, Susanne Linke demonstrates that women's liberation has not yet reached its goals.

Johann Kresnick also produced a 'woman's ballet', premiered last February, *Frida Kahlo*. In scene after scene, Kresnick retold the tragic story of the Mexican painter caught between the illnesses and tragedies which dominated the life of the artist. If in past works such as *Lear* and *Ulrike Meinhof* Kresnick opted for a directness in stage design, in *Frida Kahlo* his approach to the tableaux was more poetic, a manner which resembled the scenic development of his biographical *Sylvia Plath* (1985). Kresnick concentrated on the suffering, passion and rebellion of individuals who are forced into mental hospitals. The uncompromising willpower of Kahlo, her self-healing through her paintings in spite of all her physical torments, were presented on stage through dynamic group and ensemble scenes contrasting with more intimate individual moments.

The new generation of tanztheater has not yet hinted at giving the genre any new impulses. From amongst the young independent choreographers and companies only a few warrant mention. **Urs Dietrich** continues to develop his own dance language, although it cannot be described entirely as 'tanztheater' as developed by the older generations of the '60s and '70s. The group **S.O.A.P.**, which works from the Frankfurt Theatre in Mousonturm also deserves a mention. This theatre is a state subsidized alternative performance space which, last season, had the luxury of being able to develop a company in residence. The Portuguese choreographer Rui Horta developed a repertoire for them which showed originality. Rui Horta's background and influences, however, are not with German tanztheater, but with the modern ballet choreographer William Forsythe. The evening *Measure for Measure* consisted of three thematically independent pieces, which won one of the prizes at Bagnolet, and revealed Horta's distinctive sense of movement flow, physical dexterity, a brilliant choreographic use of the body, and a good sense of theatrical staging. The novelty of S.O.A.P. lies in the serious thematic content of their pieces which are presented through strong dancing and compelling poetic imagery. This is what many of the other independents groups tend to neglect. Ideas alone do not create a dance: they must be translated into a successful theatrical idiom. Thus, most of the activity of the season remained with the 'older' generation, in spite of the many festivals of independent dance – such as 'Meeting New Dance' in northern Westfalia, 'Utopia of the Body' in Berlin, or 'Euroscene' in Leipzig – which have been created to support the independent dance scene.

German tanztheater is not in a period of revolution but one of stability. This is also true of the dance activity in East Germany. Since reunification, free dance groups have not taken root in the main cities. In cities like Leipzig and Dresden the tendency is for a more 'modern dance' style. The **Tanztheater Ensemble** at the Leipzig Playhouse, under the direction of Irina Pauls, created a grotesque ballet called *McMozart* which deserves mention. However, the term 'tanztheater' in East Germany does have the same meaning as in the West – it is used to describe ballet with an added touch of 'modern'.

119

Hungary

Livia Fuchs

A season as eventful as the last one would have been unimaginable a few years ago. The main reasons are that Hungarian contemporary dance life has been shaken up, and that there are more visiting ballet and modern dance groups, which bring a freshness after the isolation of past decades. Although the companies performing in Budapest were not internationally first-rate, several notable companies performed last year. The **English National Ballet**, led by Hungarian Iván Nagy, performed at the Interballet 92; then in the early season we saw the **Maggio Musicale** ballet company, of lower standard but with a valuable repertory of Balanchine and Tudor pieces, and the **Göteborg Stora Teatern** company (of moderate standard) performing works by Robert North and Ulf Gadd. Another guest at Inter-ballet 92 was the company of the **Lyon Opera**, bringing with them two pieces by William Forsythe, one of the most important choreographers of today – the first time his work has been seen in Hungary. At these guest performances, the Hungarian audience can savour the many different and divergent flavours of the ballet world; guest performances are also important, because this variety can hardly be seen in Hungarian ballet companies. The **Hungarian National Ballet** of the Budapest State Opera under the leadership of Gábor Keveházi, has totally closed its doors against up-to-date dance trends: there is no twentieth-century Western European or American choreography in its repertory. Soon, only Hungarian choreographers' works will be shown – moreover, independently of the artistic value of the pieces. Although the excellent ballets of László Seregi (*Spartacus*, *Romeo and Juliet*, *A Midsummer Night's Dream*) run successfully on any great stage of ballet world, and stamp a hall-mark of quality on Hungarian ballet, the same cannot be said about Antal Fodor's still celebrated rock ballet, *The Rehearsal*, which seems to be permanently on the repertory.

The premieres of this season were by Hungarian dancers, with little or no experience of choreography. Viktor Róna, with an international dancing career going back to the 1960s, staged a new version of Petipa's *Sleeping Beauty* last April, a hard task for the company since there has not been a work requiring such clear classical knowledge in the repertory for a long time. Róna has shortened the mime parts so it became a two-act ballet, but preserved the dance qualities of the earlier Pyotr Gusev version. Róna's main innovation was to cast Carabosse as a dangerously beautiful witch, an equal to Aurora in character.

The creator of the autumn premiere, Lilla Pártay (the most expressive ballerina of the Opera company in the past decade), staged a full-length dance-drama based on Tolstoy's *Anna Karenina* to pieces by Tchaikovsky. Pártay has previously only choreographed short, plotless ballets – and having seen the two-act *Anna Karenina*, it seems that her main choreographic skill is in composing emotional chamber scenes, while her choreography in more decorative scenes is poorer.

The announced third premiere of the season staged at the Opera, was a fiasco. For me *Cristoforo* was mainly an artistic fiasco, although the creators (music by Bela Szakcsk Lakatos, libretto by Ildikó Kóródy, choreography by Gábor Keveházi) announced it as an economic one. The cancellation of the world tour was most painful for them since the sponsors had given an unbelievably large amount of money with high hopes for this two-act ballet, relying on the attractive cast of Nureyev, Ananiashvili and Pikieris. Above all I regretted the artistically poor performance of the company, the great dancers – György Szakály as Cristoforo, Ildikó Pongor and Katalin Wolf as India and America – loafing about in dramatically confused situations and uncomposed roles, trying to turn the shoddy movements into an endurable work.

Last season a new era started at two of our regional ballet companies. In June a sharp conflict broke out between Iván Markó and his company, the **Győr Ballet**, during its twelfth season. Markó left the company and prohibited the performance of his works – which were the only ones the company performed. Thus the company suddenly had no leader and no repertory. It is a wonder that the dancers not only remained together, but also arranged three premieres, mainly choreographed by the dancers. In August they collectively staged the *Legend of St Margaret of Árpéd Dynasty* on the occasion of the Pope's visit to Hungary. Then in the autumn they produced a three-act fairy-tale ballet, each act choreographed by different dancers. *Gulliver's Travels* fortunately helped the company through the difficulties of this season, becoming a successful children's ballet – a rare thing on our stages. The new director and founder member, János Kiss, aimed to find a permanent choreographer within the company, but neither William Fomin, nor Otto Demcsák showed any great talent in their first one-act pieces shown in the spring. However, the guest choreographer on the same programme, the Czechoslovak Libor Vaculik, composed a very nice, emotional, neoclassical one-act piece, *Sea of Tears*, to music by Mahler, in Kyliánesque style.

Imre Eck and Sándor Tóth, the founder and co-director of **Pécs Ballet**, stepped aside, so since May the company has been led by a new director, István Herczog, who had worked in Germany for two decades. Herczog has already choreographed two ballets for the Pécs company this season, including a special version of *Romeo and Juliet*, with Friar Lawrence as the central character. In which direction will Herczog lead the Pécs Ballet

121

(which had an avant-garde profile in the 1960s)? Next year we may find out, since Herczog has given opportunities to three young choreographers. Two of them, László Körmendy and Gábor Hajzer, dancers of the company, also created one-act works last year, while György Szakály, soloist of National Ballet, created his first piece, *Death of a Faun*. Thus the situation of Pécs is similar to that of Györ: there is not only a new director but also a new generation of dancers and choreographers, together determined to forge a new company style.

The five-year-old **Szeged Ballet**, with high standards and a definite choreographic direction towards contemporary dance theatre, is progressing steadily. Zoltán Imre, the artistic director and recently the sole director, always opened the doors wide for guest choreographers. This year the company invited Bertrand d'At and Bernd Schindowski from abroad to teach their one-act pieces *The Night* and *Firework*, while among Hungarian choreographers, Katalin Lörinc, and the extreme experimentalist, Yvette Bozsik, had the opportunity of a workshop. Zoltán Imre composed only one work, *Four Seasons 1939*, performed the same evening on which young Tamás Juronics made his choreographic debut, a work matured in the company's workshop. Imre seems to understand too well (having been a novice choreographer in Stuttgart, and later at Ballet Rambert) that a choreographer's talent needs to develop in workshops. Therefore he may offer the opportunity of free experimental workshops to Tamas Juronics and Yvette Bozsik, both of whom hold promise to become powerful and original choreographers.

A new mark on the Hungarian dance scene is the appearance of independent groups in the field of ballet and folk-dance on the one hand and modern dance on the other. The great dancers of the Opera – Katalin Hágai, Timor Kováts, Angéla Kövessy, Mariann Venekei, Tibor Eichner amongst others – cooperated with two young choreographers – Jozsef Gajdos, a freelance musical performer who started his career as a folk dancer, and Tamás Tengler, a dancer at the Opera – and arranged two programmes based on their works. It was a great success, because the Hungarian dance world lacks the show style and these small-scale works, though choreographically of little value, filled this gap with refined performances.

At first **Veszprém Theatre** did not found a permanent company but contracted dancers for one or two productions a year, as in the programme 'Perpetual Motion Existence', which consisted of one-act pieces in contrasting styles by György Krámer, Katalin Lörinc and Erika Fincza. Krámer also premiered a work with another company, the **Rock Theatre Workshop**, which had its first original dance evening of its ten years of existence with Krámer's triple bill, which was aimed mainly at a young audience.

These three groups are probably not really independent, because each is

The Szeged Ballet in Zoltán Imre's *The Four Seasons 1939*.

associated with a theatre company. The real independents in Hungary today, without any support, are representatives of modern dance awaking after a forty-year artificial sleep. The most successful representative of this young performing and creating generation is Yvette Bozsik of the **Collective of Natural Disasters**. She has toured throughout the world with her experimental solo works, which rely mainly on visual effects. She performed a mature new production in April, 'The Syndrome of the Sleeping Beauty', dealing with the conflict between dream and reality, the *Dreamtime*, directed and with music by György Árvay, the other member of the collective. In *The Turul* (a mythical bird of Hungary), a new work of **Artus Dance and Jump Theatre**, Gábor Goda created a mordant, east European, grotesque theatre play using contact improvisation. **Budapest Dance School** founded in autumn, forms a source for groups like **Berger** or **Sarbo** companies, being the only Hungarian school to train professional contemporary dancers. Iván Angelus, the director, was able to compare his distant dreams with other schools of greater standing when the Essen Folkwang School and the Angers National Centre for Contemporary Dance performed in Budapest this season.

Petöfi Hall was the venue for the east European semi-finals of the Rencontres International de Bagnolet. Among the six groups performing here, **Tranz Danz**, led by Péter Gerzson Kovács, has had deserved success with its up-to-date approach to folklore material, which has since been shown in a complex theatre atmosphere at the Bagnolet final. At Petöfi Hall, a contemporary arts venue, we could see an old avant-garde celebrity, **Carolyn Carlson**, and an American representative of newest trends, **Elizabeth Streb**'s group. However the real surprise was **DV8 Physical Theatre**'s Budapest world premiere of *Strange Fish* at the Making Waves festival.

Recently there have been International Contemporary Dance Festivals connecting Budapest with the dance world at the Petöfi Hall during June. Last year the Japanese **Saburo Teshigawara** and the Spanish **Lanónima Imperial** were hits, while this year the French **Christine Bastin** and the American **Doug Elkins**' works have had great success.

Lastly I must also mention a unique event. As is well-known, Isadora Duncan made her debut at the Budapest Uránia Theatre exactly ninety years ago. In memory of this performance which began a fantastic career, the Hungarian 'orchestica' group which preserves the system of Valéria Dienes (who had been Raymond Duncan's student), together with Barbara Kane and her group from London, Eva Blazickovás' young dancers from Prague and the American Lori Belilove, tried to revive the impossible – Isadora's fascinating personality. Although they could not recreate the art of this great rebel of dance, her spirit may arrive in Hungary again. Thus the modern tendencies of free dance can grow beside traditional classical ballet and folk-dance trends.

Israel

Giora Manor

According to an official statistical survey of 1989/91 published by the National Arts Council, there were eight professional dance companies active in Israel. (This number does not include the many semi-professional or amateur folk dance companies.) Each season about 250,000 spectators attended dance performances.

In 1989/90 the companies performed 85 works by 43 choreographers, about 40% of whom were Israeli artists, the rest guests from abroad; the accompanying music for 13 of the works was by Israeli composers. The companies employed 217 workers, of whom 68% were artists, the rest administrators, stage-crew, and so on.

In the 1990/91 season, 108 works were performed, created by 45 choreographers, 49% of whom were native Israeli; as were 31% of the 67 composers involved. The situation hasn't changed significantly since.

1992 marked the twenty-fifth anniversary of the founding of the country's only classical ballet company, the **Israel Ballet**, founded and directed by Hillel Markman and Berta Yampolski, the latter also being the chief choreographer of the company.

It was also the five-hundredth anniversary of the expulsion of Jews from Spain in 1492, when there was a dramatic transition from the Golden Era (the interdenominational flourishing of Moslem, Christian and Jewish culture on the Iberian peninsula), to the enforced conversion of the Jews to Christianity, the Holy Inquisition's *auto da fé*, when the Maranos ('new Christians') were burned at the stake. This culminated in the expulsion of Jews from Spain, and then from Portugal. A flurry of works commemorated these fateful events, including the dances pieces *Eternal Return* by Moshe Efrati and his **Kol Demama Company**, and *Angelos Negros* ('Black Angels') by Rami Be'er, principal choreographer of **Kibbutz Dance Company**.

Before *Angelos Negros*, Be'er created an evening-length work about kibbutz life, called *Real Time*. Both works marked a new phase in his choreography: he used decor to elevate his dancers to different heights above the stage, thus creating a spatial structure which connects his recent work to early twentieth-century constructivism.

Ohad Naharin, the artistic director of **Batsheva**, brought the company several steps further to a new company style – or rather a Naharin style – in two pieces of great impact. His *Kyr* ('Wall'), to original music by himself and a noisy rock-trio (The Tractor's Revenge) had a very Israeli atmosphere, even using most effectively a traditional Jewish folk song from the Passover Seder meal. His recent *Mabul* ('Deluge'), which concluded the 1992 Israel Festival in Jerusalem, was a strong, sometimes fascinating and surprising work, which, apart from some acrobatic, dangerous moments, includes a duet of sorts for a man and a hamster, in which the little animal responds to the dancer as if it understood the choreography, as well as the live singing performance of another member of the company who possesses a remarkable countertenor voice. Naharin has attained a mastery of composition technique, which allows him to realize the demands of his fertile imagination.

Batsheva's junior group, the **Batsheva Ensemble**, directed by Iris Lahad, premiered several works by the gifted young choreographer Itzik Galili, as well as pieces by some of its own dancers.

Shirim, choreographed by Domy Reiter-Soffer, danced here by Ania Brud and Vladimir Russkov of the Bat-Dor Dance Company.

Batsheva de Rothschild's **Bat-Dor Company** found itself in a serious crisis, when it was announced that the Rothschild coffers were, after all, not bottomless, and that if government financial assistance was not forthcoming the company could face closure. The company is now functioning on a much-reduced scale, as the 600,000 Shekels promised in aid by the Ministry of Education and Culture have not as yet materialized, and the company's future is still in jeopardy.

After ousting its venerable founder and chief choreographer Sara Levi-Tanai and appointing Rena Sharett as its new artistic director, **Inbal Dance Theatre** has yet to show what new direction it is taking. During the season two interesting works were premiered, both endeavouring to deal with aspects of Israeli history. Choreographer (and dance critic) Gaby Eldor, in collaboration with stage director Sinai Peter, created *Tonight We Dance*, which follows the historical events of Israel since the end of World War I to the present, as reflected in the happenings and changes in the style of social dancing in a café in Jaffa. In the dance-theatre piece *To Know the Earth*, Amir Kolben tried to depict the difficulties of new immigrants in the 1920s adjusting to their surroundings.

Kolben's group, **Tamar**, situated in Jerusalem, has been served notice by its main supporter, the Jerusalem Fund, to vacate its premises by next year, because of strong objections by its ultra-orthodox religious neighbours to such a profane and 'sinful' institution as a dance company in their midst and its school active in their quarter. On top of that the Jerusalem Fund has also announced the curtailing of its financial support of Tamar – which may mean the demise of the company.

The 1991/92 season saw a large contingent of dance from France; the Cultural Department of the French Embassy in Tel-Aviv sponsored a mini-festival of videos and films showing some of the proliferating modern dance companies of France as well as some guest performances. In the framework of the Israel Festival in Jerusalem the company of **Josef Nadj** performed its impressive *Comedia tempio*, and **Le Ballet du Fargistan** also appeared.

Also in the festival, the Canadian group **La La La Human Steps** danced its violent, repetitive piece *Infante – c'est destroy*.

Susanne Linke's company from Germany showed its powerful dance-theatre piece for men *Ruhr-Ort*, and her dance for women *Frauenballett*, was performed by the Kibbutz Dance Company. Both dances deal with work processes, and surprisingly enough, these two companion-pieces were performed together for the first time ever in Jerusalem.

At the fifth annual Karmiel Festival, taking place in July 1992 the 'real Bolshoi Ballet' is scheduled to perform. After the by now ubiquitous Russian 'Stars of. . .', '. . .City Ballet' – haphazardly put together ensembles which caused many disappointments – the St Petersburg (formerly Leningrad) Maryinsky Opera and Ballet (formerly Kirov) and the Moscow Bolshoi have finally arrived on these shores.

In May, the first international modern dance competition took place at the Susanne Dellal Center in Tel-Aviv. Dancers from twelve countries participated and though no future stars were discovered, the organizers must have learned a great deal from this experience, so the next competition (to be held in 1994) will, one hopes, prove to be much better.

The duo of dancer-choreographers **Liat Dror–Nir Ben Gal** have, for the first time in their by now international career, gathered together a company of their own, and created for their ten performers (most of whom had no prior dance training), a strong, emotional, sexy piece called *Circles of Lust*, which has already toured in Europe.

Italy

Freda Pitt

As has become habitual in Italy since dance activity became more wide-spread a couple of decades ago, the performance picture was a patch-work of sporadic outbursts for the most part. There was an unhealthy concentration of dance in the earlier part of the summer, followed by a well-nigh total absence throughout the country from the second half of August until well into the autumn.

Classical and modern ballet appeared largely in two rival series of video-cassettes on sale at news-stands; much less was available live. The greater concentration of homegrown 'nuova danza' was exemplified in the pro-grammes of the (now biennial) Reggio Emilia festival in September 1991, dubbed 'Italia Danza'. The Teatro Valli (renamed after the famous actor Romolo Valli) has, because of its reduced budget, sharply cut down the number of dance programmes during the season, but the festival offered a large number of groups, sufficient to enable any reasonably assiduous spectator to acquire a good all-round impression of what was available round the country; but none of the works shown was new. Despite a forceful presentation, it was clear that financial considerations had played a large part in the theatre's choices, since it was admitted that the opera-house companies had been omitted for lack of funds.

Notwithstanding the national label, most of the influences came from outside: **Carolyn Carlson** (who is highly esteemed in Italy; some of the members of her now defunct Venice company have set up on their own); **Pina Bausch**; **Maguy Marin**; and French 'nouvelle danse' in general. Liter-ary sources, frequent recourse to speech, and little regard for music in the majority of the now almost unavoidable recorded collages, were recurring features.

As in several other towns of limited size, the Valli has a captive audience, the other (smaller) theatre, the Ariosto – where late-night performances were given by some of the more experimental groups, for a hardier audi-ence – being under the same management. As a result, it can take risks that would scarcely be feasible in a town with numerous theatres. Some of the performances at the Ariosto were sparsely attended; the most popular were those involving on the one hand Alessandra Ferri and on the other Carla Fracci, Luciana Savignano and Paolo Bortoluzzi. (**Aterballetto**, the resident company, was prominently featured on both occasions.) The net result was a showcase for contemporary dance in Italy. Two of the chore-ographers taking part – Massimo Moricone and Virgilio Sieni – also turned up in an evening of contemporary Italian dance given by the Scala Ballet at the Teatro Lirico in Milan the following spring. They, and Enzo Cosimi, Adriana Borriello, Raffaela Giordano, Michele Abbondanza and Antonella Bertoni, already possessed a cult following, which is gradually being enlarged.

The only choreographer to demonstrate an appreciable theatrical flair during the festival was Micha van Hoecke (half Belgian, half Russian), much of whose Gogol-inspired three-part *Prospettiva Nevsky* was decidedly entertaining besides being well-crafted. His group came to the small Teatro del Vascello in Rome in December with a double bill; his setting of *Peter and the Wolf* embodying some ingenious episodes, performed with gusto by his **Ballet-Théâtre l'Ensemble**.

Lucia Latour's original and inventive *Anihccam* ('macchina' backwards) was presented not at Reggio Emilia but at the Teatro Olimpico in Rome (after earlier performances in Paris and at the previous Rovereto festival). Rovereto houses the museum dedicated to Futurist artist Fortunato Depero, whose designs inspired Latour's largely tongue-in-cheek work. Performed by her small, mostly female **Altroteatro** group, it brought out various facets of Futurist activity, taking in Depero's fascination with advertising and the chorus lines he saw in the USA. Luigi Ceccarelli provided a suitably eclectic electronic score, and the Depero-derived designs were generally admired.

Another experimental work seen in Rome was *Tratado de Pintura*, given at the Vascello by the **Centro Nacional de Nuevas Tendencias Escenicas**. These performances formed part of a Spanish beano (reciprocating a previous Italian celebration in Spain), also involving art exhibitions, and a *zarzuela* at the Teatro dell'Opera in Rome. The **Spanish National Ballet** came to Milan and Naples, and **Cristina Hoyos**' company brought a popular evening of flamenco to the Teatro Sistina in Rome.

The Gino Tani commemoration awards (Tani was a noted dance, theatre and television critic) were also presented at the Sistina, where the audience had the opportunity to see Maximiliano Guerra for the first time and to admire Sylvie Guillem in Maurice Béjart's *La Luna*. **La La La Human Steps** and, later, Mikhail Baryshnikov's **White Oak Dance Project** also appeared at the Sistina, which is more commonly the home of the growingly popular American musicals.

Earlier in the season, the Accademia Filarmonica Romana, which owns the Olimpico, earned the gratitude of Rome dance-lovers by alone providing them with nourishment. Visitors included **Alwin Nikolais**' group, the **Lyon Opéra Ballet** in Maguy Marin's *Cendrillon*, the ever-irresistible **Georgians**, and fashionable **Angelin Preljocaj**'s *Amer America*.

It is rare for a year to pass without the presence of the two most famous French choreographers, Roland Petit and Maurice Béjart. Petit's affectionate homage to Charlie Chaplin, *Charlot danse avec nous*, toured Italy for some months, spending a few weeks at the Teatro Eliseo in Rome in spring 1992, after visiting a number of smaller towns and before concluding the tour in Milan and Turin (the busy Teatro Nuovo). Elisabetta Terabust took all the female roles brilliantly, Luigi Bonino persuasively recalled Chaplin, and slick support was supplied by a small group of dancers from the **Ballet National de Marseille**.

While the Chaplin work was warmly received everywhere, the thirty-minute *pas de quatre* Petit made at the Rome Opera pleased less. This flawed but very interesting piece formed part of an all-Petit programme, the other works being familiar from the Marseille repertory. Dominique Khalfouni, Terabust, Kader Belarbi of the Paris Opéra Ballet and Cyril Pierre of the Marseille company made a formidable quartet for this piece using Sibelius music. *The Swan of Tuonela* inevitably took a conspicuous part; inevitably, since author Pierre Combescot had in the text that inspired the choreographer referred to swans as well as Wagner, mad King Ludwig of Bavaria and the Mayerling trio. The dancers represented this ghostly quartet to start with, but then, rather disconcertingly, devoted themselves to an impressive display of classical technique – hence the flaw.

As for **Béjart**, apart from taking some popular works around before disbanding his large company, in October he provided the first dance programme – his Mozart epic commissioned in Austria, *Death in Vienna* – at the newly rebuilt Teatro Carol Felice in Genoa. Ironically, the celebratory opening (with a Verdi opera) coincided almost to a day with the destruction by fire of the Teatro Petruzzelli, which had built up a keen, steady audience for dance of many kinds in Bari.

Other visiting companies included **Nederlands Dans Theater** (Genoa and Reggio Emilia), the **Monte Carlo Ballet**, the **Momix** group, **American Ballet Theatre** at Palermo for the Teatro Massimo's summer season, the **Martha Graham Company** in Milan and Pompeii, **Karine Saporta**'s group and a return visit by the **Paris Opéra Ballet** to the RomaEuropa summer festival and a small **Bolshoi-Kirov** group at the Teatro Brancaccio in Rome with Ekaterina Maximova and Vladimir Vasiliev, while Rudolf Nureyev appeared in late May 1991 at the Teatro Filarmonico in Verona with the resident company in Flemming Flindt's ballet *Death in Venice*. In addition, **Pina Bausch** first took her Tanztheater to the Teatro La Fenice in Venice with a revised version of *Viktor* (originally made for Rome), and then – in early June 1992 – she came with the combined forces of the Wuppertal Opera. The orchestra, singers and dancers appeared in her unaltered 1974 production of Gluck's opera *Iphigenia in Tauris*, the power of which earned it full houses and an excitedly enthusiastic reception in both Turin (Teatro Regio) and Rome (Teatro dell'Opera). In Turin, talking-shops, showings of videos and other activities were also organized. The **Regio**'s one ballet programme of the 1991/92 season broke new ground for Italy by presenting a double bill of ballets by Frederick Ashton (in January), audience response being gratifyingly warm. *Les Deux Pigeons* (with Sandra Madgwick and Michael O'Hare) was better liked, *Façade* causing tricky stylistic problems for the resident dancers who nevertheless threw themselves wholeheartedly into what was for them quite an adventure. Guest Elisabetta Armiato of the Scala Ballet had a field-day with the role of the Gipsy Girl in the two-act ballet and also danced elegantly and brilliantly in the Polka in the Walton piece.

A less 'important' Ashton ballet (also taught by Faith Worth) had its first Italian airing the previous summer at the Scala, where *Jazz Calendar* was introduced in a triple-bill that also included Agnes de Mille's *Fall River Legend*, with Carla Fracci as Lizzie. Now in her mid-fifties, Fracci shows no signs of reducing her activity. Much of this is the brainchild of her theatre director husband Beppe Menegatti; one of his most successful productions has been *Il Vespro siciliano*, with Verdi's music (from several operas but above all *I Vespri siciliani*) arranged by Francesco Sodini, choreography by Derek Deane (now ballet master at the Teatro dell'Opera in Rome) and scenery and costumes by Luisa Spinatelli. This was premiered at the Teatro Massimo in Palermo in the spring of 1991 and resurfaced in the autumn at three theatres in the north: the Teatro Grande in Brescia, the Donizetti at Bergamo (both of which offer a single, imported ballet production each season) and also at the Teatro Ponchielli in Cremona, where **Lucinda Childs'** and other contemporary groups appeared also.

Fracci as the combative Benvenuta and Raffaella Renzi as her sister Benedetta both had good roles. In spring 1992, again for the Palermo opera house, the **Fracci-Menegatti Compagnia Italiana di Balletto** put on an ambitious multi-sourced version of *Phaedra* (naturally with Fracci in the title-role), to Honegger music. This proved less effective.

Fracci appeared as Juliet again in John Cranko's version, when it was revived at the **Scala** in autumn 1991. The same choreographer's *Taming of the Shrew* was also revived. After a programme dedicated to Spain, the Scala company (now directed by Giuseppe Carbone) gave its best – but not always sufficient – energies to Natalia Makarova's production of *La Bayadère*. Although, unsurprisingly, it did not surmount this forbidding hurdle completely successfully, Makarova worked wonders in disciplining the *corps de ballet*, and the results were decent, if not exactly thrilling. Isabel Seabra danced with Julio Bocca on the first night, and Alessandra Ferri (also with Bocca) came in at the second performance.

Ferri has been appearing all over Italy, not always in roles to which she was suited, and not always in roles worthy of her. This has applied on both counts in Florence, where she seems – with varying results – to have been used (as elsewhere) to bring in a larger audience. With the opera-house company, Eugene Polyakov's **MaggioDanza**, she has danced Giselle (a role she also performed at the San Carlo in Naples), Terpsichore in Balanchine's *Apollo*, Caroline in Tudor's *Jardin aux lilas* and the title-role in Polyakov's film-world-based *Cinderella*. In April 1992, the company finally revived Peter Schaufuss' fine production of *La Sylphide*, with himself and Christine Camillo.

As for the over-important summer festivals, the general tendency has become for the big long-established ones either to abandon dance altogether or (as at Spoleto) to reduce it to a minimum, so that the newer, all-dance festivals have moved to the forefront in satisfying more seriously interested dance-goers. Currently the most prominent ones include Turin, Vignale (also in Piedmont), Fiesole and Castiglioncello in Tuscany, Abano Terme near Padua, Lugo near Ravenna, and refreshing Rovereto, north of Verona, in September. The resuscitation of the Nervi Festival (again directed by Mario Porcile), triumphantly inaugurated by the **Australian Ballet**, must also be saluted.

Japan

Kenji Usui

C an you imagine how many ballet and dance competitions are held in Japan each year? Last year we had ten ballet or dance competitions. But most of them were not the what you might imagine.

For instance, on one occasion, the minimum age of entry for the modern section was four years old! For the average ballet school, such a small child is not accepted even for the preparatory class. For the classical ballet section (minimum age 11) the candidates had to dance a variation from a nineteenth-century classic for just one minute! Why only for one minute? Because the competition is so popular and too many participants gather from all over Japan – usually over 800 children – that there is not enough time to dance a whole variation each.

Other competitions were slightly better. The child could show the whole variation at least, so it looked more like a competition – if you can stand to watch an eleven or twelve-year-old girl perform the Princess Aurora or Black Swan variations, that is. But in one case, competitors performed the same variation from the first to the final round. Each candidate prepared just one variation through the year for the competition. It was not necessary for her to prepare different variations or a modern number. Can a judge see the quality of a candidate from only one variation?

Why are such competitions so popular in Japan? Because we have a competitive character? Or because of an erroneous notion that dance education should start as early as possible? Judging from the older competitors, between eighteen and the early twenties, I am sure that the lack of a real professional ballet company is the reason. The youngsters, trained for many years in private ballet studios, have no place to show the results of their endeavours. In this climate, a one-variation competition sponsored by a leading newspaper, *Tokyo Shimbun*, is regarded as an authoritative competition. In the spring of 1992, it reached its forty-ninth anniversary! It is really the oldest dance competition in the world, and consists of ballet, modern dance and Japanese dance sections.

Two other ballet competitions looked more like other competitions in the world. For the Asian Pacific Ballet Competition, sponsored by the Japan Ballet Association, competitors came from Australia, New Zealand, the Philippines, Taiwan, Korea and Hong Kong; the Australians and Koreans were very successful. For some reason, China sent nobody for this competition, which is held every other year, in mid-August.

Another international competition was the Private Concours of Mrs Masako Ohya, held in Osaka in early November. The jury consisted of such famous people as Askold Makarov of Russia, Gedeon Dienes of Hungary, and John Gregory of England. This was a *pas de deux* competition, in which the marks of both dancers were put together – so sometimes, because of an inferior partner, a good dancer failed to win a prize. Another characteristic of this competition was that every pair should dance the *Corsaire pas de deux*, because this is one of Mrs Ohya's favourites. Aschen Atalyanz and Konstantin Kostfulkov won the first prize.

There was an unusual choreographic competition in late August, sponsored by the Min-On Organization. This organization usually works as an impresario, and is connected with a new Buddhist sect called Soka-Gakukai. Amongst the judges were such world-famous names as Helgi Tomasson, Jack Carter and Patricia Neary. Leda Bantecours of France received the first prize.

Because of widespread competition fever, the ballet audience in Japan tends to flock to performances such as the so-called 'Gala of the Stars of the World'. The most popular series was 'The Sixth World Ballet Festival' from 30 July to 7 August 1991. The impresario, Mr Sasaki gathered stars such as Nina Ananiashvili, Evelyn Hart, Marcia Haydée, Monique Loudières, with partners such as Andris Liepa, Farukh Ruzimatov, Patrick Dupond and Nikolaj Hübbe. And the famous Kabuki travesti actor Bando Tamasaburo

Yukari Saito (right) and Naoki Takagishi (left) of the Tokyo Ballet as moon-viewers in *Seven Haiku of the Moon*, choreographed by John Neumeier. PHOTO: K. HASEGAWA

danced a new Japanese *pas de deux* with Jorge Donn. The Festival is held every third year, and is immensely popular with the Japanese audience.

Other projects like this were similarly successful. In November 1991 there was 'Ananiashvili and Friends' with Farukh Ruzimatov and Vadim Pisarev. The 'All Star Ballet Gala' with Ludmila Semenyaka, Lubov Kunakova, Irek Mukhamedov, Ruzimatov again and Andris Liepa was held in January 1992. In May 1992 there was 'Maya Plisetskaya with Vladimir Malakhov and Friends'. Plisetskaya danced *Isadora* with Japanese children, and Malakhov danced the solo from *Narcisse*, to music by Tcherepnine, with choreography by Goleizovsky, with great success.

Of course, there were more serious projects by Japanese choreographers. One of them worth mentioning was the one-act ballet called *Dim Light – the Diary of Anne Frank* by Sachiko Goto performed on 16 November 1991. This ballet depicts the shuttered life of the hiding Jewish family and the raving Nazi militarism outside, with music by Richard Strauss. The choreographer handled the theme with subtle care and good taste and the result was so successful that the ballet received many prizes, including one from the Ministry of Culture.

The stagings of the Ashton version of *La Fille mal gardée* by the **Asami Maki Company** on 19 and 20 October 1991 and Ninette de Valois' *Checkmate* by the **Noriko Kobayashi Company** on 25 and 26 October should be applauded, as they educate the Japanese audience in how the tradition of ballet is traced from the nineteenth-century classic to the present day.

The bold attempt by the **Japan Ballet Association** to stage *Anna Karenina* by André Prokovsky to Tchaikovsky music was also praiseworthy. It was a very good chance to show to the Japanese audience that pretentious, modernist-attired ballet is not the only kind of modern ballet. Prokovsky told this famous story tactfully and carefully, with flowing dance movement and story-telling, avoiding conventional mime. It was a great success among the critics – but, unfortunately, not for the box office, because the Japanese audience is still sticking to nineteenth-century classics and the exhibition of bravura technique.

Another important event was the staging of *Giselle* by Konstantin Sergeyev and Natalya Dudinskaya for the Osaka branch of the Japan Ballet Association. In Japan, this ballet is widely known and even the smallest ballet school in the countryside might stage *Giselle* for its annual studio performance. But this Maryinsky version, performed on 23 and 24 January 1992 in Osaka, with the leads of Setsuko Tagami and Shigeru Saeki, established a standard for Japan.

There were very few performances of ballet with a Japanese theme this year. I will mention the staging of *Lady Galatia of the Lord Hosokawa* on 17 January in Tokyo. Lady Galatia was the first aristocratic lady to convert from Buddhism to Christianity, and was later martyred. The ballet portrayed her agony in dances based on the classical idiom mingled with Japanese dances. The choreographer was Shuntoku Takagi. It was later shown in Canada.

Another energetic attempt by a young choreographer was Jun Ishii's staging of his own triple-bill performance, including *Magnificat* and *Midnight Child* on 6 November 1991 in Nagoya. He also staged *Blood Wedding* based on Lorca's play, on 30 November in Osaka.

There were many visiting foreign companies from all over the world, but, if there were a strong Japanese national ballet, with dancers like Miyako Yoshida from the Birmingham Royal Ballet, Tetsuya Kumakawa of The Royal Ballet, Gen Horiuchi of New York City Ballet and Kaori Nakamura of Les Grands Ballets Canadiens, and a well-balanced repertory including authentic Japanese ballets, Japan would no longer be such a paradise for visiting companies.

The Netherlands

Eva van Schaik

The greatest events of the last ballet season in Holland were certainly the Holland Dance Festival in the Hague (November 1991) and the homage to Hans van Manen programmes during the Holland Festival in Amsterdam (June 1992).

Much attention was given by the international press to the unprecedented initiative of Jiří Kylián to start a company for dancers over forty, the **NDT3**. He commissioned Forsythe, van Manen, Ek and himself to create a piece upon four older dancers, with whom they are very well acquainted: Sabine Kupferberg, Alida Chase, Niklas Ek, and Gerard Lemaître. Their first programme was a tremendous success and proved to be about what everybody had already presumed: 'once a dancer, always a dancer'; wrestling with the boredom of routine; the end of a career; the reminiscences of youth whilst remaining evergreen. Honoured for his productive career as a choreographer, which started 35 years ago, 15 of the more than 80 ballets by van Manen were presented in three Amsterdam theatres by the **NDT1** and **NDT2**, the **Dutch National Ballet** and by several modern dancers. At the end of these festivities van Manen was honoured with the title of Officer of the Order of Orange-Nassau, the highest royal rank attainable by an artist in the Netherlands.

Besides the broadcasting of several of his ballets and a unique video profile, two books were published: one with several essays about different aspects of his craftsmanship, and one with a compilation of van Manen's lectures held in the year of his professorship at the University of Nijmegen (1986–87). Van Manen's own contribution to these performances was a splendid music-ballet for 14 NDT dancers, to Prokofiev's violin concerto, which he called *On the Move*. This title is apt not only for van Manen's views of his own career, but also the last ballet season in general. A lot of changes in the general management took place: at the NDT, Carel Birnie, its well-known Cerberus since the start of this company, was replaced by a new director, Michael de Roo. Meanwhile, general management director Anton Gerritsen, after 25 years of duty, left the Dutch National Ballet, to be succeeded by Dick Hendriks. So after a year of warming up for Wayne Eagling, the successor to Rudi van Dantzig, these two youngsters (one very experienced with the Dutch National Ballet, the other with the Royal Ballet) have to lead this company into new stormy waters. They will have a hard job, as they were not able to prevent severe financial cuts to their budget by the government. In June, parliament settled the so-called 'Kunstenplan' (arts project) for the next four years. And although the budget extracted for theatre-dance was not lowered, the biggest company in the capital will have to give in to smaller dance institutions in the regions, in spite of its fervent lobby to gain an extra DF 4 million. Instead, the Arts Council advised them to reduce the number of dancers from 86 to 68.

The experimental modern dance sector was particularly subject to severely damaging blows. The political urge to regulate the artistic scattering of too many small dance initiatives into one platform organization failed after strong opposition from the dancers and choreographers themselves. The consequences of the long, tiresome debates were quite disastrous: the older companies of Bianca van Dillen (**Dance Production**) and Jacqueline Knoops (**New Dance Group**) will no longer receive any subsidy from the state or city, and their scattered younger colleagues, including a new generation of experimentalists, are faced with sad prospects. The cry for independence, artistic identity and autonomy has been severely punished. The companies which were more lucky with the results of the proposed shifts in the dance budget were the smaller ones in the region, amongst them **Introdans** (Arnhem), **Rotterdamse Dansgroep** and **Reflex** (Groningen).

In spite of the infertile prospects and political consequences for the next four years, theatre dance in the Netherlands still prospers very well, although the boom of the last ten years has flattened out. At the Dutch National Ballet the three-pillar policy was continued with reprises of *Romeo and Juliet* and *Swan Lake*, a Balanchine programme, new Ashton and Page ballets, and the premieres of new works by Ted Brandsen and Toer van Schayk. Brandsen's ballet proved especially successful and promising. That cannot be said about the annual workshop results, which were amazingly dull and outdated. If workshops are symptoms of the pulse and spirit within a company, then DNB seems to be dreadfully uninspired.

The opposite is the case with the NDT (1 & 2) in The Hague. The company is an amazing storehouse of creativity, no doubt caused by the fact that this company not only attracts the most ambitious dancers from over the world, but also has the fruitful interaction of Kylián, van Manen, Forsythe, Naharin and Ek under its roof: they are the quintet and quintessence of classically-based contemporary choreography.

At the **Scapino Ballet** important moves were revealed by the unexpected withdrawal of Nils Christe, its artistic director for two years. Due to stress and internal problems he is *ad interim* replaced by the other resident choreographer Ed Wubbe, who had a very productive season with his triptych *Parts I, Perfect Skin* and *Parts II* to Bach violin concertos. Meanwhile the preparation of the move from Amsterdam to Rotterdam still lingers on. The commission by Daniel Ezralow turned out to be a rather expensive mistake.

Of the smaller companies in Arnhem, Rotterdam, Tilburg and Groningen, the last one (Reflex) had the most successful season, with new works by Joaquin Sabate, Itzik Galili, Michele Noiret and Marc Vanrunxt, under the new artistic leadership of Patrizia Tuerlings.

At the Rotterdam company of **Kathy Gosschalk** an atmosphere of revalidation can be sensed, due to new works of Amanda Miller, Gosschalk herself and Ton Willems. In Arnhem, the residence of Introdans, Ton Wiggers and Hans Focking continued with success, as they showed a good sense for public expectations. This year they celebrated their twentieth birthday with a gala performance, a clear symptom of their metamorphosis from restless rebellious spirit into a more restorative attitude now, with new ballets by Philip Taylor, Tamara Roso and Mirjam Diederich.

The reception of the world at war (Gulf War, Gorbachev's fall and the slaughters in Yugoslavia, Armenia under the Kurdish People and so on) was reflected by several modern dance companies. The solo performer **Truus Bronkhurst** expressed her sorrow and anguish in *Blood*, while the artistic director-choreographer of **Raz**, Hans Tuerlings, started a four-year project about militarism, industrialism, colonialism and emancipatory movements against oppression in general. His first programme was called **Journey,** after the book by Celine, *Voyage au bout du nuit*.

The sense of a threatening monster above peoples' lives was expressed in **Krisztina de Chatel's** newest production, which she called *Weep, Cry and Tangle*. To music by Shostakovich she continued her passion for repetitive phrases of movement, kaleidoscoping the world of her seven dancers under the overseeing tentacles of a huge insect-robot, designed by Bart Stuyf.

Bianca van Dillen, felt the necessity of survival too. In her latest and perhaps last evening-long programme, *Stamina*, she cooperated with composer Henk van der Meulen, to lift a part of the veil of her own dance history, being one of the pioneering protagonists of modern dance in Holland. The taste was rather bitter, *Stamina* being her swansong as artistic leader of a company which she began in 1977.

Another swansong was to be heard in the spring dance production of **Concern**, in which cinéaste-writer-sculptor Eric de Kuyper ventured onto the field of choreography, with the melodramatic help of five former dancers of Dance Production, now clustered in Concern. In their *Real Clichés* they re-enlivened the years of the 1950s under the Pax Americana: with Ladies Home Journal, McCall, Life, Paris Match and the new washing machines, hairspray, prefab kitchens and so on, as the heralds of misguided feminism.

Amongst the upcoming dance generation given place and space in the Spring Dance Festival 1992, **Karin Post, Haryono Roebana, Wim Kannekens and Adele van der Weide, Susy Blok and Chris Steel, Gonnie Heggen** represented new Dutch choreography. Only the first two managed to withstand the test. More indicative for the status quo of new dance was the Choreography Concours in Groningen, which ended in a mess, due to

Sabine Kupferberg and Alida Chase of Nederlands Dans Theater 3 in Kylián's
Obscure Temptations.   PHOTO: HANS GERRITSEN

Introdans in *U.L. Unidentified Light*, choreographed by Mirjam Diedrich. The dancers are (left to right): Tony Vandecasteele, Hilde Machtelinckx, Lauro Marcenaro, and Frank Holstein.   PHOTO: HANS GERRITSEN

the French and Finnish members of the jury. The Prize of the Public was given to Itzik Galili, an Israeli choreographer, who finds himself in the footsteps of Naharin, Duato and Kylián, but also presents a clear authentic approach. In spite of the jury who accused him of appropriating the same theme as Wim Vandekeybus, he certainly has to be reckoned with in the near future. NDT has already commissioned new work from him next season.

Last but not least in this survey is the name of **Beppie Blankert**. With her follow-up to *Charles*, her male duet to scores by Charles Ives, she completed her production with a second part to songs and instrumental pieces, which she called *Ives*. Due to her private investment in a studio for dancers and choreographers, and as a result of her expressed intentions to become the artistic leader of the scattered field, she will probably benefit from all the quarrels around, about and above her. In the next year it will be more clear what has become of her plans and prospects. Meanwhile Dutch dance is on the move, though slower and less spectacularly than last season, faced with severe cuts in its finances and facilities. All workshop-studios will be closed, two established modern dance companies will not be able to go on,

and the scattered field desperately searches for new grounds of cooperation. Meanwhile the two main companies in Amsterdam and The Hague are
'punished' for their success and will have to suffer for the improvement of
smaller provincial companies.

Obituaries

With the death of **Corrie Hartong** in August 1991 and **Karel Poons** in
March 1992 the Dutch dance world lost two of its outstanding pioneers in
the field of education. In the 1930s, Hartong established the first professional dance academy in Rotterdam, while Karel Poons was director of the
Scapino Dance Academy in Amsterdam, which he started in 1959 and
directed until 1977. Both directors were educated in the tradition of Mary
Wigman, Kurt Jooss and Yvonne Georgi, but this did not prevent their
interest in classical ballet, modern dance and experimental dance. Most
important, however, was their warm interest in the development of their
pupils, as they regarded the art of dance as an expression of humanity and
individuality. Both were responsible for the professionalization of dance
education, and were regarded as important advisors. Corrie Hartong died
at the age of 80, Karel Poons at 79.

Erna Droog died of cancer, much too young, at the age of 49. After her
career at the Dutch National Ballet she became leader of the Amsterdam
Ballet Academy in 1981. Here she was a firm defendant of ballet technique,
but never lost sight of the human interests of her students.

New Zealand

Jennifer Shennan

The new artistic director of **The Royal New Zealand Ballet**, Ashley
Killar, was appointed in 1992. Harry Haythorne remains as director
emeritus for nine months in a bridging capacity, and also to perform
character roles. Poul Gnatt, who founded the company in 1953 and directed
it for over a decade, has subsequently worked in Scandinavia but has now
retired to New Zealand. The scene is thus set for next year's celebrations of
the company's fortieth year, culminating in a move into their (first ever)
own theatre.

A highly successful tour of Jack Carter's *Cinderella*, with a witty exploration of the Prokofiev score, was a coproduction with the New Zealand
Symphony Orchestra. Kerry-Anne Gilberd and Anne Anderson alternated

141

in the charming title role; outrageous comedy came from Lee Patrice and Karin Wakefield as Ugly Sisters and Jon Trimmer as the Stepmother.

The 'Forging Ahead' season included four newly-commissioned works: *The Season of Sorrow* (music by Larry Sitsky) based on Oscar Wilde's life, and movingly performed by Eric Languet; *Les Galanteries* by Tim Gordon, a clean and elegant work inspired by Bach music for solo cello; *Artemis* by Shona McCullagh in a provocative work to Bulgarian vocal music, the title role created by Karin Wakefield; and *The Empty Fortress* by Eric Languet, set to a hauntingly beautiful dance poem by René Char, and using the whole company.

The small company **Jon Trimmer and Friends** toured to smaller centres. Its repertoire included a delightful *Les Petits Riens* by Patricia Rianne; Peter Boyes' ascetic and interesting *Ramifications* to Ligeti's music; *Love Sonnet* by Garth Welch, and a fine production of Limón's *La Malinche* by Louis Solino.

The Royal New Zealand Ballet season for the International Festival of the Arts in March 1992 saw a revival of Graeme Murphy's *Orpheus*, generally thought not to have weathered so well since its 1981 premiere. Also included were Douglas Wright's controversial and brilliant work, *The Decay of Lying*, to music by Lully and texts by Oscar Wilde; and a highly acclaimed production of Rudi van Dantzig's *Four Last Songs*. (The company was also associated in an entrepreneurial role with the **Compagnie Maguy Marin** who performed *May B* to great response in the same festival.) A return of Veredon's beautiful *Wolfgang Amadeus* was, if anything, stronger than in its first season, with Kilian O'Callaghan and Jane McDermott developing a lyrical partnership. This work is to tour to Australia in 1992; together with *Coppélia* and a triple bill, it will tour to the USA in 1993. More recently there has been a triumphant success with the premiere season of *Hamlet*, choreographed by Jonathan Taylor, to a setting of Renaissance dance music. Superb performances were given by Eric Languet, Karin Wakefield and Anne Anderson. This powerful work will tour to Europe (including England) in 1992.

Building on the enterprise in their earlier dance programming, the International Arts Festival brought **Douglas Wright** and his Auckland-based company of seven dancers to perform *A Far Cry*, a dark and brave new work (to Bartók violin and piano). Its dramatic and sculptural searching was chilling and memorable and much in contrast with the double-billed return of Wright's celebratory *Gloria* (to Vivaldi).

In the same festival, **Mary Jane O'Reilly** created *A-4*, a series of four dances developed around Mark Baldwin, a New Zealander with the Rambert Dance Company. **Footnote Dance Company's** season included *Fields of Jeopardy* choreographed by Michael Parmenter. Later in the year Parmenter's own company, **Commotion**, expanded to 15 members, performed *The Race*, an epic exploration of the creation of good and evil. Lisa Densem's

Karin Wakefield (left) and Lee Patrice as the Stepsisters in The Royal New Zealand Ballet's production of *Cinderella*.

outstanding design and leading performance, together with Ann Dewey, Helen Winchester and Taane Mete, will feature in a televised edited production.

Susan Jordan's choreography *The Rest is Silence*, a dance-theatre essay on *Hamlet*, with four performers in a multi-tiered space, and design by Tony Geddes, was commissioned by the Court Theatre in Christchurch.

Kilda Northcott made a remarkable first choreography in *Mirror Fragments*; **Lyne Pringle** performed *Crone*, an impressive solo show; **Bronwyn Judge** and **Carol Brown** toured *Manuhiri*, dances inspired by dramatic South Island landscapes. Maori legend inspired a duo, **Merenia Gray** and **Katya Wilson** to perform *Hono Tai*, which was well received. **Sally Stopforth** and **Andrea Sanders** choreographed *Into Orbit*, a hilarious slap-stick gun-running cabaret.

Paul Jenden had great success with *The Hairy Maclary Show* based on a highly popular series of children's books by Lynley Dodd, performed by the **New Zealand School of Dance**. In June 1992, a fine *Konservatoriet* with a music trio performing on stage and completing a cameo-like perfection, was staged by Poul Gnatt on the students from the New Zealand School of

143

Dance in a gala performance to celebrate the twenty-fifth anniversary of the school. On the same programme **Taiaroa Royal** performed what is possibly the most significant solo of the year in his own choreography, *Te Po*. Wielding a Maori *taiaha* (long weapon), he danced out the warrior of old and the dancer of tomorrow in a superb and skilful display. On the strength of this performance Tai has been invited to join the Royal New Zealand Ballet and perform this work on their American tour early in 1993.

Russell Kerr, now retired from Dance South, is freelance choreographing and producing, both in New Zealand and in Hong Kong. 1993 will see his definitive production of *Petrushka* for the Royal New Zealand Ballet. **Shona Mactavish** has reconstructed and filmed several of the compositions from the 1940s by pioneering modern dancer, Gertrud Bodenweiser.

Developments within dance education have included the transfer from the Arts Council to the Ministry of Education of funding for the New Zealand School of Dance, where Nicholas Carroll has been appointed assistant director. The Performing Arts School in Auckland continues to develop tertiary dance training with an emphasis on Polynesian community dance. The Dance Archive has commissioned the taped Oral History interview of Poul Gnatt which has been deposited, alongside that of Alexander Grant, in the National Library. The two historic dance masters' manuscripts, which were kept for many generations in a New Zealand family collection before being deposited in the National Library, have now been edited and published by Pendragon Press, New York (*Workbook of Kellom Tomlinson*, 1708, and the *Journal of Joseph Lowe*, 1850).

The Maori proverb 'Ka tú, ka ora; ka noho, ka mate' translates as: 'Standing upright, one is strong and well; sitting or lying down, one is sick or as good as dead.' The dance profession could be said to be standing upright. For that, considerable credit may be given to Susan Paterson, the dynamic and sympathetic director of dance programmes at the Arts Council. Although there is never a dollar to spare, Susan has channelled the resources effectively and thereby raised morale.

Obituaries

Ashley Lawrence, one of the world's greatest ballet conductors, died in Tokyo. Born in Hamilton in 1934, he spent three years at the Royal College of Music in London, studying piano and conducting, and later took a conductor's course under Rafael Kubelik in Swizterland. In 1962 he joined Britain's Royal Ballet, and was soon conducting at Covent Garden. In September 1966 he became musical director of the Deutsche Oper Berlin, and in 1971 was appointed music director of the Stuttgart Ballet. The same year, he returned to the Royal Ballet as principal conductor, and was the company's music director from 1973 until 1987. In recent years was a frequent guest conductor with the Paris Opera Ballet, and worked with them on tour in Russia. In 1982 and 1990, Lawrence returned to New Zealand to tour with the Sadler's Wells Royal Ballet. He revisited New Zealand in 1988 to conduct the New Zealand Symphony Orchestra for the Royal New Zealand Ballet's production of *Romeo and Juliet*, and had agreed to return for *Cinderella* in 1991, but unhappily, that could no longer be.

Norway

Trond Aglen

D espite the general economic crisis, as always affecting the dance and ballet scene more than any other area, a certain optimistic wind seems to blow all over dancing Norway.

The **Norwegian National Ballet**, under the dynamic direction of Dinna Bjørn, has gone through a very active year. The autumn season opened explosively with a festival dedicated to the memory of Diaghilev's Ballets Russes. This homage to Diaghilev and the other geniuses of his era resulted in an artistic as well as a box-office success. Above all it was a ballet event of a sort that has never before occurred in Norway. During the two weeks of the festival in October 1991, ten different ballets were presented. The nucleus of the festival was Swedish choreographer Ulf Gadd's 'documentary ballet', simply called *Ballets Russes*, a full-length work that has been in the company's repertoire since 1985. The new festival ballets stretched from Fokine's *Petrushka*, *Les Sylphides*, *Le Spectre de la rose* and Balanchine's *Apollo* via Tetley's *Daphnis and Chloe*, *Rite of Spring* onto Cranko's *Jeu de cartes*, Ashton's *Monotones*, van Manen's *Trois Gnossiennes*. Stravinsky's music was also present in two ballets by British choreographer Michael Corder, *Rhyme nor Reason* and *Party Game*. Corder is now staging a completely new version of Prokofiev's *Romeo and Juliet* that opens next season, with Nadine Baylis's decor and costumes.

As we can see, the festival's aim was not only to present the Ballets Russes as a historical phenomenon, but also to show its influence on times to come. Four of the ballets presented were Norwegian premieres, and one, in fact, was a world premiere: Dinna Bjørn's own choreography to Ravel's *Tzigane*, a solo with the veteran Indra Lorentzen. Lorentzen also gave a marvellous performance in another Ulf Gadd work, the full-length dance-theatre piece *Tango Buenos Aires* (1987). Gadd is now living permanently in Bali but returns to Oslo regularly.

This season the company also brought back Kjersti Ålveberg's wonderful *Volven*. A triple-bill in March included *La Somnambule*, Rudi van Dant-zig's *Vier letzte Lieder* and Ailey's *Night Creature*. *Apollo* was added to the bill, and what I really remember from that night is young Richard Suttey in the lead, showing a remarkable development since the festival. Dinna Bjørn wants her ballet out and about: during the season the company toured across Norway and abroad. Last May its trademark *The Tempest* had great success in Wiesbaden, Germany. Among her numerous activities as artistic director, Bjørn has this year been arranging official hearings on the situation of Norway's biggest ballet company. In times of financial prob-lems the Norwegian state tends to support business banks, not ballets. Another paradox is that when abroad the company is presented as the Norwegian National Ballet, but at home its official name is The Opera Ballet, a fact revealing its status as an appendix to the Opera House. Bjørn's question is clear: do we need a national ballet? The answer is still blowing in the wind.

Much worse off in status and money are the dozen independent compa-nies, most of them Oslo-based. Activity, however, continues with almost undying force. In fact, the fringe dance scene seems to survive better than does the fringe theatre. In Oslo the scene of the crime is Black Box, a theatre with two flexible stages that works as an umbrella for most fringe perform-ances, theatre included. Black Box Theatre now also co-produces with national and international companies. The latest example is Stockholm-based **Remote Control**, which appeared Expo 92 in Seville. Next is *Pino-cchio* and *Glass* with **Collage Dance Company**, which celebrated its fif-teenth birthday by moving into new premises. *Untitled* is a new work by Kristin Gjems, and Collage has invited Karine Saporta for the next Ibsen Festival in Oslo.

Another rather new Oslo stage is Scenehuset, a rehearsal and performing place for **Scirocco** and **Dans Design**. Ultra-modern Dans Design is success-fully touring abroad with *Love's Loneliness* and *Temple Sleep*.

The butoh influence is rather prevalent in Norway. Lately several groups have been to Japan, and Japanese masters have been here. This season, choreographer Anzu Furukawa staged one memorable performance with **Zakraz**, entitled *Under the Window*. And other butoh projects are coming up. But inspiration not only comes from afar; some look to Norwegian sources, too. Amidst a majority of female and rather globally-orientated choreographers, is Anderz Døving, echoing a song of the roots. But only Kjersti Ålveberg has been exploring themes from Norse mythology and folklore. She is also the one responsible choreographer of the 1994 Olympic Winter Games in Lillehammer, a performance that probably will have a national touch to it. *Honi soit qui mal y pense!* Most certainly Ålveberg will not do it to the point of cliché, and we hope she will be provided with enough money to carry through her ideas fully.

Halldis Olafsdottir, Terje Tjøme Mossige of Nye Carte Blanche in *Forvirringens Ulemper*, choreographed by Ina Christel Johannessen.   PHOTO: ØYSTEIN KLAKEGG

In expansive old Bergen the young regional company **Nye Carte Blanche**, fully-subsidized like the Opera Ballet, continues to seek its form and profile. This search, however, has been interrupted because the company also continues to change its leadership every year. Since January, the new artistic director after Jessica Iwanson was Fredrik Rütter, a former soloist with The National Ballet. With him are twelve dancers, among them Haldis Olafsdottir and Arne Fagerborg, now also a choreographer. This year's hit, *Inconvenience of Confusion*, was by Ina Johannessen. Nye Carte Blanche tours the west coast of Norway and sometimes visits Oslo, other cities and abroad. In Bergen there is also the independent company **Riss**; and **BIT** (Bergen International Theatre) co-produces dance productions.

The Association of Norwegian Ballet Critics gave its annual prize of 1991 to the independent dancer and choreographer **Jane Hveding** for her solo *Poems*, which was accompanied by Peter Lodwick.

Obituaries

The Norwegian dancer **Tutte Lemkow** died last year at the age of 72, in London, where he had been living over the last 35 years. Along with his varied and adventurous dancing career, he worked most of the time as a movie actor and screen-writer. His breakthrough was as the Fiddler in the movie *Fiddler on the Roof*, a part for which he will be remembered internationally.

The Philippines

Nestor O. Jardin

Dance dominated the performing arts scene during the 1991/92 period. In retrospect, it was an exciting season that showcased a wide variety of outstanding works from various local and foreign dance companies.

Ballet Philippines premiered choreographer Agnes Locsin's full-length contemporary *Encantada*, which many critics hailed as one of the year's most outstanding dance productions. The piece deals with a subject matter that Filipino nationalists have long decried - the rape of Philippine society under the 400-year colonial rule by Spain. Many choreographers have produced ballets on this topic, but except for a few like Alice Reyes' *Itim Asu*, these works have not really created an impact comparable to that of *Encantada*. What perhaps made the work outstanding is the very successful synergy among the members of the artistic team of Locsin, composer Joey Ayala and librettist Al Santos, who worked for over a year in a painstaking collaborative process of research, discussion and experimentation. *Encantada* best exemplifies the neo-ethnic dance origin that is evolving out of the works of several young Filipino choreographers today.

The resurgence of new choreographic expression dealing with social, political and environmental concerns was another remarkable development during the period. Among the successful productions were Enrico Labayen's *Lab Projekt*, Hazel Sabas' *Daragang Magayon* and Denisa Reyes' *Neo-Filipino*. Many of these works were created in close collaboration between visual artists, composers, choreographers, dancers, designers and actors. The results have been refreshing forms that sometimes put dance in a supporting rather than central role in the presentation.

On the classical and neo-classical scene, the **Philippine Ballet Theatre** premiered its full-length production of *Madame Butterfly* based on Puccini's opera. Choreographed by Tomas Pazik with beautiful set designs by Arturo Cruz, the ballet proved to be a wonderful vehicle for principal dancer Lisa Macuja and guest artist Rinat Gizatulin, who alternated in the lead role with Nicolas Pacana. Another highly successful production was Harold King's restaging of his version of *La Sylphide* for the Philippine Ballet Theatre, featuring Anna Villadolid alternating with Lisa Macuja in the lead role.

Yoko Morishita returned to the Philippines for the fifth time to dance with the American Ballet Theatre's Wes Chapman in Ballet Philippines' *Swan Lake*. Dancing together for the first time, the two guest artists produced an electrifying chemistry that drew raves from the Manila audience. Remarkable too was the *corps de ballet* for its precision. Alice Reyes, artistic director emeritus of Ballet Philippines, restaged her own version of *The Nutcracker* set in turn-of-the-century Philippines and featuring some prominent members of Manila society.

The Cultural Centre of the Philippines (CCP) in cooperation with the Asia Pacific Dance Alliance (APDA) hosted the 1991 Manila International Festival of Dance Academies and International Dance Conference, events which were previously held in Hong Kong. The festival featured the **Beijing Dance Academy, CCP Dance School, Jeune Ballet de France, Hong Kong Academy for Performing Arts, Dancers' Guild of Calcutta. Kuala Lumpur Dance Theatre, Jerusalem Folklore Ensemble** and the **USA Dance Repertory Theatre**. The conference, attended by 1100 delegates from the Philippines and eight other countries, discussed topics related to 'Traditions and Transformations'. A positive result of these events was the establishment of APDA Philippines, a national alliance of dancers, choreographers, teachers and scholars from the various dance disciplines.

The period also saw a French dance invasion when three major groups of diverse styles performed in Manila under the auspices of the CCP. First to visit was the **Compagnie Brumachon** which performed Claude Brumachon's *Texane*, an intense and very energetic work that drew a very enthusiastic response from the local audience. The **Ballet du Rhin** came next with an international repertoire of Anthony Tudor's *Dark Elegies*, Kurt Jooss's *Green Table*, Claude Brumachon's *La Complaint du Gerfaut*. The **Jeune Ballet de France** returned and undertook a three-week residency programme with Ballet Philippines II, that included workshops, joint performances and the creation of two new pieces – Agnes Locsin's *Paglalakbay* and Claude Brumachon's *Les Funambules du désir* – which were performed by artists from both groups.

Some of the country's leading dance companies, namely **The Ramon Obusan Folkloric Group, Bayanihan Philippine Dance Company,** Ballet Philippines, **Philippine Baranggay Folk Dance Company, Dagyaw Dance and Theatre Company** and Ballet Philippines II went on foreign tours during the period. However, the biggest touring project was organized by CCP at the Seville Expo 92 in celebration of the Philippine week. A total of 21 performances and cultural events featuring the Bayanihan Philippine Dance Company, the Philippine Madrigal Singers and some of the country's prominent musical artists were held over the eight-day period in various venues at the Expo.

The immediate future looks brighter for dance in the Philippines. The new government has made some pronouncements that arts and culture shall be given a wider role in national development. An implication is a substantial increase in the present meagre government support for the arts. The dance artists are keeping their fingers crossed.

Russia

Moscow
Elizabeth Souritz

From early summer 1991 to early summer 1992 so many things have happened in the country that one can hardly believe only twelve months have gone by. Of course most of the events were political, like the August putsch, the dissolution of the communist party or the breaking up of the Union of Soviet republics; or they had to do with economics. But even ballet can not escape the influence of politics; even less can it be independent of circumstances provoked by the economic crisis.

The transition between an organized system of government support for the arts and an independent existence, in which one is supposed to provide for oneself, is quite dramatic. Last year even big companies, like the **Bolshoi**, had difficulties. One can guess that the liberation of prices in January 1992 and their subsequent rise by 30 to 40 times have not helped. The press has discussed both the financial situation of the Bolshoi and its state of disrepair, which, as some experts have claimed, makes it dangerous to use the building. We are told that when scaffolders went up to have a look at the railing of the huge chandelier hanging over the stalls, it proved to be in such a state of decay that at the first touch a piece of it fell down. We are also told that a joint enterprise with some Italians had been proposed to deal with the reconstruction of the Bolshoi, but their terms were unacceptable. Meanwhile the Moscow government does not have the $80 million needed for repairs. To help the theatre survive, a public fund for the development of the Bolshoi has been organized, and a German oil firm was the first to subscribe.

The Bolshoi is so hard-up that after having negotiated with John Neumeier and with someone in Copenhagen for new ballet and a revival of *Sylphide*, it had to renounce the plan. I've been told that the problem is hard currency. Not only is it impossible to pay the choreographers, but also, hotels and air-fares, because Intourist and Aeroflot don't accept rubles when they deal with foreigners. So for next year the company plans a native *Don Quixote* revival.

The Bolshoi ballet also has artistic problems, such as losing its best dancers to the West. Semenyaka is one of the latest 'casualties', and Ananiashvili is seldom seen in Moscow. Nevertheless, this season the company had two important premieres - the revivals of *La Bayadère* and *Le Corsaire*. Another work was the revival of Leonid Lavrovsky's *Walpurgisnacht* for the new production of the opera *Faust*. Reviving the nineteenth-century classics is, I think, a wise decision. The Bolshoi has been gradually losing all the old ballets out of its past repertory - likewise nineteenth-century productions by Fokine, Gorsky, and Soviet ballets by any choreographer other than Grigorovich. The result has been not only an extreme paucity of the Bolshoi repertory, but an inability to master any different style of choreography (Bournonville or Goleizovsky included). So it will do the company good to dance some St Petersburg classics.

La Bayadère (premiered on 17 November) was revived by Grigorovich, who, as a former member of the Kirov company, is well acquainted with this version, which includes the Petipa choreography (or what is left of it and is attributed to Petipa) and the new variations added in the 1940s, in particular by Vakhtang Chabukiani. The changes Grigorovich made are not important, and apparently this time nothing of the old choreography is lost. Now Gamzatti dances throughout the ballet on pointe, while traditionally in her first confrontation with Nikiya she wears heels, thus distinguishing her from the romantic heroine; and her part has been enriched by new variations. A dialogue between the two rivals (Nikiya and Gamzatti) is also in dance instead of being mimed. As he did earlier in *Giselle*, Grigorovich has organized the processions rhythmically, the participants moving in a dancing step instead of just walking. But these small changes are not so important as to distort the style of the ballet. Some are even a slight improvement on the traditional version, the audiences nowadays getting tired of long mime episodes and expecting more dance and more action.

Grigorovich calls his *Bayadère* revival a 'new stage version by Grigorovich' and, though faithful to tradition, does not insist on absolute fidelity to Petipa. The second revival - of the St Petersburg *Le Corsaire* - was announced as 'authentic Petipa'. Konstantin Sergeyev insisted on it when talking to critics, and even chose Petipa's anniversary for the premiere - 11 March. He died three weeks later and his ill-health may be one of the reasons why the revival was not entirely satisfactory. Another reason was a bad choice of designer - Irina Tebilova - for decor and costumes, which look absolutely 'kitsch': a hideous clash of colours in the tutus of the 'Jardin animé', not the least feeling of romantic mood in the sets. But the worse mistake made by those who reconstructed the ballet (Sergeyev was helped by Natalia Dudinskaya and several *répétiteurs*) was to think of Petipa only in terms of variations and *pas de deux* and not in terms of the ballet as a whole. It is true that the romantic *Corsaire* that Jules Perrot produced on the Maryinsky stage in 1858 had been reworked by Petipa several times (in 1863, 1880, 1899), the dance-drama about the reckless corsair Conrad gradually becoming a ballet about the beautiful maiden Medora, the ballerina's dances coming to the fore at the expense of all the others. But Petipa always knew how to combine mime and dance and make the story of his ballets intelligible. His ballets have a sound and well-balanced structure. That is what the new Bolshoi version lacks absolutely, the ballet having become a long *divertissement* with hardly any link between dances.

In both *La Bayadère* and *Le Corsaire* there are two casts. Both young ballerinas of the Bolshoi - Nadezhda Gracheva and Galina Stepanenko - now heading the company in the absence of their elder colleagues, dance Nikiya and Medora. Gracheva is the lyrical dancer *par excellence*, Stepanenko, the statuesque proudly confident one. With so many Bolshoi male dancers either working abroad permanently or touring on their own, Alexei Vetrov danced in both ballets, while Yuri Posokhov understudied him as Solor and Marc Peretokin as Conrad.

Leonid Lavrovsky choreographed *Walpurgisnacht* in the 1940s. Later it was danced not only in opera performances, but also in highlight programmes, especially when the company toured abroad. To tell the truth I never was a great admirer of this production, either of its sugary duets or of its athletic feats in the Soviet bravura manner. Now, I think, it looks even more old-fashioned. Should this act have been revived? As a historian of ballet I say 'Yes', because it is a fine example of a certain style, a Soviet 'classic', one of the most famous works of a famous choreographer. As a member of the audience I disagree. I would rather see some fresh choreography.

The **Stanislavsky** ballet company had nothing new to show us this season. This does not mean it was idle. The musical theatre named after K. S. Stanislavsky and V. I. Nemirovich-Danchenko has gone through troubled times. The trouble was mostly with opera. When the conductor Yevgeny Kolobov left in the autumn, taking most of the musicians with him, the opera had to stop performing and the ballet danced practically every night to tape recordings. There were also some weeks when no performances were given at all. Accordingly this season was shorter than usual. It opened in October and closed in May, the stage of the theatre then being used for filming.

The ballet company of the **Palace of Congresses**, which is at the end of its second season, continues to work under Andrei Petrov and with the collaboration of Vladimir Vasiliev and Yekaterina Maximova. In June 1991 it presented a new version of Prokofiev's *Cinderella* with choreography by Vasiliev, and with Maximova in the title role. Vasiliev played the Stepmother. For this production the famous fashion house Nina Ricci presented the company with costumes designed by Gerard Pipart. These were splendid, extravagantly rich costumes, some of enormous volume, in fabrics of the most beautiful colours, shining and shimmering, all decorated with lace, embroidery, feathers, innumerable spangles. The beauty of the French textiles was the first and strongest impression one got from the production. And, in contrast to this arrogant opulence, was the unaffected simplicity of Maximova, pathetic in dramatic moments, playful in moments of bliss, enchanting the audience by her gentle charm. As for the choreography, I think Vasiliev was carried away by the idea of stressing the grotesque and the eccentric in Prokofiev's music. Maybe one of the reasons was that this angle of approach gave him an opportunity to amuse himself playing the comic part of the Stepmother, which in this production is very prominent. And he overdid it. There are too many comic episodes, some of them not in good taste, especially when the Prince is being put to sleep by grotesque doctors with huge syringes, like in a Molière *bouffonade*; too much clowning, too many people rushing about and grimacing, too much affectation. The romantic love story, the story of selflessness, tenderness, and forgiveness engendering magic, was lost. Also lost were the beautiful Prokofiev waltzes, some delicately moving, some full of elation, some triumphant. On one hand Vasiliev made a point of preserving the integrity of the Prokofiev score (at the 1945 premiere some changes were made of which the composer did not approve), but on the other, he failed to convey

153

through dance its versatility and its deep meaning. But should the choreographer be blamed for it, or is it that the Palace of Congresses - its vast stage with all its technical equipment, its huge auditorium - incites the ballet-masters to create pompous *féeries*, grand shows, extravaganzas? This question arose after seeing another premiere by the same company, *Ruslan and Ludmila*, in March 1992.

The plot of *Ruslan and Ludmila*, Alexander Pushkin's youthful poem, is absolutely appropriate for a magic opera or ballet. Mikhail Glinka's opera is well-known, but since Adam Glushkovsky and Charles Didelot staged their ballets in the 1820s (when Pushkin was still alive) no other choreographer has turned to this story. It tells us of Princess Ludmila abducted during her wedding feast by the evil magician Chernomor, and of her bridegroom, Ruslan, together with two other knights (one of them a comic figure) pursuing the kidnapper. Eventually, after many adventures, Ruslan reaches the castle of Chernomor and liberates Ludmila.

The choreographer, Andrei Petrov, asked the composer Vladislav Agafonnikov to rework Glinka's music and make a ballet, which he staged himself on lavish scale. The costumes, though not as extravagant as the ones presented by Nina Ricci, were rich and colourful. The many changes of decor, designed by Marina Sokolova, made a brilliant spectacle. Petrov tried to match the splendour of decor and ingenuity of stage effects by producing an abundance of dances. I would even say overabundance, as they follow one another non-stop, and at moments one wishes for respite. I think the ballet would gain by being cut.

The company, headed by Natalia Kasatkina and Vladimir Vassilyov (actually called Moscow State Theatre of Classical Ballet) celebrated its twenty-fifth anniversary. In early spring it had a season at the Palace of Congresses to show all the ballets in its repertory.

There have been some other jubilees.

In April 1991 the great virtuoso dancer of the 1930s, Vakhtang Chabukiani was ninety years old, and a gala performance to honour him was held at the Bolshoi. Some dances from his ballets were performed, but the most interesting part of the evening were excerpts from old films with Chabukiani himself dancing. Sadly he survived his jubilee only by one year, dying in April 1992.

In March 1992 we celebrated the centenary of Kasyan Goleizovsky (1892–1970). The Goleizovsky Foundation (comprising his widow, the dancer Vera Vassilieva, his son - an art historian - Nikita Goleizovsky, a former Goleizovsky dancer Lin Su An and other actors and ballet historians) has arranged an exhibition, a conference (with the help of the Russian Institute of research in the arts and of the Theatre Union) and some concerts of Goleizovsky's works. The exhibition showed the many talents of this man, who was not only one of the most gifted choreographers, but also a designer, a sculptor and a poet. The exhibition had, along with photographs and designs for Goleizovsky's ballets, also many of his drawings and paintings and a series of wooden sculptures, mostly characters of ancient slavic mythology - water-sprites, wood-goblins, and so on. At the conference, researchers from various Russian towns analysed Goleizovsky's choreography, people who worked with him recalled their experience (one of the speakers was Igor Moiseyev), Nikita Goleizovsky gave a lecture about his father's library and art collection, and films were shown. The Foundation invited two American scholars, Marilyn Hunt and Nancy Reynolds, who explored the issue of Goleizovsky's influence on choreographers of the next generation, and some videos of Balanchine's works were shown. Two dance programmes were prepared for memorial performances, one by the Bolshoi, the other by the Foundation. The Bolshoi gave a concert with Goleizovsky's *Polovtsian Dances*, and dances reconstructed mostly by Vera Vassilieva and performed by Bessmertnova, Mikhalchenko and Ilse Liepa. The Foundation gave another concert of dances reconstructed by Vassilieva and Lin Su An and, which I found particularly charming, some dances Goleizovsky choreographed for children. They were revived by Margarita Yusim for the children of the school at the 'October' cultural centre. One of these dances was *The Chickens* (to music by Mussorgsky) featuring an oldish hen (Vitautas Taranda) and a flock of tiny yellow chickens, hatching out of eggs and being taught by mummy how to behave.

This year was rich in events such as festivals, competitions, prize-givings, gala performances. The first competition in Moscow was at the end of February: a competition of choreographers followed by a festival of 'chamber ballets' (meaning small independent dance companies). The competition showed that we are poor in choreographers - which is certainly no news. But the festival also showed that one should look for new people and new ideas not in the large so-called academic companies and not in the capital, but rather in the provinces, where some small groups are doing experimental work. There was, for instance, the **Studio of Chamber Dance** headed by Olga Bavdilovich from Vladivostok, a big port on the eastern coast. Bavdilovich is interested in Oriental philosophy and religion, and her dances are meant to reflect different relations between man and the world. Through combinations of angular movements and clustered, jerkily moving bodies one gets the feeling of an ecstatic mood, gradually building into a ritual.

Another competition - in March - was to honour Diaghilev and was organized by the Diaghilev Centre with the assistance of the Association of Dance Workers of Russia (president Olga Lepeshinskaya). It was an international competition with an international jury, and an enormous amount of money was spent on it: on programmes and booklets, on the arrangements in the Tchaikovsky Hall, on entertainments, including a closing supper party. To justify the title (Diaghilev Competition) the prizes were named after dancers who worked with Diaghilev: Anna Pavlova, Tamara Karsavina, Ida Rubinstein, Olga Spessivtseva, Vaslav Nijinsky, Mikhail Mordkin, Léonide Massine, Serge Lifar. This was not a very good idea, because it resulted in some critics expressing doubts as to whether the recipient of the prize was really as good as the dancer after whom the prize was named. As I was away from Moscow, I did not watch the competition, but I am told a twelve-year-old Japanese girl, Tomomi Nakaguti (Tamara Karsavina prize) was something of a sensation, while a boy from Kiev, Alexei Ratmansky (Vaslav Nijinsky prize), showed the greatest artistry.

From late May to early June a competition was held not in Moscow, but in Perm, but Moscow dancers Maximova and Vasiliev provided money for the prizes (along with Baryshnikov and Makarova) and Vasiliev headed the jury. The prizes were not in rubles, but in dollars, which made the competition something special. It was the Moscow company headed by Viatcheslav Gordeyev that took away most of the prizes. The grand prix went to a Japanese working with this company, Ivata Moribiro, the first prize, to Yana Kasantzeva and Dan Sasaki (another Japanese) and the prize for the best choreography to Gordeyev himself. Thus the Gordeyev company, hitherto considered second rate, now moves into the limelight.

A special prize named after Diaghilev was given to our eminent ballet historian, Vera Krassovskaya. I think that is great news and well deserved. Not only is she the greatest contemporary Russian writer on ballet, but she was the first to speak of Diaghilev's importance to Russian ballet at a time when he was either criticized or not mentioned, in her book *Russian Ballet at the Beginning of the Twentieth Century* (1971).

Another prize, that some reviewers called a 'ballet Oscar' that really got its name (Benois prize) from the Benois family, went, after the decision of an international jury, to the choreographer John Neumeier and to the dancers Nadezhda Gracheva, Alexander Kølpin and Julio Bocca. The presentation of the prizes was at the Bolshoi on the international day of dance (Noverre's birthday). The prize itself is a statuette of a couple dancing. The sculptor is Igor Ustinov, son of Peter Ustinov, also belonging to the Benois family.

All this active social life - and ballet is just a small part of it - all these festivals, competitions, gala performances, fashion balls - how is it compatible with the acute economic crisis we are suffering? To answer this question one must give an idea of the changes our society is undergoing. What we are witnessing now is a dramatic differentiation into rich and poor. Before we were, at least at first sight, a rather homogeneous society. What the upper classes (that is to say, the communist bosses) possessed was never exposed to the eye, but hidden behind the walls of the guarded country houses, in the secret '200th section' of the department store GUM, where for little money the privileged could buy things that other people never as much as saw. The poor did not even realize how poor they were, and were generally satisfied with the little they got practically free from the state. Now everything has changed. The 'terrible social contrasts' that were always attributed to capitalism have become a part of our life. Millions of families have suddenly found that their income keeps them well below the poverty line. Streets and underground passages swarm with beggars and the homeless. And at the same time 'commercial shops' are open all over the town, where goods are sold either for hard currency or rubles, but at prices absolutely out of reach of those who live on a regular salary. Since the government has permitted free commerce, squares and sidewalks in the centre of Moscow have become a huge black market. Walking to the Bolshoi on the first night of a Petipa revival one had to break through a dense crowd selling food, cosmetics, clothes - anything. Some do it to survive, selling what they have stored before the prices rocketed. Many are profiteers. Commerce in itself is not shameful, but one can't help being worried when thousands of people, especially the young, have no desire to produce goods, because they find it so much easier to buy cheap and then sell for a higher price.

Of course we all realize that the socialist system did not work and we need to move toward another one - the free market. But one does wish it were more civilized: without museums making place for hard-currency cafés, without theatres and libraries being forced to close, without printing houses having to print wallpaper instead of books. And that is no exaggeration: it happened at the St Petersburg publishing house 'Iskusstvo', which for years had been printing all our ballet books. Now dozens of manuscripts, including those by the most eminent ballet historians, like Vera Krassovskaya or Galina Dobrovolskaya, absolutely ready for print, are being refused, as the publishers do not expect to cover their costs. It is reminiscent of Lopakhin in Chekov's *Cherry Orchard*, who wants to destroy the beautiful blossoming cherry orchard in order to profit from the land.

These new Lopakhins, these new rich people - can't ballet profit from them? After all Russian ballet has prestige all over the world, ballet is an attraction. Some attempts have been made to get them interested in dance. A firm that calls itself 'W' ('double v'), and has a ballet slipper in its emblem, inaugurated a series of dance concerts. The first was by Farukh Ruzimatov in May, then the Scottish Ballet and Viacheslav Gordeyev's company in June and Eldar Smirnov's company in July. The firm issued season tickets to the concert-hall 'Rossiya', setting very high prices and thus emphasizing that these performances were not for the average ballet-lover, but for the rich. The best-known Moscow businessmen were approached and invited to buy tickets. Going to the opening gala performance and having been told that the more expensive tickets were all sold, I expected to see evening dresses, maybe even white tie and tails - something exciting and unusual. But there were many empty seats in the stalls, and the audience looked no different from the ordinary ballet fans. So it does not look as if the prospective sponsors have been lured to the ballet. At the next performances tickets were distributed freely not only to the press (which, by the way was never a custom in Russia), but even at the entrance of the theatre. We are told that some were also given freely to orphanages.

The **Scottish Ballet** has been on tour to Russia also under the auspices of the 'W' firm. At the press conference, the head of the firm, Valery Sergeyev, complained bitterly of the difficulties that the official organization 'Gos-concert' (hitherto a monopoly in the business of presenting foreign companies in Russia and Russian companies abroad) created in order to prevent this tour. He also thanked those who helped him: on the Russian side the Association 'Rossiya-concert' and the Russian Association of Dance Workers; on the English side, the British Council and the British Embassy. The company danced in the huge Palace of Congresses (seating 6000), which of course was not full. Probably a smaller theatre would have been more practical. But we have been told that the 'W' firm managed to get a place for the company to dance largely through the courtesy of Natalia Kasatkina and Vladimir Vassilyov, generous enough to cancel three performances of their own company to help the Scottish Ballet. The company gave three programmes with some ballets familiar to our audiences, such as *Who Cares?* (which we have seen danced by New York City Ballet), two Kylián ballets, North's *Troy Game* and two ballets new to us: *Vespri* by André Prokovsky, which was quite a success, and *Brief* by Amanda Miller, which few people seemed to enjoy. Of course the audience greeted the ex-Kirov ballerina Galina Mezentzeva warmly.

Coming back to the problem of publishing ballet books, I want to mention a brave little publisher called ART (Actor-Régisseur-Theatre) under Sergei Nikulin (who was the editor of the famous Vadim Gayevsky book *Divertissement* banned in 1981 for a couple of sentences criticizing Grigorovich) which has started to publish a series of ballet memoirs. Two are already on sale: Mathilde Kschessinska's and Nina Tikanova's, and others are planned - Lifar's, Serge Grigoriev's and possibly Bronislava Nijinska's *Early Memoirs*.

St Petersburg

Arkady Sokolor-Kaminsky

The Soviet ballet is dead. Long live . . . Ballet!

The decline and fall of the Soviet Empire, the dramatic and painful disruption of the former republics, the priority of politics, cannot have failed to influence our cultural life and its values, what with the present economic muddle and inept reforms. Despite all prognoses and promises, prices have rocketed sky-high and are dozens or hundreds of times higher. As a result, the cost of producing a new performance is astronomical. Small groups are always on the look-out for a sponsor who could help cover expenses, otherwise a new performance is an impossibility. Troupes which do not have a stage of their own on which to perform are in an especially critical position, the rent of a theatre being sometimes so high that the profits do not cover expenses. Hence the paradox - the more active the troupe, the heavier the losses. It seems it's much more profitable not to perform at all - but that would mean the artistic death of any troupe. That's why small groups appear and vanish quickly, but it does not mean that their artistic level or competitive abilities are not high enough.

As for the spectator - alas! burdened with his everyday troubles and hardships, he is not so eager to rush to the theatre. Now he won't be lulled so easily by a dream or a fancy, tired as he is of various political games. Even the most prestigious theatres, filled to capacity in the past, can seldom boast a full house. The tickets are seven or ten times more expensive. Visiting companies' prices are higher still. We find it all so strange, having been brought up on the slogan: 'Art is for the people!' In the past the state saw to it that a visit to a theatre, a museum or a cinema was a possibility. These times have passed and economics demands its rights. The city's transport is unreliable, the roads are bad or under repair - and have been in this condition for years, so it's a problem to get to the Theatre Square for the Maryinsky and Conservatoire. Besides, it's not safe to stay out late - crime rates are growing. So is it the right time to enjoy oneself? The theatre opens half an hour earlier, but it doesn't help much. The problems are legion; most of them have nothing to do with art.

Well, what about the creative work of our artists, of the artistic life itself? Haven't they been buried under the debris of the old state system, which was sluggish and slow, but cemented hard by lies, blood and deceit?

The events of the August 1991 coup all but ruined the first night of the **State Theatre of Ballet** directed by Boris Eifman, for in those terrible days of suspense and fear all kinds of shows which gathered a lot of people together were forbidden. Fortunately, the shadows of the past lived a short life and then vanished; we were spared the menace of the old dictatorship.

As for Eifman's production, we enjoyed his wise and mature creation, *Requiem*, inspired by the immortal Mozart. On 21 August 1991, its first night, the largest concert hall (Oktjabrsky) was almost full; thus the public demonstrated both its interest in the new ballet and its protest against all kinds of regulations on private life, such as a visit to the theatre, that the ill-starred leaders of the Emergency Situation State Committee wished to impose on the people.

Requiem, produced by Eifman, is a passionate confession of a long-suffering human soul. Man comes into the world, each time discovering

159

anew the torments of a seeking soul, the wisdom of eternal truth, the bliss of love and the bitterness of inevitable losses. At the beginning you see a child who, supported by his mother, is making his first steps. He gradually grows stronger, testing his might, and boldly confronts the unfamiliar elements of life, which at times caress him or strike him. The subject doesn't seem new and is reminiscent us of Balanchine's *Apollo*. But the musical revelations of Mozart and the originality of the poetic dance by Eifman add a new meaning to the eternal theme of seeking the purpose of life. Free plastic movements are alternated with the traditional ones of the classical dance, and this plastic combination shows the tense strife of the two antagonistic principles, the dramatic nature of life. A youth is in the centre of the one-act ballet. He has two images - one is a youthful creature, the other, a mature battle-hardened man. Especially good is A. Gordeev, a recent gain for the troupe whose dance is free and manly - he was to dance the second part of the role. The design by Semion Pastookh is to my mind extremely good, awakening our imagination and turning the events on the stage into a grandiose universal mystery-play.

The second new production of the Eifman company - *Giselle* - was shown to us on 25 June 1992. It is a conscientious translation of the well-known version of the ballet, which is in the repertory at the Maryinsky, with an attempt to accentuate the romantic nature of the performance somewhat corrected by the academic-prone Petipa. The fact that even small, modern-orientated troupes like this one include classical ballets in their repertory is easily explained: it's a sheer necessity, for foreign tours are a means of survival, and abroad they cannot imagine Russian ballet without its traditional classical performances.

The Maryinsky, now as before, is the stronghold of classical ballet. We hardly had time to get used to 'St Petersburg' as the wave of fashionable 'renamings' rolled up to the Kirov Theatre. So, get used to it too - since January 1992 it's been the Maryinsky again!

The last season of the Maryinsky ballet company was unlike any other before. The beginning was strange: it was not the main company that opened the season on 22 September but the so-called **Maly Kirov Ballet** ('Minor Kirov Ballet') with a programme of Jacobson pieces. This 'Maly Ballet' sprang up from the ruins of the 'Chamber Kirov Ballet' and the 'Leonid Jacobson Fund' and is indebted to the commercial genius of Oleg Vinogradov. As the chief choreographer he has already won fame first as a businessman, rather than as an artist, and he graciously accepted the proposal to head the company together with Irina Jacobson.

It was the price paid for permission to use the chic name 'Kirov' or 'Maryinsky'. The deal went through. There followed no artistic revelations. The links between the Kirov Theatre and the Maly Ballet are quite loose. The troupe itself is mixed and changing, and is comprised of dancers ranging from pensionable age to beginners, with the former predominating. The companies represented in it are diverse. And it is 'aliens' who form the main body of the Maly Ballet troupe.

The splendid choreography of the brilliant master Leonid Jacobson was unrecognizable and quite disappointing. I pity those spectators who never saw the masterpieces performed by past generations of first-class dancers at the Kirov Theatre. Some of the producer's accents were shifted, lighting effects changed, the costumes inadequate - all this was disastrous. Poor Jacobson! If he were alive now, he would give these 'reformers' a piece of his mind!

The next production of the Maly Ballet was Petipa's *Harlequinade* based on the score by Drigo. Its appearance is fully in the spirit of a society worried by its economy. Again a classical ballet is a life-saver: it can be shipped abroad. A charming dainty little thing, restored in its time by Piotr Gousev for the Maly Opera Theatre, it has been scrupulously copied by Natalia Jananis. Leaving aside the problem of authenticity of choreography and the degree of changes made by successive restorers, we shall only remark that, however different from the original, *Harlequinade* presented a chance to glimpse Petipa's playful creation. The colourful scenery by Semion Pastookh and costumes by Galina Solovieva created the atmosphere of a festive masquerade. The choice of dancers was more successful, and though they were somewhat lacking in artistic expressiveness, the performance as a whole left a favourable impression. It might have been specially produced for Petipa's jubilee - the 175th anniversary of his birth will be marked in 1993.

And what about the main - 'legitimate' **Maryinsky** ballet company? Its activities this year were going on under the unfavourable conditions of a hard struggle for supremacy between the chief conductor Valery Goergiev and chief choreographer Oleg Vinogradov. Goergiev decided to play first fiddle in the artistic management and subjected all activity to the interests of the opera and orchestra. And he succeeded. For the first time in the history of the Maryinsky the play-bill demonstrated threatening gaps: for weeks at a stretch there were no performances at all, because the stage was occupied by opera rehearsals. The ballet, alas, had to be content with the position of a poor Cinderella, though to a great extent it was the ballet company that earned the hard currency which afforded the theatre the luxury of not raising the curtain every night.

Vinogradov's repertoire policy was to give the troupe access to western repertory. This time the Petersburg audience first applauded Antony Tudor and George Balanchine, and later Jerome Robbins.

Tudor's *The Lilac Garden*, to Chausson, and *The Leaves are Fading* to Dvorák, and Balanchine's *Apollo*, to Stravinsky, were shown in one programme on 26 January 1992. The refined choreography was not adequately

realized for the sophisticated taste of the select audience. The sweet femi-
ninity of Altynai Asylmuratova compensated to a certain degree for the
lack of psychological subtlety in her splendid duets in *The Leaves are Fading*,
whereas other dancers hadn't even that. The tough, cold-hearted Tatiana
Terekhova, the pretentious, even insincere Larisa Lezhnina, the hapless
Anna Polikarpova, all failed to penetrate the poetic world of Tudor. The
male dancers were equally colourless. The spectators of the older generation sadly recollected the unforgettable impressions of Tudor's choreography which they enjoyed at the performances of foreign companies. The
young generation had to be content with watching just the framework of
well-known productions. It's frightful to say, but *Apollo* seemed almost
obsolete and formal. Jerome Robbins was luckier, maybe because the choreographer himself had supervised the rehearsals. As a result *Les Noces* to
music by Chopin (the first night was on 18 March 1992) appeared to be a
lyrical meditation about the many forms of love, of its inexhaustible wealth
that links people together, however different their feelings might be. The
most memorable duet was that of Makhalina and Kurkov who demonstrated dramatic, highly emotional dance.

Acquaintance with first-rate western choreography, though, is sometimes not easy for our dancers - unfortunately they know so little about it
- but it is, I am sure, extremely instructive, and will bear fruit in the future.

Instead of producing a new ballet, Vinogradov preferred to stage his
Coppélia for the Maryinsky, done 19 years ago for the Maly Opera Theatre.
He complicated the choreography, slightly revised it, and the designer
Vacheslav Okunev saw to the picturesque decor. The young dancers enjoyed dancing their roles, and the ballet seemed to have gained new life,
become colourful and gay. The mastery of the experienced Gabriella Komleva, who was chosen by the choreographer as the main ballet-mistress,
contributed a lot to the expressiveness of the dance. The two main roles,
danced by the fascinating and funny Elvira Tarasova (Coppélia) and the
saucy and attractive Larisa Lezhnina (Swanilda), were a great success.

The only new production by the **Maly Opera Theatre** (now vainly subtitled 'named after Mussorgsky' - though the great composer never had
anything to do with the Theatre in his life) is a two-act ballet, *Petersburg*,
staged by Nikolai Boyarchikov after the novel by Andrey Bely. The first
night was on 14 June. The music by S. Banevitch, known as the composer of
several operas and ballets for children, submerges one into an atmosphere
of phantasmagoria and tremulous illusory visions that can melt away at
any moment. The scenery by the talented designer R. Ivanov combines the
fictitious and the real, whimsically mixed and managing to coexist side by
side. The choreographer, in my opinion, succeeded in presenting the image
of the mysterious capital of Russia, where creatures born of poetic inspiration live as active a life as real characters, who may, however, turn into

fantastic ghosts. Between them they form both horrific and attractive rings interspersed with the *corps de ballet* of white women in coruscating shimmering robes and enormous white hats as was the style at the beginning of the century.

The wreathed dance of the women is reminiscent of our magical 'white nights'; of the capricious Muse of the Poet, who may inspire him or leave him; of the visions of our future that appear in this providential mirage and can be either distinctly or just vaguely discerned. Alas! They are not for everyone to behold. V. Adjamov (Nikolai Ableukhov) was an indisputable success. The highly-strung dancer with a picturesque mass of black hair managed to combine meditative lyricism with dramatic intensity.

Our magical 'white nights' are present not only in the ballets. Now, in June, they envelop the city and the people, creating that poetic aura of which dance and music are part. They seem to have sprung at the command of a magic wand, the magician being St Petersburg. Here is an example: a wonderfully poetic concert held in the exquisite white-and-gold State Choir Hall with its charming ornaments and moulding. Through the upper windows streams the light of the 'white nights' turning the hall into a glowing pearl, and promising the delights of artistic splendour. The choreographer G. Alexidze and the artistic director of the Choir, V. Chernushenko have revived here the lost tradition of the 1960s. At that time the young choreographer and well-known musicians combined their efforts to create visual images showing the union of music and dance. The concerts were an artistic revelation, the more so because the brightest stars of Kirov ballet danced in them - Osipenko, Makarova, Komleva, Kolpakova, Fedicheva.

The performance on 12 June 1992 proved that the original idea had remained vital. The concert was performed by the **Ballet of St Petersburg Choir**, specially organized for the occasion, and the best dancers of the Maryinsky - Kunakova, Efteeva, Danukaev.

Music of all ages and styles was played, both instrumental and vocal. Mozart, Vivaldi, J. S. Bach, Tchaikovsky on the one hand, and Stravinsky, Messiaen, Schönberg, Ives, on the other - were friendly neighbours here. The musicians played different instruments - a gothic harp, a 'cello, a guitar, an organ, a piano, wood and brass wind instruments. They sat on the stage and watched the dance performed before their eyes. The dance was picturesque and varied, with many aspects - funny, absurd, tragic. The choreographer did his best to invent plastic representations of musical ideas. The greatest impact was made by the pieces staged after the 'Choir concert in memory of A. Yourlov' by G. Sviridov and 'The Angel's Voice' by P. Tchesnokov for a choir and a soprano - musical pieces of supreme emotional intensity and slavonic might.

The concert ended. The magic of the 'white nights' continued. I left the hall - before me were the Palace Square and Winter Palace. The Pushkin memorial flat is a minute's walk from here, as well as the Winter Canal. I walked along Nevsky, didn't feel like going by the underground. Near the Kazan Cathedral, on its steps, a choir is singing! Free of charge, for passers-by. They sing beautiful church music. I walked on. Near the building of the former 'Duma' (The City Council) rock musicians are giving a concert too. The town, despite holes in the roads, its neglected buildings with peeling plaster, lives its own life. And I live my own life, too.

Could it be the that heavier the burden of unsolved problems, the more eagerly we turn to Art?

Obituaries

In June 1991 our famous Ballet School in St Petersburg got the statute of the Academy of Russian Ballet named after Vaganova. Now it is an institution of higher education. Its graduates will be qualified as ballet teachers. In future new specializations may appear. **Konstantin Sergeyev** was elected first President of the Academy. Unfortunately he held this post for less than a year. On 1 April 1992 he died unexpectedly, just two weeks after the first night of *Le Corsaire*, which he staged at the Bolshoi Theatre. He was 82. The last of the Mohicans of great Russian ballet is gone. His knowledge of the classical repertoire and the style of Russian ballet was brilliant. He was an excellent dancer and actor, the 'lyrical tenor' of Leningrad ballet. He was a partner to Galina Ulanova and Natalia Dudinskaya. A number of classical ballets which he supervised are still in the repertory of the Maryinsky and other theatres of our country and of the world. For a long time he was at the head of the Kirov ballet company, then artistic director of the Ballet School; he also choreographed several ballets, Prokofiev's *Cinderella* among them. Sergeyev is buried in the Volkov cemetery, not far from Vaganova.

Three days later **Vachtang Chabukiani** died - 'the fiery Vachtang', who began his brilliant career as a dancer and choreographer in Leningrad at the Kirov Theatre. After the War he became chief choreographer of the Tbilisi Opera and Ballet Theatre, and later was artistic director of the Ballet School there. His dance was temperamental and made even the most sober people lose their heads. His performances in *La Bayadère* and *Don Quixote* became a legend. The ballets he directed such as *The Heart of the Mountains*, *Laurencia* and *Othello* made it possible for him and other dancers to excel in superb choreography.

Last year, unfortunately, abounded in deaths: **Tatiana Vecheslova** and **Marina Shamsheva,** who had been with the Kirov Ballet for many years, died last summer. At the end of April 1992 **Vacheslav Kuznetzov** died. He was not yet 62. He was an excellent dancer and actor. The great go. May the young generation be as great.

On 7 March 1991 **Asaf Mikhailovich Messerer** died, aged 88. He was one of the most famous Bolshoi dancers from the 1920s to the 1940s, and later was a most distinguished teacher. He started ballet rather late, at the age of sixteen, and was a student of Alexander Gorsky's at the Moscow ballet school from 1919–21. Small in stature, but well proportioned, he acquired a perfect technique: extraordinary lightness of elevation, and great speed in all kinds of turns and pirouettes. He became a virtuoso *demi-caractère* dancer (Basil in *Don Quixote*, the Chinese god and Jungler in *The Red Poppy*, Philippe in *Flames of Paris*), excelling also in comic parts and dances (*The Football Player* for example). Messerer also produced some dances and ballets of his own (*Ballet School* to music by Shostakovich, *Spring Waters* to Rachmaninov), and some revivals (*La Fille mal gardée*, *Sleeping Beauty*). As early as the 1920s he had started teach, gradually becoming one of the most famous teachers in Russia and the West. He taught classes at the Bolshoi from 1946, and all the famous Bolshoi dancers worked with him. Messerer wrote a book on ballet technique, *Classes in Classical Dance* (1967), and a book of memoirs, *Dance, Thought, Time* (1979).

South Africa

Amanda Botha

Due to the progress of the political reform process in South Africa and the subsequent lifting of the almost two-decade art boycott against the country, the performing arts in general and the world of ballet and dance in particular, had a year of great artistic bloom which was marked by a new vigour in performances. South Africa welcomed many overseas artists on their first visit to the country and was even able to employ international dancers as ballet mistresses and teachers on contract. There was also an exciting surge of new black talent and the formation of new dance groups.

Invitations were also offered to South African dance groups to perform at international festivals. The Cape Town based **Pace Dance** group of nine dancers and five musicians will participate in the Festival de Confolens in France in a programme of contemporary and traditional African dances. A traditional tribal dance group was also invited to appear at Expo 92 in Seville, Spain.

These developments are of great importance to the future of South African dance and ballet. Not only do they offer new inspiration to dancers and choreographers, but they also contribute significantly to building future audiences for both the classical school as well as the traditional and

165

modern dance genres. South Africa is now truly in a position to develop and foster a unique South African dance style, especially in modern and jazz dance.

Although during the moratorium years South African dancers made their way as individuals in international companies such as the New London Ballet, Scottish Ballet and Salt Lake City Ballet, talented dancers now have the opportunity to compete internationally. There is also potential for future international exchange programmes and opportunities for international companies and individual dancers to be guest artists here.

In the Black townships, dance classes amongst youngsters seem to bloom. There is great interest in both modern and classical dance. Ballet is also introduced as a school-leaving subject and there are excellent facilities for the training of young dancers.

Several international dance academies have existed for several years, and each has played a significant role in the development of dance. The Royal Academy of Dancing of South Africa is deeply rooted in the history of South African dance. The first studio was established in 1927 in Johannesburg and at present 18,000 children receive training at 600 studios run autonomously by member teachers of the RAD. Teachers are given an in-depth training to attain a teacher's certificate, which entitles them to register with the RAD.

The doyen of South African dance, Marjorie Sturman, was honoured for her contribution to ballet by the Johannesburg City Council at a special function to celebrate her ninetieth birthday on 18 February 1992. Marjorie Sturman, one of South Africa's great dance pioneers, was born in London in 1902 and came as a young child with her parents to South Africa. She opened her own studio in Pretoria in 1922. Together with the late Poppy Frames and Ivy Conmee she was responsible for the RAD method being taught for the first time in a country outside England, introducing the Royal Academy of Dancing to South Africa.

The first Russian ballet company toured South Africa and presented a programme which highlighted the supreme artistry of several Russian companies, among them the Bolshoi Ballet. The company of twelve dancers was brought to Namibia and Cape Town by the Russian Friendship Association. The ballet master was Boris Miagkov, an ex-Bolshoi soloist. This was a historic visit as diplomatic contact between the two countries had ceased in 1950.

PACT Ballet presented ten programmes/productions during the year under review. The hundred performances had an overall attendance figure of 98,256. Amongst the highlights of the year were the world premiere of the full-length ballet *Christmas Dream*, choreographed and produced by Graham Gardner, whilst the Bolshoi ballerina Alla Mikhalchenko danced in the centenary production of *Giselle*. This production, which enjoyed high

PACT Ballet's production of *Giselle*, with Leticia Müller as Giselle and Johnny Bovang as Albrecht.   PHOTO: HÉLÈNE CILLIERS

critical acclaim, was also filmed for South African Television's Arts programme.

In addition to Mikhalchenko, two dancers from the Royal Ballet made their South African debut. Errol Pickford and Nicola Roberts danced in Ashton's *La Fille mal gardée* whilst Michael Coleman, formerly from the Royal Ballet, produced Fokine's *The Firebird*. Another visitor was the British conductor Francis Rainey who conducted *La Fille mal gardée*.

PACT Ballet also presented the following productions: *War and Peace* (Valery Panov), *Romeo and Juliet* (Nicholas Beriozoff), *The Three Musketeers* (André Prokovsky), *Swan Lake* (Petipa/Ivanov), *Anna Karenina* (Prokovsky) and *The Sleeping Beauty* (Petipa). In addition, a programme of four short ballets – *Vespri* (Prokovsky), *Le Spectre de la rose* (Fokine), *L'Après-midi d'un faune* (Gardner) and *The Firebird* (Fokine) – were presented, as well as a one-act ballet, *Configurations* (Choo-San Goh).

The company enjoys the services of two orchestras: the National Symphony Orchestra and the Transvaal Philharmonic Orchestra. Company headquarters are the modern State Theatre in Pretoria, but it also performs at different venues in the Transvaal, including schools, and recently it has

Penny Swain as Zuki the Village Maiden, with John Simons as Menze, in CAPAB
Ballet's *Wushe's Lament*.   PHOTO: PETER STANFORD

used a 'touring stage' fixed on a large truck to take ballet to the townships
and rural areas.

Dawn Weller-Raistrick, OMSS, is the artistic director and Bruce Simpson
and Nicola Middlemist act respectively as ballet master and mistress. The
company consists of 26 soloists and 50 *corps de ballet*.

CAPAB Ballet, with its headquarters in Cape Town, celebrated its
twenty-first anniversary at the Nico Malan Opera House – the first state
subsidized theatre complex in South Africa. Tight budgetary controls prevented the company from staging a new major ballet. The productions in
the period under review were mainly well-established works that guaran-
teed good audience attendances.

Veronica Paeper, South Africa's foremost choreographer, succeeded
David Poole as artistic director, and faced a formidable task of rebuilding
and restructuring the company. Now she has placed her own hallmark on
this company, and despite a shaky start, she has managed to uplift the
artistic standard, largely due to the appointment of the Russian dancer
Nadia Krylova as ballet mistress.

Five full-length ballets choreographed and produced by Paeper were
amongst the twelve productions offered, a new production of *The Nut-*

cracker, sponsored by the Balletomanes, among them. The Bolshoi ballerina Daria Klimentova, as the Sugar Plum Fairy, danced some performances of *The Nutcracker*. Other Paeper ballets were *The Merry Widow, Don Quixote, Carmen* and *The Tales of Hoffman*.

Other full-length ballets were *Giselle* and *Swan Lake*, and five programmes of triple-bills were presented. In memory of Margot Fonteyn *Les Sylphides* was presented, and in a special programme homage was paid to Frank Staff (1918–1971), a pioneer of South African dance and choreography. Two of his highly acclaimed works – *Transfigured Night* and *Peter and the Wolf* – were produced. Paeper also paid homage to Mozart in his bicentenary year with a one-act work based on *Eine kleine Nachtmusik*. She also wrote the divertissement *Un Grand pas de deux*. Three Cape-based choreographers also wrote one-act ballets for CAPAB. Norman Furber presented *Stardust*, a nostalgic journey to the 1920s and 1930s, while Mzonke Jama, the only black professional classical dancer and choreographer in South Africa, wrote *Sithandwa* based on the Xhosa initiation ceremony. Erica Brumage choreographed a humorous zoological fantasy entitled *Carnival of the Animals*.

South African choreographers John Cranko (*Pineapple Poll*) and Gary Burne (*Variations in Space*) were also remembered.

Apart from 199 performances in the Nico Malan Opera House, which attracted 118,282 people, the company also went on tour in the Eastern and Western Cape with *The Merry Widow* and *Giselle*. A number of school performances were offered, as well as an information programme, *Ballet Boutique*, which focused on the work of international choreographers such as Balanchine, Petipa, Ashton, Robert North, Martha Graham, Jerome Robbins and Gene Kelly.

The CAPAB company enjoys the services of the CAPAB orchestra with Terence Kern was resident conductor. Kern was previously a conductor of the Joffrey Ballet in New York, as well as a guest conductor with the Royal Ballet and Salt Lake City Ballet. Phyllis Spira, OMSG, is principal balletmistress. Nadia Krylova and Keith Mackintosh are respectively balletmistress and master. There are 48 dancers in the company.

NAPAC Dance, with Garry Trinder (previously artistic director with Hong Kong Ballet) as artistic director is stationed at The Playhouse Theatre in Durban. The past year was a year of transition for the dance department. There were several changes in the top structure of the company and Trinder introduced many novel ideas to the company. He advocates a policy of reaching out to the broader communities and making his company's resources more accessible to the people of Natal. With this in mind, the former NAPAC Youth Dance Company was reformulated and the **NAPAC Dance Company 2** was formed on 1 January 1992. This company will not only augment the main company in all major productions but is playing a vital role to further the outreach programme by presenting innovative South African works to the community at large, as well as touring specially created educational programmes to schools. This company has ten members.

In addition, a company named **Kwasa**, which in Zulu means 'it dawns', was formed. Kwasa has a fourteen-member workshop group for talented potential performers who will be trained in a specially created one-year 'internship' course in the performing arts – free of charge. The dancers will then return to their communities, pass on their skill and generate further theatrical activities.

NAPAC Dance presented varied programmes of great classical and contemporary works. Owing to financial restraints many recent revivals had to be presented. Ashley Killar's *Giselle* and *Romeo and Juliet* were very well received. The mixed bill – 'Dance Panorama', featuring Balanchine's *Tchaikovsky Pas de Deux* and *The Four Temperaments*, as well as Jack Carter's *Witchboy* and Sonja Mayo's *Requiem*, was the highlight of the year. 'Dance Tapestry' was another mixed-bill season featuring the works of South African choreographers. An opportunity was also offered to company members to choreograph ballets for the company, which were presented as 'Dance in the Studio'.

In addition to schools and educational programmes, two children's ballets were presented, and January saw the introduction of the scholarship classes for children. Two classes are held each week with the aim of identifying talented children from this region.

Two international dancers were invited artists. Vincent Hantam returned from the Scottish Ballet, and Ayako Yoshikawa made her South African debut in *Giselle*, and both accepted contracts as soloists with the company. The NAPAC Dance Company presented two seasons of Spanish dance programmes in association with Linda Vargas: *Taverna Flamenco* and *Teatro Español*. The **Taipei Folk Dance Troupe** was presented in association with the Embassy of the Republic of China.

During the period under review the NAPAC Dance Company presented 148 performances which were attended by 56,437 patrons.

The large geographical area of South Africa means the companies have to tour extensively in order to reach the community at large. There are good theatres and facilities in the bigger towns outside the main centres, but in rural areas, use has to be made of local facilities such as school and church halls, as well as libraries.

Obituaries

David Poole (1925–1991) was born in Cape Town on 17 September 1925, and received his ballet training from Dulcie Howes and Cecily Robinson at the University of Cape Town Ballet. In 1947 he joined Sadler's Wells Theatre

Mark Hawkins and Selva Hannam of the NAPAC Dance Company, in Hawkins' work *Waiter, Separate Checks Please!*   PHOTO: VAL ADAMSON

Ballet, and after an extensive tour through America with the company he returned to Cape Town in 1952 as guest dance and producer. He then rejoined Sadler's Wells Ballet at Covent Garden. After another tour of America with the company, he became a member of Ballet Rambert in London. In June 1957 he returned to Cape Town to produce *Beauty and the Beast* and *The Firebird* for the University of Cape Town Ballet. During that year he also worked with the Eoan Group. He returned to Europe the following year to dance at the Edinburgh Festival. In 1959 he joined the staff of the University of Cape Town Ballet School, for whose company he choreographed three-act versions of *The Nutcracker* and *Sylvia*, and produced, among other ballets, Cranko's *Pineapple Poll* and Rodrigues' *Blood Wedding*. For the Eoan Group he choreographed *Pink Lemonade* and *The Square*. When The CAPAB Ballet Company was formed in 1963, Poole was appointed balletmaster. He succeeded Dulcie Howes in 1970 as artistic director of the company. In 1973 he was appointed director of the University of Cape Town Ballet School, retaining his association with the CAPAB Ballet as artistic advisor. The same year he did several productions for the CAPAB Ballet, including *Giselle* and *Le Cirque* (for which he received the first Choreographic Prize from the Department of National Education) as well as a new work, *Rain Queen*. He was awarded the Nederburg Prize in that year. Poole was appointed an associate professor by the University of Cape Town in 1980, and in 1983 he became the first professor of ballet in South Africa. In 1983 he was appointed Vice-President of the Royal Academy of Dancing in London. He retired as Director of the University of Cape Town Ballet School and was appointed artistic director of CAPAB Ballet in the same year. In 1987 the title artistic director was changed to director of CAPAB Ballet. After his retirement on 31 December 1990, he devoted much of his time to the work of the David Poole Ballet Trust, which was established to assist with the training of black dancers in the Cape Town townships. David Poole died of cancer on 17 August 1991.

Pamela Chrimes' (1922–1992) illustrious career in ballet took her all over the world, initially as a dancer, and later as a teacher, choreographer and producer. She received her ballet training in 1936 at the University of Cape Town Ballet School under Dulcie Howes. She later went on to become the first South African to join Sadler's Wells Ballet in 1945. In the same year, she returned to South Africa and joined the staff of the University of Cape Town Ballet School until her retirement in 1992. She worked with the Bolshoi Ballet in 1956 on their first performances outside Russia, and later studied ballet training methods at the Bolshoi School in Moscow, and at the Maryinsky School in Leningrad. She was invited to the United States as guest lecturer and producer for several ballet companies. She also visited Israel where she was a guest teacher at the Bat-Dor and Batsheva companies.

Christian Thorburn (1958–1991), an ex-soloist of the CAPAB Ballet company, died on 22 December 1991 in a drowning accident in the Breede River. He received his training at the University of Cape Town Ballet School under David Poole. He danced in many roles in ballets choreographed by Veronica Paeper for the CAPAB Ballet. He retired from dancing in 1988, and joined a Cape-based advertising agency.

South-East Asia

Daryl Ries

At the ebb of the nineties, we see a new age emerging in South-East Asia. The need to seek fresh meanings from the trials of the past has meant unhinging the shackles of Chinese history without abandoning its rich cultural heritage. A major transformation has been concern with contemporary themes and an experimental approach to traditional theatre. Dance is reflecting and, in part, provoking changing attitudes toward Chinese culture.

Insularity has been replaced by interaction amongst Asian dance companies and new artistic connections have crossed political borders between Hong Kong, Taipei, Singapore and China, the motherland.

Hong Kong

Nowhere has the potential for change been greater than in the climate of economic growth that has given impetus to cultural exchange and artistic freedom. With the advent of China's takeover in 1997, local companies are at the crossroads of a new era and look to each other for artistic and moral support.

Willy Tsao, founder of the **City Contemporary Dance Company**, which has thrived for a decade in Hong Kong, has been appointed artistic director of the Guangdong Modern Dance Company based in the southern city of Guangzhou (formerly Canton) in China. This symbiotic relationship may help the two walk the tight-rope between Hong Kong and China, but they must steer a careful course between western influence and the censorship of the Chinese government.

The City Contemporary Dance Company shares its original, eclectic works with the Guangdong dancers, who have in turn been trained by artists sent by the American Dance Festival (ADF). CCDC completed its

The Hong Kong Ballet in Peter Darrell's *Tales of Hoffman*, with Jiang Qi (guest artist) and Stella Lau (principal ballerina).

own tour of Chinese communities in the United States last year, while the Guangdong Company made its American debut at ADF in July 1991.

The **Hong Kong Ballet** has been stepping up performances in Asia with return engagements in China and Singapore. In keeping with its policy of promoting links abroad, *Paquita* staged by former Royal Ballet dancer, Petal Ashmole Miller, featured Ballet West principle, Jiang Qi, from Beijing.

174

He also performed in the Hong Kong debut of Peter Darrell's *Tales of Hoffman* that opened the autumn 1991 season.

In collaboration with the **Singapore Dance Theatre** the company opened this year's Singapore Festival of Arts with a salutation to Choo San Goh. The late Singaporean choreographer's *Forbidden Territory* has become the signature work of the Hong Kong Ballet, and was performed in conjunction with artistic director Bruce Steivel's *Good Times* for the Festival.

A measure of the company's success has been its ability to stimulate a broader interest in ballet among the general public. World-class ballets have been brought in by each of the company's directors. Garry Trinder, who ended his five-year term as artistic director, was succeeded in the new year by American Bruce Steivel, formerly ballet-master for the Basel Ballet and Ballet du Nord, and artistic director of the Stadttheater in Bern. He has continued to keep the Hong Kong Ballet's high profile as an 'eye-opener' for contemporary ballet in Asia by bringing in Karin von Aroldingen to direct Balanchine's *Who Cares?* and Jean-Paul Comelin, director of Ballet du Nord, to set his piece, *Les Nuits d'été*.

It is also not generally known that China has never seen *The Nutcracker*, and the Hong Kong Ballet hopes to bring its exquisite Peter Darrell version there. Throughout its thirteen-year history, the company has sought to maintain close relations with China's major companies for exchanges of artists and performances. Mainland artists have been sought to fill lead roles and the Hong Kong Ballet has introduced audiences from Shanghai to Guangzhou to a new generation of western ballet.

International cultural exchange has been the key for local companies and no one knows this better than Hong Kong's avant-garde, **Zuni Icosohedron**. Their controversial dance theatre, confronting China–Hong Kong relations, has been put on the shelf by the government, which is more eager to support ballet and mainstream modern dance. Zuni is anathema in China and thrusts its work abroad, where it is in demand in Europe, America and Japan. After the world premiere of their version of *One Hundred Years of Solitude, Mirage* at the Mito Arts Tower in Tokyo, they performed at the Mitsui and Toga International Festivals this year.

Gaining entrance, as well, into video and film performance, Zuni finds some financial support from collaborations with Japanese artists and festival projects, but they still appeal at home for greater democracy in arts funding.

Nurturing the new generation of performers, choreographers and teachers in Hong Kong, is the **Academy for the Performing Arts**, where a degree programme has been instituted this year in conjunction with a professional diploma course designed to attract professionals and graduate students from abroad.

The Bachelor of Fine Arts degree curriculum in dance follows a three-year course in which students will continue in their major study of ballet, modern dance, Chinese dance or musical theatre dance with a concentration on performance, choreography, direction or teaching.

Overseas applicants are sought to fill the quota, and response from Asian-Americans is most usual. However, the new degree programme could have wide appeal to Asians here looking for international accreditation.

Taiwan

The **National Institute of Arts** in Taipei is host to the International Festival of Dance Academies 92, conceived by Carl Wolz, dean of dance at the Hong Kong Academy in 1986. This annual festival is accompanied by an international dance conference. This year's topic, 'Trends in Dance in Asia', reflects the current concern with the preservation and transformation of traditional forms, cross-cultural influences and contemporary developments.

'No government can guide the direction of culture', says the former chairman of the Institute and founder/director of the **Cloudgate Dance Theatre**, Lin Hwai-Min, 'but there has been an enormous change in prevailing attitudes since the lifting of martial law.' According to Lin, even the once-decimated culture of Taiwan's aboriginal tribes is being restored, and indeed, features strongly in his own dance works.

Shooting the Sun, an aboriginal tale choreographed by Lin for his company and performed at the IFDA 92, is a dance-drama inspired by the Atayal tribe. Cloudgate, Taiwan's foremost dance company was disbanded after a pioneering decade, and reinstated with government funding and by popular demand last year. They have always drawn, despite their Graham training, from traditional roots, but change is vital.

Like his counterparts in South-East Asia, Lin regrets the upheavals in his country, in China and in Hong Kong, but believes it is a 'necessary thing' to express these times in their work. 'Considering that in China for the last 2000 years you never got a chance to do this, it is a birth pang', he says and sums up current sentiments in the region by acknowledging China as the 'motherland of my ancestors and of my culture, but not of our (political) future.'

With the intention of reaffirming international links and indicating the prestige of Cloudgate in the world dance community, Cloudgate made its 1991 debut with Paul Taylor's *Aureole*.

Singapore

For Singaporeans, it was a fitting tribute to 'the finest Asian choreographer of the twentieth century'. Choo San Goh's legacy resides in the repertory of the **Singapore Dance Theatre**, which performed the award winning *Momentum* for the opening of the Singapore Festival of Arts, June 1992. Goh's ballets are a blessing for the company, which sees his work as not only inspirational, but as identifiably Singaporean with their infusion of Oriental expression.

SDT seeks to commission local choreography, and in their eighth season performed two world premieres: *The Breath of Time* by Timothy Gordon and *Moon Flight* by Ying E. Ting. The company will present *The Nutcracker* as its first full-length ballet, in conjunction with the ballet's centenary.

In its fourth year, and with 12 members, the SDT is stretching its wings and touring four cities in China in summer 1992.

Over the years, there has been a bond formed between the SDT and Hong Kong Ballet that bodes well for the ballet in South-East Asia. Frequent exchanges and joint programmes have added to the constructive activity of both companies.

Guangzhou, China

The **Guangdong Modern Dance Company** based in Guangzhou, (formerly Canton), is slowly overcoming the stigma of modern dance as a foreign art form with its home-grown choreography newly fused with a contemporary identity. Very much in the vein of the modern dance that began to flourish in Hong Kong and Taiwan over a decade ago, Guangdong exhibits a cautious approach to individual expression and to social and political commentary. The result is a tentative step toward a dance language that breaks with the concept of art as the utilitarian servant of a controlled society.

An unprecedented example of the government's relaxed grip over China's regional arts groups, the Guangdong Company is the first 'glasnost experiment' to be officially sanctioned. Its inaugural performance on 6 June, at the newly expanded Guangdong Academy, marks a new age in the development of contemporary expression in China.

According to Madame Yang Mei-qi, director of the company and principal of the affiliated Guangdong Academy, modern dance cannot be separated from the growth of a modern culture in China. 'We are not producing American clones', she insists, 'but transplanting American creative principles that will give Chinese dancers ideas to draw upon. Our choreography will unify Chinese characteristics with modern techniques that will carry greater meaning for the Chinese people.'

The Guangdong Modern Dance Company is the result of a four-year plan linking the American Dance Festival with the Asian Cultural Council in a joint programme to stimulate and support this unprecedented project.

177

Spain

Laura Kumin

Seville's Expo 92 World's Fair, the Olympic Games held in Barcelona and Madrid's designation as Cultural Capital of Europe made 1992 a gala year for Spain. These celebrations produced a temporary increase in the number of new productions. Little has changed however, as far as theatre facilities and dance programming are concerned and prospects look less bright for next year. The recession affecting Spain has already caused budget cutbacks this autumn, with more austerity in sight for 1993, and many of the companies described in this article may be hard-pressed to survive the anticipated reductions in government grants.

The **Ballet Nacional de España** did not present its annual winter season at Madrid's Teatro de la Zarzuela last year, and most of the company's touring took place abroad in 1992, to Mexico, the USA, London, the Orient and Buenos Aries, with former principal dancers Antonio Alonso and Lola Greco featured as guest artists. Greco continued her collaboration throughout the year. New works included *Romance de Luna*, two flamenco pieces, *Romeras* and *Soleá por Alegrías*, and *La Vida Breve*. All were choreographed by company director and star dancer José Antonio, who recently announced that he would not be renewing his contract in 1993. No successor has been announced as yet.

Cristina Hoyos and her company presented the dancer's second production in Spain last May at Expo 92's open-air auditorium before taking it on the road throughout Spain and Turkey, and finally to the Edinburgh Festival, where it was enthusiastically received. Hoyos, who received Spain's 1991 National Dance Award, collaborated with choreographer Manolo Marin for *Yerma* and *Lo Flamenco*, the former based on the García Lorca play of the same name, while the latter is a series of dances in the traditional Flamenco style. Hoyos' company, undoubtedly the most successful of Spain's private flamenco ensembles, has also been affected by the difficult economic situation, and she has followed a standard procedure among traditional Spanish dance companies by temporarily disbanding the group until May 1993, when bookings will resume.

Antonio Canales, a former soloist with the Ballet Nacional and a featured dancer in many international gala events, founded his own company in 1992, with six dancers and eight musicians. This powerful performer premiered *A Ti, Carmen Amaya*, a tribute to the legendary flamenco dancer, in Bilbao last January, and gave it again in Madrid in July. His was one of the very few flamenco companies to emerge this year.

Merche Esmeralda and the **Ballet Región de Murcia** presented their new repertoire this year, with a mixed programme that included classical works by Rosita Segovia and Victoria Eugenia. Also presented was Marco Berriel's *El Cielo Protector*, based on Paul Bowles' novel *The Sheltering Sky*, adapted by dance critic Victor Burrell and the choreographer, with music by Rafael Reina. Participating guest artists included flamenco dancer Joaquín Cortés, and Julia Olmedo, formerly with Béjart's Ballet du XX Siècle. Major changes are in store for the company in 1993: in August Merche Esmeralda announced her resignation as artistic director and ballet-mistress and no replacement has yet been named.

Carmen Cortés premiered and toured her *Cantes de Ida y Vuelta* with funding from the Comunidad de Madrid and Spain's Quincentennial Commission. *Cantes de Ida y Vuelta* are flamenco songs and dances that were produced by the melding of musical traditions of Spain and her former colonies, a theme that has inspired several flamenco artists in 1992.

In Seville, **Mario Maya** and his company had a new programme to offer this year, *3 Movimientos Flamencos*, in which a rhythmic study and two narrative episodes are combined. Maya was chosen by the Spanish Ministry of Culture as the 1992 recipient of the country's National Dance Award, while outstanding veteran dancer and choreographer Antonio was honoured for his lifetime achievements with a Gold Medal of Merit in Fine Arts.

Flamenco enthusiasts should be aware that Madrid's club La Zambra Flamenco Tablao occasionally schedules a month of late-night performances by some of the country's most outstanding young dancers. A recent programme included Cristobal Reyes, El Grilo, El Toleo, Adrián and Joaquín Cortés, with nine musicians. As the crowd which fills the room at 2 am indicates, the dancing is well worth missing a few hours of sleep.

The 1991/92 season was a difficult one for classical ballet in Spain. Nacho Duato, director of the **Ballet Lírico Nacional**, kept the contemporary focus of the company, trimmed the existing ranks, and invited some new dancers to join the ensemble. The company toured Spain, Italy, Mexico and Venezuela, giving about 75 performances. It's December 1991 season introduced Hans van Manen's *Bits and Pieces* and Jirí Kylián's *Stamping Ground* to Madrid audiences, while adding Duato's *Rassemblement* (created for the Cullberg Ballet in 1990 to music by Haitian composer Toto Bissainthe), and the world premiere of Duato's *Coming Together*. The season was marred by a strike by numerous company members in protest against the abandonment of classical ballet repertoire, the failure to renew several contracts, and the reduction of the number of active dancers in the current programmes. Enough of the cast remained to carry out the performances, but conflicts between management and some dancers remained unresolved.

Another Madrid season at the Teatro Albéniz in April included *13 Gestures of a Body* by Portuguese choreographer Olga Roriz, co-produced by

Madrid Cultural Capital of Europe 1992. The company performed at the Teatro de la Zarzuela in July, with a programme featuring Duato's *Mediterrania*, a choreographic homage to his native Valencia. *Mediterrania* is composed of several segments, each devoted to one aspect of the regional character. The choreography was sponsored by a business venture of the same name that promotes tourism in Valencia, one of the few examples of private funding for dance in Spain. *Mediterrania* was premiered in Valencia, and later toured to Seville and Barcelona among other Spanish cities.

Duato remains a popular figure in Spain and the Ballet Lírico Nacional's new direction has attracted the interest of a wide and appreciative audience. In 1993 the company will officially change its name to Compañía Nacional de Danza, thus reflecting the ensemble's new identity.

The dilemma of who is to carry on with the traditional classical ballet repertoire in Spain is far from solved, however, and distresses many dance lovers, critics, and dancers concerned about their career prospects Spain. Economic pressures forced veteran teacher María de Avila to disband her promising young ballet company. The 1992 Itálica International Dance Festival in Seville opened this year with a gala dedicated to her in which several of her famous pupils, including Trinidad Sevillano and Ana Laguna, performed.

The **Ballet de Victor Ullate** continues to be the most promising private ballet company in the country. The dancers display a level of technical assurance and polished performances worthy of many more mature ensembles. The company's repertoire continues in the line of European neoclassicism and contemporary ballet, although it was announced that for December 1992 several works by Balanchine would be added. The company's season at Madrid's Teatro Albéniz last April showcased Mischa van Hoeke's creation for the young company, *Saeta*, an evocation of the choreographer's impressions of post-war Spain and her people, set to music by Miles Davis and Gil Evans, and beautifully performed. Another addition to the repertoire was principal dancer Eduardo Lao's *Gula Gula* (Mother Earth), a reverent and vigorous paeon to the land, with music by Laplander Marl Boine Persen. Although in this, his second work, Lao displays a strong influence from the Dutch neoclassical school, he shows great promise and is one of the few young choreographers working in the ballet idiom.

Luis Fuente, a principal dancer with the Joffrey Ballet for many years, returned to his native Spain, established a school and, briefly, a company, later collaborating with the Ballet Nacional Clásico in 1983. Currently he directs a young company of his advanced students, who perform his neoclassical/contemporary ballets. The ensemble is beginning to perform in and around Madrid. One of their pieces is *Con Rosalía*, a suite of short dances to well-known Spanish singer-songwriter Amancio Prada's musical adaptation of poems by Galician writer Rosalía de Castro.

The **Ballet de Zaragoza** added the full-length *Coppélia*, with choreography by artistic director Mauro Galíndo, to its repertoire last March. New works to be set on the company include John Cranko's *Opus One*, and *Death and the Maiden* by Robert North.

In Barcelona **Cristina Magnet i Burch**, who uses a neoclassical ballet vocabulary, presented her second full-length production, *Vinyes Verdes Vora el Mar*, inspired by the works of several renowned Catalonian poets, all related by a common, and very Mediterranean theme – the sea. The company's previous work, *Brahms*, toured Catalonia in 1992 and was the subject of a programme filmed by Catalonian regional television.

In the Basque country, the **Ballet de Euskadi** presented their newest production, *Matices*, in Bilbao in October. Choreographed by artistic director Rafael Martí, the ballet consists of a series of neoclassical variations followed by an adaptation of Bizet's *Carmen*.

Russian prima ballerina Maya Plisetskaya, former director of the Ballet Lírico Nacional, gave a series of master classes at Madrid's Teatro Albéniz with a focus on the interpretation of major roles in classical ballet. During the closing ceremony Plisetskaya had harsh words about the fate of ballet in Spain and urged teachers and students to fight for the creation of a national classical ballet company if the Ballet Lírico Nacional continued in its present vein.

Amid the gloomy prospects for Spanish classical ballet, one bright note was the first prize at Lausanne's 1992 International Dance Competition won by 19-year-old Spaniard Yuri Yanowsky, son of dancers Anatol Yanowsky and Carmen Robles, directors of the Canary Islands' Ballet del Atlántico (now no longer in existence).

The year 1992 has seen intense activity for many of Spain's contemporary dance choreographers. The demand for new productions increased along with possibilities of local or national coproduction, because of the special events scheduled in Madrid, Seville and Barcelona. While some companies may have benefited from additional international attention focused on Spain because of the Quincentennial of Columbus's voyage to America, little has changed regarding the possibilities of survival for these dance companies, or the creation of a much-needed theatre network for dance.

Expo 92 left Seville with an immense open-air auditorium and the smaller, more flexible Teatro Central–Hispano, which has been devoted to new trends in theatre and dance since its inauguration in April. In this capacity it coproduced several new works by local and international choreographers. Unfortunately, plans for turning the theatre over to the Centro Andaluz de Teatro include little or no provisions for dance programming. Expo 92 offered Spanish choreographers another performing outlet through 'Jóvenes Valores del Siglo XX' (Young Talent of the 20th Century), coordinated by singer/actor Miquel Bosé. This showcase for young performers gave nine Spanish contemporary dance companies an opportunity to present their work this summer before a large audience in an informal setting.

In other parts of Andalusia **Malaga Danzateatro**, directed by Josep Mitjans, presented resident choreographer Thome Araujo's full-length *Cronocromía*, the company's fifth production, during a week-long programme of contemporary dance at that city's Teatro Municipal Miguel de Cervantes.

Valencia's two major dance companies, **Ananda Dansa** and **Vianants Dansa** each presented new works this season. Ananda's *Borgia Imperante* explored the Borgia dynasty through the effective amalgam of dance and theatre that has become the company's trademark. It opened at the Teatro Central–Hispano in June, coproduced by Expo 92 with regional and national cultural councils. Gracel Meneu's Vianants Dansa initiated a choreographic partnership with Valencian choreographer Antonio Aparisi (first prize winner of the Certamen Coreográfico de Madrid 1990) for π, closely based on Carlos Santos' vibrant, sometimes antic musical and vocal score. **Vicente Sáez** also worked out of Valencia last winter before premiering *Uadi* in Gerona and Madrid. *Uadi* uses the primitive and timeless sensuality of the desert as a motivating force, and was coproduced by government agencies from Valencia and Barcelona, as well as the Biennale de la Danse de Lyon.

Madrid's designation as Cultural Capital of Europe during 1992 provided local companies with several new choreographic events and reinforced dance programming throughout the year with over a dozen performance series and initiatives. A retrospective look at some of the capital's young contemporary dance companies held at the Teatro Pradillo in January and February kicked off a year of unprecedented activity for the city's dance ensembles. Eight local groups participated in an audience development programme that reached over 15,000 youngsters, with more than 50 ballet, contemporary and Spanish dance performances. During the city's annual 'Madrid en Danza' festival six Madrid-based choreographers created site-specific works, performed at various intervals on the same day throughout the city. The project captured the attention of 2500 spectators, as well as heavy media coverage. In September and October an exhibition was held that brought part of dance impresario Juan María Bourio's immense collection of Spanish dance memorabilia (spanning a period from 1930–1980) to the dance world's attention, a first attempt to create some sort of dance documentation in the field in this country. Dancer-choreographer **Ana Yepes** brought her *Zarandanzas*, created in collaboration with Ris et Danceries and Francine Lancelot, to Madrid's Festival de Otoño in October. The Franco-Spanish coproduction illustrates the mutual influences and

Gracel Meneu dancing in her own choreography, *Solos*, for Vianants Danza.

PHOTO: P. P. HERNÁNDEZ

development of Baroque dance in both countries. During November a total of 33 companies participated in the 'Tribuna de la Danza', a showcase held at the Centre Cultural Galileo, created to offer local groups a long-awaited opportunity to present their latest productions to Madrid audiences and presenters. The other major event in November was a week-long project devoted to the Escuela Bolera, Spain's eighteenth-century dance style in which elements of popular dance and classical ballet were melded. Danced in soft slippers and with castanets, the Escuela Bolera undoubtedly influenced the classical ballet repertoire. The event, presented by Madrid Cultural Capital of Europe and the Spanish Ministry of Culture's National Institute for Performing Arts and Music (INAEM), included conferences and seminars, master classes, an exhibition, a catalogue and special performances at the Teatro de la Zarzuela with the Ballet Nacional and guest artists. It was the first project devoted to this aspect of Spanish dance heritage.

Also in Madrid, **Blanca Calvo** premiered her second full-length work, *Detrás del Viento*, at the Sala Olimpia in October 1991, coproduced by the Festival de Otoño. The Centro de Difusión de la Música Contemporánea produced a compact disc of composer Javier López de Guereña's original score.

Madrid's contemporary dance companies, although suffering from the same economic and touring problems as always, did manage to be quite visible at local theatres. This year's 'Madrid en Danza' festival was devoted almost entirely to Spanish contemporary dance. **10 y 10** presented their newest production *Alguien Ha Sido Herido*, which comprised two pieces, one each by artistic directors Pedro Berdäyes and Mónica Runde. Both dealt with issues of human sexuality and individuality, using striking visual elements and images.

Veteran teacher and choreographer **Pilar Sierra** received a grant from the Comunidad de Madrid to restage *Las Brujas*, conceived in the style of German expressionism. It was presented in Madrid in November. **Sierra and Tomeu Vergés** each premiered a quartet on a shared programme at the Sala Olimpia during 'Madrid en Danza', thus completing an annual series of commissioned work by the INAEM.

Béjart alumnus Marco Berriel regrouped his company **Foro's**, collaborating with outstanding young Flamenco dancer Joaquín Cortés, together with Lola Greco and Julia Olmedo. *De Amor y Muerte. . .* featured three short works: *Romance del Amargo*, a duet for the choreographer and Cortés based on García Lorca's famous poem; a solo for Lola Greco to music by young composer Rafael Reina; and *Trio*, inspired by Sartre's *No Exit*. Foro's was one of the most popular companies with 'Madrid en Danza' audiences, attracted by these four excellent performers.

Olga Mesa, a former Certamen Coreográfico de Madrid prizewinner, premiered *Lugares Intermedios* at the Teatro Pradillo during 'Madrid en Danza'. This very personal, intense and moving solo was taken to Glasgow in November.

Debra Greenfield, first prizewinner of the Certamen Coreográfico de Madrid 1991 was invited, as is the custom, along with her company **Fuga**, to perform a full programme at the 1992 Certamen. This year's jury, headed by Jennifer Muller, awarded first prize to Iñaki Azpillaga, while second and third prizes went, respectively, to Roberto Gómez from Tarragona, and Susana Casenave from Madrid. In 1992 the Laban Centre in London contributed a new scholarship to this national choreography competition organized by Paso a 2.

The Sala Olimpia continued its 'Danza en Diciembre' winter series. In 1991 it included a mixed evening of short works by local choreographers Antonia Andreu, Blanca Calvo, Carmen Werner, María José Ribot and Carmen Senra, as well as 10 y 10. Also included was *Julieta*, by **Pablo Ventura** (born in the Canary Islands and trained at London's The Place). *Columpio*, by **Adolfo Vargas** and **Helena Berthelius** (former Certamen Coreográfico de Madrid winners) was also presented, as was **Lanónima Imperial**'s *Afanya't a Poc a Poc*, choreographer Juan Carlos García's latest full-length piece for the Barcelona-based company. *Afanya't* toured extensively in Europe in 1992. Lanónima later presented an unusual mixed bill with choreography by artistic director García, Clara Andermatt and Artur Villalba, during Barcelona's Olympic Arts Festival this summer.

Also in Catalonia, Toni Mira and his modern company **Nats Nus** performed Mira's fourth production *Esta Tarde VI Llover* at the Olympic Arts Festival, a coproducer, after a preview in Heidelberg last May.

The **Ballet Contemporani de Barcelona** took part in 'Madrid en Danza' last May with *Fetitxe*, by artistic director Amelia Rolunda. The piece featured an acoustically sensitive floor that played an active part in both the choreography and the score. *Aquí No Hi Ha Cap Angel*, **Ramón Oller**'s newest choreography for his company, continues in the tender and poetic vein that characterizes Oller's recent work, this time taking his inspiration from texts by Catalonian novelist Mercé Rodoreda.

Danat Danza's *Kaspar* examines the legend of Kaspar Hauser in choreographers Sabine Dahrendorf and Alfonso Ordóñez's vigorous and inimitable style. One of Spain's most popular contemporary dance companies with international audiences, Danat tours extensively abroad and is noted for its seamless integration of both dance and production values. In October the company won a special mention from UNESCO as the outstanding dance production at Expo 92.

More than ever, dance from Spain was present at international festivals.

Jacob's Pillow and the American Dance Festivals, among the most prestigious dance events in the US, both devoted special attention to Spain this past summer. Barcelona's **Mal Pelo, Senza Tempo, Mudances** and **Danat Danza** all performed at Jacob's Pillow, in addition to Madrid's **Mónica Valenciano and Marga Guergué**, whose duet *Constanza* was coproduced by the Pillow. ADF extended an invitation to Danat and Valenciano, also staging a shared programme with Flamenco dancer **José Greco Jr.** and young tap dance star **Savion Glover**.

By far the most extensive international event devoted to Spain was this year's Biennale de la Danse de Lyon, held in September 1992, in which 18 different Spanish ensembles performed, in addition to international companies such as the Cullberg Ballet and the Ballet Nacional de Cuba, which gave programmes with Spanish themes.

Space for dance continues to be an important issue in Spain. The closing of studio/performance space La Fábrica two years ago left Barcelona without a venue for informal presentations. In 1992 the city also lost Teatre Obert, a government-funded production agency that had nurtured many young choreographers. Last June, however, the Generalitat de Catalunya opened L'Espai, a small theatre which will book only local dancers and musicians. A few hours drive north in Gerona, La Nau 18, directed by Anna Rovira is playing an active role in promoting new dance and theatre. In Madrid the Ministry of Culture's Centro Nacional de Nuevas Tendencias Escénicas (Sala Olimpia) and the privately-run Teatro Pradillo lent much-needed support to contemporary dance companies . The Pradillo's future is uncertain at the time of writing; it would be a great loss for the profession if it were to lose this intimate performing space.

The Asociación de Profesionales de la Danza de la Comunidad de Madrid continues to publish its magazine *Por la Danza* as frequently as its budget permits. A new bimonthly magazine for dance has recently appeared on the scene. *Ballet 2000* is the latest in a series of sister publications (*Ballet 2000* in France and Italy's *Balleto Oggi*). This year the Comunidad de Madrid also published the country's first comprehensive guidebook for students and professional dancers.

A one-day national strike by performing artists in December 1991, and the continued efforts of dance professionals to achieve improved touring and funding possibilities (via annual events such as Dansa a Valencia) have yet to produce substantial changes for dance in Spain. Now that the euphoria over the country's spectacular 1992 events has waned, and the effects of a recession are emerging, the dance community will have to reassess its position and strategies for securing those fundamentals necessary for the survival of this art in Spain.

Sweden

Peter Bohlin

The Swedish 1991/92 dance season aroused an unusual number of mixed feelings. Among the wonderful surprises was Goesta Berling's *Saga* (for me the performance of the year), a five-hour piece with two intervals, based on the Nobel Prize-winner Selma Lagerloef's masterpiece of the same name. Staging it in a large barn close to Lagerloef's home in west Sweden's woodlands, Leif Stinnerbom, a folk dance and music specialist and the leader of the small countryside Teater Västanå, chose the three-beat folk dance polka to be the underlying frame of the play, making the actors move and talk in fluent harmony with the live music.

The greatest expectations of the year were evoked by Mats Ek's new creation for the **Cullberg Ballet**: *Carmen*, a one-act ballet (to Shchedrin's hour-long suite) coupled with his *The House of Bernarda Alba* to make a full Spanish evening. I rank *Bernarda*, created in 1978, as one of Mats Ek's *chefs d'oeuvre*: it's still boiling with the passionate, physical eloquence that made me gasp when I first saw it. *Carmen* leaves another impression, appealing, as it were, more to the intellect than to the senses. Again Marie-Louise Ekman's (Ek's long-time design partner) costumes and sets are striking, and again Ek had found a perspective quite his own. His Carmen is a cigar-smoking, liberated woman of modern society, Don José a man of more traditional values, who wants to marry and settle down. Thus Ek has set out, again, to play an exchange game of male and female attitudes.

The ballet starts with Don José's execution. He is brought in blindfolded; the firing squad enters and the men start aiming their guns. But instead of shots there explodes a fiesta. It's an excellent start, and a great surprise. But in the long run the ballet's characters prove to be surprisingly shallow – I miss the passion – and the story is at times interrupted by seemingly meaningless dances performed by girls in candy-box metallic colours. Ek has abandoned a successful way of telling a story (in *Bernarda* no one is ever asking why), while looking for something else. I'm not sure he found it.

The Cullberg Ballet also introduced Kylián's *Stamping Ground* to Sweden. It's the first company outside his own to which Kylián has entrusted the ballet, and the dancers honoured this privilege by dancing it splendidly. Over the years the Cullberg Ballet and the Nederlands Dans Theater have been in close co-operation, exchanging both dancers and pieces.

The Cullberg Ballet is a part, since its creation in 1967, of the National Swedish Theatre Centre, an organization started in 1933 which aims to provide live theatre performances for the whole country. During this season, the centre also produced *Cyberpunk*, an impressive, dynamic creation for young audiences, with choreography, designs, music, heaps of texts, and direction by Patrik Sörling, and a touring triple-bill, *Cascade – a Concert for Dancers*, by Greta Lindholm, in a musical, gentle style quite her own, where the dancers often provide the music themselves. There were also two highly contrasting works by Birgitta Egerbladh, who stops at nothing to make her points: when the subject is vanishing rural society she might cram the stage with objects seldom or never seen in dance, in order to provoke a mix of compassion and laughter.

The Royal Swedish Ballet premiered five pieces. Nils Christe's new *Organ Concerto* was beautiful, although very similar to his previous piece for the company, *Before Nightfall*, with flow, speed and energy. It was given in a dual bill with *Elvira Madigan* by Regina Becks-Friis (the learned specialist in historical dance), who created a truly 'grand spectacle' with a wealth of roles, including those for a full circus, with a tight-rope dancing girl and a ballerina sharing the role of Elvira (who at the turn of the century danced on a rope in a circus in Sweden and ran away with a married officer). The drama ended, like *Mayerling*, with a double suicide.

The ballet was visually superb, in David Walker's elaborate costumes and sets, and the choreographer quite successfully adapted the story to Mahler music, mainly the Fourth Symphony. To the finishing soprano song, little children were playing in heaven, which gave a sweet touch (certainly better than it might sound) to the end. But somehow, the passion got lost, and that's unfortunate in a love story which Sweden is almost legendary in Sweden, and has been the inspiration for many artistic creations. Shortly after the actual bloodshed there was an enormously popular song, and right now there seems to be quite a demand for Elvira Madigan productions: there is one played in a circus tent (with a talkative clown who makes people roar with laughter), a new Swedish musical is announced for autumn 1992, and Robert North, the new artistic director of the **Gothenburg Ballet**, mounted his *Elvira Madigan* for the company. His second full-length ballet this season was a new *Living in America* in three acts devoted to, in proper order, the wild west, the period between the world wars, and today's society. The Gothenburg Ballet also danced the Swedish premiere of North's *Death and the Maiden* and, in a studio performance, gave a contribution to the 1492 celebrations with *Vikings*, a hilariously comic ballet subtitled 'Why the Vikings didn't discover America' – they soon had enough and sailed back home.

For the Royal Swedish Ballet, again, Per Jonsson created two pieces: *Clamavi*, a solo performed only once (to music by Arne Nordheim for the Nordheim Festival in Bergen, Norway) and *Aya's Eye*, a one-hour piece for

Östgötabaletten's *The Firebird,* choreographed by Vlado Juras to music by Igor Stravinsky. The dancers here are Julia Sundberg as the Firebird, and (covered) Joacim Keusch as the Prince.   PHOTO: LESLEY LESLIE-SPINKS

eighteen Royal Ballet dancers, with the addition of a few dancers from Jonsson's own company. The powerful music was specially composed by Sven-David Sandström – the two have worked together successfully on several occasions – but the choreography, frankly, seemed not quite completed. Jonsson's remarkable flow was there all right, but there were many ideas that vanished into thin air.

At the eighteenth-century Drottningholm Theatre Ivo Cramér created, for the 1992 summer season, *Figaro or Almaviva and Love,* in style after an eighteenth-century libretto. Some Royal Ballet dancers showed themselves at their best: Göran Svalberg, back after three years with Béjart Ballet Lausanne in a style new to him; and, above all, Pär Isberg in the role of an elderly man who desperately want to marry. Avoiding all clichés, Isberg acted with wit and choice control.

Indeed, Cramér's year was a busy one. In summer 1991 he premiered *Pantalone and Colombine,* a light ballet pantomime to Mozart music on his own libretto, and in February he premiered, in Strasbourg, *Jason and Medea,* the first Noverre reconstruction in modern times.

The Swedish Ballet School is continually providing new talents. The full-length production of *Don Quixote* was the school's greatest venture so far, and it turned out to be a superb performance, with a treasure of upcoming dancers. The ballet was mounted by Valentina Savina from Moscow, now ballet-mistress at the Royal Swedish Ballet. Hers was the stroke of genius to put girls of all sizes, even the tiniest ones, in the white act, and she had selected a long solo dance for a small ten-year-old girl, who looked like an angel with a ballet technique to match. It's a delight to watch Savina rehearse little Swedish kids, who happily obey her orders in Russian and Spanish: a testimony, again, to ballet's truly international nature. The tenth anniversary of the school's reorganization and integration with the ordinary Swedish school system was also celebrated during the year, with a breathtaking three-hour gala, performed by a remarkable selection of the school's graduates.

In contemporary dance outside the institutions, **Efva Lilja** continues her investigations of water, in creations like *The Well* and *Fara* (which means both 'travel' and 'danger'). *Fara* was performed on a platform attached to four rowing boats hidden under the water surface, in a late evening performance during the 1991 Stockholm Water Festival. Other companies that often perform outdoors are **Tiger** in Stockholm and **Rubicon** in Gothenburg, but the latter also has a permanent stage, Unga Atalante.

The **Modern Dance Theatre** in Stockholm, which has made the winter solstice, and from 1992 also the summer one, the occasion of once-only performances of unexpected concoctions, offered many pieces of contemporary character during the year. Among the most interesting were Claire Parson's staging of Beckett's play *What Where* and her choreography *Quad*.

In the New Swedish Choreography Competition at Stockholm's House of Dance, Parsons attracted the attention of the Eurodance organizers from Mulhouse, and was invited there with *Aria*, in which she plays, as often in her work, conspicuously and deliberately with male versus female attitudes, and with dance versus non-dance. The competition was won by Lena Josefsson, who was born in Zaire of missionary parents, and received her dance education there. With its African background, her contemporary style is a delight in its own right, and her creation *Broken Pieces*, earned her an invitation to the 1992 Bagnolet competition. Also in the competition was Jens Östberg, with his *Drokk* – it doesn't mean anything in Swedish either. Later, during the Dancin' City's Scandinavian Choreography Competition in Copenhagen, he deservedly won the audience's award: he had created a knock-out piece, and the young dancers performed it with all necessary power.

Other Swedish competitions were the 'Young Dancers' Competition' won by Reniie Mirro, and a 'Swedish Folk Dance Composition Competition' won by Eva-Mia Sjölin, who has repeatedly excelled at similar functions.

At the House of Dance in Stockholm, the Dance Museum arranged a video dance festival and the Association Européenne des Historiens de la Danse symposium 'Renovators of Dance and the Genesis of Dance Languages'. The theatre, which in principle is not a producing one, had a first successful try at coproducing with *Hinagata, The Language of the Sphinx*, by Carlotta Ikeda and her all-female butoh company **Ariadone**.

The House of Dance also arranged its first Folk Dance Festival, for which Aleksander Dybowski created *Open Senses*, a folk dance suite stressing parallel and similar ideas in different European traditions.

Margaretha Åsberg was appointed the first professor of choreography at the National College of Dance – but at the same time her theatre subsidies were cut by half!

Indeed, there were some serious set-backs during the season. The **Wind Witches** were strangled by financial difficulties, ironically just after one of their best performances ever, *Swimming in a Lonely Night*.

In **Malmö**, the City Theatre's ballet didn't have a single premiere, and there was an open war declared between politicians and artistic directors of the theatre. In the end Jonas Kåge, the ballet director, decided he got good enough terms and agreed to stay for another three years.

Vlado Juras, the best director the **Norrkoeping-Linkoeping Ballet** has ever had, decided he had had enough of the theatre's mismanagement, and left. With never-ending enthusiasm and conviction, and with sound ideas (he created a *Firebird*, to Stravinsky's music, aiming at audiences from six years old!), he brought out the best in the ballet, found new audiences and selected a good repertory – such that at the 1991 celebration for Nadine Gordimer, Nobel Prizewinner for Literature, the company was invited to dance Mats Ek's *Soweto*. But when the theatre started to get into economic difficulties, the ballet was the first to suffer.

But worst of all was the collapse of the idea of the House of Dance in Stockholm. The intended trinity of a dance museum, theatre and resident company (the Cullberg Ballet) came to nothing when Mats Ek, having asked an additional favour and not got it, offered his resignation (effective from summer 1993) from the post as artistic director of the Cullberg Ballet and decided to keep the company at the premises in south Stockholm. The fact that he had turned Cullberg Ballet into an attraction for the whole world apparently was not enough.

Switzerland

Richard Merz

Three of the Swiss ballet companies in state-run theatres started under new directorship in the autumn. For the small group of dancers in Berne this was the end of three years of constant change; whereas in **Basel** it meant the end of their greatest epoch of dance history, and the audience was very sceptical if they would see any dancing of a level comparable to which they had been accustomed for almost twenty years with Spoerli and his company.

So Youri Vàmos was starting from a very difficult position in Basel. Luckily, he is especially capable in the field of full-length ballets, the kind of dance performance the audience likes most – and even produced three of them in his first year. Since, from the beginning, he was able to present a company highly skilled both in technique and expression, plus exciting soloists – above all the brilliant Joyce Cuoco – he won his audience round with flying colours. *Spartacus* as well as *Vathek* were successful as well as exciting dancing shows, whereas in *Lucidor* Vàmos convincingly showed his skill in telling a story. Those looking for something 'new' were not much pleased with this work, but those who appreciated a well-constructed piece liked the performance. On the whole, Vàmos's first season met with tremendous success with Basel audiences.

Story-telling ballets were also the goal of the new director at **Berne**, François Klaus. Being a comparative newcomer to choreography after an outstanding career as a soloist with Neumeier in Hamburg, he clearly lacked the skill to get a story across to the audience. In *The Little Mermaid* he was not of course the first choreographer to prove helpless with the problem of dealing with legless sea creatures. For his *Juans Traum* ('The Dream of Juan'), bringing the subject of Don Juan on stage, he had the interesting idea of showing a modern young man who, because of his actual difficulties with women, sees himself in his dreams as Don Juan. But unfortunately Klaus did not find a convincing enough form to make this idea work. Nevertheless, in both productions he presented colourful pictures and scenes of easy-flowing dancing in Neumeier style, with a promising company and a wonderful soloist, Martin Schläpfer.

Whereas in both Basel and Bern the audiences were enthusiastic (or at least very pleased) with the ballet on their stages, Bernd Roger Bienert's work in **Zürich** met with highly mixed feelings. He is almost obsessed with the grey old idea that the highest goal in art is to be 'new' and 'different'. Thus he uses the bodies of his dancers in such a twisted, aggressive way

The ballet company of the Stadttheater Bern in *Hamamelis Coxinus, Zauberer*, with Marc Rosenkranz, Stephanie Black, Paul de Masson and Sônia Melo.

PHOTO: G. ELMER

that people begin to feel sorry for them, and become rather concerned for their health. Given these impressions during performances, the widespread rumours of unusually heavy tensions in the company – even for the ballet world – astonished no one. And there is no way to get any useful information about the situation – the opera house refuses to talk about it, and the dancers are scared to make public statements.

So ballet only seemed to go on smoothly and without problems on the happy stage of Zürich opera house; first in a new scenic work, *Unruhiges Wohnen* (which means something like 'Restless Homelife') to words by Elfriede Jelinek and music by Roman Haubenstock-Ramati, full of strong, depressing images of cruelty in human relationships. It had a rather strange approach to Mozart, bringing together the Piano Concerto KV 482, the *Requiem*, and huge movements of heavy pieces of decor behind the restless dancing and running company. Then there was *Josephs Legende*, full of tremendous power and sensuality; Joseph being raped in every imaginable way by the wife of Potiphar, sexually completely out of her mind. The character of the legend was completely lost, its place being taken by some kind of ennobled sadomasochistic porn, which would probably have been considered outrageous as a video, and thus forbidden in Switzerland, but

193

Compagnie Philippe Saire in Saire's 1990 piece *Don Quixote*.   PHOTO: Y. LERESCHE

as a piece of culture on the stage of an honourable opera houses and to a score by Richard Strauss, was rather highly acclaimed.

Bienert uses music in the same way as Béjart: as something to be used for his own purposes in any way he wants. It may be no coincidence that in the companies of these great users, dancers meet with considerable problems. Some years ago, moving from Brussels to Lausanne, Béjart felt like having a big company with lots of dancers, 60 of them – and of course he got it. Now his mood has changed, he does not 'like the word "company" ' any more. No, he wants to have a school in Lausanne and a related 'ensemble of 20 professional dancers'. The 40 others are simply dropped. There is no further use of them. So the era of the exciting, highly skilled but on the whole rather phoney Ballet Béjart Lausanne came to an unexpectedly sudden end this summer; a fact which was considered by one Swiss critic to be no great artistic loss, but a heavy social one, since the gathering for a Béjart performance was always a big social event with people so delight-fully mixed: made-up, in expensive Versace model dresses, or in blue jeans and redeemer sandals.

In **Lucerne** another era came to an end after three years of directorship by Ben van Cauwenbergh. The era of his predecessor, Riccardo Duce, had been marked by important choreographic achievements. Choreographi-cally, neither van Cauwenbergh nor much less Valery Panov could excel, both of them looking, whatever the music and the plot, simply for occa-sions to develop effective dancing. But dance-wise, Lucerne never had such a great time. This small group showed classical dance on a high virtuoso level, and also presented an authentic-looking *West Side Story*. And of course, Lucerne has never had before (and probably never will have again) a Kirov ballerina as a company member for three years, as they have now with Galina Panova.

In this fast flow of beginning and ending eras, only in **St Gallen** and **Geneva** was there a steady building up of a well-trained company to give a high standard of performance. Both directors, of course, are fighting with difficulties: Marianne Fuchs in St Gallen has to overcome all the problems of the severely limited possibilities of this small theatre; Gradimir Pankov has the constant threat of his company being disbanded through lack of money in the budget of the poor city of Geneva.

The dance profession has always faced financial problems, but now the situation has grown much tighter, as cultural budgets are being cut back everywhere. Of course, the independent scene is the first to suffer from this situation: to survive as an independent company is more difficult than ever. Some choreographers who gave all their energy to dance for years have given up or are considering it. But even in these times some are going on, are finding their way, like **Philippe Saire** with his small company, founded in 1986. In 1990 his *Don Quixote* met with success both with critics and audiences, but it is with his *Vie et moeurs du cameleon nocturne* that he showed a really well-structured and vividly performed choreographic work in the otherwise somewhat dull landscape of independent dance in Switzerland. The question remains: how to be fresh and innovative in choreography, and strong and bright in performance, when most of the energy is spent getting money to survive?

United Kingdom

The Birmingham Royal Ballet
Mary Clarke
The Birmingham Royal Ballet, now so happily settled in its new home, the Birmingham Hippodrome, describes the theatre as its 'best date', drawing excellent houses and with a sold-out *Nutcracker*, in Peter Wright's staging, at Christmas. The number of performances has been increased from five to six weeks, and there was also widespread touring throughout the country. A disappointment was that there was no Covent Garden season in 1992, and although the company paid return visits to Sadler's Wells – where it retains a devoted audience – the small stage meant that one of the company's great achievements of the year, the revival of Massine's *Choreartium*, could not be shown in London.

It had long been an ambition of Wright's to stage *Choreartium*, Massine's great symphonic ballet of 1933, especially after the success of Tatiana Leskova's revival of the same choreographer's *Les Présages* at the Paris Opéra. Leskova, who knew the ballet from her days with de Basil's Ballet Russe company, came to supervise the staging, and the result was not only a triumph for the company, but also did much to reinstate Massine as one of the most important choreographers of this century. (His reputation, once so great, diminished in recent years as he came to be regarded merely as the creator of *ballets bouffes*.)

Choreartium, danced to Brahms' Fourth Symphony, was the second of Massine's symphonic ballets, and one of the most powerful, employing vast resources to state heroic themes and strong emotions. The revival was faithful to the choreographer – it was rewarding to find that Leskova's contemporaries, the ballerinas and dancers of the 1930s, recognized the authenticity of the staging – but in place of the original designs by Terechkovich and Lourié, never much liked, new ones, similar in style but cleverly adapted to the taste of today, were provided by Nadine Baylis.

The first programme, on 2 October 1991, shared a programme with

196

Balanchine's delectable *Divertimento No. 15* and the company's fine production of *Petrushka*. It reaffirmed Peter Wright's policy of keeping a balanced repertory of full-evening ballets with mixed programmes representing different choreographers, and BRB seems to have succeeded in the difficult task of 'selling' the triple bills.

In that same October season, Kenneth MacMillan restaged and revised an early work, *The Burrow*, based on the Kafka story, which had given Lynn Seymour her first major creation. In new designs by Nicholas Georgiadis, it proved a fine addition to the repertory, and gave Marion Tait, the senior ballerina of the company and an artist of rare quality, a superb role as The Woman, the one character who faces up to the grim fatality of the ending.

MacMillan was also to give the company a full-evening ballet, namely a revival, in new designs, of his *Romeo and Juliet*. First staged in Birmingham on 1 June 1992, the production suffered from a number of injuries and recasting, but brought a delightful reading of Juliet from Nina Ananiashvili. She should have been partnered by Alexei Fadeyechev of the Bolshoi, but he was injured, so Kevin O'Hare had to step in at short notice, and even Peter Wright's bold decision to give a chance, as Juliet, to his promising young ballerina Monica Zamora, was thwarted by injury.

The new designs were by a young designer, Paul Andrews, who set the ballet in the early fifteenth century, and turned for inspiration to Italian paintings of that time. The choreographer does, of course, dictate the shape of the settings and also the necessity to provide a production that will tour easily to the larger theatres where the company appears. The permanent set and the more intimate scenes were well realized and the costuming for both nobles and townspeople effective realizations of period dress. Andrews has not yet, however, found a way of dressing the classical dancers in costumes which allow freedom of movement but blend convincingly with the more realistically dressed ensembles.

Education work in the Birmingham area continued and the spread of Junior Associate classes for youngsters hoping for entry to the Royal Ballet School was welcome. Wright again found time for choreographic experiment and showed new pieces by Graham Lustig (*Inscape*, to music by Peter McGowan with designs by Henk Schut), and Oliver Hindle, whose promising *Sacred Symphony* was followed by *Dark Horizons* (made possible by Peter Wright's Digital Premier Award of 1991) which dealt with American Indians forced to live on reservations. It was for an all-male cast, and not so much a narrative work as an attempt to evoke the misery of a conquered race. Danced to Shostakovich's Chamber Symphony in C, in evocative designs by Peter Farley, which suggested the great plains, the choreography drew on primitive dance traditions but not specifically on the rich resources of the American Indian inheritance.

For the first time, and as an indication of BRB's new identity, the press

197

Samira Saidi and members of The Birmingham Royal Ballet in their production of Massine's *Choreartium* staged by Tatiana Leskova.   PHOTO: LESLIE E. SPATT

conference for the 1992/93 seasons was held in Birmingham. The plans announced indicated a continuation of present policies, with a revival of Kurt Jooss's *The Green Table*, an international dance season to be hosted in Birmingham, and a collaboration with The Birmingham Conservatoire to encourage young conductors in the art of conducting for ballet.

English National Ballet
Jann Parry

In the two years of Ivan Nagy's artistic directorship, English National Ballet's once-interesting repertoire has dwindled into banality. Nagy inherited an alarming financial deficit from his predecessor, Peter Schaufuss, which has meant that no money has been available to commission expensive new productions. The deficit had been substantially reduced by the end of the 1991/92 season – but the company cannot justify its continued existence if it fails to offer audiences (as well as its own dancers) fresh insights into ballet as a creative art form. Other companies with equally stringent financial constraints (Northern Ballet Theatre and London City

Ballet, for example) have found ways of refreshing their repertoires with stimulating approaches to the 'classics'.

ENB sorely needs new productions of *Swan Lake* and *The Sleeping Beauty*, which Nagy intends to introduce as soon as he can. The company relies on *The Nutcracker* as a box-office family favourite, with a profitable annual Christmas season at the Royal Festival Hall in London, as well as a tour of the regions. Schaufuss's over-complicated production has been replaced by Ben Stevenson's version, adapted from his Houston Ballet production. It is a safe, traditional account of the ballet, with a more boisterous family party than the sedate Royal Ballet affair at Covent Garden, and an attractive snowflake scene.

Stevenson's *Cinderella*, however, cannot bear comparison with Frederick Ashton's version for the Royal Ballet, with which it has much in common, including the same designer (David Walker). Stevenson's account first entered the (then) London Festival Ballet repertoire in 1973 and has never been a great artistic success, though the title alone draws families with young children. ENB has plenty of promising Cinderellas, none of whom could make much impression in the 1992 revival: the best they can do is dance prettily and unmemorably, just as they do in *The Nutcracker*.

During the 1991/92 season, which could have been the occasion to salute Europe and Britain's presidency of the European Community, ENB acquired or revived no fewer than five ballets by Ben Stevenson, who has worked in the United States since 1968 (when he left London Festival Ballet). Nagy seems intent on turning a company that now calls itself English National Ballet into a replica of a regional American ballet troupe. His only attempt at innovative programming, at the London Coliseum in June 1992, included two joke-pieces by American David Parsons (*The Envelope* and *Sleep Study*) and Stevenson's all-male *L*. Stevenson was thanked in the programme note for donating the ballet (made as a tribute to Liza Minelli) but one jaundiced British reviewer suggested that he should be paid to take it right back.

There were, however, two commissioned works on the same programme by choreographers who could count as British or European. Robert North's *A Stranger I Came* covered much the same emotional and choreographic ground as his *Death and the Maiden*, made more than a decade previously: Schubert songs and piano music, the figure of Death claiming his mortal victim. Danish-born Kim Brandstrup (who trained and has mainly worked in Britain) based his *White Nights* on a short story by Dostoyevsky. A young man, updated as a photographer who sees the world only through his camera lens, falls in love with a girl whose heart belongs to another. The man is forced, briefly, to confront the real world before retreating into isolation. The commissioned score, by British composer Gerard McBurney, uses piano music by Mussorgsky, which puts the

199

work in the same romantic vein as North's Schubert ballet: both choreographers chose Josephine Jewkes for the leading woman's role, which made for an ill-balanced programme.

Jewkes, who was finally made a principal in mid-1992 after ten years with the company, brings emotional depth to her roles (which include Juliet, Tatiana in *Onegin* and Anne Frank) after a career held back by injury. Another home-grown asset is Freya Dominic, who rejoined ENB in 1985 to perform character roles while pursuing an acting career at the same time. Among the newcomers developing within the ranks is Rebecca Sewell, obviously gifted but still immature as an interpreter. The brief return of Trinidad Sevillano, now with Boston Ballet, to dance Ashton's Juliet was a reminder of how much ENB lost with her departure.

Nagy brought in a number of young Cubans, most of whom – Carlos Acosta, Ana Lobe and Lourdes Novoa – returned home after the summer of 1992. José Manuel Carreño, who has become an elegant romantic lead as well as a virtuoso technician, remains as a resident guest artist. He has usually been paired with Maria Teresa del Real, from Miami, who is a feisty, reliable dancer, but no Giselle or Odette. Yelena Pankova, ex-Kirov, who is a lovely Giselle, left ENB in 1991, and Ludmila Semenyaka, ex-Bolshoi, in 1992. There were no challenging roles for her to dance, so, like other guest artists, she was unable to contribute much to younger dancers' development.

The company's greatest assets include two married couples who complement each other admirably: Renata Calderini and Maurizio Bellezza, who first joined ENB in 1981 and who were invited to return in 1990; and Agnes Oaks and Thomas Edur from the Estonian State Ballet, who joined in 1990. Both couples have benefited from dedicated coaching before they joined ENB, but there has been little opportunity for them to show their range, other than in Cranko's *Onegin* and *The Taming of the Shrew* and some of the Fokine repertoire (which has not been seen at its best for quite a while).

The ENB School, established by Peter Schaufuss in 1988, continues, although its principal, ex-dancer Lucia Truglia, was abruptly asked to leave in the summer of 1992. She has been replaced by Kathryn Wade, an experienced teacher from the Royal Ballet School.

London Contemporary Dance Theatre
Judith Mackrell

For London Contemporary Dance Theatre early 1991 to mid-1992 was a time of retrospection and planning, celebration and uncertainty, consolidation and change. The period began with the death of its figurehead, Martha Graham; it encompassed the radical upheaval of a new artistic director, Nancy Duncan, and it was concluded with an unwelcome question mark as Duncan announced that she was leaving the company in June 1992.

When Martha Graham died in April 1991 the world rushed to pay tribute to her monumental life and career. Coincidentally though, one indirect celebration of Graham's immense legacy had been planned months before she actually died – in London Contemporary Dance Theatre's April 1991 season *10 for 1*. This was officially launched as a tribute to Robin Howard – the man who had fallen in love with Graham's work in the 1950s and who had dedicated his life to getting modern dance established in this country. It was he of course who founded the Contemporary Dance Trust, of which LCDT is one part – and *10 for 1* was a testimony to the vision that had motivated him. It showed three decades of new choreography which had been created by dancers nurtured through the Trust and it showed a company of performers who ranked among the finest in the world as instruments of modern dance.

Yet the season also celebrated the woman who had first inspired Howard, for at the core of its first two programmes was a performance of Graham's seminal 1930 solo *Lamentation*, a credo of the intensely expressive and unsparing dance which she was to make her own. More history was reconstructed in Kate Coyne and Sheron Wray's shared performance of *Harmonica Breakdown*, the 1938 work by Jane Dudley who danced with Graham in the 1930s and 1940s and who was appointed Director of Contemporary Dance at the London School of Contemporary Dance in 1970. And almost all the rest of the season was made up of work created by members of the company, who have all been variously indebted to the Graham legacy.

Robert Cohan artistic director of LCDT from 1967/89, and a long-time dancer in Graham's own company, was represented by *Forest*, one of his finest, most evocative and sensuous works. Made in 1977, its knotted sculptural shapes suggest a primitive and preconscious form of life; its wary, quivering movements evoke the wildness of animals, and a secret erotic duet at the centre of the work speaks powerfully of some profound ritual coupling.

Among Cohan's first generation of students was Richard Alston, an art student who came to the London Contemporary Dance School with little dance training but big ambitions to be a choreographer. The second piece of dance that Alston made there, *Something to Do* (1969), was taken into the company repertoire and was revived for this season. In many ways it stands as a rejection of the whole Graham basis of his training – a piece about nothing but the activity of dancing. Yet Alston's determination to pursue his own vision, leaving LCDT in 1972 to set up his own company, was entirely in the Graham spirit of single-minded artistic rebellion.

After Alston, the school continued to produce new choreographers, including Darshan Singh Bhuller, Jonathan Lunn, Kim Brandstrup and Yael Flexer, who were all represented in April's three programmes. The season also saw the launch of a new Robin Howard Trust, designed to fund the creation of more new choreography and to pave the way for more Cohans, Alstons, even a future Graham. Yet for all its deservedly triumphant celebration of past successes, *10 for 1* took place at a time when the company itself was in a state of limbo, – its previous artistic director Dan Wagoner having left after less than two years with the company, and leaving no new director in place.

At this point, the company was not only looking for a new director, it was also looking for a new direction, for during the 1980s many critics were starting to feel that its repertoire was increasingly out of touch with new developments in modern dance. Nancy Duncan, who finally took over as director in August 1991, was appointed largely because of her long experience in discovering and commissioning new work. Though she had never run an enterprise as big as LCDT, she had, since 1982, run a small repertory company called CoDanceCo in New York. Here she had presented early works from a number of important choreographers, including Mark Morris and Susan Marshall.

Unlike Cohan and Wagoner though, Duncan was not a choreographer, so the vision she would be imposing on the company would not be that of a creator. Around the time of her appointment there was talk of an association with Mark Morris who would work closely with the school and mount some works on the company. Unfortunately this fell through and Duncan was left with the task of forging a new image for the company by herself.

Her first autumn season had to be assembled at very short notice, and was never meant to be a statement of intent. Duncan simply added to the repertoire three American works which were both available and familiar to her – Nina Wiener's *Wind Devil*, Arnie Zane's *Freedom of Information (Section 3)* and Dan Wagoner's *Flee as a Bird*.

Of these, *Wind Devil* proved the most interesting, a whirl of impulse and energy that invoked the power of desert whirlwinds. Wagoner's piece was an amiable and characteristically eccentric re-run of familiar jazz dance motifs, while *Freedom of Information* was a stylish, exhausting and ultimately trivial work-out for the dancers.

Critically, this choice of repertoire wasn't a huge success, though everyone commented on how good the dancers looked – very un-British in their fast, hard and rangy energy. It was generally acknowledged too that Duncan had a difficult job in front of her in creating a brand new image for the company – one that both encompassed the sharp end of new dance and also remained accessible to the audience. Part of Duncan's problem lay in the fact that most of today's dance radicals (Anne Teresa De Keersmaeker, Wim Vandekeybus or Lloyd Newson) work with their own hand-picked group of dancers. They very rarely work with, or give their choreography to other companies.

Duncan's plans for the 1992 autumn season, though, did show initiative. She managed to secure Mark Morris' *Motorcade*, a work set to music by Saint-Saëns, which was first choreographed for Baryshnikov's White Oak Project; also Christopher Bruce's *Rooster*, a mix of classical and modern dance set to the Rolling Stones; and a brand new work from Amanda Miller, a choreographer much admired in Europe though scarcely known over here.

With Duncan's departure however, the unfortunate sense of limbo which preceded her arrival is likely to return and to dog the rest of LCDT's year. Questions will doubtless be asked about why a company with so much prestige, with so many resources, with so many fine and committed dancers, cannot keep an artistic director. Is it simply LCDT's future that seems precarious or the whole future of large modern repertory companies?

Yet, uncertain as LCDT's identity currently looks, the rest of the Trust's activities have continued to go from strength to strength. The Place Theatre has remained a crucial support to the modern dance scene – not only showing important new British work but forging extremely promising links with European and American choreographers. The School too has been prominent in the foreign scene, with students participating in the International Theatre School Festival in Amsterdam during June 1992, and with members of the teaching staff beginning work on a three-year British-Czechoslovakia Dance Project. Thus, whatever internal troubles may currently be afflicting LCDT, the Trust itself remains faithful to Howard's vision – nurturing a British dance scene that looks not only forward but outwards, not just to the present but to the future too.

Northern Ballet Theatre
Bill Harpe
How many of the world's classical ballet companies have yet come to terms with the fact that the most powerful art form of the century has been film? Britain's Northern Ballet Theatre has certainly recognized that important fact since 1987 when Christopher Gable – former Royal Ballet dancer, former actor, and former film star – took over as artistic director.

Not that the company repertoire since his arrival looks like it has been put together in Hollywood. Indeed the two major creations since his arrival have been full-length ballets which feature in the repertoire of almost all of the world's great ballet companies. But it is the way in which Northern Ballet Theatre has recreated *Romeo and Juliet* and *Swan Lake* which makes the difference.

Romeo and Juliet (which entered the company's repertoire in February 1991) follows the familiar Shakespearean scenario and is set to the familiar rhythms and melodies of Prokofiev's score. But the story is told in contemporary fashion. The young lovers may at times be conventionally romantic but they also live out some of today's eroticism on stage. The costumes may be replete with historical references but they also look as if Michael Jackson might take a shine to them. The fighting scenes may involve swords and daggers but they also have a touch of the realism of television drama about them. However, the undoubted popular appeal of this production lies not only in the fact that the individual scenes set in ancient Verona are presented in a new and accessible way. The key to the production is in the way in which these scenes are connected. For the story-line moves like a feature film – cutting, mixing, and fading from scenes of violence to scenes of love with the flowing choreography of the cinema. And it is these links with today's world of film which enable the work to communicate so directly both to audiences who are familiar with dance, and to audiences who, though unfamiliar with dance, are familiar with film. And since virtually all of today's audiences are familiar with film, Northern Ballet Theatre's repertoire is virtually accessible to all.

Whereas, *Romeo and Juliet* effectively united commentators, promoters, and audiences in the most enthusiastic of welcomes, the company's most recent production, *Swan Lake* (premiered in Leeds at the Grand Theatre on 8 February 1992) did not. For this new production of *Swan Lake* – as contemporary, as accessible, and as cinematic as the earlier *Romeo and Juliet* – proved popular with audiences and promoters, though a good deal less popular with commentators and critics.

The reason for this divide – between those paying to see the performance and those being paid to comment on the performance - is really quite simple. For while Northern Ballet Theatre's contemporary recreation of *Swan Lake* has been touring the length and breadth of England to popular acclaim, and to some muted and some less than muted critical disapproval, one simple fact has to be stated. This is not *Swan Lake*. This is a different work. It's a new work. It's an all-dancing all-acting musical set in nineteenth-century Russia with a soundtrack by Tchaikovsky.

The Prince's companions, or posse, are now a bunch of high-living fast-drinking officers – their birthday party manoeuvres focus on a chorus girl in crimson leotard, tassles, and black fishnet tights – and their officers' mess cabaret takes the form of a large-bosomed drag act on roller skates. This is not at all your familiar *Swan Lake*.

Meanwhile the captive lakeside creatures to whom the Prince is attracted are not so much swans as pliant and eloquent extra-terrestrials with qualities which are simultaneously human, alien, and bird-like. And the villain – separating the tender leader of these creatures from the romantic soldier Prince – is a would-be military dictator with a physical infirmity and a grasp on power and on glamour (in the shape of his daughter dressed for the nineteenth-century equivalent of a yuppie cocktail party).

Inevitably a great deal of the richness of meaning of the original *Swan Lake* is lost. The image of creatures who spend their days as captive and elegant swans only to escape at night to become passionate women – surely a metaphor for the position of aristocratic women in nineteenth-century Europe – is lost. The image of men as romantic courtiers in the palace and as determined hunters in the forest by the lake – hunting with cross-bows for swans who are also women – is also lost. And the battle of wills between the Prince, seeking true love, and his mother, seeking an arranged marriage for her son, gets lost or confused in the power play with the would-be military dictator.

In some respects the very heart of this meaningful fairy-tale has been lost. But then, so it has been in so many contemporary productions of *Swan Lake*. When did we last see those passages of expressive mime which graced productions three or four decades ago? When did we last see Odette, the Swan Princess, reveal the essential meaning behind the very title of the work as she mimes to the Prince – 'I was born on the lake of my mother's tears'?

Productions of *Swan Lake* by many companies throughout the world have been scaled down, simplified, pruned, and more often than not rendered vehicles for dancing at the expense of meaning. So it may be that Northern Ballet Theatre has taken a brave step in seeking to render its new work both modern and dramatic. And if there have been losses in taking this step, there have also been gains.

For this new work allows us to see nineteenth-century Russia through the eyes of the twentieth century musical. The exuberant and sensitive choreography is by Dennis Wayne, an American dancer and choreographer with a spectacularly American biography: soloist with the Harkness Ballet, the Joffrey Ballet, and American Ballet Theatre; creator of Dancers, a contemporary ballet company, with Joanne Woodward; choreographer and director of a weekly television variety series; guest artist on auspicious occasions in Scotland, Japan, Australia; and most recently creator of a tribute to Fred Astaire for the 1992 Olympic Games in Barcelona. His choreography is an all-American phenomenon, classy and showy. It's as if *Swan Lake* had been choreographed by an American artist following on from the achievements of Michael Kidd, Bob Fosse, and Jerome Robbins.

Northern Ballet Theatre has now matured into the work – they are clearly at home in Lez Brotherston's sweeping military marquee, in his red, gold, and glass ballroom, and by the side of his hauntingly blue-neon lake. And the action, directed by Christopher Gable, connects from scene to scene like a piece of seasoned cinema – with principals and ensembles moving their audiences to laughter and to tears because they are clearly moved themselves.

The company's plans for the autumn 1992 season include the creation of another full-length work, to be based on Charles Dickens' moving Christmas story which has already inspired a number of memorable films (the most recent with George C. Scott as Scrooge, the parsimonious old skinflint who is transformed into a genial and generous employer and friend through the visitations of three seasonable ghosts). The creative team being lined up for *Christmas Carol* – director Christopher Gable, choreographer Massimo Moricone, and designer Lez Brotherston – brings together the trio who made such a success of *Romeo and Juliet*. We may expect the company not only to dance but also to sing Christmas carols on stage!

Further ahead, the company's plans for spring 1993 season include a new triple bill – with a revival of *A Simple Man* by choreographer Gillian Lynne, based loosely on the life of the north of England painter L. S. Lowry, and a new classical work commissioned from choreographer Graham Lustig. Significantly, the trio of ballets is to be completed by a new jazz-influenced work commissioned from Jamaican-born dancer and choreographer Derek Williams (now resident in America).

Now if there are two cultural forms which have their roots in America then they are the feature film and jazz. It may be no accident that Northern Ballet Theatre, creating and extending a repertory of dramatic full-length ballets which are essentially cinematic in form, is now seeking to represent in its repertory that musical form which has been the greatest influence on popular music this century, namely jazz. It may also be no accident that young American choreographers, Dennis Wayne and Derek Williams, are contributing to the company's repertory.

For the greatest influence on British culture is American culture. It could just be that Northern Ballet Theatre, having reached out to new audiences in Britain with ballets which are simultaneously classical, dramatic, and cinematic could do just the same equally successfully in America. And it may soon have an opportunity to do so. For it seems likely that the company may be entering America as early as spring 1993, for its first New York performances – Northern Ballet Theatre could turn out to be in tune with America; it could turn out to be a British company with a special appeal to audiences in New York.

Rambert Dance Company
Angela Kane

In the current economic climate, even the most adventurous artistic directors must keep an eye on the box office. The degree to which audiences influence company policy varies, but Rambert Dance Company seems more resistant to market forces than most – the concept of Rambert as a creative company has ensured that new commissions and collaborations continue to dominate repertory.

Nine new works were presented during the 1991/92 season. Of these, six

Paul Old and Glenn Wilkinson of Rambert Dance Company in Merce Cunningham's *Touchbase*, a production made possible by Cunningham's Digital Premier Award.   PHOTO: MARK ELLRIDGE

were by choreographers new not only to Rambert but also to Britain's modern dance mainstream, while the remainder were by the trio responsible for shaping the company's present style – artistic director Richard Alston, associate choreographer Siobhan Davies, and the company's most important outside influence, Merce Cunningham. In true Rambert tradition, two works were by company dancers. Mark Baldwin's *Island to Island*, and *Still Dance* by Paul Old were developed from pieces presented in workshops. Clearly, the dancers have been inspired by Alston's directorship. Both works reveal distinct movement styles – Old particularly is attempting to find his own dance energy and phrasing through choreography without accompaniment, as Alston did in his early career.

Alston created his best work when alternating between a full-time commitment to one company and freelance commissions. Eclecticism has characterized his choreography and it has also influenced his repertory choices. As director, he has exposed Rambert to a range of dance possibilities while simultaneously providing opportunities for young choreographers to gain experience beyond the confines of a single company. In 1991, he commissioned two works from choreographers at opposite ends of the dance spectrum. *Completely Birdland* by Laurie Booth extends Rambert's interest in dance performance as process rather than product. The six dancers receive separate instructions before each performance but, to date, few permutations have been evident in their various realizations. The accompanying score and backcloths (by, respectively, Hans Peter Kuhn and Graham Snow) are both powerfully 'fixed' in performance and these too conflict with any notion of indeterminacy. Booth has, however, introduced new physical concerns – unlike William Tuckett, whose violent, empty choreography in *Slippage* seems more an exorcism of his Royal Ballet training than a response to Rambert's high-level skills.

Other new works have been *Phillidor's Defence* by the Dutch choreographer Guido Severien; *Cat's Eye* by Alston, *Winnsboro Cotton Mill Blues* by Davies; and *Touchbase*, the first work created by Merce Cunningham for a British company. (Another work, by the French choreographer Hervé Robbe, was created for the 1991 Danse-à-Aix Festival but it has yet to be performed in Britain.) During the year, Rambert also revived two works by Alston and Davies. Since neither *Wildlife* (1984) nor *Plain Song* (1981) have been seen for several years, their revival provides interesting comparisons with present choreography.

As if to highlight parallels, *Wildlife* was performed during Rambert's 1992 London season alongside Alston's newest work, *Cat's Eye*. In both, channels of dance space are created and transformed by a movable set. In *Cat's Eye*, a serrated screen opens to reveal several banks of colour behind, and, like *Wildlife*, the solo protagonist seems to control the structure's space-time changes. *Cat's Eye* takes its title from David Sawer's score, which includes similar sonorities and animal-like sounds as Nigel Osborne's music for *Wildlife*. The choreography, too, prompts comparison with *Wildlife*, but whereas subsequent Alston works (such as *Zansa* and *Strong Language*) revealed an increased mastery of dance-music-design associations, *Cat's Eye* is a reminder, rather than a refinement, of former ideas.

Wildlife was the precursor not only of later Alston works, but also of his commissioning decisions as artistic director – particularly his belief in movement as subject matter and his encouragement of new choreography as a three-way collaboration with music and design. Though Alston has juxtaposed different perspectives on dance-making, he has also sought a coherent repertoire. The appointment of Davies as associate choreographer has further consolidated his aims.

During the early 1980s, Davies worked with London Contemporary Dance Theatre and her own smaller-scale company (and its successor, Second Stride). Then, her most innovative choreography was with her own group of dancers, as *Plain Song* proved. Today, she again has her own company and the freedom to create in a more flexible environment, but her best choreography has been for Rambert – most notably when developing ideas first explored with the smaller-scale group. Davies's recent work confirms this. *Winnsboro Cotton Mill Blues* develops many of the rhythmical complexities and spatial concerns of *Different Trains* (created for the Siobhan Davies Dance Company in 1990). It also furthers Davies's fusion of public comment and intimately moulded choreography. With just ten dancers and simple lighting (by Peter Mumford), she conjures up scenes of mass mechanization. The coupling of tape-recorded loom sounds with Frederic Rzewski's piano score completes the industrial landscape. (Rzewski wrote *Winnsboro Cotton Mill Blues* in 1979 as a reaction against the poor working conditions in North Carolina's textile mills.) Individual movement phrases are performed repeatedly, often with dancers positioned in a production-line chain. Occasionally, one dancer slumps or is carried by others, but the larger picture of workforce anonymity predominates.

Technology of a different kind initiated *Touchbase*. Using computer-generated images (from the software programme 'Life Forms'), Cunningham began structuring his choreography before the seven Rambert dancers began rehearsing with him in New York. Alongside two casts from Cunningham's company, they developed the dance in rotation – Cunningham would create material with one cast; they would then teach it to the second while Cunningham worked with the third cast on a new section. The production was made possible by a Digital Premier Award, and it enabled the two companies to come together to create different interpretations. (Colleagues who have seen all three casts suggest that the greatest degree of difference is not between the Rambert and Cunningham companies but between the latter's two versions.)

While *Touchbase* draws upon computer technology, in performance the most literal connection between title and choreography is Mark Lancaster's design. An upstage gate becomes 'home'. The dancers move to and away from it, sometimes turning the gate on its post as they pass by. Both the setting and costumes are summery, but unlike other Cunningham works, such as *Fabrications*, where glimpses of lazy, rural idylls mix with long sections of non-literal choreography, in *Touchbase* the dancers remain separate, from their surroundings and each other. Like *Doubles* (the last Cunningham work to enter Rambert repertory), *Touchbase* demands extreme composure, not only because of its long sections of stasis, but also because of its luminous focus on all seven dancers as soloists. The Rambert dancers found this unnerving in *Doubles*, but in *Touchbase* they bask in such singular attention. Working directly with Cunningham has given them a boost. The seven Rambert dancers now have a more assured approach to other choreography too, and, by example, their new-found confidence has enlivened the entire company.

Touchbase was premiered during Rambert's season at the Royalty Theatre, London, in June 1992. Though the season failed to produce exciting programme combinations (which Alston usually achieves so well), the company danced wonderfully throughout. The stage at the Royalty is ideal for Rambert's dancers – wide, open and with sufficient distance between stage and auditorium for the full stature and sweeping momentum of their dancing to be absorbed. Alston's decision to relocate Rambert from Sadler's Wells (the company's regular venue since 1973) could benefit other companies too – until London gets its own dance house, the Royalty is a more suitable theatre for middle- to large-scale performances in the capital.

Rambert arrived at the Royalty Theatre through trial and error. In April 1991, the company presented three programmes at Riverside Studios, and although the fifty-foot wide stage solved many of the problems of Sadler's Wells, it brought other restrictions. The technical resources of Riverside could not accommodate the designs for two recent works. (Alston's *Roughcut* was performed without Tim Hatley's hanging perspex poles, but *Four Elements* by Lucinda Childs was excluded from the season.) Also, the more intimate audience-performer context caused many of Rambert's dancers to wither from such close-up scrutiny.

The shortcomings of Riverside led Alston and his administrative director, Roger Taylor, to find another London venue – one prepared to open its doors to dance instead of a long-running musical or drama. After several months research, they decided on the Royalty which, built on the site of the former Stoll Theatre, had presented seasons of ballet. Situated in the heart of London's theatreland, Rambert's first season there was in October 1991. It included the first London performances of *Completely Birdland*, premiered in Leicester the previous month, *Signature* by Siobhan Davies, and *Four Elements* – both of which had been performed on tour for some time.

Before rediscovering the Royalty as a venue for dance, Rambert's repertory was best displayed on tour. Many theatres outside London offer better conditions for dance performance, and this is particularly true of some abroad. During the year, in addition to the regular round of touring in Britain, Rambert performed at five international festivals – in Aix-en-Provence, Florence, Salzburg, Turin, and at the Spoleto Festival in Charleston, USA. Also, the recession has meant that Rambert is increasingly involved in fund-raising activities. Galas and events for business sponsors have become part of the company's schedule. Yet despite the extra demands, both administrative and on the dancers, Rambert continues to encourage 'in-house' choreographers.

In May 1992, six dancers presented new work at Riverside Studios. (Although the Royalty has become Rambert's London home for repertory, Riverside continues to be the regular venue for company workshops.) The choreography ranged from first-steps musings to more mature expositions, and, significantly, the most developed work, *Gone* by Mark Baldwin, will enter the repertory in October. New choreography and a sense of Rambert's past have spearheaded Alston's seven years as director. And, refreshingly, the new rather than novelty remains the determining factor for repertory.

The Royal Ballet
Mary Clarke

The repertory of The Royal Ballet continues to be dominated by full-evening ballets which obstinately sell better at the box-office than do mixed programmes – no matter how good they may be. It is galling that whereas works like *Manon, Swan Lake, Romeo and Juliet*, and, of course, *The Nutcracker*, consistently draw full houses, a triple-bill as fine as Nijinska's *Les Biches* and *Les Noces* with Ashton's *Scènes de ballet* as the central work found many empty seats. It was not until almost the last performance that the public seemed to wake up to the fact that this was an evening of superlative choreography. And, as if to rub salt into the wound, the company commissioned a new full-evening ballet from David Bintley, *Cyrano*, first staged on 3 October.

It was given a lavish production with many complicated scene changes, properties galore, over 200 costumes and nearly as many hats, designed by Hayden Griffin, to create, as the publicity put it, a 'lavish seventeenth-century romantic adventure'. The score, by Wilfred Josephs, did nothing to help matters, and it remained a mystery that it should ever have been accepted by Covent Garden. The basic trouble, however, was the choice of subject. Bintley said in his programme note 'Cyrano loves Roxane, and she him, through his words'. Take away Rostand's words and the story has to be told in gesticulation and mime; Cyrano loses not only his poetry but his wit.

Bintley followed the shape of the play fairly closely, and the first two acts were the best. He did find some dancing for Cyrano in love, and there was some vitality in the scenes in the Hotel de Bourgogne and Ragueneau's bakery. But the garden scene was mostly mimed 'words' until Roxane descended to dance a somewhat conventional *pas de deux* with Christian. In the last act, the battle scene and the nunnery scene were run together, contrasting the wartime ferocity of the first with the tranquillity of the second. But by then Bintley seemed to have run out of choreography altogether, and the death scene was milked to the hilt for sentimentality.

Bintley was saved, just, by two magnificent casts. Both Stephen Jefferies, for whom it was made, and Irek Mukhamedov, who followed him, did all that was possible for Cyrano, while Lesley Collier and Viviana Durante and Bruce Sansom and Stuart Cassidy did the same for Roxane and Christian. It was thanks to them that the ballet was mostly well received, but it was no sell-out, and although it opened the 1991/92 season it seemed unlikely to enjoy long life.

For the first time The Royal Ballet acquired a work by William Forsythe

– In the middle, somewhat elevated – first shown at Covent Garden on 13 February. Created originally for the Paris Opéra Ballet, and later given in Frankfurt, it is danced to music by Thom Willems, in designs by Forsythe. Sylvie Guillem, still a permanent guest of the company, danced the role she created. The ballet succeeded in winning an award, but had a very mixed reception from the critics. However, it survived in the repertory and delighted the fans of Mlle Guillem.

Balanchine was well represented, his joyous *Symphony in C* (Bizet) joining *Agon* and *Stravinsky Violin Concerto* in the repertory, and all, thanks to the vigilance of The George Balanchine Trust, meticulously rehearsed. Ashton was less well represented, but his *La Fille mal gardée* continued to delight; and a delightful guest as Lise was Nina Ananiashvili from the Bolshoi, who is cementing her links with the company and obviously enjoys dancing a new repertory. Another welcome guest, this time from St Petersburg, was Altynai Asylmuratova, who danced a ravishing Juliet. And for the first time dancers from Arthur Mitchell's Dance Theatre of Harlem appeared with the company.

Harlem was involved, too, in an exciting joint project called 'A Chance to Dance' aimed to identify talented eight- and nine-year-old children from all ethnic backgrounds and give them, in their own schools, basic training to enable them to audition for ballet schools, including the Royal Ballet School, at the appropriate age. The children responded with glee, the boys as enthusiastic as the girls, and before long the Covent Garden programme could announce that the small black child playing the Changeling Boy in *The Dream* was a member of this scheme.

Young choreographers were also represented. William Tuckett's *Present Histories*, to music by Schubert in designs by Andy Klunder and Lucy Bevan, was a sort of 1930s cocktail party piece, in which ambiguous sexual relationships were explored. On its own terms it was effective, if sometimes mystifying. Jonathan Burrows, subsequently to leave the company to found one of his own, was represented with the quartet from his longer work *Stoics*. His is an original and lively talent, and his departure, both as performer and choreographer, a loss to the company.

The year under review ended with what was, tragically, to be the last major work from Kenneth MacMillan (who died on 29 October 1992), but it was one of his very finest. *The Judas Tree*, which was first performed on 19 March, is a ballet about betrayal, but in no sense a biblical story. The title comes from a Mediterranean tree that produces red flowers on the bare wood, like tears of blood, and is called the Judas tree. Working in the closest collaboration with the composer Brian Elias – new to ballet music, but a great admirer of MacMillan – and the designer Jock McFayden, the choreographer created a work that seemed to say betrayal and Judas are part of the human condition that exists even today. The ballet is for fourteen men

The Royal Ballet's Irek Mukhamedov and Viviana Durante in MacMillan's last
work, *The Judas Tree*.   PHOTO: LESLIE E. SPATT

and one woman, and the setting a rough, contemporary building site –
scaffolding, ladders, broken-down cars, and a backcloth that placed it
within sight of Canary Wharf, which winks in the distance.

The central figure is The Foreman, Irek Mukhamedov, and the solitary
woman, Viviana Durante, whom he considers 'his' although she refuses
submission and has a vicious, sexual temperament of her own. She is first
seen under a white sheet, an image which recurs as if to suggest that
beneath the sexual bravado of much of her behaviour there is a vulnerable
human being. The image is reinforced at the end as she dons the sheet to
grieve over the bodies of The Foreman, hanged, and his gentle friend,
whom he has betrayed, lynched. Lynching and multiple rape figure powerfully in the piece, which is violent, horrible at times, but dreadfully true
of the darker, brutal character of the rough urban world of today. The Royal
Ballet danced it with passion; the men in their work outfits looking as if
they might have strayed from any building site – not a ballet classroom! The
searing performances of Mukhamedov and Durante were perfectly complemented by Michael Nunn as the friend.

The Judas Tree was given on a triple-bill starting with *Stravinsky Violin*

213

Concerto and ending with *Symphony in C* – an excellent example of intelligent programme building. In the second movement of *Symphony in C*, Darcey Bussell, who all season had been growing in ballerina stature, found one of her most beautiful roles; even more promise of things to come.

On balance, The Royal Ballet seemed to be regaining its true status. Optimism was in the air.

Smaller British companies
Lesley-Anne Sayers

Most of Britain's choreographic innovation is coming out of our smaller companies; overall the standard of work has probably never been higher. It sometimes seems difficult to reconcile this fact with claims of underfunding. Intense competition for funds may well promote professionalism amongst those that attract support, but the recession and inadequate investment in the arts are crippling the emergence of new talent.

Dance is currently coming to the forefront of the avant-garde by proving its potential to provide visually exciting metaphors for our time; the mixture of performance arts that make up so many of the 'dance' works of today is a potent medium. The most successful groups however, are those that present a niche market with the images they want, providing a sort of sub-cultural identity much as do pop stars. That the work is also more than this does credit to the creativity of our choreographers who have to jostle the need for media attention and fashionable advertising images with their own artistic integrity. The current emphasis on product rather than process however, and on audience numbers as a criterion for evaluation, needs to be moderated: we must consider the long term effects of this kind of commercialism on our experimental theatre. There is much to celebrate, providing we can retain a balance of works and approaches and seek to enable artists rather than ever-more elaborate productions.

The performance event of the year has surely been **DV8**'s *Strange Fish*. Commissioned for Expo 92 Seville, this work enjoyed a great success at the Making Waves festival in Budapest before opening in the UK. DV8, led by choreographer Lloyd Newson, take this performance to the outer limits; it's searing images etch themselves into the memory, and the commitment and integrity of the performers is outstanding. *Strange Fish* presents its themes through characters, using speech as well as movement. Their playfully creative and darkly destructive interactions hurtle from one metaphor to the next against a background of incredible stage effects including an avalanche of stones, an erupting floor and a female Christ on the cross. *Strange Fish* explores its themes from the social level to the apocalyptic. It is powerfully poignant and the intensity of its performance is shattering.

Collaborative performance work that crosses boundaries between the arts can be difficult to classify. Recognizing the importance of such work, the Arts Council set up a new funding area specifically for productions of this type. This is what saved **Second Stride** last year, and it is good to be able to report that they are now on three-year funding from this source. This enables them to make some relatively long-term plans. We are promised a lot of exciting new collaborations, including a major new dance work where Ian Spink will work with two other choreographers, Ashley Page and Aletta Collins. This year Spink collaborated with writer Martin Duncan on *The Four Marys* a curious piece that transports Mary Queen of Scots and four of her courtiers (also called Mary) into the twentieth century. It's the synchronicity of it all that inspired Spink and Duncan; the narrative is practically incidental. It works through its poignant and amusing use of juxtaposition. Parody and absurdity are never far away, deriving either from a combination of events or from the text itself. '. . . don't let your mother eat plants growing by the wayside', we're advised,'one mouthful may not be fatal but it a very bad habit'. It's very postmodern, a sort of celebration of our awareness that meaning can only be expressed as a self-conscious parody of itself. Spink tells his audience to make what they will of it, and doing so is never less than engaging; Second Stride produce some of the most stimulating theatre around.

Lea Anderson, one of our most prolific choreographers, brought her two companies, **The Cholmondeleys** and **The Featherstonehaughs**, together this year for the first time since *Flag* (1989). *Birthday* revolves around the idea of celebrations with the usual Anderson style of humour. Some critics bemoan her refusal to break out of a rather limited movement range, thought of as earth-bound and thumpy. Anderson is revered however, for her ability to find movement from everyday body language and then build this basic inspiration into distinctive and original choreography that is both witty and insightful. The Featherstonehaughs, our only all-male group, seek to explore male stereotypes. They come from a variety of performance backgrounds and they sing, dance and chat their way thorough some wonderfully entertaining material. In *The Big Feature* they draw on the format used by rock bands in addressing the audience directly, introducing themselves and each short piece in turn. *Giant Jesus Baby Heater*, set to open at the Hawth Amphitheatre at the time of writing, promises to be visually spectacular with the company appearing at the windows of a giant advent calendar like moving frescos on their way to enlightenment. Meanwhile Anderson's all-female group, The Cholmondeleys, are planning a new collaboration with writer Anne Rabbit which will fuse dance and dialogue in a series of short dances and plays.

Adventures In Motion Pictures remains one of our most popular groups. Their choreographer Matthew Bourne trained, like Anderson, at the Laban Centre, which has now produced so many of our most distinctive choreographers and performers. Bourne has wit, elegance, style, ingenuity and an irreverent sense of humour. All of these attributes were much in evidence in this year's production *Deadly Serious,* an entertaining tribute to the films of Alfred Hitchcock. In his planned new version of *The Nutcracker* we are promised Dr Dross and his spoilt daughter Sugar, and a sticky ending in the Kingdom of the Sweeties. This will mark the centenary of the original production; Petipa, Ivanov, Tchaikovsky, turn in your graves.

This year **Michael Clark**, yawnfully known as the *enfant terrible* of British ballet, returned to centre stage, after an absence of several years, with a new work modestly entitled *Modern Masterpiece,* or *Mmm...* as it later became. It was good to see him back after his much-reported drug problems. The work, however, featured all his old preoccupations in a combination of homoerotic and sadomasochistic imagery. The bare-breasted presence of his mother, Bessie Clark, contributed to the interest value, but was otherwise pointless. No doubt it is all subversive and meaningful to Clark; but then he's not known as an intellectual and seems more concerned with his image as a sex object. Presenting himself in terms of the images produced by a society fascinated by what it considers perverse, Clark enslaves his talent to self-obsession and ends up reinforcing some highly questionable stereotypes. Aside from all the tiresome foreplay however, the hub of this work, which is a new interpretation of Stravinsky's *Rite of Spring*, is awe-inspiring in terms of its power and physicality. The high point is the solo work for the Chosen Girl. The splayed movement has a violence and intensity that is breathtaking and vividly encapsulates the themes of the music. Clark's distinctive vocabulary derives in part from his classical ballet training informed with the qualities of contemporary dance, and the head-led, off-balance, jerk dynamics of punk. It takes more than a few minutes of brilliance however, submerged in a cloud of old hat, loud music and hype to make a modern masterpiece. *Mmm...* was the more apt title.

Rosemary Butcher's *Of Shadows and Walls,* a collaboration with film maker Nicola Baldwin, brings a new physicality into her work. She has termed this development 'athletic realism' after the biotechnic exercises used by Russian actors in the 1920s, who were investigating new forms of expression. The emphasis is on dedication to performance seen as an expression of the life force. Perhaps Butcher is taking up the challenge, in a sense, posed by the preponderance of more dramatic approaches to dance; her quietly abstract and conceptual style must inevitably be affected by the almost alien context in which it now finds itself. She has recently won a Barclays New Stages award for *The Body as Site, Image as Event.*

This year **Jonathan Burrows** left the Royal Ballet in order to devote his energies to his own small group. Burrows has been choreographing for a group of fellow ballet dancers for some time now, and has met with a lot of critical interest, even acclaim. Works such as *Hymns* (1988) and *Stoics* (1991) evoke a warm and compassionate sense of absurdity. His vocabulary ap-

Birthday, performed by The Cholmondeleys and The Featherstonehaughs, choreographed by artistic director Lea Anderson.   PHOTO: CHRIS NASH

217

pears casual, one movement flowing easily from the next in a playfully relaxed style. His background, in classical technique and as a dancer in some of Rosemary Butcher's most successful works, such as *Touch the Earth* (1987), is richly diverse and he dislikes what he considers arbitrary distinctions between forms. Something of a rising star, Burrows is currently choreographing a new work, *Very*, funded by a Digital Dance Award, will be premiered in October 1992 and toured Europe-wide in the spring.

Siobhan Davies is enjoying a particularly productive year. Aside from *Winnsboro Cotton Mill Blues* for Rambert she has managed two new works for her own small company. The haunting *White Bird Featherless* explores movement with a more vigorous dynamic than is usual in her work. The music, composed by Gerald Barry for two pianos and countertenor, is made up of restructured sequences from his opera *The Intelligence Park*. Music is always of crucial importance to Davies, and she likes to work very closely with her collaborating composers. Her second new work, *Make-Make* will premiere in the autumn at the Tramway, Glasgow. The vocal score is said to layer the sounds and rhythms of Innuit game songs, Pygmy polyphonies and Celtic keening.

Yolande Snaith's group, **Dance Quorum**, was one of four dance companies to win one of nine Barclays New Stages awards this year which will fund a new work, *Diction*. This year's work, *No Respite*, is surprisingly pared-down. The energy she usually puts into the development and elaboration of her material, often with forays into mixed media, here goes into restriction. It opens with the clacking of clogs crossing the floor in the darkness. Snaith sits playing cards at a magical table which, together with a giant, slanted chair was designed by Barnaby Stone. Behind her, two others are involved in a movement ritual. The three battle for possession of the cards, or a place at the table, or in the game wherever it is located. By the end however, *No Respite* is too true to its title; the movement does not in itself sustain interest and there is minimal development of idea. Snaith is capable of much more.

Shobana Jeyasingh Dance Company's *New Cities Ancient Lands* has enchanted audiences this year with its stimulating triple bill. *Speaking of Sakti* was commissioned from Madras-based choreographer Chandralekha, who strips off the decorative elements of Bharatha Natyam and seeks to explore women's oppression in India through movements of enslavement to empowerment. Jeyasingh's own concerns are more formal, combining her language of Indian classical dance with her contemporary Western experience. In *Late* and *Byzantium* she continues her collaborations with contemporary Western composers to stunning effect. With her wonderfully fluid and rhythmic movement and her obvious intelligence, Jeyasingh is forging new contexts for both the Indian dance and the Western music on which she draws.

218

Space permitting, there are many other groups that could be mentioned here. Some, such as **Amici**, are doing inspiring work based in the community, as well as the theatre. Overall, Britain currently has much to contribute to the international dance culture.

Dance Umbrella
Elizabeth Charman

In 1991, as is usual with this festival, Dance Umbrella presented British audiences with work from a variety of countries, and as always there was an air of hopeful expectation surrounding the work of the US choreographers – particularly prior to the performance by **Doug Elkins Company** at Riverside Studios. Elkins's work proved to have some real sparkle, with a hotch-potch collection of references to a whole range of dance forms thrown together with ingenuity, although his air of self-conscious frippery became tiresome. With a visit from **Trisha Brown** playing to good houses, and work by choreographers from New York's PS 122, the USA was well represented, with the real gem being presented by **Eiko and Koma** at The Place Theatre.

Although others felt that this was not their best work to date (see also Robert Greskovic's article, pp. 230–243), *Land* was a most absorbing performance. It is rare to see such density of meaning expressed in such minimal movement. Every moment of motion was carefully considered and executed, each continuing organically from the previous action. This work was evidently more concerned with 'message' than other works: accompanied by live native American music, *Land* dealt with the landscape and culture of the Pueblo Indians of New Mexico. This was a sideways address, however, and more than imparting a message, the work was quite simply bewitching. Lying on the red earth, with the backdrop the bluish hue of lichen, the two figures moved slowly together, heads turned away from us or faces to the floor, rolling and wriggling on their bellies, shuffling forward on their elbows against the rough earth. The whole was exquisitely poignant and painful, and quite unlike anything else in the Umbrella.

Eiko and Koma are Japanese, but have been living in New York for fifteen years, so their work reflects their experiences within a variety of cultures. There were others whose work arises from similar circumstances such as **Shobana Jeyasingh** (see Lesley-Anne Sayers' article, pp. 214–218) and **Valli Subbiah**. The latter, with her company of three dancers, showed *Trikonam*, a work choreographed by Savitry Nair and Maurice Béjart. In contrast to some beautifully performed pure dance passages of intricate rhythmic foot patterns, which made up solo material to open the performance, *Trikonam* was a farcical story which was something like a Euro-Indian romantic ballet in which a slumbering Koen Onzia (guest artist from English National Ballet) awoke, amazed to find himself transformed into an

Indian dancer, his body involuntarily taking the shapes of the Bharatha Natyam vocabulary. An Indian sylphide then entered, with whom Onzia danced an 'anything you can do I can do better' duet, pitching the bravado of classical ballet against the intricacies of Bharatha Natyam.

If Eiko and Koma were amongst the best in Umbrella and Valli Subbiah and Company the silliest, **L'Esquisse** was quite possibly the most offensive. The work had an unsettling misogynous feel despite its being co-created by a woman. It took as its premise the self-destructive nature of humanity, and certainly the hour-long work relentlessly pursued its bleak view of human relationships, with women the willing victims of man's baser instincts, and with men powerless to prevent themselves being the perpetrators of women's suffering. It was a terribly one-dimensional work and, for me, did overstep its remit, resorting to gross and cheap portrayals of women. A man removed a woman's dress to the sounds of a child crying; the women were hung from a metal bar from which they then swung like corpses, dressed in restrictive corsets, as crowds cheered; women grovelled in dirt that men cast on the ground – and so on. What was objectionable about the work was that it did not have a clear sense of *how* to address the issues that it sought to illuminate. From the sanitary whiteness of the opening scene – with the women stylishly dressed, as ever, in tight dresses and heels – to the dirt and sweat of the close of the piece, the performers and audience travelled on a journey – but a journey that, on balance, I would rather not have made.

A tiresome trek was made at Chisenhale Studios in the company of **Gaby Agis** and fellow performers in *Cold Dark Matter: an Exploded View*. A collaboration with installation artist Cornelia Parker, the work lumbered on in usual Agis style with no apparent purpose and certainly no interest, though the installation, which was made up of everyday rubbish and commonplace objects, provided a welcome distraction from the dross that surrounded it.

And as Agis showed us the worst of improvisation, **Laurie Booth** and Julyen Hamilton showed us the best. In *New Text/New Kingdom*, Booth worked with his regular partner Russell Maliphant, plus two additional dancers, Ellen van Schuylenburch and Jo Chandler, both past members of Michael Clark's company and both performers of ability. The gentle acrobatics of Booth and Maliphant, however, translated less comfortably onto Schuylenburch and Chandler. Maliphant has readily absorbed Booth's style and provides an ideal counterpart to him – neither dominates the other on stage – but Chandler could not find his way in the work and Booth's movement did not suit Schuylenburch's physique. She is a beautiful dancer but looked at odds with the harmony created on stage by Booth and Maliphant, her presence suggesting a male/female dialogue that was not being addressed in the work. *New Text/New Kingdom* became locked in its narrative as it proceeded, with a text that threatened to overwhelm the dance. This was a quasi-mystical piece, inspired by *The Egyptian Book of the Dead*, with a set made up of a sail-like curtain and moveable painted screens, carried on and off by the dancers, but there were too many trappings and not enough direction; and the work was less substantial then last year's Umbrella piece, *Spatial Decay II*.

Julyen Hamilton is an improviser of extraordinary ability and has been working steadily on the continent for over ten years, although his work is rarely seen in Britain. The problems which Booth encountered with text in his work, were certainly no hindrance to Hamilton, who used an extract of prose written by Elizabeth Pike with great delicacy, wit and integrity. A performer who is so confident and so relaxed on the stage is quite something to watch – open to every nuance, Hamilton moves so freely that every moment seems a wonderful surprise both to him and to his audience, leaving us staggered by the ingenuity of his imagination.

In contrast with the endless range of movement possibilities explored by Hamilton, **Rosemary Butcher**'s evening of work was well-crafted but nevertheless insipid – though since she was forced to present the work with one dancer too few (owing to injury), it is perhaps unfair to judge too harshly.

Less inventive, as well as less well crafted, was the work presented by the Japanese contingent – **Pappa Tarahumara** and **Saburo Teshigawara and Karas**. The extensive use of props and stage effects with little else in addition was the link in the work of these two companies. Teshigawara and Karas was particularly dull, ploughing pointlessly on through a barrage of sound, as goldfish swam in bowls uncomfortably positioned at the front of the stage under the hot lights.

Obituaries

Henry Bardon (died 19 July 1991) came to Britain as a refugee from the German invasion of his native Czechoslovakia. He trained at Dundee College of Art and was subsequently employed as a scene-painter at Perth Repertory theatre. After moving to Stratford-upon-Avon the quality of his work attracted the attention of Lila de Nobili who did much to promote his career as a designer in his own right. She recommended him to Ashton to devise the setting (with David Walker responsible for the costumes) for *The Dream* in 1964. This team collaborated on many subsequent productions, including nineteenth-century ballet such as *Beatrix* for London Festival Ballet and *Swan Lake* for the Royal Swedish Ballet; they also redesigned Ashton's *Cinderella* in 1965. Bardon's decors for Peter Wright's 1968 production of *The Sleeping Beauty* were beautifully complemented by de Nobili's costumes and Rotislav Doboujinsky's masks.

Bice (Beatrice) Bellairs (died June 1991) was a teacher and choreographer. She founded the Grant-Bellairs School in London with Pauline Grant in 1935, but moved to Guildford in 1939 where she continued to teach. She also choreographed shows in Windsor and Coventry, and was responsible for the choreography of Ken Russell's memorable 1966 BBC TV programme *Isadora Duncan: The Biggest Dancer in the World*.

Richard Collins (died 19 September 1990) was a latecomer to dancing, having first read history at Magdalen College, Oxford. His single-minded determination to take up ballet led him to become the first Western dancer to train for four years with the Bolshoi in Moscow, where he mastered a number of spectacular feats, but, perhaps inevitably, lacked a secure technique. He performed for short periods with London Festival Ballet and with the Irish Ballet, but found his true metier as a teacher in Norway, London and the United States. In 1990 he was promoted from ballet master to artistic director of Cincinatti Ballet, and seemed to be restoring the fortunes of the company when he was killed in a car crash. Collins was also the author of *Behind the Bolshoi Curtain*, a description of his experiences in Moscow, the novel *Minka*, and the hit musical *Pinko* which ran for four years in Warsaw.

Richard Davies (died 17 October 1991) was a broadcaster and writer on dance as well as a schoolteacher. He was dance editor for *Classical Music*, to which he contributed an important series of interviews with choreographers and dancers. He also did a great deal to encourage the development of dance in education.

Desmond Doyle (died 9 July 1991), a South African by birth, was a valued member of the Sadler's Wells Royal ballet 1951–75. A stylish soloist and secure partner, he created a variety of roles including the Husband, shifty, rapacious, remorseful, in MacMillan's *The Invitation*; a fierce and menacing Tybalt in MacMillan's *Romeo and Juliet*; Jaeger, loyal and self-effacing in Ashton's *Enigma Variations*; and the untiring Ballet Master in *Jazz Calendar* – nicely apt casting, since in 1970 he was appointed ballet master (jointly with Jill Gregory). In 1976 he moved to Brazil where he continued to teach, and became ballet master of the Ballet do Teatro Municipal de Rio de Janeiro (1981–87).

Anita Heyworth (died 8 November 1991) was the pupil and partner of Madge Atkinson and former principal of the London College of Dance and Drama from which she retired in 1973. She appeared in a number of Atkinson's Natural Movement choreographic works in Manchester theatres early in the century, and was noted for her expressive qualities. However, it is for her dedicated teaching and inspired training of teachers that she is best remembered, and more recently for her revitalization of the Natural Movement branch of the Imperial Society of Teachers of Dancing, for which she was an examiner, committee member and later chairman. In 1988 she presented her extensive personal archive on Natural Movement to the National Resource Centre for Dance.

222

Anna Ivanova (Nancy Hanley) (died 23 April 1992) began her career performing with Anna Pavlova's company, the State National Theatre in Belgrade, and Nicholas Sergeyev's company, but it is as a teacher that she is best remembered. After the demise of her own studio, established with Mary Skeaping, she taught for companies internationally from Cuba to Turkey, including Sadler's Wells Ballet and Ballet Rambert. In teaching she drew on her experiences with Trefilova, Egorova and Kchessinskaya in Paris in the 1920s, and she welcomed the opportunity to serve as ballet mistress for eight years with Antonio's company in Spain, where she developed her personal interest in Spanish dancing. Her book *The Dancing Spaniards* was published in London in 1970.

Edward Kelly-Espinosa (died 13 October 1991) and his sister **Yvette Espinosa** (died 5 May 1992) were the children of Edouard Espinosa and Louise Kay (Eve Kelland) of the famous Spanish-Jewish dancing dynasty established in the nineteenth century. After both had had successful careers in the commercial theatre, they devoted themselves to teaching, in particular to the British Ballet Organisation founded by their father.

Isabel Lambert (died 27 January 1992), a painter in her own right, is generally best known as a model for other painters and sculptors – Epstein, Derain, Picasso, Giacometti, and many times for Bacon. In 1947 she married the already-ailing Constant Lambert, and partly through him and partly as a result of the first post-war exhibition at the Hanover Gallery, she was invited at Leonor Fini's suggestion to design Ashton's ill-fated *Tiresias* (for which Lambert composed the score). Her decors did little to enhance the production although her Minoan-style costumes were striking. Much more successful was the second ballet she designed for Ashton (and for which the music was composed by her third husband, Alan Rawsthorne), *Madame Chrysanthème*, which drew on Japanese art. She also designed *Blood Wedding* and *Jabez and the Devil*.

Joan Moriarty (died 2 January 1992) did all in her power to put Ireland on the dance map. Having studied with Marie Rambert she established her first school in 1944 and her performing organization, the Cork Ballet Group, first appeared in 1947. It went through a number of names and guises, but achieved greatest success as the Irish Ballet Company 1974–1989. This company performed versions of the classics, usually with guest artists, and works choreographed for its own dancers, usually by Moriarty. Most successful was her full-evening dance version of *The Playboy of the Western World* (1978) which, with music by The Chieftains, also won international acclaim in New York and London.

Sir Andrzej Panufnik (died 27 October 1991) was a Polish-born but naturalized British composer and conductor. He was music director of the City of Birmingham Symphony Orchestra from 1957 to 1959, but preferred to devote his time to composing, and appeared only intermittently as a conductor. He was a prolific and eclectic composer, mostly for orchestra, and he had eight symphonies to his credit. His music has been set by a number of choreographers including Gerald Arpino (for *Elegy*), David Bintley (for *Homage to Chopin, Adieu,* and *Polonia*) and Kenneth MacMillan (for *Cain and Abel,* and *Miss Julie*).

John Piper CH (died 28 June 1991) was one of the most versatile and essentially English artists of this century. He worked in a very wide range of media, but is perhaps best known for his architectural and topographical studies. He remained a modernist, but his early experiments in abstraction ceded after 1937 to a more representational neo-romanticism, deeply felt and rich in colour and texture; and he was an altogether an apt choice to design Ashton's patriotic pageant *The Quest* in 1943. His decor for this ballet, as for other theatre works, derived from his own paintings; but, ever the generous collaborator, he acknowledged Ashton's advice on costume design, although he had his own clearly-formulated ideas on what was appropriate for dancers. Piper's first contact with the stage came in the 1930s when he worked with the experimental Group Theatre, an experience fruitfully repeated in 1952 when he joined Cranko, MacMillan and others to mount a dance season in the neglected theatre at Henley-on-Thames (the town near which he made his home for more than fifty years. Piper redesigned de Valois' *Job* in 1984, and worked on several of Cranko's most interesting ballets, including *Harlequin* in April and the first *Prince of the Pagodas* (for which Desmond Heeley designed the costumes) with its intriguing mobile decors. He also designed many of Benjamin Britten's operas, including *Albert Herring, Gloriana,* and *Death in Venice*.

Joan Potter (died 9 June 1991) was a member of the Borovansky Ballet in Australia 1945–50 and 1954–58, but otherwise her career was with London Festival Ballet as a dancer and then until 1982 as ballet mistress. As a soloist she is remembered for the roles she imbued with her character and charm, including a Junior Pupil in *Graduation Ball*, a Village Dancer in *The Snow Maiden*, and then more recently Lotte in Ronald Hynde's production of *The Nutcracker*. As a teacher she was responsible for training children for Festival Ballet's productions and she worked closely together with Vassilie Trunoff whom she married in 1950. They frequently performed together and during Beryl Grey's directorship were the backbone of her ballet staff. They also mounted productions together (mostly from the Ballets Russes repertory) both in Britain and Australia.

Colin Sharp (died April 1992) worked in the administration of London Festival/English National Ballet from 1982 to 1990. Appointed assistant company manager by John Field, he rose to become artistic manager with Peter Schaufuss. He had considerable flair for dealing with people, and helped both Schaufuss to manage his exhausting schedule, and guest choreographers to settle in with the company.

Brian Shaw (died 2 April 1992) was a virtuoso dancer and his interpretation of the Bluebird in *The Sleeping Beauty* remains unsurpassed for its precision, line, speed and musicality. He joined Sadler's Wells Ballet in 1944, and when only 17 created a role in Ashton's *Symphonic Variations*. Shaw's medium stature prevented him from being recognized as a *danseur noble*, but Ashton used him in *Birthday Offering*, *Ondine* and *Monotones II*. He is also remembered as the Blue Skater in *Les Patineurs*, spinning ever-faster as the curtain falls, and more recently as a lively Widow Simone in *La Fille mal gardée* which he continued to perform until 1989. Shaw had been one of Vera Volkov's star pupils when she taught in England (1943–1950) and he in turn became the Royal Ballet's Principal Teacher from 1972 to 1991.

Adrian Ward-Jackson (died 23 August 1991) was a successful art consultant whose love of painting and sculpture was complemented by his enthusiasm for dance, and resulted in his eager encouragement of fine artists to design dance productions. His interest and dedication made him an ideal Chairman of Rambert's board of directors from 1986–90, and he was also a Governor of the Royal Ballet and a member of the Royal Opera House Trust. As a patron of dance he devised means to nurture new talent (choreographers and composers as well as designers), and was instrumental in establishing the Frederick Ashton Choreographic Award (which recognized the talent of Ashley Page and Jonathan Burrows) and the Frederick Ashton Memorial Trust to commission new works for Rambert Dance Company. In 1990 he was appointed Chairman of the Arts Council's Dance Panel where he was energetically campaigning to improve the status of dance until forced to resign in May 1991 by the onslaught of AIDS.

USA

Chicago
Cerinda Survant
Dance in Chicago reflects the city's racial, ethnic, and cultural diversity: one finds teenagers busking on the State Street pedestrian mall, Bharatha Natyam performed in a suburban temple, American Indian pow-wows, and annual tours by classical ballet companies from the US and abroad. Few dancers in Chicago earn a living dancing; some hold administrative jobs in various aspects of the performing arts, many teach, and the vast majority labour outside the field. Continuing economic instability threatens individuals and companies alike.

Chicago has never attracted and maintained a resident ballet company commensurate with the city's other performing arts institutions: the Chicago Symphony Orchestra and the Lyric Opera of Chicago have achieved critical, popular, and financial success around the world, while an entire series of ballet companies has floundered and failed at home. Four-year-old **Ballet Chicago**, directed by Daniel Duell, continues to experience great difficulty realizing laudable artistic goals. After cancelling their 1991 spring season at the Civic Opera House, Ballet Chicago presented their autumn season at the Dance Center (a small, state-of-the-art performance space several miles north of the theatre district), then returned downtown to present their 1992 spring season at the proscenium Civic Theatre.

Ballet Chicago's appearance in the Dance Center's small, bare, black theatre was memorable: the lack of distance and illusion of the proscenium forced the dancers to reveal themselves, both technically and emotionally. The large stage maintained the scale and spacing of the company's choreography while the theatre's extraordinary intimacy bared every uncertainty and failure of technique. Ballet Chicago bore such brutal scrutiny well: though the men's ensemble dancing lacked the ease and musicality of the women's, all the dancers' very human pleasure and absorption in the act of dancing was equally obvious, especially in Balanchine's *Allegro Brillante*, and resident choreographer Gordon Peirce Schmidt's *Scenes from an Italian Songbook*.

The Balanchine corpus stands at the centre of Ballet Chicago's repertoire, but the company regularly commissions and produces new works. During the 1991/92 season, they premiered Schmidt's *Brahms Quintet in G Major* and *The Sleep of Reason*, Duell's *Time Torque* and *Verdi Divertimenti*, and David Parson's *A Hairy Night on Bald Mountain*. They also performed *Allegro Brillante*, *Tchaikovsky Pas de Deux*, and *Square Dance*. *Hansel and Gretel*, choreographed by Duell and Schmidt and set to the Humperdinck opera arranged by Kimberly Schmidt, is scheduled for the 1993/94 season.

Schmidt's chosen vocabulary owes as much to Tudor and Arpino as Balanchine, but the dark psychic universe he creates in his dances is uniquely his. *The Sleep of Reason*, premiered last autumn, is forbidding and ambiguous, a dance of passivity, objectification, and manipulation, set to music by Ravel. The dance begins as an oddly detached duet; the two dancers remain in nearly constant physical contact, but their eyes never meet. They slide and slither against each other in precarious lifts and peculiar partnering; the continual distortion of line suggests a relationship devoid of both emotion and consciousness. A second man enters, swooping and circling, hovering at the perimeter of the space they share. Schmidt never attempts to resolve the triangle; rather, the dance turns back upon itself, an icy and interminable fantasy.

Joseph Holmes Chicago Dance Theatre has also suffered: the eighteen-year-old multiracial modern dance company cut its twelve dancers' contracts from 52 to 34 weeks and reduced off-season administrative staff. However, both apprentice and scholarship programmes remain, and the company continues to present its scheduled programming.

The company's immense popularity stems from the strength and virtuosity of its dancers and an eclectic, accessible repertoire. Holmes set many works to popular music, particularly jazz fusion and pop vocals. *He and She*, set to a score by Pat Metheny and Earl Klugh, is still part of the company's active repertoire. *Unarmed*, artistic director Randy Duncan's new work, a solo set to a recording of Sinead O'Connor's 'I am Stretched on Your Grave', explores the tension between expressive movement and its accompanying musical text. The dance cages the performer in a rectangle of light as sharp and insistent as the score's martial drum. The movement is taut, bound. Forearms claw through heavy space or shield the dancer's face; he hurtles to the floor, leaps, and plunges back again; his torso straightens only with the greatest effort. He escapes the limits of his narrow box, only to collapse.

As in *Unarmed*, the musical text of *Copeland Motets* plays an essential role in the coalescence of imagery. Both movement and costumes emphasize the uniformity of the three dancers' height and line, rather than gender. The three performers – one woman and two men – are partners; together, they accomplish lifts and balances impossible for one or two. The movement suggests that any one may support another, any two may lift the third, any one may disentangle the others. The dance hints at a shared journey into light, a journey realized only through the strength of mutual support and the transcendence of conventional gender roles.

Hubbard Street Dance Company, under the artistic direction of Lou Conte, remains Chicago's most solvent, most popular and best-known ensemble. Created in 1975, Hubbard Street has grown from four dancers performing in nursing homes and community centres to an ensemble of nineteen salaried dancers and apprentices appearing throughout Europe, the US, and in an annual two-week engagement at Chicago's Civic Opera House. In 1988, Hubbard Street began to depart from a successful repertoire of romantic duets and showcase ensemble works in the company's characteristic ballet-based jazz vocabulary. Margo Sappington's angry, wrenching *Step Out of Love*, Bill Cratty's dark narrative *The Kitchen Table*, Daniel Ezralow's murderous *SUPER STRAIGHT is coming down*, and allusive, athletic *Read my Hips* began the transformation of company style: these accomplished technicians now display an expressive range beyond sensuality and self-consciousness.

The Tharp Project – the company premiere of *Sue's Leg* and *The Fugue* in 1990, of *Baker's Dozen* and *The Golden Section* in 1991, and *Nine Sinatra Songs* scheduled for the 1992/93 season – continues this transformation.

Hubbard Street's dancers now use weight and space as never before; their individual performances are increasingly transparent, relaxed, self-contained. Yet the premiere of Bob Fosse's *Percussion Four*, the solo from the Broadway musical *Dancin'* that Gwen Verdon restaged as a men's trio, suggests that Hubbard Street's hallmark presentational brio remains intact.

Danger inheres in the Tharp Project, notably the danger that Hubbard Street will be damned because they are Hubbard Street and not Twyla Tharp's original company. Restaging and maintaining works of historical import also diverts energy and resources from the creation of new dances; the Tharp and Fosse works illuminate dancing and our recent past, but they are not important new works that resonate with the whole context of contemporary culture.

Muntu Dance Theatre has accustomed mainstream dance audiences in Chicago to consistent, exceptionally high standards of choreography, performance and staging in African dance. The company celebrated their twentieth anniversary with two premieres: *Ole Time Religion*, a collaboration between artistic director Amaniyea Payne and percussionist Chief James Hawthorne Bey exploring the parallels between African-American gospel music and traditional Yoruba forms; and *Muana Mbenga* by Biza Sompa, a dance from the northern Congo celebrating a fisherman's miraculous catch. Muntu's superlative dancing and teaching dominated the first Dance Africa/Chicago: Honoring the Source, a week-long festival combining ritual, educational, and presentational forms. Dance Africa also featured the **Ko-Thi Dance Company** from Milwaukee, Wisconsin, and the **African-American Dance Ensemble** from Durham, North Carolina. Dance Africa/Chicago 1992: A Cultural Jubilee will feature **Urban Bush Women** from New York, Chicago's **Alyo Children's Dance Theatre** and **NAJWA Dance Corps** as well as Muntu and the African-American Dance Ensemble.

Chicago's smaller modern dance companies continue to present innovative and well-crafted work. Shirley Mordine, artistic director of **Mordine & Company Dance Theatre**, created two new works this season in collaboration with performance artist James Grigsby: *Stream of Recollection*, a large ensemble dance for the company, and *Here and There*, an intimate, intricate performance work for Grigsby and Mordine.

The atmosphere of *Here and There* recalls a folk tale or a fable. Grigsby and Mordine create characters so engrossed in their books, that they circle and support each other without even making eye-contact. They read Darwin, wear the stylized powder and rouge of Pierrot, and move with a peculiar courtly grace. Suddenly drawn to their Day-Glo garden, they lose each other while darting through eerie anthropomorphic trees and shrubs. An intruder, a masked Mordine, enters and leaves with one of their precious books. *Here and There* evokes the triangle of Harlequin, Columbine, and Clown, and eschews any easy resolution.

Like a stream of consciousness, *Stream of Recollection* locates the viewer in the mind of its central character. She walks into a tableau – a family group in turn of the century costume, posing for a photograph. The movement grows out of the dancers' posture and position, sketching character, suggesting relationships and events: ambivalent siblings, a wary marriage. The set alternately conceals and reveals the choreography; the dancers slip behind black velvet curtains, spread them, pull them aside, reshaping the performance space as recollection reshapes life. As the photographer narrates, she emphasizes memory's power to revise and conceal, suggesting that recollection is a futile, but fully human, endeavour.

Jan Erkert and Dancers' *About Men . . . About Women* probes both present and past, juxtaposing the performance of personal text with ensemble movement that combines abstract and gestural motifs. The evening-length work comprises four separately titled, mutually allusive dances: *Portrait of Five Men* and *Glass Ceilings* were created for this concert; *Ways of My Fathers* was restaged as four short dances; and *Sensual Spaces* was remade, incorporating movement drawn from the other three dances into its existing choreographic structure of kaleidoscopic duets, trios, quartets, and unison movement.

Sensual Spaces has been danced by a female cast and by a company of men and women, in a university chapel and in a stripped theatre, to Tomas Luis de Victoria's *Missa Ave Maria Stella* performed onstage by a large vocal ensemble and to tape. This version of *Sensual Spaces* contrasts vigorous ensemble choreography with a recurring, restrained duet: the two dancers animate the others – initiating a phrase of reaching and falling, repeating and altering an embrace – and embody a stillness of almost ritual intensity. *Sensual Spaces* evokes an image of the divine that is both male and female.

In *Portrait of Five Men*, the automobile serves as metaphor for sex, for mastery, for autonomy. At a spoken signal, the dancers burst out of their black folding chairs, grunting, muttering, and calling, boys against the girls in a physical free-for-all mixing American football, boxing, and contact improvisation. Erkert's comic timing and the text's arch double-meanings soften her sardonic treatment of men and male relationships. The movement that accompanies the text's portrayal of the first youth is all stereotypical posturing; of the young lover, a composite of common games. For the father, a Detroit Ford engineer forced into early retirement, a peculiar, powerful solo suggests withdrawal and alienation even as the performer moves downstage toward the audience. For the ninety-year-old grandfather, a doubled duet – two young professionals and two mature non-dancers – evokes both an old and resilient friendship and the contrast between youth and age.

Florida

Florence Fisher

The **Sarasota Ballet of Florida** is a welcome addition to the US dance scene. Relocating in November 1990 from Montreal, along with part of his former company, Ballet Eddy Toussaint, artistic director and choreographer Toussaint has succeeded in reaching the high level of his original ensemble. Adding new young dancers who fit well into his particular style, he has formed a vital, technically superior troupe. Combining ballet techniques with modern dance movements, Toussaint has created new dances of widely varied themes.

Reflecting the influence of Florida's subtropical sea and sky upon the choreographer's perceptions, *Florida Suite*, danced to a Delius score, premiered in November 1991. The same year, at the other end of the spectrum, *Bodies*, an acrobatic *pas de deux* to an exotic score by Brian Eno and David Byrne made its debut. *Cantate* for seven male dancers to music by Bach, and *Bonjour Brel*, to Jacques Brel's songs, were seen in August 1992. In March 1992, in collaboration with the Florida West Coast Symphony Orchestra, Toussaint created *Requiem* to Mozart's final masterpiece.

Principal dancers Sophie Bissonette and Denis Dulude, of the original Montreal company, were the romantic lovers in *Brel*. Kathryn Dandois and Alexei Dovgopoiyi danced *Bodies*. A new principal this year, Diane Partington, was featured in this year's performance of *Florida Suite*. Other featured dancers were Jeff Merckle, Stephen Austin, Nancy Street, and Jennifer Franklin.

In and around New York

Robert Greskovic

Money and politics continued to distract dance and its organizations, moving the real business - Art - of this fine art business off to the side. In political terms, the focus of this shift was sometimes to the right, and other times to the left. Compared with the previous year, however, there was some easing in the making of art and artists into ping-pong balls for politicians. The much discussed and beleaguered National Endowment for the Arts (NEA), which awards paltry amounts of funding compared with most other 'civilized' countries, had a cautious year and an even more cautious amount of funds to dispense - $8.5 million for dance in 1992. A political high point came in March, when President Bush announced the 'resignation' of John Frohnmayer, the NEA's beleaguered chairman, who spent his two-year tenure trying to please both sides of the impassioned art-versus-official art issue. This move came amid our Presidential Primary Election process, and followed uncannily in the wake of vociferous, anti-NEA rhetoric from Bush's shrill right-wing challenger for the Republican Party's presidential nomination, Patrick Buchanan. Frohnmayer's replacement, Anne-Imelda Radice, has, in her veto power over panel-approved grants, made her once-maligned predecessor look less meddlesome.

Meanwhile, real money (i.e. that gained from private and/or corporate funding and from box office revenues), while not fraught with so much rhetoric as public money, remains in related short supply. With the economy in a malaise, the arts bind gets stalemated: less outside funding means raising ticket prices, but less personal income leaves fewer takers for those costlier seats. While dance activity - so-called modern, experimental, classical, and folkloric - was fairly brisk in and around New York, there remained tell-tale signs of corner-cutting measures and of increased marketing ploys.

With its new, first-ever production of *The Sleeping Beauty*, **New York City Ballet** took a costly gamble that appeared to have paid off, at least in monetary terms. At an expense of nearly $3 million, balletmaster-in-chief Peter Martins mounted a two-act version of the 1890 Tchaikovsky/Petipa masterwork. David Mitchell's illustrational scenery, augmented by numerous slide projections indicating the various time and locale changes in the libretto, makes a fairly pretty and historically authentic setting for this well-known fairy tale. Patricia Zipprodt's lavish and carefully detailed costumes mostly compliment and support Mitchell's work. Martins' staging aims to present much of the Petipa choreography already known to the world from British and Russian sources, and embroider it with details and tempi he thinks appropriate to his dancers and his understanding of Tchaikovsky's intentions. The results are mixed. This *Beauty* tells its libretto story and makes some theatrical points, but is wanting in leisure and texture. It lacks breadth and, especially in the case of its brisk tempi, often seems breathless and graceless. It's high point is the 'Garland Waltz', credited to George Balanchine (1981), even though it is dressed with some of Zipprodt's least successful costumes and is somewhat cramped on a stage choked off by a balustraded walkway and staircase. Just how big a pay-off (in terms of box-office revenues), this spectacle proves to be has yet to be seen. Though its debut two weeks were virtually all sold out, its three-week return this year, to start a tradition for opening the annual spring season, was not the sell-out the company had hoped for. Martins' echt-Petipa *Sleeping Beauty* is nowhere near the equivalent of Balanchine's echt-Petipa/ Ivanov *Nutcracker*, in terms either of artfulness or of popularity.

With Jerome Robbins out of the picture as both balletmaster-in-chief, and, for the time being at least, as choreographer, New York City Ballet is decidedly all in Martins' hands. The four new ballets he created since overseeing the *Beauty* reveal no advance over his previous work, but tend, rather, to reinforce their serious limitations. Each work has a would-be air of efficiency and practicality to it. In the specific cases of the works to contemporary scores (all too frequently the all-too-contemporary Michael

231

Torke), there is an added scent of self-conscious chic and trendiness, Danish modern you might say. *Ash* (to Torke) is a high-energy dashing-about exercise for four interchangeable ensemble couples and one central couple. Made to feature Wendy Whelan and Nilas Martins (the choreographer's son), the work is a microcosm of Martins' NYCB: his sometimes efficient but rarely inspired dancers doing energetically efficient but artistically deficient motion. *A Musical Offering* (J. S. Bach) is Martins' formula in a more stately vein, one dictated by its more 'serious' music. Cast with four couples of principal dancers, it has the air of dutiful democratic thinking - a little something for everybody involved. But Martins' evident motivation to keep everyone happy here appears to stalemate. The chosen dancers - Judith Fugate and Peter Boal, Lourdes Lopez and Jock Soto, Kyra Nichols and Lindsay Fischer, Heather Watts and Damian Woetzel - have sometimes classical/sometimes quirky material that looks almost interchangeable. As has happened with Martins' multiple-couple ballets in the past (*Les Petits Riens* and *Mozart Serenade*, for example), this equal opportunity thinking yields a theatrically numb affair. *Delight of the Muses* is Martins' response to the Mozart bicentennial year. However imaginative the project was on paper - to make a Mozart ballet to contemporary music, (in this case a pastiche composition by Charles Wuorinen) - the end result was more sour and laboured than anything else. This goes for both score and choreography, which pits uneven numbers of unevenly matched dancers against each other with ham-handed jokes about ballet steps and ballet partnering.

Martins' *Jeu de cartes* is a re-do of most of what he's done before. Taking the same Stravinsky score that others had used (originally Balanchine himself), and discarding its accompanying Stravinsky card-game scenario, Martins made a busy, one-ballerina/three-partners work that descends noticeably from NYCB's Stravinsky ballet canon, complete with recycled Balanchinisms, and references to Martins' own *Concerto for Two Solo Pianos*.

If there was no news nor much interest in this newest work, it was presented in a newsworthy context. Martins' premiere was one of eleven new works unveiled during a week-long special event called 'The Diamond Project.' Put together by the balletmaster to focus on new, classical choreography for his company, the project managed to elicit interested public attention and to show the company happily, if not always valuably, at work. All the choreographers, some new to the company some not, were selected by Martins. In the end their works ranged from the dubious to the dutiful to the rewarding. William Forsythe was the biggest name and his work, *Herman Schmerman*, was the most formulaic and predictable. This prominent light in would-be contemporary ballet - I call it anti-classical ballet - was a kind of aesthetic guru. More than one other 'Diamond Project' creation looked to Forsythean dynamics or decorative elements, or both, for inspiration. John Alleyne made the most Forsythe-derivative work, while Alexander Proia, Martins himself, and to a slightly lesser extent Robert LaFosse, each made works that showed signs of admiration for and emulation of Forsythe's one-note, brash and glib view of ballet dancing. Works by Lynne Taylor-Corbett and Bart Cook showed more standard use of the classical canon, but in the case of the former the result was playful and common; and in the case of the latter, awkward and illegible. David Allan and Tony Pimble, both located on the West Coast, made energetic perpetual motion pieces. Allan's was more rigorous over all; Pimble's, more sentimental. The two ballets that made the best showings in terms of value to their casts and to the company's repertory were Miriam Mahdaviani's *Images* (to Debussy) and Richard Tanner's *Ancient Airs and Dances* (to Respighi). Mahdaviani's six-woman/six-man work is a lyrical rite of spring, shaped by supple statuesque women and youthfully fresh men. It has dimensions of ritual, community, and memory, and hints that the whole twelve-dancer affair is really the filigreed reverie of one woman, the one who enters first, solitarily (Romy Karz, whom Mahdaviani newly reveals here). Tanner's cast of three leading and six ensemble couples configures a finely wrought suite of moods, all of which seem coloured by the aura of dusk and beyond.

With the company announcement of a large-scale Balanchine festival next year to mark the tenth anniversary of the balletmaster's death, the current state of this bedrock repertory bears assessing. The value of this body of work has been stressed in the company since Balanchine's death, and its dominance in the repertory has reflected this accent. The problem, becoming more and more evident as the years pass, is that this mighty catalogue of work is mightily complicated, and filled with difficult challenges. As the Balanchine-tutored dancers leave the company, their places are taken by others differently schooled, and many of the roles in the canonic repertory are beyond their skill. This goes for partnering as much as for specific dance execution. So far Martins has tended to oversee the maintenance of NYCB repertory all by himself, alongside a permanent staff of underling balletmasters and mistresses. Whether the special preparation for the Balanchine Celebration will involve the particular participation of individual personnel who have been specifically connected to the ballets included remains to be seen. Until now, Martins has shown no interest in getting such 'outside' help, and NYCB repertory has been the worse for it.

The past year for **American Ballet Theatre** was one of beginning and ending. It began with what was in essence the first of Jane Hermann's seasons as the artistic director since she replaced Mikhail Baryshnikov in the autumn of 1990. While in place for about a year, Hermann had to live through the long-range time-lag that arts organizations all work by. Now she was running a show she had personally arranged. Then, by the end of

233

June 1992, her tenure was ended; she had resigned her position, reportedly because of a lack of wholehearted support from the Board of Directors, and was left to shepherd the troupe as a 'lame duck' for a couple of transitional months. What happened in between these demarcations was about a year's worth of mostly commendable dancing, primarily by personnel chosen and schooled in the Baryshnikov years. (Blossoming most prominently was Julie Kent, whose beauty and serenity distinguished almost all the roles she was given.)

All this fine and admirable dancing was framed, all too frequently, by retrograde or artistically lackadaisical additions Hermann made to the repertory. The company's somewhat signature store of so-called full-length ballets was augmented by a dramatically and musically lame-brained version of *Coppélia*, one originally staged for the company in 1968 by Enrique Martinez. Vladimir Vasiliev staged an echt-Soviet version of *Don Quixote*. This rather sprawling spectacle, which used the company's Santo Loquasto designs from Baryshnikov's production, was poorly received by most of the critical establishment, many of whom preferred Baryshnikov's tightly timed staging. But Vasiliev's staging revealed a pervasive sense of leisure that was refreshing and, if you gave in to it, beguiling. Instead of the normally busy months of touring and rehearsing between lengthy spring/summer engagements at New York City's Metropolitan Opera House, ABT had a spotty time. Because of funding problems, and cancelled production plans, a proposed new staging of *The Nutcracker* was postponed and performance dates connected to this were lost.

To open what became her last season at the helm of ABT, Hermann presented a new *Peter and the Wolf* and a rare staging outside England of Frederick Ashton's *Symphonic Variations*. The former was a serious misfire. Laboured efforts to update and upgrade the 'introduction to the orchestra' scheme of the work acted only to make it suitable for neither adults nor children. Larry Gelbart's overly clever libretto was often inadequately delivered. Neither Tony Walton's one-note set nor Willa Kim's predictably busy costumes signified much. Michael Smuin's choreography, fitted out with stage apparatuses and gimmicks that hardly paid off, ranged from the mundane to the insignificant. The decision to add kiddie cartoon sound effects over the orchestral sounds that give the work its *raison d'être* was cynical to a degree. The Ashton revival was as distinguished as the Smuin concoction was fatuous. With two solid casts, weak only in the role of central male partner (originally Michael Somes, who supervised the re-staging), ABT performed Ashton's rich and demanding classicism with sure strength and unaffected purity. Also new was Ulysses Dove's *Serious Pleasures*, a ghastly Forsythe-like affair, that reeked of desperate chic - sleek, black costuming; busy but pointless, stark lighting; an overwrought set of peek-a-boo louvred doors; and a metallic, electronic score sounding

Greg Lara and Lance Gries in Trisha Brown's *Astral Convertible*.

PHOTO: LOIS GREENFIELD

incidentally like noisy plumbing. As frantic as it was empty, this nine-dancer work was merely an indulgent display of one-note, hysterical dynamics.

The revivals from ABT's own past were a mixed lot. *The Firebird* (by Fokine, in a production by Nicholas Beriozoff) made little impact on the Met's stage, and seemed more rote work than anything else. *Undertow*, Anthony Tudor's Joycean creation, got too few performances - three all told - to hit its stride, but the company gave the classical centre of this personally classical choreography a special sheen that was rewarding, and probably unprecedented. Glen Tetley's empty *Le Sacre du printemps* was the same gruelling spectacle it was when first created for Baryshnikov in 1977. *Grass* by Mats Ek proved to be an inane battle-of-the-sexes duet in which the very

235

gifted Wes Chapman and Kathleen Moore appeared to be escaping from the bristles of a giant toothbrush.

Veteran ABT choreographer Agnes de Mille and novice John Seyla gave the repertory premiere works. De Mille's ballet, *The Other*, is a reworking of her previous explorations of a 'Death and the Maiden' theme to Franz Schubert. This version is a confused affair in which the figure of Death is ambiguously presented, especially so when Carld Jonassaint, a solitary black dancer in the cast, lends this pivotal character inadvertently racial overtones. Seyla's *Moondances* is an eccentric, slightly unfocused suite of dances set to the homespun philosophizing of a New York City street poet and musician. With the youthful choreographer himself taking on the mime role of the aged poet, cutting through ensemble dancing of dashing physicality, the work had a gentle bittersweetness.

Noticeably gone from ABT's offerings was the mini-repertory of Twyla Tharp pieces that had been given high profile ever since Tharp was brought in by Baryshnikov to be an artistic associate in 1988. The spring/summer season of 1991 saw the final ABT performances of these works - which included most of the pieces Tharp made especially for the ballet company as well as those she had made for her own company. Hermann and Tharp could not, it seemed, come to an agreement on the status of these ballets in ABT - no one was spelling things out 'on the record' - so Tharp left, taking all her works with her. (Hermann's few official comments about her concerns for the company's classical base alongside Tharp's modernist bent rang false when one saw what Dove had wrought for her dancers as classical choreography.)

Tharp's ballets were shown during this period, however, sometimes to great acclaim. One result of ABT's abandonment of this body of work was the relicensing of some of them to the **Boston Ballet**. (Previously, Hubbard Street Dance Company had acquired a separate body of Tharp's earlier, non-ballet pieces.) Two of Tharp's bigger dances, *In the Upper Room* (originally made for her own company, when it included classical dancers on pointe) and *Brief Fling* (originally created for ABT), became major entries on Boston Ballet's March and April programmes billed as 'On the Edge'. This run of two different programmes made up of 'contemporary' dance included works by Ralph Lemon, Monica Levy, Susan Marshall, Elisa Monte and Mark Morris, plus world premiere creations by Bill T. Jones and Bebe Miller. Elsewhere the Boston Ballet bill-o'-fare included offerings of 'standard' ballet repertory, such as *Giselle*, *The Nutcracker*, *A Midsummer Night's Dream*, and *Swan Lake*.

The biggest concentration of Tharp ballets came about by way of a new 'project' the dancemaker herself directed. Begun in October at Ohio State University, with residencies and workshops, the little company included some former Tharp dancers and a few one-time classical ballet dancers, mostly for NYCB. The project climaxed with a two-week New York City season. By this time Tharp had also engaged several dancers from the Paris Opera Ballet. The four-programme repertory included some works from Tharp's past, and some premiere pieces. Overall the newest pieces became the most rewarding, but a reworked revival of *Deuce Coupe*, originally made for the Joffrey Ballet and Tharp's own company in 1973, proved winning and affecting in its own way. NYCB's Robert LaFosse shone brightly in a season that included mostly superb dancing from the guesting Parisians and from the newest Tharpians. *Octet* and *Sextet* were both new dances that featured the highly schooled ballet dancers Tharp has become increasingly interested in working with. The first, to a dark and mellow jazz-like composition by Edgar Meyer, looks as if it comes from the 1920s; it involves four teasingly self-important young men and four inherently important bathing beauty ballerinas à la Nijinska. The other is a more outgoingly high-spirited affair (set to colourful south-of-the-border carnival music by Bob Telson) in which LaFosse and Isabelle Guerin figure most prominently. The season's most newsworthy work was *Men's Piece*, which marked another of Tharp's returns to the stage. Continuing a line of works in which the choreographer voices thoughts about her field and her part in it, this Manifesto about Woman and Man as a dancing couple was more zany Tharp double-talk than thoughtful final analysis.

One reason for Tharp's not wanting to head her own company is the great financial cost that goes along with such an organization today. The **Joffrey Ballet**, automatically ranked as the country's third most prominent ballet group, had a year of problems that illustrate Tharp's point. After a hurriedly put on two-and-a-half-week season of *The Nutcracker* - normally a sure money-maker - failed to sell especially well, the already financially strapped troupe had to cancel a planned winter season in New York City. Instead, it put its energies and finances toward a spring season in Los Angeles, where it would unveil several new ballets and give the premiere performances of its reconstruction of *Les Présages*, a major step toward a proposed all-Massine evening. Subsequently this four-and-a-half-week season had to be cancelled because of social unrest and turmoil in the southern California area where the theatre was located. In addition to these financial and happenstance problems, the company has lost Tina LeBlanc. The world-class classicist who was the Joffrey's crown jewel was recently married and, citing interest in being close to her West Coast husband, joined the **San Francisco Ballet**.

With the acquisition of LeBlanc, San Francisco Ballet, has a roster of dancers second to none in the States. An October visit by the company to NY's City Center Theatre revealed that the company, which had experienced a reported rejuvenation under its current director, Helgi Tomasson, was a brightly-toned ensemble of fresh and elegant dancers. Whatever disappointments there were in repertory terms - and there were a good many - the company was a well-oiled dancing entity that beamed forth with freshness and eagerness and skill. Tomasson's strong suit is his inherent ability to inspire and develop male dancers - the NY season featured among his already solid ranks a highly gifted 'defector' from the Royal Ballet, Bruce Sansom. With the prodigious Elizabeth Loscavio and, now, LeBlanc under his direction, his strength regarding ballerinas stands on equally firm footing.

While media and funding focus is still concentrated on such big institutions as NYCB, the levelling-off of high standards that helped gain the company its stature makes attending the offerings of smaller organizations more than just idle curiosity. **Pennsylvania Ballet**, which was saved from the brink of extinction last year by the work of ex-NYCB dancer Christopher d'Amboise, then its new director, continued to stay alive. His repertory additions continue the pattern of many medium-sized ballet companies around the country: new works by its dancer-turned-artistic director counterbalanced by acquisitions of more tried and popular twentieth-century ballets. This year d'Amboise added *The Prodigal Son* to his company's long-standing repertory of Balanchine ballets. **Houston Ballet**, continuing the British connection maintained by its English director Ben Stevenson, added Ashton's *The Two Pigeons* to its repertory. **Feld Ballets/NY** continues to represent Big Ballet's Obstreperous Kid Brother. Though its omnipresent director Eliot Feld continues to lose dancers, it seems, with each season, he still maintains his company, sometimes filling in with dancers from his own school - The New Ballet School, which recently received a $250,000 grant from the Mellon Foundation. This year the ever-scrappy Feld showed three new works: *Clave*, a now-familiar Feldian exercise in repetition for his chief muse, the ever-beautiful Buffy Miller; *Endsong*, a dramatically and pictorially interesting group work, that gained some extra drama from the necessity of performing it without its intended music - Richard Strauss - because of difficulties with the estate; and *The Wolfgang Strategies*, an almost angrily anti-classical absurdist answer to the would-be classic call for a Mozart anniversary creation.

After a period of financial and organizational uncertainty, **Dance Theatre of Harlem** returned with a full-fledged season at the Brooklyn Academy of Music. Two weeks of four programmes offered little in terms of significant new repertory but much in terms of fresh dance talent. With the veteran Virginia Johnson out due to injury, some of Arthur Mitchell's younger women got prime time. Both Judith Rotardier and Felicity de Jager stood out exceptionally.

East Coast visitors included the **Royal Ballet** and the **Kirov/Maryinsky Ballet**. After an earlier visit to Kennedy Center the Royal played two weeks at the Metropolitan Opera House and proved eagerly interesting once more to NY audiences. The Dowell/Sonnabend *Swan Lake* was a sore disappointment, both in terms of details and by virtue of what it said about Royal classicism - it seemed more verismo and illustrational than classical and lyrical, so did much of the dancing. None of the new ballets was especially engaging - MacMillan's *Winter Dreams* and Bintley's *Still Life at the Penguin Café*. Paris Opera guest Sylvie Guillem proved the artistic cipher she had been in her guesting with ABT; Laurent Hilaire performed warmly but danced untidily at his repertory's most demanding spots. But Bruce Sansom and, most especially, Darcey Bussell gave great performances, and great pleasure. Other unfamiliar Royal dancers found followings, even if none proved so profound as Sansom or Bussell. Irek Mukhamedov, looking unfortunately heavier than he did here with the Bolshoi Ballet, still managed to win admiration for his warmth and power. The Kirov, first in DC in the autumn and then in NYC this summer, is very much a group in transition if not turmoil. Director Oleg Vinogradov's new *Swan Lake* is as dispiriting, in its way, as the Royal's. The refurbished production of *La Bayadère* was in good shape; Lavrovsky's *Romeo and Juliet* was given with the proper leisure, but lacked something in character detail. There is a definite lack of male talent overall, and the very talented Igor Zelensky is about to join NYCB for at least a year. Upper-level women are also not in great supply, with only the sometimes brash Yulia Makhalina consistently scaling new heights. The company's performing of the Balanchine, Tudor, and, most recently, Robbins, is individually uneven, but works like these show the dancers and their dancing in a new and mostly rewarding light.

Two visiting companies played locally and offered different visions of Forsythe-mania. Alonzo King's **LINES Contemporary Ballet** performed a week of one bill of its director's ballets. These showed a physically feisty but artistically numbing aesthetic that I can only ascribe to what I call 'Billy Blight'. **Scapino Ballet Rotterdam**, with a week's worth of a programme of ballets by Nils Christe (artistic director) and by Ed Wubbe (resident choreographer), made a more reasonable show of this line of working in Wubbe's *Rameau*, mostly because its dancers were so appealing and its echt-Forsythe work more plastically interesting and physically varied.

Our own School of American Ballet and the Paris Opera's Ballet School performed within a month's time in NYC. Both showed that dancers were still being trained with a rigour not always wanted by the companies ready to hire them. The appearances by the pupils from the Opera included a day-long lecture-demonstration and then three performances of shockingly frivolous ballets. One was, a mangled bit of Russophilia, *Le Prisonnier du Caucase* by George Skibine; another, a cynical and decadent 'living art' stunt, *Entre deux rondes* by Serge Lifar; and then *Arcades*, a clumsy, 'école de ballet' showcase by Atillo Labis. Essentially this display reinforced the school's strength and emphasis on masculine technique and its lack of finesse on the female side. The School of American Ballet made a better showing as performers, even if one suspects it would make a lesser showing of a strict classroom display like the Parisians put on. This programme showed strong performances of Balanchine's *Allegro Brillante*, especially in the ballerina role with Tara Keim; and slightly less strong ones of the choreographer's *Who Cares?*, which of course needs *three* strong ballerinas. The *pas de trois* from Bournonville's *La Ventana* had alternate casts and alternately successful performances. A truncation of Peter Martins' *Mozart Serenade* suitably tested, without inspiring, its eager and adept casts.

Washington DC's Kennedy Center continues to showcase ballet companies both from the States and abroad. The most newsworthy aspect of its presentations is an ongoing programme to commission new works for half a dozen American ballet companies who play at the centre. Lately these commissions have yielded a not-quite-original *Age of Anxiety* by John Neumeier (to Bernstein) for **Ballet West** and *American Gesture* by Lar Lubovitch (to Charles Ives) for **Pacific Northwest Ballet**. The logic here is to provide funds for new works by choreographers that the companies might not otherwise be able to afford, and to offer the finished commissions to all six companies participating in the project. Of course, the works may go into the choreographer's own company repertory as well, and in the cases of Paul Taylor and Lubovitch have already done so.

Lubovitch's company gave a one-week season and made much, in publicity terms, out of the fact that budgetary constraints forced it to perform the new *American Gesture* (a Kennedy Center commission) without the designs originally prepared for the work. *Waiting for the Sunrise*, which Lubovitch made originally for the White Oak Dance Project, was given happy performances here, with especial excitement generated by the intense and fine performing of Scott Rink.

In his annual two-week local season, **Merce Cunningham** showed three new works, each one a special beauty revealing the special beauty of his current company. *Beach Birds* is lushly pictorial and nearly illustrational of its poetic title. *Loosestrife*, in which the maestro himself is surrounded by all fifteen of his company dancers, is a compelling composition of both solo focus and group energy. *Change of Address* is a work for the full company, minus the choreographer himself, and it takes off and keeps taking off in directions rather different from the harmonious unpredictabilities Cunningham has been known for. There is a rawness and a volubility here quite unlike anything Cunningham has created up to now.

The **Paul Taylor Company**, whose financial problems prevented it from performing in NYC for an unusually long time, finally had a two-week season (an annual four-week season had been standard) and showed two new Taylor works of different, but equally intriguing, focus. *Company B*, an immediately popular work that emanated from the Kennedy Center's commissioning project, uses Andrews Sisters songs and is a social dance/social comment suite. *Fact & Fancy*, like the Andrews Sisters work, uses recorded music (and saves on musician costs) and was seemingly as bewildering as its companion premiere was beguiling. It's a dark and would-be shambling affair, but its design plan is firm and its ability to fool the eye and the mind is impressive.

Baryshnikov spiced up the **Martha Graham Dance Company**'s NYC season, its first since its founder/mentor died in April, by performing in *El Penitente*. The other news in the season was *The Eyes of the Goddess*, billed as Graham's last work, having its premiere in the wake of her passing. Designed, oppressively, ex-post-facto by Marisol, and set to a score chosen by Graham's heirs, the result was a sprawling occurrence, diffuse even in terms familiar for very late Graham. As they have been for a while now, the company dancers are an uneven ensemble, lacking both real force and real power, which is misconstrued as forced performing and over-emoting.

Gorgeous dancers and dancing is definitely the rule of Judith Jamison's tenure as artistic director of the **Alvin Ailey American Dance Theatre**. Even the air-headed *Escargot*, the Louis Falco revival that was featured in the Ailey winter season, looked substantial on these dancers. Jamison's own choreography tends to be insubstantial, but it does not dominate the repertory. And, with Masazumi Chaya as her right hand, Jamison is keeping the Ailey repertory in tip-top shape all the while she's adding pieces that, as in the case of Donald Byrd dances for example, nicely showcase the company's considerable gifts.

The **Mark Morris Dance Group** played a two-week stint of two programmes in a Grand Ballroom converted to a little theatre. His first NY season since his departure for Brussels in 1988, this repertory reclaimed his following, who acclaimed both his mixed bills. The first featured quality, live music - from Vivaldi's *Gloria* to a Lou Harrison piece for piano and violin. The second, more profane than the sacred air of the first, used either pre-recorded music or silence. The newest pieces, *A Beautiful Day* (to Schubert) and *Polka* (to Harrison), were complementarily rich - the former, a mysteriously serene duet; the latter, a vehemently slap-happy round dance/ritual.

Folkloric dance companies included the world-famous, block-buster ensemble of the **Moiseyev Dance Company**, which played Radio City's mammoth Music Hall, as well as small-scale Russian groups concerned with 'authentic' rather than theatricalized folk material. The Moiseyev season gave everyone pause to consider the future of such huge state-subsidized troupes in the light of the disintegration of the state that formed them. The company proved to be young, strong, and seemingly bottomless of depth. The more home-spun group's included the **Gulyane Folk**

241

Project, from various regions of the former Soviet Union, and the **Dancing Teens** from Voronezh. Both were part of 'Russian Partners', a project run by Bonnie Freundlich and David Eden, that aims to show authentic Eastern European folk dance and music in community outreach situations of a lecture-demonstration/get-together format.

In between these visits the **American Indian Dance Theatre** presented a second local season, showing its theatricalized versions of dances native to the indigenous peoples of North America. Some of these presentations are more effective than others, but none is more bravura than the hoop dance, in which a male dancer works with what look like hundreds of hoops to the effect of some continually transmuting mating dance of a fabulous bird of display.

The closest we come to such spectacle on our standard theatrical circuit is the **Pilobolus** family of performers. This year saw visits from **Momix**, a marvellous offshoot of the unclassifiable mentor group, and of **Iso**, an offshoot of this offshoot, which better understands the letter than the spirit of its inspiration. Momix played a month of varied programming and showed that its major difference from Pilobolus stems from the strong effect of the women in the troupe. With their not-quite dance concoctions Pilobolus *et al.* often look like Denishawn for the late twentieth century. Thus, Momix has a St Denis slant; Pilobolus, that of Shawn.

The hundredth anniversary of Ted Shawn's birth was actually celebrated this year with a little touring company of dancers called **Men Dancers: The Ted Shawn Legacy**. Trying to be too many things - a homage to Shawn's work, to his spirit, and to our men dancers - the programme, with uneasy framing numbers choreographed by Ann Carlson, lacked firm focus and substance.

The ostensibly independent companies of **Alwin Nikolais** and **Murray Louis** shared a season and programmes this winter, since neither could afford a lone run. Both proved to be doing what they have been known to do over the years, and a generation of dance/theatre aspirants with a bent for media still stands to gain a formidable visual education studying the visual/physical surround conjured up by Nikolais.

The American Dance Festival, honouring and furthering the so-called Modern Dance, continued to be both a historical reference point and an inspiration for new work in this vein. Last summer was noteworthy for the for the debut appearance of the **Guangdong Modern Dance Company**, China's first such group, established with assistance from ADF. The festival's prestigious Scripps prize was awarded to **Anna Sokolow**.

The ninth instalment of Brooklyn Academy of Music's Next Wave Festival included two monumental pieces by **Pina Bausch**: the almost iridescent, 'exterior' *Palermo, Palermo*, and the dark, 'interior' *Bandoneon*. **Eiko** and **Koma**'s *Land* had its undeniable beauties but, perhaps due to the relinquishing of some production elements to others outside this very gifted husband and wife team, it lacked the ultimate Eiko and Koma signature, an unbeatable blend of the raw and the exquisite. **Wim Vandekeybus and Ultima Vez** produced *Always the Same Lies*, a pretty but not fully gripping spectacle built around hammocks and eggs. **Garth Fagan Dance** presented *Griot New York*, and once again showed, here on a grand scale, that Fagan's wilful eccentricity is no substitute for artful mystery.

Meanwhile the less glamorous and less grand venues around the area continued to show the work of less heralded artists. Words often overwhelmed deed in a spate of works that spoke up for various racial, gender, and sexual orientation causes. A choreographer who manages to approach such 'subjects' and yet keep dancing as his main mode of expression is **Demetrius Klein**, a Floridian who visits here all too infrequently. His low-profile appearances with his dance group this year included the showing of his new rendering of Ravel's *La Valse*. This pungently musical, physically alive work cuts through the time, space and history of its score with unshakable confidence and highly personal theatrical vision. A group calling itself the **Rhythm Technicians and Rock Steady Crew** gave some performances of a their street dancing manoeuvres in an ill-conceived and hopelessly naive work called *So! What Happens Now?* Their intense amateur acrobatics have some of the impact of real folk art, but their part in a viable theatrical showcases has yet to arranged.

Starting what might well become a tradition, Movement Research, a NYC service and presenting organization, this year started an autumn, winter, and spring series of free evening performances in the now august surround of the Judson Church. Once the site of some now-landmark activity in so-called postmodern dance, this airy church sanctuary provided a congenial and blessedly un-hyper setting for some of the year's most jewel-like performances. Each evening was a shared programme, sometimes by two, other times three artists. This writer went whenever possible and will not easily forget such magical sights as **Susan Rethorst and Vicky Shick** pacing elegiacally through a little dance for two calm, but precise women wielding silver tea spoons as if they were infallibly magic wands. Or **Keely Garfield**, leading a trio of white-clad fellow performers through a delicately zany ritual that involved each working with an enamel skillet and a single, buck-wheat pancake. Or, **Scott Heron**, a gaunt slip of a young man, starting his piece like a solemn high priest crowned with a story-high cocoon of transparent balloons, and continuing his journey by way of entering a little plot, outlined by a string of bare light bulbs, wherein he cued a terrific clatter from some musician friends stationed in the choir loft. What a racket ensued, and what a marvellous event Heron oversaw.

San Francisco

Paul Parish

We in San Francisco are in the embarrassing position of seeing our ballet puffed up beyond its merits by the New York press; it's not been a great year. One suspects that Helgi Tomasson is being used as a stick with which to beat Peter Martins by those who are forced, day in day out, to notice that New York City Ballet does not look like it did under Balanchine. Though our dancers may have a sunnier energy than those at NYCB – and they certainly look happier than the kids at ABT or the Joffrey did when they toured through here – it feels like the vision at **San Francisco Ballet**, though optimistic, is merely sentimental, decorative, mannerist.

Perhaps one feels this way because it is the first disappointing year since Helgi Tomasson took over the company seven years ago. Every year the dancing had looked brighter, cleaner, the corps and soloists revealed greater fluidity in linking long chains of steps into phrases that lift and expand your sense of the world; in short, they made one very happy, especially dancing the Balanchine repertory, but also in Tomasson's new stagings of *Sleeping Beauty* and *Swan Lake*. And as we've waited for ballerinas to emerge who could be put in front of these dancers and carry the figurative responsibilities for the ballet, the sense of a groundswell of talent has allayed misgivings about the mannerist tendencies in Tomasson's repertory choices.

This year did not feel like an advance: the great fun again came from the corps and soloists, especially in Balanchine's *Who Cares?* I did not see the performance led by Joanna Berman, but I firmly believe it was the climax of the year, since she combines technical mastery, vulnerability, and wit in a unique way and could make 'Fascinating Rhythm' as hilarious as Patricia McBride did originally. And certainly the corps and soloists understand how to infuse classical amplitude with the pelvic accents of jazz, and they hear the music in the dancing.

It's in Balanchine that they really shine, as dance-musicians, like orchestra-players. As we watched them rise up through the ranks, we were all imagining the future of the company, as we saw bright kids get larger responsibilities: Shannon Lilly, Katita Waldo, Grace Maduell, Kristen Long, Jennifer Karius; most of all Elizabeth Loscavio, who's now a ballerina, with absolute triumphs under her belt in Balanchine's *Ballo della Regina*, and in *Sleeping Beauty*. But this year, Loscavio could not make it look so promising. She had it nailed in her debut in Balanchine's *Theme and Variations*, but the performance lacked amplitude; normally our most musical dancer, in this she was rushing, and the *pas de chats* (for example) – which are set like diamonds and should crown the quick arcs of her phrases, but didn't – snapped shut and were already gone when their facets should have been most open and intense.

Loscavio was a delight as Lise in Ashton's *La Fille mal gardée* (in the repertoire since 1968, and deservedly popular all along), especially her variation in the Fanny Elssler *pas de deux*. This was probably the prettiest dancing we saw all year: such gusto in her leaps, expressed with such sweetly shaded *épaulement* as she swept up her arms and lifted her breast into the air. Good as that was, both she and Stephen Legate (a thrilling Colas, though he dances *too* big – his legs look ten miles long in *sissonnes*) rushed the mime and stood around with time on their hands as their music played out. The real star of the show was Christopher Stowell as Alain, who built the character very much in dance terms. Stowell, our cleanest technician and most scrupulous stylist of either sex, is perhaps our most interesting dancer; but he's hard to cast, not just because he's short, but more because of something insatiable in his temperament that makes him look unhappy onstage and self-absorbed, ungenerous as a partner. In this part that was not a problem, and Stowell's energies have never glowed brighter. Alain's idiosyncrasies shaped every move, especially when Stowell was in the air, and were never clearer than in the dancing itself: he shaped his trajectories so that when he 'stuck' his landing in a pose of exquisite silliness (that was simultaneously a beautifully rotated attitude), the image became an icon. The comic line was drawn with as sure a sense of the ridiculous and as little regard for the necessities imposed by gravity as if he were Mighty Mouse or Bugs Bunny.

It did not feel like the Royal Ballet. One hesitates to tell the English about Ashton, but when I was at Oxford, I went up to London and saw the Royal Ballet a lot in 1969 and 1970. (I'd say I formed my taste on the Royal Ballet, on Nureyev, Sibley and Dowell, Monica Mason, and Alexander Grant.) Though Grant supervised this production, Stowell does Alain his own way – I missed the overtones of sadness I remember with Grant, and that Shakespearean sense that 'the fool knows more than we do' about the mysteries of life. Stowell gave fewer suggestions of a holy fool, but he was sublimely silly nevertheless. He wanted more to get the girl, he had more ambition in that direction; with Grant, you were as relieved for him as you were for Lise that she ended up with Colas.

There were other high points to the season – the most intense, because it came as such a revelation, was Grace Maduell's sublime dancing in the penultimate solo of Tudor's *Dark Elegies* ('Oft denk ich, sie sind nur ausgegangen'). It's a ballet nobody else at SFB seems to know how to dance. They're all trying very hard to look wooden, stoical, impersonal; they look browbeaten, like they don't get it. But Maduell looks like Kathleen Ferrier sounded when she sang the song: vulnerable, grateful for a form into which she could pour her grief. She moved as if through a heavy medium: as her body opened into an expressionist attitude and then contracted powerfully, it felt like she was pulling her way through pain, like a manta ray pulling itself through water. Suddenly, chills went up my back, tears sprang to my eyes, I started from my chair.

Nothing like that happened in the three *Swan Lake*s I saw. Sabina Allemann, a house ballerina with a large repertory and some following, looked deadly dull to me. Muriel Maffre, a stunning French ballerina (built like Sylvie Guillem though even taller), who's had terrific success in roles as varied as Bournonville's *La Sylphide*, Forsythe's *In the middle, somewhat elevated*, and Balanchine's *Bugaku* and *Symphony in C*, had a sensational act as Odile, but looked bizarre as Odette: partly because she emphasized the bird to the point that she seemed to be indulging her glamour and had forgotten that Odette wants to *get out* of this spell (which may be the French way); and partly because she is so skinny, and her tutu fits so badly, that there were times one could not look at her.

One had looked forward to Loscavio's debut: many found it satisfying, found her Odette passionate and assertive. It didn't look that way to me. She is a natural for Odile (that act went dazzlingly) – in fact, at the bows she looked at times more like Odile than Odette.

There may not be any great American Odettes; I didn't see Cynthia Gregory do it more than a few times, but I did not like her. I can't say about the Balanchine ballerinas, either, though since his version is only Act II, they don't have the burden of carrying her impact through Act III to the end – so that one sees *her* through Odile (and doesn't merely 'see through' Odile), and sees her reflected 'in mirrors more than one' in the swans' choric dances of grieving *for* her in Act IV.

Tomasson's staging sentimentalizes Odette. The production blurs things by relocating the action in a scene from Fragonard, which is exquisitely realized both in costumes/sets (by Jens-Jacob Worsaae) and in the gallant manners the dancers affect – but this relocates the deep action in a post-heroic period of *liaisons dangereuses*, not in the heroic period of chivalric devotion. (Of course, decors don't rule: a great dancer can always make decor disappear if she imagines a world more vivid than the sets and acts, as if that's her reality, especially if the choreography clothes her in nobility.) The greater problem is Tomasson's final scene. It's not like Ashton's, where the choric dancing carries a weight like the great Greek tragic odes, or the choruses in *Fidelio*, and establish a public dimension of sympathy with the protagonists and their values. Instead, Tomasson quickly banishes the chorus: to Tchaikovsky's *Serenade Mélancolique*, he has made a sentimental *pas de deux* for just the two of them, reprising images from Act II (including the 'my mother's tears' gesture from Ivanov's great mime scene, which Tomasson has mistakenly suppressed). It weakens these images to bring them back for no more reason than to let Odette have a good cry.

Odette does not need her hand held: kissing it won't make it better – though that's very much an 'Age of Sensibility' sort of attitude to take, and

(Left to right): Susan Taylor, Christina Buenocamino, and Joral Schmalle, in Oakland Ballet's 1989 production of Emily Keeler's *The Awakening*.

PHOTO: MARTY SOHL

suits the decision to replace the chivalric code with the code of sentiment. But that turns *Swan Lake* from a tragedy into melodrama, from granite to sugar-loaf – and from Odette's victory into Odile's. In Ashton's version, the climax came at the last moment. Indeed, it came after the last moment, in the apotheosis; it wasn't just sad, it was tremendous, a vision of eternity: yes, that's who they are, that's who they made of themselves, that's glorious.

The fault is not in the dancers, it's a problem of artistic direction, and it's showing up all over the place, in a lot of strikingly executed, empty choreography that substitutes anxious concern for surface clarity for the kind of significant form which emerges from deep coherences. Probably one-third of the current rep at SFB falls in this category: David Bintley's *Job*, James Kudelka's *The End*, Tomasson's *Aurora Polaris, Haffner Symphony, Beads of Memory*, are laboured, unmusical movement studies with occasional flashes of inspiration.

Well, it's not news that ballet choreography has entered a mannerist phase, internationally. Everyone is trying not to complain – they're doing the best they can - but it was shocking, when Baryshnikov brought his **White Oak Dance Project** here, to see that *every piece* on his two programmes was a good ballet. One recalled that when he was director of American Ballet Theatre, Baryshnikov commissioned good work from David Gordon, Merce Cunningham, Karole Armitage, Twyla Tharp, Mark Morris, modern dancers familiar with ballet – that's where good choreography is nowadays – and made ABT once again a real part of the cultural life of New York. Tomasson has made some gratifying moves in this direction. (His own best work, the exquisite *Meistens Mozart*, is in this vein.) Some work by Mark Morris would be especially welcome. (Baryshnikov has remade himself, by the way, into a very good, but not a great, modern dancer, although in Mark Morris's solo, *Ten Suggestions*, he looked like the god of play, forever young.)

The most successful new ballet around San Francisco last season was made by a modern dancer, Margaret Jenkins, for the scrappy **Oakland Ballet**, who performed *Sightings* on both sides of the Bay, on the wide shallow stage of Oakland's Paramount Theater and on the narrow, deep stage at Theater Artaud (a converted warehouse in the Mission district, and the home of the avant-garde in San Francisco) for Jenkins' home season. The dancers looked splendid on both occasions. The ballet is like music by Elliott Carter: it feels like there are several ballets going on at once in the opening section, as the stage fills with dancers who are strangely convincing in their separate concerns and trajectories. It becomes more fun in the trio and duets which follow, where wry, tender greetings and support are exchanged. In the finale things get crowded again: it's remarkable how clearly one can follow several lines at once, and how much they seem to belong to the same world though they don't seem to greet or even acknowledge each other.

What's impressive is that Jenkins studied the dancers, found what's theatrical about the way each one moves, found ways to expand that, and to develop phrases with a big rhythm that rise from each individual's own impulses into clear, complex forms; so the dancers came into bloom.

Jenkins' *Strange Attractors*, for three of her own dancers moving inside a gorgeous set (by Alex Nichols) which surrounded the stage with fringes of tan linen string, floor to ceiling, was even more successful, poetically. Their brief costumes were knit of the same soft linen, and they seemed like the Bride of Frankenstein and her two best friends on a warm soft day. Miss Klopp, in particular, looks quite mad, though not at all dangerous, and explores the space autistically, like Giselle without a grievance. In the middle the music becomes expansive, and they sweep around the room softly.

One has assumed that an international readership will be most interested in our ballet company, since it has a wide reputation already. The modern dancers and performance artists, however – although they did not face the heroic physical challenges our ballet dancers did – have developed modes of movement inherently more interesting than much of what we saw at the ballet. A short list of those performers would include **Remy Charlip**, **Liz Ozol**, **Jon Weaver**, **Robert Henry Johnson**, all of whom perform solo and, as is a fashion, to verbal texts; and **Joanna Haigood**, who redefines space like a constructivist, finding planes to dance on (such as upside-down on the ceiling and falling out of windows) along the lines that Trisha Brown did back in the Judson days.

Obituaries

Charles 'Cookie' Cook, part of the vaudeville tap-dance act 'Cook and Brown' and well-known tap teacher, died at 77 in August 1991. Besides touring the States and Europe as part of the vaudeville team, Cook also did solo appearances. Some of America's current tap artists name Cook as an important mentor and teacher. He died of kidney failure.

Robert Irving, conductor and music director, died aged 78 in Winchester, England in September 1991. Beginning as conductor for the BBC Orchestra and then for Sadler's Wells Ballet, he eventually settled in New York City where, since 1958, he was conductor for New York City Ballet. He also conducted part-time for the Martha Graham Dance Company. He gave up his post as Principal Conductor and Music Director of City Ballet due to illness in 1989. He died of coronary arrest.

Roman Jasinski, Polish-born dancer, former star of the Ballets Russes companies, died aged 83 in April 1991. After working as a dancer with such choreographers as George Balanchine, Michel Fokine, Léonide Massine and Bronislava Nijinska, he founded Tulsa Ballet Theatre in 1956, with his wife, ballerina Moscelyne Larkin. In addition to reviving well-known works from his own past, he also worked diligently to revive Balanchine's little-known *Mozart Violin Concerto*. He died of heart failure.

Lydia Joel, former editor-in-chief of *Dance Magazine* and head of the dance department of the School of Performing Arts in New York City, died aged 77 in May 1992. Trained as a dancer in both ballet and modern dance, Joel performed in the late 1930s in the work of Hanya Holm. After her career as dancer and company director, she worked as an editor, historian and journalist. She died of leukaemia.

Robert Kovich, choreographer and teacher who first came to prominence as a dancer in the Merce Cunningham Dance Company died in April 1991. After eight years as a Cunningham dancer, during which time his precise and strong dancing was regularly recorded in Cunningham's dance films and videos, he started to do his own work. Kovich performed his original dances primarily in France and in the States. He died of cancer, aged 40.

Deni Lamont, long-time soloist and member of the artistic staff of New York City Ballet, died aged 59 in November 1991. After a career as principal dancer with Ballet Russe, he danced for American Ballet Theatre and then joined City Ballet. Notable among his created roles there was Pierrot in Balanchine's *Harlequinade*. He died of lung cancer.

Irina Nijinska, dancer, teacher, and balletmistress, primarily of works created by her mother Bronislava Nijinska, died in July 1991, aged 77. A Russian emigré who was schooled in Europe, she settled in Hollywood in 1940. Having assisted her mother in restagings of her work toward the end of her life, Irina became the guardian of Bronislava's work upon the choreographer's death in 1972. In addition to the works that survived complete, those thought not to have survive increasingly occupied her attention, when she became increasingly involved with reconstructions, such as *Le Train bleu*. She died of complications following a stroke.

Ruth Page, long-time champion of ballet as a dancer, teacher and choreographer, died aged 92 in April 1991. Having studied and worked with both ballet and modern dance theories, Page was one of the first choreographers to use American themes in her work. As a performer, she danced the role of Terpsichore in the very first staging of Stravinsky's *Apollo* by Adolph Bolm in 1928. Founder of the Chicago Opera Ballet, the company with which Rudolf Nureyev made his American debut, Page kept Chicago as her home base. She died of respiratory failure.

Gertrude Schurr, Latvian-born modern dancer and teacher, died aged 88 in January 1992. A product of the Denishawn school, and a student of Doris Humphrey, Charles Weidman, and Martha Graham, she appeared as a dancer for all these choreographers at some point in her career. Joining

Graham's group in 1930, she appeared in many of its premieres. In 1982 she helped Graham revive *Primitive Mysteries*. She also danced for May O'Donnell. She died of heart failure.

Olga Spessivtseva, legendary Russian ballerina, whose career was cut short by mental instability, died in September 1991, aged 96, at the Tolstoy Foundation Nursing Home, where she had resided since 1963. During the 1920s and '30s she was an acclaimed interpreter of the ballerina roles in *Giselle, Swan Lake*, and *The Sleeping Beauty*. In 1927 she created the lead role in George Balanchine's *La Chatte*. Serge Diaghilev, in whose company she came to prominence, stated a preference for her over Anna Pavlova. She gave her last performance in 1937. She died of pneumonia.

S. Cobbet Steinberg, dance writer, historian, and film-maker died aged 42 in August 1991. Closely associated with the San Francisco Performing Arts Library and Museum, he was the author of eight books and monographs on the arts, chief among these a volume on the San Francisco Ballet. He also curated exhibitions and codirected a national seminar on *Swan Lake*. He died of complications from AIDS.

Burt Supree, dance writer and editor, died aged 51 in May 1992. After a career performing in experimental dance and theatre, he began writing about dance in 1976. Since 1973 he had been writing a weekly column called 'Kids' for the *Village Voice*, where he then became dance editor and critic. His work in both capacities often championed experiments of beginning artists. He died of a heart attack.

Clark Tippet, principal dancer and choreographer with American Ballet Theatre, died aged 37 in January 1992. Once his repertory of principal roles in many of ABT's full-length ballet productions started to yield to a repertory of principal mime roles, Tippet began to work as a choreographer. Encouraged by the workshop Mikhail Baryshnikov instituted at ABT, the choreographer saw five of his ballets enter the company's repertory, often to great interest and acclaim. He died of complications from AIDS.

PART IV

The Statistics of
Dance Companies

Australia

THE AUSTRALIAN BALLET

2 Kavanagh Street, South Melborne
Victoria 3205
Tel: (03) 684 8600
Fax: (03) 686 7081

Artistic dir.: Maina Gielgud

Administrative dir.: Ian MacRae

Visiting choreographer(s): Glen Tetley

Guest teacher(s): Jurgen Schneider, Dame Sonia Arova, Mr Wang Jiahong, Madame Tang, Johnny Eliasen, Denise Schultze

Principal dancers: David Ashmole, Miranda Coney, Steven Heathcote, Greg Horsman, Timo Kokkonen, Adam Marchant, David McAllister, Lisa Pavane, Colin Peasley, Fiona Tonkin

Guest dancers: Henriette Muus, Alexander Kølpin, Christine Dunham, Gary Norman, Marilyn Jones, Michela Kirkaldie, Edna Edgley, Dame Margaret Scott, Valrene Tweedie, Juliet Day

No. of dancers: 30 male, 34 female

No. of performances: 186

Tours to: Italy

Premieres:

Apollo 3/5/91, Sydney
Ch.: Balanchine. *M.:* Stravinsky. *L.:* William Akers.

Of Blessed Memory 18/10/91, Melbourne
Ch.: Stanton Welch. *M.:* Joseph Canteloube. *D.:* Kristian Fredrikson. *L.:* William Akers.

Symphonic Poem 21/2/92, Melbourne
Ch.: Timothy Gordon. *M.:* Suk. *D.:* Kenneth and Victoria Rowell. *L.:* William Akers.

Nutcracker 12/3/92, Sydney
Ch.: Graeme Murphy. *M.:* Tchaikovsky. *D.:* Kristian Fredrikson. *L.:* John Montgomery.

AUSTRALIAN DANCE THEATRE

120 Gouger Street
Adelaide, SA 5000
Tel: (08) 212 2084

CHRISSIE PARROTT DANCE COLLECTIVE

PO Box 8278
Stirling Street
Perth, WA 6849
Tel: (09) 227-9463
Fax: (09) 227-9190

Artistic dir.: Chrissie Parrott

Administrative dir.: Drew James

Principal/associate choreographer(s): Chrissie Parrott

Visiting choreographer(s): John McLaughlin, Jenny Newman-Preston, Jon Burtt, Stephen Petronio

No. of dancers: 4 male, 4 female

No. of performances: 53

Pay rates: A$510 per week

Premieres:

Terra 20/6/91, His Majesty's Theatre, Perth
Ch.: Chrissie Parrott. *M.:* Various, David Pye. *S.:* Andrew Carter. *C.:* Cordula Albrecht. *L.:* Kenneth Rayner.

Empire 12/2/92, His Majesty's Theatre, Perth
Ch.: Chrissie Parrott. *M.:* Michael Nyman. *C.:* Brett Grant. *L.:* Kenneth Rayner.

Factory 12/2/92, His Majesty's Theatre, Perth
Ch.: Chrissie Parrott. *M.:* Various. *S.:* Andrew Carter. *C.:* Brett Grant. *L.:* Kenneth Rayner.

Surrender II 12/2/92, His Majesty's Theatre, Perth
Ch.: Stephen Petronio. *M.:* David Linton. *C.:* H. Petal. *L.:* Ken Tabachnik.

Dreams of a Circus Sleeping 15/6/92, Playhouse Theatre, Perth
Ch.: Jennifer Newman-Preston. *M.:* David Hobbs. *C.:* Cordula Albrecht. *L.:* Stephen Wickham.

Abbreviations
C., costumes; *Ch.*, choreography; *D.*, design; *dir.*, director; *L.*, lighting; *M.*, music; *S.*, set

From the Heart 15/6/92, Playhouse Theatre, Perth
Ch.: Chrissie Parrott. *M.:* Various. *S.:* Chrissie Parrott. *C.:* Cordula Albrecht. *L.:* Stephen Wickham.

Rev 15/6/92, Playhouse Theatre, Perth
Ch.: Jon Burtt. *M.:* Lee Buddle. *D.:* Katie Lavers. *C.:* Katie Lavers, Cordula Albrecht. *L.:* Stephen Wickham, Katie Lavers.

Repertory:

Software Dragon
Ch.: Chrissie Parrott. *M.:* Cathie Travers. *S.:* Andrew Carter. *C.:* Chrissie Parrott. *L.:* Kenneth Rayner.

Terminal Velocity
Ch.: Chrissie Parrott. *M.:* David Pye. *C.:* Janelle Cugley. *L.:* Jacqueline Molloy.

DANCE NORTH

PO Box 1645
Townsville, QLD 4810
Tel: (077) 722549/722828
Fax: (077) 213014

Artistic dir.: Cheryl Stock

Administrative dir.: Lorna Hempstead

Principal/associate choreographer(s): Cheryl Stock

Visiting choreographer(s): Nanette Hassall, Jane Pirani, Karen Pearlman, Richard Allen

Guest teacher(s): Nanette Hassall, Leigh Warren, Wendy Wallace, Terry Simpson, Anthony Shearsmith, Ann Roberts, Debbie Costigan, Brenda Knucky, D'Esley Jeffries, Richard Allen, Karen Pearlman, Harold Collins, Lynette Denny, Sue Street, Pam Buckman, Maggie Sietsma, Natalie Weir, John Byrne, Peter Lucadou-Wells.

No. of dancers: 4 male, 3 female

No. of performances: 78

Pay rates: Dancers Award

Premieres:

A Moon of Our Own 9/4/91, Townsville
Ch.: Cheryl Stock. *M.:* Robert Keane. *D.:* Anneke Silver. *L.:* Norman Kupke.

Gods of Sand 9/4/91, Townsville
Ch.: Jane Pirani. *M.:* Philip Glass. *D.:* André Reynard. *L.:* Norman Kupke.

Wind Prints 9/4/91, Townsville
Ch.: Nanette Hassall. *M.:* Kevin Volans. *D.:* Margaret Wilson. *L.:* Norman Kupke.

Cross Your Heart 28/11/91, Townsville
Ch.: Bradford Leeon. *M.:* Paul Horn, Culture Beat. *D.:* Bradford Leeon. *L.:* Rebecca Palmer.

Lost and Found 28/11/91, Townsville
Ch.: James Cunningham. *M.:* Philip Glass. *D.:* James Cunningham. *L.:* Rebecca Palmer.

Orchid Sky 28/11/91, Townsville
Ch.: Bernadette Walong. *M.:* Jon Hassell, Brian Eno. *D.:* Bernadette Walong. *L.:* Rebecca Palmer.

Repertory:

If War Were a Dance
Ch.: Richard Allen, Karen Pearlman. *M.:* Danny Blume, 1940s recordings. *D.:* Michael Pearce. *L.:* Norman Kupke.

Take It As It Comes
Ch.: Tim Kay. *M.:* Paranormal Music Society. *D.:* Tim Kay. *L.:* Rebecca Palmer.

Tom Tom Box
Ch.: Brett Daffy. *M.:* Tuck & Patty, Tom Tom Club. *D.:* Brett Duffy. *L.:* Rebecca Palmer.

Women's War Too
Ch.: Cheryl Stock. *M.:* 1940s, various. *D.:* Michael Pearce. *L.:* Norman Kupke.

DANCEWORKS

PO Box 274
Albert Park
Victoria 3206
Tel: (03) 696 1702
Fax: (03) 696 1650

Artistic dir.: Helen Herbertson

Administrative dir.: Sandra Matlock

Principal dancers: Nicky Fletcher, Michael Collins, Ros Warby, Dianne Reid, Brett Daffy, Toby Bell

No. of dancers: 3 male, 3 female

No. of performances: 70

Pay rates: Equity Award

Premieres:

Backlash 11/4/91, Beckett Theatre, Melbourne
Ch.: Helen Herbertson. *M.:* Carl Vine. *D.:* Anna Borghesi. *L.:* Margie Medlin.

Common Touch - Eve's Dance 11/4/91, Beckett Theatre, Melbourne
Ch.: Beth Shelton. *M.:* Andrée Greenwell. *D.:* Anna Borghesi. *L.:* Margie Medlin.

255

Last Stand - dance for a dying woman 11/4/91, Beckett Theatre, Melbourne
Ch.: Helen Herbertson. *M.:* Carl Vine. *D.:* Anna Borghesi. *L.:* Margie Medlin.

Percy and the Antelope 11/4/91, Beckett Theatre, Melbourne
Ch.: Beth Shelton. *M.:* Andrew Byrne. *D.:* Anna Borghesi. *L.:* Margie Medlin.

No Physical Injury 18/7/91, Beckett Theatre, Melbourne
Ch.: Helen Herbertson. *M.:* Ian Chia. *S.:* Simon Barley. *C.:* Amanda Johnson. *L.:* Margie Medlin.

Web 18/7/91, Beckett Theatre, Melbourne
Ch.: Beth Shelton. *M.:* Ian Chia. *S.:* Simon Barley. *C.:* Amanda Johnson. *L.:* Margie Medlin.

Private Life-Public Place (a vertical wall dance) 12/9/91, Forecourt, Victorian Arts Centre, Melbourne
Ch.: Helen Herbertson, Dianne Reid, company members. *M.:* Fred Frith, Gary Clail, Tom Waits, David Byrne, Brian Eno, Lester Bowie's Brass Fantasy. *S.:* Simon Barley. *C.:* Danceworks. *L.:* Margie Medlin. *Projections:* Ian de Gruchy.

Magdalene 7/11/91, Extensions Studio, Carlton
Ch.: Ros Warby. *M.:* Helen Mountfort. *C.:* Ros Warby. *L.:* Tim Preston.

My Friend the Chocolate Cake 7/11/91, Extensions Studio, Carlton
Ch.: Ros Warby. *M.:* Helen Mountfort. *C.:* Ros Warby, Dianne Reid. *L.:* Tim Preston.

Off the Beam 7/11/91, Extensions Studio, Carlton
Ch.: Michael Collins, Nicky Fletcher. *M.:* Ben Grieve. *C.:* Michael Collins, Nicky Fletcher. *L.:* Tim Preston.

Rose Minni - Matilda Redwood 7/11/91, Extensions Studio, Carlton
Ch.: Nicky Fletcher. *C.:* Nicky Fletcher. *L.:* Tim Preston.

Trans End Gen Dance 7/11/91, Extensions Studio, Carlton
Ch.: Michael Collins. *M.:* Bradley Barnett, Stephen Jones, Nicky Fletcher, Brian Parker, Toni Roberts. *C.:* Toni Roberts. *L.:* Tim Preston.

Wings of Summer 11 2/12/91, Gasworks, Art Park and South Melbourne Beach
Ch.: Beth Shelton, Meme McDonald. *D.:* Tim Newth. *C.:* Danceworks and South Melbourne Community. *L.:* Liz Pain.

Physical Business 16/4/92, Merlyn Theatre, Melbourne
Ch.: Helen Herbertson. *M.:* Patrick O'Hearn, Les Negresses Vertes, Linsay Cooper. *S.:* Simon Barley. *C.:* Danceworks with Tricia Simmons. *L.:* Mini Hogan.

Human to Human 13/6/92, Beckett Theatre, Melbourne
Ch.: Helen Herbertson in collaboration with Nicky Fletcher, Michael Collins, Ros Warby, Dianne Reid, Brett Dafffy, Toby Bell. *M.:* Astor Piazzola, Andrew Byrne, Peter Sculthorpe. *S.:* Simon Barley. *C.:* Danceworks with Tricia Simmons. *L.:* Rachel Burke. *Projections:* Ian de Gruchy.

MERYL TANKARD COMPANY

Gorman Houslie, Avenue Braddon
ACT 2601
Tel: (06) 247 3103

ONE EXTRA COMPANY

2/15 Broughton Street, Milsons Point
NSW 2061
Tel: (02) 957 4590
Fax: (02) 957 4938

Artistic dir.: Graeme Watson, Julie-Anne Long (associate)

Administrative dir.: Rosemary Jones

No. of performances: 69

Tours to: Indonesia

Premieres:

Dancing Demons 14/9/91, Denpasar, Bali
Ch.: Graeme Watson, Kim Walker, Julie-Anne Long. *M.:* Tony Lewis. *C.:* Meredith Lucy. *L.:* Dean Winter. *Director:* Kai Tai Chan.

Bite Pull Suck 19/3/92, Sydney
Ch.: Sue Healey, Sue Peacock, Julie-Anne Long. *D.:* Eamon D'Arcy. *C.:* Belinda Gilmour. *L.:* Karen Norris.

QUEENSLAND BALLET

Corner Drake Street and Montague Road
West End, QLD 4101
Tel: (07) 846 5266
Fax: (07) 846 5261

Artistic dir.: Harold Collins

Administrative dir.: Kay Francis

Principal/associate choreographer(s): Jacqui Carroll, Natalie Weir

Guest teacher(s): Graeme Collins, Pamela Buchman

Principal dancers: Michelle Giammichele, David Kierce, Martin Michel, Rosetta Cook

No. of dancers: 10 male, 10 female

No. of performances: 92

Pay rates: A$400—4600 per week

Premieres:

Pirates! The Ballet 12/4/91, Brisbane
Ch.: Daryl Grey. *M.:* Arthur Sullivan. *D.:* Christopher Smith. *L.:* David Whitworth.

Intersections 5/7/91, Brisbane
Ch.: Graeme Watson. *M.:* John Adams. *D.:* Eamon D'Arcy. *L.:* David Whitworth.

Transfigured Night 5/7/91, Brisbane
Ch.: Jacqui Carroll. *M.:* Schönberg. *D.:* John Nobbs. *L.:* David Whitworth.

The Taming of the Shrew 27/3/92, Brisbane
Ch.: Harold Collins. *M.:* Scarlatti. *D.:* Christopher Smith. *L.:* David Whitworth.

Medea 25/6/91, Brisbane
Ch.: Natalie Weir. *M.:* Samuel Barber. *D.:* Bill Haycock. *L.:* David Whitworth.

12 Feet Repeat 25/6/92, Brisbane
Ch.: Andris Toppe. *M.:* Gottschalk. *D.:* Andris Toppe. *L.:* David Whitworth.

Repertory:

Cinderella
Ch.: Harold Collins. *M.:* Rossini. *D.:* John Stoddart. *L.:* David Whitworth.

Frankie and Johnny
Ch.: Andris Toppe. *M.:* David Pyle. *D.:* Bill Haycock. *L.:* David Whitworth.

A Midsummer Night's Dream
Ch.: Harold Collins. *M.:* Mendelssohn. *D.:* Christopher Smith. *L.:* David Whitworth.

Othello
Ch.: Jacqui Carroll. *M.:* Tchaikovsky. *D.:* John Nobbs. *L.:* David Whitworth.

Pas de quatre
Ch.: Anton Dolin, after Perrot. *M.:* Pugni. *D.:* Natalie Karvoska. *L.:* David Whitworth.

Pulcinella
Ch.: Harold Collins. *M.:* Stravinsky. *D.:* Bill Haycock. *L.:* David Whitworth.

The Summer of our Memories
Ch.: Harold Collins. *M.:* Graeme Koehne. *D.:* Richard Jeziorny. *L.:* David Whitworth.

SYDNEY DANCE COMPANY

**The Wharf, Pier 4
Hickson Road
Walsh Bay, Sydney
NSW 2000
Tel: (02) 221 4811
Fax: (02) 251 6904**

Artistic dir.: Graeme Murphy

Administrative dir.: Derek Watt

Visiting choreographer(s): Alfred Williams, Kim Walker, Paul Mercurio, Adrian Batchelor, Gideon Obarzanek, Stephen Page

Principal dancers: Until Jan 1992: Janet Vernon, Lea Francis, Ross Philip, Paul Mercurio. *From Jan 1992:* Jan Pinkerton, Kathryn Dunn

Guest dancers: Kim Walker, Luciano Martucci (guest actor)

No. of dancers: 11 male, 10 female

Tours to: France, Venezuela, Colombia

Pay rates: Negotiated for principals and senior members of more than 3 years service. Similar to award rates for first and second year members.

Premieres:

The Shakespeare Dances 4/7/91, Seymour Centre Theatre, Sydney
Ch.: Graeme Murphy, Gideon Obarzanek, Stephen Page, Alfred Williams, Adrian Batchelor. *M.:* John Dankworth, Laibach, David Page, Benjamin Britten, Mike Caen. *S.:* Ross Philip. *C.:* Jennifer Irwin.

Edgeing (sic) 27/5/92, Drama Theatre, Sydney Opera House
Ch.: Paul Mercurio. *M.:* Seal/Not Drowning, Waving. *S.,C.:* John Senczuk. *L.:* John Rayment.

Monkey See 27/5/92, Drama Theatre, Sydney Opera House
Ch.: Kim Walker. *M.:* Steve Reich, David Byrne. *S.:* John Senczuk. *C.:* John Senczuk. *L.:* John Rayment.

Piano Sonata 27/5/92, Drama Theatre, Sydney Opera House
Ch.: Graeme Murphy. *M.:* Carl Vine. *C.:* Jennifer Irwin. *L.:* Roderick van Gelder.

Repertory:

Afterworlds
Ch.: Graeme Murphy. *M.:* Colin Brumby, Francis Poulenc, Propaganda. *S.:* Alan Oldfield. *C.:* Anthony Jones.

Nearly Beloved
Ch.: Graeme Murphy. *M.:* Graeme Koehne. *S.:* Stephen Curtis. *C.:* Anthony Jones. *L.:* Roderick van Gelder.

Poppy
Ch.: Graeme Murphy. *M.:* Carl Vine. *S.:* Kristian Fredrikson, George Gittoes, Gabrielle Dalton. *C.:* Kristian Fredrikson. *L.:* John Drummond Montgomery.

Some Rooms
Ch.: Graeme Murphy. *M.:* Canteloube, Keith Jarrett, Francis Poulenc, Benjamin Britten, Samuel Barber. *S.:* Graeme Murphy, Graeme Johnson. *C.:* Anthony Jones. *L.:* Roderick van Gelder, after original design by John Drummond Montgomery. *Film and slides:* Michelle Mahrer, Brett Cabot.

A Streecar Named Desire
Ch.: Graeme Murphy. *M.:* Alex North. *S.:* Angus Tattle. *C.:* Jennifer Irwin. *L.:* Roderick van Gelder.

Viridian
Ch.: Graeme Murphy. *M.:* Richard Meale. *L.:* John Rayment.

WEST AUSTRALIAN BALLET

PO Box 7228
Cloisters Square
WA 6850
Tel: (09) 481 0707
Fax: (09) 324 2402

Artistic dir.: Barry Moreland

Administrative dir.: John Catlin

Principal/associate choreographer(s): Barry Moreland, Elizabeth Hill, Edmund Stripe

Visiting choreographer(s): Chrissie Parrott

Guest teacher(s): Irina Kolpakova, Vladilen Semyonov, Arlette Weinreich, Jurgen Schneider

Guest dancers: David MacAllister

No. of dancers: 11 male, 11 female

No. of performances: 116

Tours to: Philippines

Pay rates: A$392.80 per week (1st year). A$640.00 per week (principals).

Premieres:

Perpetuum Moblie 15/3/91, Perth
Ch.: Elizabeth Hill. *M.:* Simon Jeffes. *S.:* Andrew Carter. *C.:* Chrissie Parrott. *L.:* Kenneth Rayner.

Bournonville Dances 21/3/91, Perth
Ch.: Bournonville. *M.:* H.S. Paulli. *L.:* Kenneth Rayner.

Lounge Suite 17/10/91, Perth
Ch.: Chrissie Parrott. *M.:* Stravinsky. *D.:* Andrew Carter. *C.:* Cordula Albrecht. *L.:* Kenneth Rayner.

Sinfonietta 17/10/91, Perth
Ch.: Edmund Stripe. *M.:* Janacek. *D.:* Andrew Carter. *C.:* Cordula Albrecht. *L.:* Kenneth Rayner.

Illuminations 17/10/92, Perth
Ch.: Barry Moreland. *M.:* Mozart. *D.:* Andrew Carter. *C.:* Cordula Albrecht. *L.:* Kenneth Rayner.

Austria

BALLETT DER VEREINIGTEN BÜHNEN GRAZ

Kaiser Josefplatz 10
8010 Graz
Tel: 0316/76451

BALLETT DER WIENER STAATSOPER

Opernring
1010 Wien
Tel: 51444-0

Artistic dir.: Gerlinde Dill

BALLETT DES SALZBURGER LANDESTHEATERS

Schwarzstrasse 22
5024 Salzburg
Tel: 0662/871512-0
Fax: 0622/871512-13

Artistic dir.: Peter Breuer

Administrative dir.: Freimuth Teufel

Principal/associate choreographer(s): Peter Breuer, Robert Machherndl

Visiting choreographer(s): Dinna Bjørn, José de Udaeta

No. of dancers: 10 male, 10 female

No. of performances: 55

Premieres:

Albinoni 27/1/92, Landestheater, Salzburg
Ch.: Erich Walter. *M.:* Albinoni. *D.:* Peter Breuer.

Le Corsaire pas de deux 27/1/92, Landestheater, Salzburg
Ch.: Petipa. *M.:* Drigo. *D.:* Peter Breuer.

Fatum 27/1/92, Landestheater, Salzburg
Ch.: Peter Breuer. *M.:* Tchaikovsky. *D.:* Peter Breuer.

Schéhérazade pas de deux 27/1/92, Landestheater, Salzburg
Ch.: Fokine. *M.:* Rimsky-Korsakov. *D., L.:* Peter Breuer. *C.:* Susanne Breuer.

Tarantella 27/1/92, Landestheater, Salzburg
Ch.: Peter Breuer. *M.:* Louis Moreau Gottschalk. *D.:* Peter Breuer.

Orpheus & Euridike 9/5/92, Landestheater, Salzburg
Ch.: Peter Breuer. *M.:* Gluck. *D.,L.:* Peter Breuer. *C.:* Susanne Breuer.

Repertory:

Chaplin
Ch.: Peter Breuer. *M.:* Charles Spencer Chaplin. *D.:* Peter Breuer.

Mozart und Salieri
Ch.: Peter Breuer. *M.:* Mozart. *D.:* Peter Breuer.

Paganini
Ch.: Yuri Vamos. *M.:*Rachmaninov. *D.:*Peter Breuer.

Strength
Ch.: Robert Machherndl. *M.:* Phil Collins. *D.:* Peter Breuer.

Tango Espergesia
Ch.: Peter Breuer. *M.:* Astor Piazzola. *D.:* Peter Breuer.

Belgium

CHARLEROI/DANSES

45, rue du Fort
6000 Charleroi
Tel: (071) 31 04 32
Fax: (071) 30 31 48

Artistic dir.: Frederic Flamand

Administrative dir.: Bernard Degroote

Visiting choreographer(s): Joachim Schlömer, Karole Armitage, Lucinda Childs

Guest teacher(s): Richard Glasstone, Sally Wilson

No. of dancers: 8 male, 8 female

No. of performances: 15

Tours to: France

Pay rates: 6300 FB (gross)

Premieres:

Inlets II 13/12/91, Charleroi
Ch.: Merce Cunningham. *M.:* John Cage. *D.:* Mark Lancaster.

Mercuric Tidings 13/12/91, Charleroi
Ch.: Paul Taylor. *M.:* Franz Schubert. *C.:* Gene Moore. *L.:* Jennifer Tipton.

Overboard 13/12/91, Charleroi
Ch.: Karole Armitage. *M.:* David Shea, Foetus. *D.:* David Salle, Jeff Koons. *C.:* Arole Duke. *L.:* Pat Dignan.

Das Meer in Zwei Etagen 26/3/92, Charleroi
Ch.: Joachim Schlömer. *M.:* Alfred Schnittke. *D.:* Frank Leimbach. *L.:* Dominique Sourniac.

Oopha-Naama 26/3/92, Charleroi
Ch.: Lucinda Childs. *M.:* Iannis Xenakis. *C.:* Lucinda Childs, Nan Hoover.

COMPAGNIE MICHELE ANNE DE MEY

Théâtre Varia
rue du Sceptre, 78
B-1040 Brussels
Tel: 32 2 217 41 27
Fax: 32 2 217 51 67

Artistic dir.: Michèle Anne de Mey

Administrative dir.: Christine Tinlot

Guest teacher(s): Robert Masarachi, Piotr Nardelli

Principal dancers: Nicholas Crow, Kristin de Groot, Olga de Soto, Michèle Anne de Mey, Matteo Moles, Françoise Rognerud, Gabi Sund, Andreu Bresca

Guest dancers: Mischa van Dullemen, Jordi Casanovas

No. of dancers: 3 male, 5 female

No. of performances: 50

Tours to: France, Norway, UK, Austria, Germany

Premieres:

Châteaux en Espagne 23/5/91, Brussels
Ch.: Michèle Anne de Mey. *M.:* Mozart, Haydn. *S.:* J. Daenen. *C.:* A. DuBois. *L.:* F. Gahide.

De Mey 2 21/1/92, Brussels
Ch.: Michèle Anne de Mey. *M.:* Thierry de Mey. *C.:* A. Wathieu. *L.:* F. Gahide.

ROSAS

19 Werkhuizenstraat
B-1080 Brussels
Tel: 32 2 425 36 29
Fax: 32 2 425 30 51

Artistic dir.: Anne Teresa De Keersmaeker

Administrative dir.: Guy Gijpens

Principal/associate choreographer(s): Anne Teresa De Keersmaeker, Jean-Luc Ducourt (assistant)

Guest teacher(s): Shelley Senter, Yoshida Norio, Andrei Ziemski, Piotr Nardelli, Louise Burns, Susan Alexander, David Steele, Jorge Salavisa

Principal dancers: Fumiyo Ikeda, Johanna

Saunier, Nathalie Million, Carlotta Sagna, Marion Levy, Vincent Dunoyer, Bruce Campbell, Nordine Benchorf, Cynthia Loemy, Samantha Van Wissen, Muriel Hérault, Anne Mousselet, Mark Bruce, Thomas Havert, Eduardo Torroja

No. of dancers: 6 male, 9 female

No. of performances: 76

Tours to: Netherlands, France, Germany, Austria, Finland, Norway, Portugal, Canada, USA, Switzerland, Sweden, Spain, England

Premieres:

Erts 5/2/92, Brussels
Ch.: Anne Teresa De Keersmaeker. *M.:* Beethoven, Schnittke, Webern. *S.:* Hermann Sorgeloos. *C.:* Ann Weckx. *L.:* Jean-Luc Ducourt.

Repertory:

Achterland
Ch.: Anne Teresa De Keersmaeker. *M.:* Ligeti, Ysaÿe. *S.:* Hermann Sorgeloos. *C.:* Ann Werckx. *L.:* Jean-Luc Ducourt.

Rosas danst Rosas
Ch.: Anne Teresa De Keersmaeker. *M.:* Thierry De Mey, Walter Hus, Peter Vermeersch, Eric Sleichim. *S.:* Anne Teresa De Keersmaeker, Hermann Sorgeloos. *L.:* Remon Fromont.

Stella
Ch.: Anne Teresa De Keersmaeker. *M.:* György Ligeti. *S.:* Herman Sorgeloos. *C.:* Rosas. *L.:* Jean-Luc Ducourt.

ROYAL BALLET OF FLANDERS

Keizerstraat 14
B-2000 Antwerp
Tel: (03) 234 34 38
Fax: (03) 233 58 92

Artistic dir.: Robert Denvers

Administrative dir.: Jan Vanderschoot

Visiting choreographer(s): Flemming Flindt, Rudolf Nureyev, Stuart Sebastian, Peter Anastos, and others

Principal dancers: Dawn Fay, Lucinda Tallack-Garner, Lenka Jarosikova, Hilde Van de Vloet, Chris Roelandt, Lars Van Cauwenbergh, Jan Vandeloo, Julio Arozarena, David Palmer, Rimat Imaëv

Guest dancers: Irekh Mukhamedov, Jan Broeckx, Evelyne Desutter, Danilo Radojevic

No. of dancers: 23 male, 26 female

No. of performances: 90

Tours to: Hong Kong, Taiwan, Ireland, Greece, Turkey

Pay rates: Principal dancer BF 1,100,000; soloist BF 1,000,000; demi-soliost BF 790,000; corps de ballet BF 675,000

Premieres:

Beyond Memory 27/9/91, Gent
Ch.: Mauricio Wainrot. M.: Philip Glass. C.: Carlos Gallardo. L.: Mauricio Wainrot.

Configurations 27/9/91, Gent
Ch.: Choo-San Goh. M.: Samuel Barber. C.: Carol Vollet-Garner. L.: Tony Tucci.

Cinderella 14/2/92, Antwerp
Ch.: Peter Anastos. M.: Prokofiev. D.: Roger Bernard.

Repertory:

Dracula
Ch.: Stuart Sebastian. M.: Verdi, Lanner, Vierne, Rossini, Debussy, Bizet, Rachmaninov. S.,L.: Chris Phillips. C.: Lowell Hathwich.

The Four Temperaments
Ch.: Balanchine. M.: Hindemith. L.: Johan Bielen.

Serenade
Ch.: Balanchine. M.: Tchaikovsky.

Solid Ground
Ch.: Danny Rosseel. M.: Arvo Pärt. C.: Gerdamariën and Danny Rosseel. L.: Jaak van de Velde.

Brazil

BALLET DO TEATRO MUNICIPAL, RIO DE JANEIRO

Teatro Municipal
Rua Maestro Francisco Braga no. 42/ap. 701
Rio de Janeiro, RJ
Tel: 201 2463

Artistic dir.: Tatiana Leskova

BALLET OF THE CITY OF SÃO PAULO

Teatro Municipal de São Paulo
Praça Ramos de Azevado
São Paulo SP-CEP 01037
Tel: 011-239-3883/239-1740
Fax: 011-223-5021

Artistic dir.: Rui Fontana Lopez

Visiting choreographer(s): Luis Arrieta, Oscar Araiz, Hans Kresnik, Rodrigo Pederneiras, Sergio Funari, Wilson Aguiar, Susana Yamauchi, João Maurício, Vitor Navarro, Raymond Costa

Guest teacher(s): Gustavo Molajolli, Renate Schottelius, Ilse Wiedmann, Marcos Verzani, Beatriz Cardoso

No. of dancers: 12 male, 18 female

No. of performances: 75

Pay rates: US$600 per month (13-month contract/year)

Premieres:

Mozart Concerto 6/91, São Paulo
Ch.: Rodrigo Pederneiras. M.: Mozart. C.: Freusa Zechmeister. L.: Paulo Pederneiras.

Les Noces 9/91, São Paulo
Ch.: Luis Arrieta. M.: Stravinsky. S.: Luis Arrieta. C.: Renata Schussheim. L.: Fernando Guimarães.

(ZERO)² 4/92, São Paulo
Ch.: Hans Kresnik. M.: Paulo Alvares. D.: J.C. Serroni. L.: Hans Kresnik.

Repertory:

Adagietto
Ch.: Oscar Araiz. M.: Mahler. C.,L.: Oscar Araiz.

Ausência
Ch.: Luis Arrieta. M.: Rachmaninov. C.: Margot Delgado. L.: Mario Martini.

Cantares
Ch.: Oscar Araiz. M.: Maurice Ravel. C.: Carlos Cytrinovsky. L.: Oscar Araiz.

Magnificat
Ch.: Luis Arrieta. M.: J. S. Bach. C.: Renata Schussheim. L.: Mario Martini.

Mathis o Pintor
Ch.: Oscar Araiz. M.: Paul Hindemith. S.,L.: Oscar Araiz. C.: Renata Schussheim.

Mikrokosmos
Ch.: Sérgio Funari, Wilson Aguiar. M.: Bartók. C.: Sérgio Funari, Wilson Aguiar. L.: Cacá D'Andretta.

Terrazul
Ch.: Sérgio Funari. M.: Weber. S.: Sérgio

Funari. C.: Leda Senise. L.: Fernando Guimarães.

Trindade
Ch.: Luis Arrieta. M.: Samuel Barber. D.: Luis Arrieta.

Variações Sobre um Tema de Haydn
Ch.: Rodrigo Pederneiras. M.: Brahms. C.: Freusa Zechmeister. L.: Paulo Pederneiras.

Vivaldi
Ch.: Victor Navarro. M.: Antonio Vivaldi. C.,L.: Victor Navarro.

Canada

ALBERTA BALLET

National Christie Center
11 18th Avenue South-West
Calgary, Alberta T2S 0B8
Tel: (403) 245 4222
Fax: (403) 245 6573

Artistic dir.: Ali Pourfarrokh

BALLET BRITISH COLUMBIA

Suite 502, 68 Water Street
Vancouver
British Columbia
Tel: (604) 669-5954
Fax: (604) 684-5648

Artistic dir.: John Alleyne

Administrative dir.: David Lui

Visiting choreographer(s): William Forsythe, John Alleyne, Mark Godden, William Soleau, Glen Tetley

No. of dancers: 8 male, 10 female

Tours to: Asia, Canada, USA

Premieres:

Architecture for the Poor 23/5/92, Vancouver
Ch.: David Earle. M.: Marjan Mozetich. C.: Joanne Lamberton. L.: Ken Alexander.

Isie 23/5/92, Vancouver
Ch.: William Soleau. M.: Purcell. L.: Ken Alexander.

Holberg Pas de Deux 23/5/92, Vancouver
Ch.: John Cranko. M.: Grieg. L.: Ken Alexander.

Mythical Hunters 23/5/92, Vancouver
Ch.: Glen Tetley. M.: Oedeon Partos-Hezionoot. D.: Anthony Binstead. L.: Ken Alexander.

Repertory:

Go Slow Walter
Ch.: John Alleyne. M: David Wynne

In the middle, somewhat elevated
Ch.: William Forsythe. M.: Thom Willems. L.: Ken Alexander.

Return to the Strange Land
Ch.: Jirí Kylián. M.: Janacék. L.: Joop Caboort.

Urlicht
Ch.: William Forsythe. M.: Mahler. C.: Sigrid Kay. L.: Ken Alexander.

LES BALLETS JAZZ DE MONTREAL

30 St Urbain Street
Montreal
Quebec, H2X 2N5
Tel: (514) 982 6771
Fax: (514) 982 9145

Artistic dir.: William Whitener

DANNY GROSSMAN DANCE COMPANY

511 Bloor Street West , 2nd Floor
Toronto
Ontario M5S 1Y4
Tel: (416) 531-8350

Artistic dir.: Danny Grossman, Pamela Grundy (associate)

DESROSIERS DANCE THEATRE

629 Eastern Avenue
Toronto
Ontario M4M 1E4
Tel: (416) 463-5341
Fax: (416) 463-5802

Artistic dir.: Robert Desrosiers

Administrative dir.: Ursula Martin

Principal/associate choreographer(s):
Robert Desrosiers

Guest teacher(s): Debbie Hess

Principal dancers: Robert Desrosiers, Jennifer Dick, Philip Drube, Marie-Josée Dubois, Gaétan Gingras, Robert Glumbeck, Katarzyna Kwasniewszka, Marq Levene Frerichs, Jean-Aimé Lalonde, Robin Wilds

Guest dancers: Karen du Plessis

No. of dancers: 6 male, 4 female

No. of performances: 37

Tours to: USA, Italy, Canada

Pay rates: Cdn$375-$500

Premieres:

Full Moon 10/6/91, Glory of Mozart Festival, Toronto
Ch.: Robert Desrosiers. *M.:* Mozart. *S.:* Myles Warren. *C.:* Jane Townsend. *L.:* Casey McClelland.

Full Moon (expanded version) 20/9/91, Algoma Fall Festival, Sault Ste. Marie, Ontario
Ch.: Robert Desrosiers. *M.:* Mozart, with soundscape by Eric Cadesky. *S.:* Myles Warren. *C.:* Jane Townsend, Cheryl Mills. *L.:* Casey McClelland.

Black and White 20/11/91, Premiere Dance Theatre, Toronto
Ch.: Robert Desrosiers. *M.:* Eric Cadesky. *S.:* Dan Solomon. *C.:* Robert Desrosiers, Cheryl Mills. *L.:* Casey McClelland.

Repertory:

Avalanche
Ch.: Robert Desrosiers. *M.:* Ron Allen, Eric Cadesky, John Lang. *L.:* Casey McClelland.

LES GRANDS BALLETS CANADIENS

4816 rue Rivard
Montreal
Quebec, H2J 2N6
Tel: (514) 849 8681
Fax: (514) 849 0098

JUDITH MARCUSE DANCE COMPANY

106-206 East 6th Avenue
Vancouver, BC V5T 1J8
Tel: (604) 872-4746
Fax: (604) 872-7951

Artistic dir.: Judith Marcuse

Administrative dir.: Laura MacMaster

Principal/associate choreographer(s): Judith Marcuse

Visiting choreographer(s): Lola MacLaughlin, Shapiro & Smith, Oscar Nieto

Guest teacher(s): Kenny Pearl, Daniel Shapiro, Joannie Smith

Principal dancers: Linda Arkelian, Morio Cardoso, Jean-Guy Cossette, Brigid Hoog, Carol Horowitz, David Lauzon, Marthe Leonard, John McPherson, Jennifer Pratt, Wen Wei Wang

No. of dancers: 5 male, 5 female

No. of performances: 40

Pay rates: Available on request

Premieres:

Encuentros 19/2/92, Commodore Ballroom
Ch.: Oscar Nieto. *M.:* Isaac Albéniz, Kreisler & Grant. *C.:* Oscar Nieto, Pauline Turner. *L.:* John Webber.

Tangled Web 19/2/92, Commodore Ballroom
Ch.: Judith Marcuse. *M.:* Sarah McLaughlin. *C.:* Pauline Torner. *L.:* John Webber.

Repertory:

Cadence
Ch.: Lola MacLaughlin. *M.:* Kevin Volans. *C.:* Chip Siebert. *L.:* Bruce Halliday.

Traces
Ch.: Judith Marcuse. *M.:* Arvo Pärt. *C.:*
Judith Marcuse, Carolyn Knight. *L.:* Nick
Cernovitch.

LA LA LA HUMAN STEPS

3575 St Laurent #601
Montreal PQ H2X 2TZ
Tel: (514) 845 8273

Artistic dir.: Edouard Lock

NATIONAL BALLET OF CANADA

157 King Street East
Toronto
Ontario M5C 1G9
Tel: 362-1041
Fax: 368-7443

Artistic dir.: Reid Anderson, Valerie Wilder
(associate)

Administrative dir.: Robert Johnston

Resident choreographer: John Alleyne

Visiting choreographer(s): William
Forsythe, Glent Tetley, James Kudelka,
Ronald Hynd, Desmond Heeley,
Christopher House

Guest teacher(s): Luc Amyot, Sergiu
Stefanschi, Galina Yordanova, David
Howard, Vladimir Vasiliev, Daniel Seillier,
Svea Eklof, Debra Hess, Mary Jagu,
Joysanne Sidimus, Kathryn Bennetts, Victor
Litvinov

Principal dancers: Karen Kain, Kimberly
Glasco, Rex Harrington, Margaret Illmann,
Martine Lamy, Serge Lavoie, Jeremy
Ransom, Raymond Smith, Gizella
Witkowsky

Guest dancers: Gregory Osborne, Evelyn
Hart, Fernando Bujones, Oliver Matz,
Laurent Hilaire

No. of dancers: 27 male, 37 female

No. of performances: 10

Tours to: USA, Hong Kong, Japan, Korea,
Taiwan

Premieres:

The Rites of Spring 6/5/91, O'Keefe Centre
Ch.: Glen Tetley. *M.:* Stravinsky. *S.,C.:*
Nadine Baylis. *L.:* Timothy Hunter.

Musings 10/6/91, MacMillan Theatre
Ch.: James Kudelka. *M.:* Mozart. *D.:* Astrid

Janson. *C.:* . *L.:* Stephen Allen.

Café Dances 24/10/91, Brock Centre for the
Arts
Ch.: Christopher House. *M.:* Various. *D.:*
Denis Joffe. *L.:* Stephen Allen.

Interrogating Slam 13/11/91, O'Keefe Centre
Ch.: John Allyene. *M.:* Morton Subotnick. *C.:*
Kim Nielsen. *L.:* Ken Alexander.

The Taming of the Shrew 13/2/92, O'Keefe
Centre
Ch.: John Cranko. *M.:* Domenico Scarlatti.
D.: Susan Benson. *L.:* Robert Thomson.

Split House Geometric 7/5/92, O'Keefe
Centre
Ch.: John Allyene. *M.:* Arvo Pärt. *D.:* John
Alleyne. *L.:* Stephen Allen.

O VERTIGO DANSE

4455 de Rouen
Montreal, Quebec H1V 1H1
Tel: (514) 251-9177
Fax: (514) 251-7358

Artistic dir.: Ginette Laurin

Administrative dir.: Mireille Martin

Principal/associate choreographer(s):
Ginette Laurin

Principal dancers: Ann Barry, Marc Bovin,
Estelle Clareton, Pierre-André Côté, Carole
Courtois, Jennifer Dressler, Kathleen Dubé,
Randy Joynt, Karen Kuzak, Scott Kemp,
Mireille Leblanc, Chi Long, Cameron
MacMaster, Nathalie Morin, Maryse Poulin,
Marie-Claude Rodrigue

No. of dancers: 4 male, 5 female

No. of performances: 50

Tours to: Canada, USA, Europe

ROYAL WINNIPEG BALLET

380 Graham Avenue
Winnipeg, Manitoba R3C 4K2
Tel: (204) 956-0183

TORONTO DANCE THEATRE

80 Winchester Street
Toronto, Ontario M4X 1B2
Tel: (416) 967-1365
Fax: (416) 967-4379

Artistic dir.: David Earle

Administrative dir.: Don MacMillan

Principal/associate choreographer(s):
Patricia Beatty, David Earle, Christopher
House, Peter Randazzo

Guest teacher(s): Robert Cohan

Principal dancers: Miriane Braaf, Monica
Burr, Bill Coleman, Pascal Desrosiers,
Susanna Hood, Christopher House,
Rosemary James, Laurence Lemieux, Sean
Marye, Graham McKelvie, Coralee
McLaren, David Pressault, Suzette
Sherman, Michael Trent

Guest dancers: Kate Alton

No. of dancers: 7 male, 7 female

No. of performances: 51

Tours to: USA

Pay rates: $325—575 per week

Premieres:

Early Departure 25/2/92, Premiere Dance
Theatre, Toronto
Ch.: Christopher House. *M.:* John Rea. *C.:*
Denis Joffre. *L.:* Ron Snippe.

Mandala 25/2/92, Premiere Dance Theatre,
Toronto
Ch.: Patricia Beatty. *M.:* Mark Hand. *C.:*
Denis Joffre. *L.:* Ron Snippe.

Untitled Monument 25/2/92, Premiere
Dance Theatre, Toronto
Ch.: David Earle. *M.:* Toru Takemitsu. *S.:*
Ken Shaw. *C.:* Denis Joffre. *L.:* Ron Snippe.

Repertory:

Artemis Madrigals
Ch.: Christopher House. *M.:* Stravinsky. *C.:*
Denis Joffre. *L.:* Ron Snippe.

The Court of Lions
Ch.: Christopher House. *M.:* Collage of early
music. *C.:* Denis Joffre. *L.:* Ron Snippe.

Court of Miracles
Ch.: David Earle, Christopher House, James
Kudelka. *M.:* Collage of early music. *S.:* Ron
Ward. *C.:* Denis Joffre. *L.:* Ron Snippe.

Dreamsend
Ch.: David Earle. *M.:* Webern. *C.:* Denis
Joffre. *L.:* Ron Snippe.

Fifteen Heterosexual Duets
Ch.: James Kudelka. *M.:* Beethoven. *C.:*
Denis Joffre. *L.:* Ron Snippe.

First Music
Ch.: Patricia Beatty. *M.:* Charles Ives. *S.:*
Dave Davis. *C.:* Denis Joffre. *L.:* Ron Snippe.

Fjeld
Ch.: Christopher House. *M.:* Arvo Pärt. *C.:*
Denis Joffre. *L.:* Ron Snippe.

Handel Variations
Ch.: Christopher House. *M.:* Brahms. *C.:*
Denis Joffre. *L.:* Ron Snippe.

Island
Ch.: Christopher House. *M.:* Steve Reich. *C.:*
Denis Joffre. *L.:* Ron Snippe.

Noli Me Tangere
Ch.: Christopher House. *M.:* Henry
Kucharzyk. *S.:* Claire Kerwin. *C.:* Denis
Joffre. *L.:* Ron Snippe.

Sacra Conversazione
Ch.: David Earle. *M.:* Mozart. *C.:* Denis
Joffre. *L.:* Ron Snippe.

Schubert Dances
Ch.: Christopher House. *M.:* Schubert. *C.:*
Denis Joffre. *L.:* Ron Snippe.

Chile

BALLET DE SANTIAGO

Teatro Municipal
San Antonio 149
Santiago
Tel: 6381609
Fax: 56-2-6337214

Artistic dir.: Luz Lorca

Administrative dir.: Andres Pinto

Principal/associate choreographer(s): Jaime
Riveros, Hilda Riveros

Visiting choreographer(s): André
Prokovsky, Ben Stevenson, Ronald Hynd,
Valery Panov, Vicente Nebrada, Jack Carter,
Marcia Haydée, Laszlo Seregi

Guest teacher(s): Josefina Mendez, Katalyn
Sebesteyn, Simon Motram, Rodolfo
Castellanos, Marilyn Burr, Yuri Uhmrihin,

Rosanna Seravalli, Imre Dosza

Principal dancers: Sara Nieto, Berthica Prieto, Valentina Chtchepatcheva, Claudia SMiguel, Edgardo Hartley, Pablo Ahoaronian, Vladimir Guelbet, Luis Ortigoza, Marcela Goicoechea, Jacqueline Cortes

Guest dancers: Li Cunxin

No. of dancers: 21 male, 28 female

No. of performances: 100

Tours to: South America, Europe

Premieres:

MacBeth 4/91, Teatro Municipal, Santiago *Ch.:* André Prokovsky. *M.:* David Earl. *D.:* R. Don.

Tiempo de Percusion 4/91, Teatro Municipal *Ch.:* Hilda Riveros. *M.:* Alejandro Garcia. *D.,C.:* E. del Campo. *S.,L.:* B. Trumper.

Snow Maiden 10/91, Teatro Municipal *Ch.:* Ben Stevenson. *M.:* Tchaikovsky. *D.:* P. Whiteman. *L.:* R. Yañez

La Fille mal gardée 4/92, Teatro Municipal *Ch.:* M. Burr. *M.:* Hérold/Lanchbery. *D.:* Carlos Bruna. *L.:* R. Yañez.

Firebird 6/92, Teatro Municipal *Ch.:* Marcia Haydée. *M.:* Stravinsky. *D.:* P. Nuñez. *L.:* R. Lopez.

Fuegas del Hielo 6/92, Teatro Municipal *Ch.:* Jaime Pinto. *M.:* Sergio Gonzalez. *D.:* G. Droghetti. *L.:* R. Lopez.

Repertory:

Don Quijote
Ch.: Jaime Pinto. *M.:* Minkus/Lanchbery. *D.:* G. Droghetti. *S.:* . *C.:* C. Rosati. *L.:* R. Yañez.

Four Temperaments
Ch.: Balanchine. *M.:* Hindemith.

Nutcracker
Ch.: Ben Stevenson. *M.:* Tchaikovsky. *D.:* M. Jacobs. *L.:* R. Yañez.

La Sylphide
Ch.: Ivan Nagy. *M.:* Løvenskiold/ Lanchbery. *D.:* Sergio Zapata. *C.:* Pablo Nuñez.

BALLET NACIONAL CHILENO

Compañia 1264
Santiago
Tel: 6967426
Fax: 56-2-2225116

Artistic dir.: Maritza Parada Allende

Visiting choreographer(s): Oscar Araiz, Michael Uthoff, Patricio Bunster, Hilda Riveros, Rob Stuyf, Mauricio Wainrot

Guest teacher(s): Lidia Diaz, Mabel Silvera, Micaela Taslaoanu

Principal dancers: Rosa Celis, Cecilia Reyes, Berenice Perrin, Renato Peralta, Jorge Ruiz

No. of dancers: 17 male, 17 female

No. of performances: 62

Tours to: Bolivia

Pay rates: 400-1000 US$

Premieres:

Alborada del Gracioso 16/5/91, Teatro Universidad de Chile *Ch.:* Michael Uthoff. *M.:* Maurice Ravel. *D.:* Hernán Pantoja.

Cantares 16/5/91, Teatro Universidad de Chile *Ch.:* Oscar Araiz. *M.:* Maurice Ravel. *D.:* Carlos Citrinowsky. *L.:* Oscar Araiz.

Sinfonia Danzante 16/5/91, Teatro Universidad de Chile *Ch.:* Michael Uthoff. *M.:* Beethoven. *D.:* Judanna Lynn. *L.:* Hernán Pantoja.

Anne Frank 29/8/91, Teatro Universidad de Chile *Ch.:* Mauricio Wainrot. *M.:* Bartók. *D.:* Carlos Gallardo. *L.:* Alberto García.

Ecos 29/8/91, Teatro Universidad de Chile *Ch.:* Mauricio Wainrot. *M.:* Samuel Barber. *D.:* Carlos Gallardo. *L.:* Alberto García.

Sinfonia de los Salmos 29/8/91, Teatro Universidad de Chile *Ch.:* Mauricio Wainrot. *M.:* Stravinsky. *D.:* Carlos Gallardo. *L.:* Alberto García.

Repertory:

Calaucan
Ch.: Patricio Bunster. *M.:* Carlos Chávez. *D.:* Julio Escámez. *L.:* Arturo Celis.

Carmina Burana
Ch.: Ernst Uthoff. *M.*: Carl Orff. *D.*: Thomás
Rossner. *L.*: Thomáas Rossner, B. Adaros.

Fiesta
Ch.: Mauricio Wainrot. *M.*: Maurice Ravel.
D.: Carlos Gallardo. *L.*: Alberto García.

Vindicación de la Primavera
Ch.: Patricio Bunster. *M.*: Stravinsky. *D.,C.*:
Marco Correa. *S.*: Ricardo Sepúlveda. *L.*:
Irma Valencia.

China

CENTRAL BALLET

3 Tai Ping Jie
Beijing 100500
Tel: 33 4962

CHINA OPERA AND DANCE DRAMA THEATRE

2 Nan Hua Dong Jie
Hu Fang Lu
Beijing 10052
Tel: 335215/338052

GUANGDONG MODERN DANCE COMPANY

Guangdong Provincial Dance School
Sa Ho Ding, Shui Yum Road
Guangzhou 510075
Tel: 7714523

Artistic dir.: Willy Tsao

Administrative dir.: Yang Mei-qi

Principal dancers: Qin Li-ming, Qiao Yang

No. of dancers: 8 male, 8 female

No. of performances: 35

Tours to: USA, Hong Kong

Premieres:

Coloured Relations 1/92, Guangzhou
Ch.: Shen Wei. *M.*: Steve Roach, Sarah
Hopkins. *D.*: Shen Wei. *L.*: Lin Pai-shi.

Our Sky 1/92, Guangzhou
Ch.: Willy Tsao. *M.*: Cui Jian, Qi Qin, George
Lam. *C.*: Sun Yu-Ling. *L.*: Xie Li-ming.

Red Undergarment 1/92, Guangzhou
Ch.: Yan Ying. *M.*: Chinese folk songs. *D.*:
Yan Ying. *L.*: Lin Pai-shi.

Still a Child 1/92, Guangzhou
Ch.: Shen Wei. *M.*: Chinese traditional. *D.*:
Shen Wei. *L.*: Lin Pai-shi.

Bird Songs 6/92, Guangzhou
Ch.: Willy Tsao. *M.*: Bulgarian folk songs.
D.: Willy Tsao. *L.*: Lin Pai-shi.

Heaven Quest 6/92, Guangzhou
Ch.: Shen Wei. *M.*: My Ushio Torikai. *D.*:
Shen Wei. *L.*: Lin Pai-shi.

Repertory:

Beginnings
Ch.: Qu-Xiao. *M.*: John Adams. *D.*: Qu-Xiao.
L.: Lin Pai-shi.

Cuckoo Sings Blue
Ch.: Qin Li-ming. *M.*: Sound collage. *D.*: Qin
Li-ming. *L.*: Lin Pai-shi.

Downs and Ups
Ch.: Qin Li-ming. *M.*: Gabrielle Roth. *D.*:
Qin Li-ming. *L.*: Lin Pai-shi.

Insomnia
Ch.: Shen Wei. *M.*: Collage. *D.*: Shen Wei. *L.*:
Lin Pai-shi.

The Maid
Ch.: Yin Xiao-rong. *M.*: Western opera. *D.*:
Yin Xiao-rong. *L.*: Lin Pai-shi.

Reminiscence
Ch.: Zhang Yin-zhong. *M.*: Tan Dun. *D.*:
Zhang Yin-zhong. *L.*: Lin Pai-shi.

Water Zen
Ch.: Su Ka. *M.*: Liang Ming-Yue. *D.*: Su Ka.
L.: Lin Pai-shi.

Young Bird
Ch.: Qin Li-ming. *M.*: He Jian-hau, Chen
Gang. *D.*: Qin Li-ming. *L.*: Lin Pai-shi.

SHANGHAI BALLET

1674 Hong Qiao Lu
Shanghai 200335
Tel: 2759516

Cuba

ASI SOMOS

Calle A No. 310 Apt. 7B
Entre 3ra y 5ta
Playa
C. Habana
Tel: 2-42-76

Artistic dir.: Lorna Burdsall

BALLET DE CAMAGÜEY

Carretera Central
Este esq. a 4
Camagüey 70300
Tel: 96535 - 99215

Artistic dir.: Jorge Vede

Principal/associate choreographer(s): José A. Chávez, Lázaro Martínez

Principal dancers: Pedro M. Boza, Christine Ferrando, Bárbara García, Celia Rosales, Pedro Beiro, Victor Carnesoltas, Guillermo Leyva, Orlando López, Clara Díaz, Leydis Escobar, Adelaida Gómez, Wilmian Hernández, Doris Pérez, Lídice del Río, Roberto Machado

Premieres:

Conflictos
Ch.: Menia Martínez.

Consolación de Liszt

Ch.: Menia Martínez.

Degas
Ch.: Jorge Lefebre. *M.:* Bizet. *D.:* Felix Avila, after Joel Rustaud.

BALLET FOLKLORICO DE ORIENTE

SAN FELIX NO. 407,
ESQ. SAN FRANCISCO
SANTIAGO DE CUBA

Artistic dir.: Antonio Pérez Martínez

Principal/associate choreographer(s): Antonio Pérez Martínez

Premieres:

El Aguaro de Iroko
Ch.: Antonio Pérez Martínez.

Danza del Bichet
Ch.: Antonio Pérez Martínez.

Huellas de Sangre
Ch.: Antonio Pérez Martínez.

Son
Ch.: Antonio Pérez Martínez.

BALLET NACIONAL DE CUBA

Calzada No. 510
entre DyE Vedado
C. Habana 4
Tel: 32 4625

Artistic dir.: Alicia Alonso

Administrative dir.: Salvador Frenández

Principal/associate choreographer(s): Alicia Alonso, Gustavo Herrera, Alberto Méndez, Iván Tenorio

Principal dancers: Alicia Alonso (prima ballerina assoluta), Loipa Araujo, Aurora Bosch, Amparo Brito, Sonia Calero, Marta García, Ofelia Gonzáles, María Elena Llorente, Josefina Méndez, Mirta Plá, Rosario Suarez, Rolando Candia, Lázaro Carreño, Fernando Jhones, Orlando Salgado, Andrés Williams, José Zamorano, Gloria Hernández, Rodolfo Castellanos, Pablo Moré, Francisco Salgado, Jorge Vega

Tours to: Spain, Colombia, Mexico, Japan

Premieres:

Frutas y Realidades
Ch.: Gladys González. *M.:* Leo Brouwer. *D.:* Mariano Rodríguez.

Lilac Garden
Ch.: Antony Tudor. *M.:* Chausson. *D.:* Ricardo Reymena, Salvador Fernández (after Hugh Stevenson).

Sleeping Beauty Act III
Ch.: Alicia Alonso, after Petipa. *M.:* Tchaikovsky. *D.:* Julio Castaño. *C.:* Salvador Fernández.

Swan Lake
Ch.: Alicia Alonso, after Petipa. *M.:* Tchaikovsky. *C.:* Salvador Fernández.

Tiempo Fuera de la Memoria
Ch.: Brian Macdonald. *M.:* Paul Creston. *C.:* Salvador Fernández.

Trapiz
Ch.: Iván Tenorio. *M.*: Stevie Wonder. *D.*: Umberto Peña.

BALLET TEATRO DE LA HABANA

Teatro Nacional
Paseo y 19
Plaza de la Revolución
C. Habana
Tel: 79-2728/79-6410

Artistic dir.: Caridad Martínez

COMPAÑIA DE BALLET SANTIAGO DE CUBA

Teatro Heredia
Avenida de las Americas esq. Ave de los Desfiles
Santiago de Cuba
Tel: 4-31-78

Artistic dir.: María Elena Martínez de la Torre

Principal/associate choreographer(s): María Elena Martínez de la Torre, Lázaro Martínez

Principal dancers: Osmani Montano, Melba Cedeo, Idael Jerman, Wilmer de la Cruz, Rebeca Masó

No. of dancers: 9 male, 11 female

Premieres:

Canto Vital
Ch.: Azari Plisetski.

En tu mano va mi mano
Ch.: Hilda Riveros. *M.*: Pablo Moncayo.

Majísimo
Ch.: Jorge García. *M.*: Massenet.

Manada
Ch.: Lázaro Martínez. *M.*: Paul Winter.

Por tí Argentina
Ch.: María Elena Martínez. *M.*: Charlie García, Osvaldo Pugliecci.

Ritual de la Dobles
Ch.: Lázaro Martínez. *M.*: Kreisler.

COMPAÑIA TEATRO DE LA DANZA DEL CARIBE

Santa Lucia 305
Entre San Pedro y San Felix
Santiago de Cuba
Tel: 5-224-7626

Artistic dir.: Eduardo Rivero

Principal/associate choreographer(s):
Eduardo Rivero, Jorge Abril, Eddy Veitía, Narciso Medina

No. of dancers: 14 male, 9 female

Premieres:

Desahogo
Ch.: Bárbara Ramos. *M.*: Grefal Dan.

Destellos
Ch.: Eduardo Rivero. *M.*: Juan Pinero.

Imposición
Ch.: Arturo Castillo, Arcenio Andrades. *M.*: Jean-Michel Jarre.

Mandela
Ch.: Eduardo Rivero. *M.*: Miles Davis.

Metamorfosis
Ch.: Narciso Medina. *M.*: Jean-Michel Jarre.

Okántomi
Ch.: Eduardo Rivero. *M.*: Traditional African.

Raices (Weeping Willow)
Ch.: Eduardo Rivero. *M.*: Quincey Jones.

Tribute
Ch.: Eduardo Rivero. *M.*: Bob Marley, Jimmy Cliff. *D.*: Eduardo Arrocha.

Unidos
Ch.: Lesme Grenot. *M.*: Vangelis.

CONJUNTO DE DANZAS DE GUANTANAMO

Centro de Danza
Calle Maximo Gomez No. 1607,
Entre Varona y Marmol
Guantánamo
Artistic dir.: *Elfrida Mahler*

Principal/associate choreographer(s):
Elfrida Mahler, Isaías Rojas

No. of dancers: 10 male, 14 female

Premieres:

Des Bandes
Ch.: Isaías Rojas. *M.*: Traditional Cuban/Haitian.

Camine a Dios
Ch.: Alfredo Velázquez. *M.*: Hindu/Church choral.

El Eterno Problema
Ch.: Tomás Guilarte. *M.*: Peter Gabriel.

CONJUNTO DE DANZAS ESPAÑOLES

Calzada no. 510 e
D y E,
Vedado La Habana 4

Artistic dir.: Olga Bustamente Fonte

Principal dancers: Olga Bustamente, Eduardo Veitía

Premieres:

Danzas Fantásticas
Ch.: Olga Bustamente. *M.:* Joaquín Turina.

Danzas Regionales
Ch.: Olga Bustamente, Eduardo Veitía, Danay Rojas.

Escuela Bolera Castillo de la Real Fuerza, Havana
Ch.: Carmen Elvira Fernández.

CONJUNTO FOLKLORICO CUTUMBA

Enramadas 170 alto
entre Padre Pico y Corona
Santiago de Cuba

Artistic dir.: Roberto Sanchez Vigñot

Principal/associate choreographer(s):
Ernesto Armiñán, Roberto David, Idalberto Bandera

Principal dancers: Idalberto Bandera, Cenia Jiménez, Danis Pérez, José Carrión, Juan B. Castillo, Maura Isaac

No. of dancers: 10 male, 10 female

Premieres:

Fiesta del Guamo y el Baccin (Voodoo)
Ch.: Ernesto Armiñan.

Loases (Haitian Gods)
Ch.: Idalberto Bandera.

Yaguetó ó Yautó
Ch.: Roberto David. *M.:* Haitian traditional.

CONJUNTO FOLKLORICO NACIONAL DE CUBA

Calle 4 No. 103, Entre Calzada y 5ta,
Vedado
Cuidad de la Habana 10400
Tel: 30-3060/30-4560/30-3939

Artistic dir.: Teresa González

Principal/associate choreographer(s):
Manolo Micler

Principal dancers: Margarita Ugarte,
Zenaida Artmenteros, Silvana Fabars, Alfredo O'Farril, Johannes García, Leonor Mendoza, Domingo Pau, Librada Quesada, Juan J. Ortiz, Julían E. Villa, Lucía Subiadur, Mercedes Riscart, George W. Dixon, Gerardo Villarreal

Tours to: Mexico, Switzerland, Spain, Peru, France

Premieres:

Cantata Yoruba
Ch.: Rogelio Martínez Furé.

La Jardinera
Ch.: Manolo Micler.

Rey Congo
Ch.: Alberto Villareal.

Shangó Bangoshé
Ch.: Teresa González.

DANZA ABIERTA

Gran Teatro de La Habana
Prado Promenade
Entre San Rafael y San José
C. Habana
Tel: 32-6343/32-2829

Artistic dir.: Marianela Boán

Principal/associate choreographer(s):
Marianela Boán, Victor Varela, José Amgel Hevia

Premieres:

Desolada
Ch.: José Hevia. *M.:* Enya, Vivaldi, and others.

Desnuda
Ch.: José Hevia. *M.:* Henry Purcell, Ennio Morricone.

Locomoción
Ch.: Marianela Boán. *M.:* Telemann, Joachim Bello, Steve Reich, Shostakovich. *C.:* José Hevia.

Retorno
Ch.: Marianela Boán. *M.:* Sindo Garay, Steve Reich, Tibor Zsemo *D.:* Vladimir Cuenca.

DANZA COMBINATORIA

Calle F No. 108 Apt. 3
Entre 5ta y Calzada
Vedado
C. Habana
Tel: 32-1798

Artistic dir.: Rosario Cárdenas

Principal/associate choreographer(s):
Rosario Cárdenas

Premieres:

Asunto de Familia
Ch.: Rosario Cárdenas. M.: Antonio Russer.
C.: Eduardo Arrocha.

Caballos
Ch.: Rosario Cárdenas. M.: Juan Marcos
Blanco. C.: Eduardo Arrocha.

Hombre Cadete Mujer
Ch.: José Hevia. M.: Sidney O'Connor. C.,L.:
José Hevia.

Solo Pesos y Formos
Ch.: Ana Ileana Llorente. M.: Charlie
Chaplin. C.: Ana Ileana Llorente. L.: Ramiro
Maseda.

DANZA CONTEMPORANEA DE CUBA

Paseo y 39
Plaza de la Revolución
C. Habana
Tel: 79-2728/79-6410

Artistic dir.: Miguel Iglesias

GESTOS TRANSITORIOS

Calle 8, No. 467 apt. 6
entre 9 y 21,
Vedado
C. Habana

Artistic dir.: Narciso Medina

Principal/associate choreographer(s):
Narciso Medina

Premieres:

Cantoral
Ch.: Narciso Medina. M.: Collage: Ennio
Morricone, and Spirituals.

Espacio Hombre Solo
Ch.: Narciso Medina. M.: Foklórica Cubana.

La Espera
Ch.: Narciso Medina. M.: Ennio Morricone.

Jordan y Jo
Ch.: Narciso Medina. M.: Collage

LA JOVEN GUARDIA

Centro de Promoción de la Danza
Calle 5ta No. 253, esq a E
Vedado
C. Habana 4
Tel: 32-4625/32-7752

Artistic dir.: Iván Monreal

Administrative dir.: Laura Alonso

Principal/associate choreographer(s): Iván
Monreal, Lupe Calzadilla, Lesme Grenot,
Miguel Gómez, Marta Bercy, List Alfonso,
Lázaro Noriega, Reynaldo Muñiz, Armando
Yuvero, Héctor Figueredo

No. of dancers: 24 male, 22 female

Denmark

NEW DANISH DANCE THEATRE

Meinungsgade 8D, IV
2200 Copenhagen N
Tel: 3139 8787
Fax: 3537 4998

Artistic dir.: Anette Ablidgård, Warren
Spears

Administrative dir.: Paul Richard Pedersen

THE ROYAL DANISH BALLET

Royal Theatre
PO Box 2185
1017 Copenhagen K
Tel: 33 32 20 20

Artistic dir.: Frank Anderson, Lise la Cour
(associate)

Administrative dir.: Michael Christiansen

Guest teacher(s): Jean-Pierre Bonnefous,
Sergui Stefanschi, Kevin Haigen, Adam
Lüders

Principal dancers: Kirsten Simone, Sorella
Englund, Mette-Ida Kirk, Heidi Ryom, Lis
Jeppesen, Rose Gad, Silja Schandorff, Niels
Kehlet, Alexander Kølpin, Flemming
Ryberg, Arne Villumsen, Yuri Possokhov,
Nikolaj Hübbe (on leave of absence),
Kenneth Greve, Lloyd Riggins,

No. of dancers: 44 male, 45 female

271

No. of performances: c. 110

Premieres:

A Folk Tale 20/9/91
Ch.: Bournonville. *M.:* N.W. Gade, J.P.E. Hartmann.

Concerto 24/10/91
Ch.: Kenneth MacMillan. *M.:* Shostakovich.

Napoli 27/3/92
Ch.: Bournonville. *M.:* N.W. Gade, E. Helsted, H.S. Paulli, H.C. Lumbye.

Allegro Brillante 9/5/92
Ch.: Balanchine. *M.:* Tchaikovsky.

Polacca 11/5/92
Ch.: Anna Lærkesen. *M.:* Chopin.

Repertory:

Abdallah
Ch.: Bournonville. *M.:* H.S. Paulli.

Apollon Musagètes
Ch.: Balanchine. *M.:* Stravinsky.

Caroline Mathilde
Ch.: Flemming Flindt. *M.:* Peter Maxwell Davies.

The Conservatiore
Ch.: Bournonville. *M.:* H.S. Paulli.

Delta
Ch.: Laura Dean. *M.:* Gary Brooker.

Far from Denmark
Ch.: Bournonville. *M.:* (in part) Joseph Glæser.

The Flower Festival in Genzano
Ch.: Bournonville. *M.:* E. Helsted, H.S. Paulli.

The Kermesse in Bruges
Ch.: Bournonville. *M.:* H.S. Paulli.

The Kings Volunteers on Amager
Ch.: Bournonville. *M.:* V.C. Holm.

The Nutcracker
Ch.: Flemming Flindt. *M.:* Tchaikovsky.

Serenade
Ch.: Balanchine. *M.:* Tchaikovsky.

Simple Simon
Ch.: Lise la Cour. *M.:* Bent Fabricius-Bjerre.

La Sylphide
Ch.: Bournonville. *M.:* Løvenskiold.

Tchaikovsky Pas de Deux
Ch.: Balanchine. *M.:* Tchaikovsky.

Theme and Variations
Ch.: Balanchine. *M.:* Tchaikovsky.

The Ugly Duckling
Ch.: Lise la Cour. *M.:* Bent Fabricius Bjerre.

TEATER TANGO

Vesterbrogade 62D
1620 Copenhagen V
Tel: 3124 9833/3131 0115

Artistic dir.: Rhea Leman

Administrative dir.: Mucki Nordgren

No. of dancers: 4

UPPERCUT DANCE THEATRE

Rathsacksvej 32
1862 Frederiksberg C
Tel: 3131 4841

Artistic dir.: Cher Geuetze, Sheila de Val

Administrative dir.: Kirsten Vad

Estonia

ESTONIA THEATRE BALLET

Estonia pst. 4
Tallin EE 0105
Tel: 7-0142-443-031
Fax: 7-0142-443-505

Artistic dir.: Mai Murdmaa, Viesturs Jansons, Juris Zigurs

Principal dancers: Kaie Korb, Juri Jekimov, Viesturs Jansons, Irina Härm, Hane

Raidma, Inna Sormus, Tatjana Voronina, Andrei Izmestjev, Priit Kripson, Mikhail Netschajev, Toomas Rätsepp

No. of dancers: 18 male, 25 female

No. of performances: 80

Tours to: Germany

Premieres:

Crime and Punishment 22/11/91

Ch.: Mai Murdmaa. *M.:* Arvo Pärt.

Little Symphony 15/2/92
Ch.: Mai Murdmaa. *M.:* Haydn.

Miraculous Mandarin 15/2/92
Ch.: Mai Murdmaa. *M.:* Bartók.

Paquita (divertissement) 15/2/92
Ch.: Petipa. *M.:* Minkus.

Carmina Burana 13/6/92
Ch.: Mai Murdmaa. *M.:* Carl Orff.

Repertory:

La Bayadère
Ch.: Petipa, Igor Tschernoshov. *M.:* Minkus.

Giselle
Ch.: Coralli, Perrot, Petipa, Tiit Härm. *M.:* Adam.

Last Songs
Ch.: Martin Fredman. *M.:* Richard Strauss.

Miss Julie
Ch.: Birgit Cullberg. *M.:* Ture Rangström.

Nutcracker
Ch.: Mai Murdmaa. *M.:* Tchaikovsky.

Redemption
Ch.: Mai Murdmaa. *M.:* Kuldar Sink.

Scream and Silence
Ch.: Mai Murdmaa. *M.:* Kuldar Sink.

Swan Lake
Ch.: Petipa, Ivanov, Sergeyev. *M.:* Tchaikovsky.

Variations
Ch.: Laszlo Seregi. *M.:* Dohnanyi.

NORDIC STAR DANCE THEATRE

c/o Estonia Theatre
Estonia pst.4
Tallinn EE 0105
Tel: 7-0142-444 709
Fax: 7-0142-442 584

Artistic dir.: Saima Kranig

Principal dancers: Tatjana Kilgas, Saima Kranig, Katrin Laur, Tiina Ollesk, Anu Ruusmaa, Larissa Sintsova, Ülle Toompuu, Ivar Eensoo, Toomas Jooger, René Nommik, Oleg Ostanin

Tours to: Lithuania, Russia, Finland

Premieres:

The Case 24/9/91
Ch.: Tamar Rogoff. *M.:* Cebello Morales. *D.:*

Katrin Laur, Tiina Ollesk.

The Journey 24/9/91
Ch.: Bonnie Sue Stein. *M.:* Lepo Sumera, Laurie Spiegel.

One Hand Takes from the Other 24/9/91
Ch.: Barbara Hofrenning. *M.:* David Shea.

Kisses of the Wind 26/10/91
Ch.: Jurius Smoriginas. *M.:* Lepo Sumera, Samuel Barber, J.S. Bach, Gregorian chant.

Pietà 26/10/91
Ch.: Jurius Smoriginas. *M.:* Mahler. *D.:* Saima Kranig, Toomas Jooger.

Quiet Chaos 26/10/91
Ch.: Jeanne Yasko. *M.:* Arvo Pärt.

Woman 26/10/91
Ch.: Mai Murdmaa. *M.:* Luciano Berio. *D.:* Tatjana Kilgas.

Farewell 19/11/91
Ch.: Mai Murdmaa. *M.:* Mahler. *D.:* Larissa Sintsova, Toomas Jooger, Anu Ruusmaa.

VANEMUINE THEATRE BALLET COMPANY

Vanemuine t.6
Tartu EE 2400
Tel: 7-01434-34159
Fax: 7-01434-31513/74095

Artistic dir.: Ulo Vilimaa

Principal dancers: Marika Aidla, Jelena Karpova, Heli Kohv, Mare Tommingas, Aivar Kallaste, Oleg Titov, Jura Petrov

No. of dancers: 4 male, 11 female

Premieres:

The Little Prince 9/91
Ch.: Mare Tommingas. *M.:* Peeter Volkonski.

African Sanctus 4/92
Ch.: Mare Tommingas. *M.:* David Fanshawe.

Barcelona 4/92
Ch.: Mare Tommingas. *M.:* Freddy Mercury, Mike Moran.

Repertory:

Bamby
Ch.: Ülo Vilimaa. *M.:* Lydia Auster.

Giselle
Ch.: Coralli, Perrot, Petipa, Alla Shelest. *M.:* Adam.

273

Finland

FINNISH NATIONAL BALLET

PO Box 188
SF-00181 Helsinki
Tel: (358-0) 12921
Fax: (358-0) 1292 301

Artistic dir.: Doris Laine (until 31.1.92); Jorma Uotinen (from 1.2.92)

Visiting choreographer(s): Carolyn Carlson, John Neumeier, Heinz Spoerli, Doris Laine, Jorma Uotinen, Rudi van Dantzig

Guest teacher(s): Germaine Acogny, Peter Appel, Kathryn Bennetts, Diana Carter, Viktor Rona, Marina Stawitskaja

Guest dancers: Nina Ananiashvili, Alexei Fadeyechev

No. of dancers: 34 male, 33 female

No. of performances: 93

Tours to: China

Pay rates: FIM 6785–13673 per month, depending on length of time with the company. Extra per performace, paid vacation. Pensions are 60% of full salary, after retirement at 42 (women) or 46 (men).

Premieres:

La Belle Vie 25/4/91, Finnish National Opera
Ch.: Heinz Spoerli. *M.:* Offenbach. *D.:* Ralf Forsström. *L.:* Petri Pylkkö.

Maa 31/10/91, Finnish National Opera
Ch.: Carolyn Carlson. *M.:* Kaija Saariaho. *S.,C.:* Markku Piri. *L.:* Claude Naville.

Aurora's Wedding 18/1/92, Finnish National Opera
Ch.: Doris Laine, after Petipa. *M.:* Tchaikovsky. *S.,C.:* Mark Väisänen.

Mozart, and Themes from 'As You Like It' 26/3/92, Finnish National Opera
Ch.: John Neumeier. *M.:* Mozart. *S.,C.:* Klaus Hellenstein. *L.:* John Neumeier.

Repertory:

Divertimento No. 15
Ch.: Balanchine. *M.:* Mozart. *S.:* Barbara Karinska. *L.:* Simo Järvinen.

The Faun
Ch.: Jorma Uotinen. *M.:* Debussy. *S.:* Jorma Uotinen. *C.:* Helena Lindgren. *L.:* Simo Järvinen.

La Fille mal gardée
Ch.: Heinz Spoerli. *M.:* Hérold-Hertel-Damase. *S.:* Paul Suominen. *C.:* Heinz Berner.

The Four Last Songs
Ch.: Rudi van Danztig. *M.:* Richard Strauss. *S.,C.:* Toer van Schayk.

Giselle
Ch.: Coralli/Perrot/Petipa. *M.:* Adam. *S.,C.:* Mark Väisänen. *L.:* Petri Pylkkö.

Lady of the Camellias
Ch.: Domy Reiter-Soffer. *M.:* Saint-Saëns. *S.,C.:* Seppo Nurmimaa. *L.:* Kimmo Ruskela.

Loviisa
Ch.: Tommi Kitti. *M.:* Eero Hämeenniemi. *S.:* Måns Hedström. *C.:* Måns Hedström.

Pulcinella
Ch.: Nils Christe. *M.:* Stravinsky/Pergolesi. *S.,C.:* Tom Schenk. *L.:* Kees Tjebbes.

The Ragtime Dance Company
Ch.: Gray Veredon. *M.:* Scott Joplin. *S.,C:* Carmela Wager (after Gray Veredon). *L.:* Chenault Spence.

Ronia, the Robber's Daughter
Ch.: Marjo Kuusela. *M.:* Jukka Linkola. *S.,C.:* Seppo Nurmimaa. *L.:* Matti Hietanen.

The Seven Brothers
Ch.: Marjo Kuusela. *M.:* Eero Ojanen. *S.,C.:* Måns Hedström.

Spirit Blues
Ch.: Walter Nicks. *M.:* Duke Ellington. *S.,C.:* Carmela Wager. *L.:* Chenault Spence.

Stairset
Ch.: Tiina Lindfors. *M.:* Palle Mikkelborg. *S.:* Carmela Wager/Tiina Lindfors. *L.:* Chenault Spence.

TANSSITEATTERI ERI

Yliopistonkatu 7
20110 Turku
Tel: 35821-501032/3580-7017267

Artistic dir.: Vivica Bandler

Principal/associate choreographer(s): Tiina Lindfors, Lassi Sairela, Eeva Soini

Visiting choreographer(s): Jeanne Yasko

Principal dancers: Tiina Lindfors, Suvi Pohjonen, Lassi Sairela, Eeva Soini, Andrus Kämbre

No. of dancers: 2 male, 3 female

Tours to: Sweden, Denmark

Premieres:

Soldier's Tale 30/4/91, Turku
Ch.: Tiina Lindfors. *M.:* Stravinsky. *D.:* Tiina Lindfors. *L.:* Birger Bergfors.

Tango of my Heart 4/9/91, Turku
Ch.: Tiina Lindfors, Lassi Sairela, Eeva Soini. *M.:* Old Argentinian tangos. *D.:* Dance Theatre Eri. *L.:* Jouni Heikola.

Listen 14/11/91, Turku
Ch.: Jeanne Yasko. *M.:* Arvo Pärt. *D.:* Jeanne Yasko. *L.:* Jouni Heikola.

Shots 14/11/91, Turku
Ch.: Lassi Sairela, Eeva Soini. *M.:* Crumb, Ligeti, Lurie, Saarino. *D.:* Lassi Sairela, Eeva Soini. *S.:* Jari Laurikko. *C.:* Pirjo Liiri-Majava. *L.:* Jouni Heikola.

Strings 14/11/91, Turku
Ch.: Jeanne Yasko. *M.:* Walcott/Vasconcelos. *D.:* Jeanne Yasko. *C.:* Tuula Laine. *L.:* Jouni Heikula.

Jeann d'Arc 24/4/92, Turku
Ch.: Tiina Lindfors. *M.:* Arvo Pärt, 15th-century music. *D.:* Tiina Lindfors. *C.:* Pirjo Liiri-Majava. *L.:* Jouni Heikola.

TANSSITEATTERI RAATIKKO

Viertolankuja 4
01300 Vantaa
Tel: 358-0-873 1184/873 2306
Fax: 358-0-873 3294

Artistic dir.: Marja Korhola

Administrative dir.: Ulla Jarla

Principal/associate choreographer(s): Marja Korhola, Hannu Hyttinen

Visiting choreographer(s): Kenneth Kvarnström, Marjo Kuusela, Ulla Koivisto

Guest teacher(s): Jeanne Yasko, Arnold Chiwalala, Alexander Kikinov, Juhani Teräsvuori

Principal dancers: Marja Korhola, Eevamari Kitti, Reija Vaahtera, Hannu Hyttinen, Jari Kukkonen, Marinella Reinikka, Helena Haaranen, Tiina Jalkanen, Kati Kivilahti, Peter Lagergren, Marja Leino, Kirsi Lillqvist, Ari Numminen

Guest dancers: Paula Tuovinen, Jaana-Pia Karaspuro, Jarrko Lievonen

No. of dancers: 4 male, 9 female

No. of performances: 122

Tours to: Sweden, India, Belgium

Pay rates: 3000–10,000 Finnish Marks

Repertory:

Apollo and Muse
Ch.: Hannu Hyttinen. *M.:* Stravinsky. *D.:* Hannu Hyttinen. *L.:* Mika Tertsunen.

Dancehappening for Children
Ch.: Marjo Korhola. *M.:* Collage.

Dancehappening Raatikko
Ch.: Working team. *M.:* Collage.

Feather Planet
Ch.: Hannu Hyttinen. *M.:* Heikki Sarmanto. *S.:* Tapio Tuominen, Hannu Hyttinen. *C.:* Irmeli Toivanen. *L.:* Matti Rautio.

Hairsplitter's Valse
Ch.: Ulla Koivisto. *M.:* Collage. *S.:* Kari Petäjä. *C.:* Marja Uusitalo. *L.:* Kaj Salomaa.

The Height of Sophistication
Ch.: Hannu Hyttinen. *M.:* Poulenc. *S.:* Hannu Hyttinen. *C.:* Soili Eriksson. *L.:* Risto Linnapuomi.

Mummy Ballet
Ch.: Marjo Korhola. *M.:* Collage. *S.,C.:* Marjo Korhola. *L.:* Claude Naville.

Teatro Magico
Ch.: Marjo Korhola. *M.:* Collage.

Ten Feet
Ch.: Marja Korhola. *M.:* Collage. *S.:* Arto Aromaa. *C.:* Soili Eriksson. *L.:* Uffe Dolk.

Toe Dance
Ch.: Marja Korhola. *M.:* Collage.

20th Anniversary Performance
Ch.: Marjo Kuusela, Kenneth Kvarnström. *M.:* Collage, Jörgen Adolfsson, Tommy Adolfsson. *C.:* Soili Eriksson. *L.:* Matti Rautio.

France

COMPAGNIE BAGOUET

Centre Chorégraphique National de Montpellier Languedoc-Roussillon
11 boulevard Victor Hugo
34000 Montpellier
Tel: (33) 67 60 63 72
Fax: (33) 67 60 76 03

Artistic dir.: Dominique Bagouet

Administrative dir.: Liliane Martinez

Principal/associate choreographer(s):
Dominique Bagouet

Visiting choreographer(s): Trisha Brown

Guest teacher(s): Liz Aggis, George Appaix, Priscilla Danton, Lance Gries, Véronique Larcher

Principal dancers: Hélène Baldini, Hélène Cathala, Olivia Grandville, Sylvain Prunenec, Fabrice Ramalingom, Rita Cioffi, Matthieu Doze, Dominique Jégou, Juan Manuel Vicente

Guest dancers: Catherine Legrand, Jean-Charles Di Zazzo

No. of dancers: 5 male, 4 female

No. of performances: 53

Tours to: Italy, Germany, Switzerland, Spain

Pay rates: c. 120,000 francs

Premieres:

Necesito 26/7/91, Festival d'Avignon
Ch.: Dominique Bagouet. *S.:* Danka Semenowicz. *C.:* Dominique Fabrègue. *L.:* Manuel Bernard.

One Story, as in falling 25/6/92, Montpellier
Ch.: Trisha Brown. *M.:* Alwin Curran. *S.,C.:* Roland Aeschlimann. *L.:* Spencer Brown.

COMPAGNIE CLAUDE BRUMACHON

Centre Chorégraphique National de Nantes
94, rue de la Tombe-Issoire
75014 Paris
Tel: (1) 40 44 91 21
Fax: (1) 40 44 85 85

Artistic dir.: Claude Brumachon

Administrative dir.: Agnès Izrine

Principal dancers: Benjamin Lamarche, Valerie Soulard, Sophie Torrion, Roxana del Castillo, Fabienne Saint-Patrice, Anne Minetti, Nick Pettit, Pascal Guillermie, Veronique Redoux, Yolande Limousin, Hervé Maigret, Guillaume Lemasson

Guest dancers: Christine Maltete, Marc Tetedoie, Delphine Brouard

No. of dancers: 4 male, 9 female

No. of performances: c. 75

Tours to: Italy, Germany, RDA, Poland, Yugoslavia, India, Indonesia, Vietnam, Philippines, England, Scotland

Pay rates: c. 9000.00 FF

Premieres:

Fauves 8/10/91, Nantes
Ch.: Claude Brumachon. *M.:* Christophe Zurfluh. *C.:* Martine Ritz. *L.:* Philippe Mombellet.

Repertory:

Eclats d'Absinthe
Ch.: Claude Brumachon. *M.:* Christophe Zurfluh. *C.:* Martine Ritz. *L.:* Philippe Mombellet.

Folie
Ch.: Claude Brumachon. *M.:* Christophe Zurfluh. *C.:* Claude Brumachon, P. Goudinoux. *L.:* Philippe Mombellet.

Le Piedestal des Vierges
Ch.: Claude Brumachon. *M.:* Christophe Zurfluh. *L.:* Philippe Mombellet.

Texane
Ch.: Claude Brumachon. *M.:* Christophe Zurfluh. *C.:* Huguette Blanchard. *L.:* Philippe Mombellet.

COMPAGNIE KARINE SAPORTA

Centre Chorégraphique National de Caen
10 rue Pastuer
BP 393
14009 Caen
Tel: 31 85 73 16

Artistic dir.: Karine Saporta

COMPAGNIE MAGUY MARIN

Maison des Arts
Place Salvador Allende
94000 Créteil
Tel: 31-1-49 80 55 80
Fax: 31-1-43 99 21 58

Artistic dir.: Maguy Marin

Administrative dir.: Antoine Manologlou

Principal/associate choreographer(s):
Maguy Marin

Guest teacher(s): Isabelle Missal

Principal dancers: Ulises Alvarez, Frédéric Carnet, Teresa Cunha, Christiane Glik, Athanassios Koutsoyannis, Jean-Marc Lamena, Mychel Lecoq, Françoise Leik, Yaël Orni, Cathy Polo, Isabelle Saulle

No. of dancers: 5 male, 6 female

No. of performances: 75

Tours to: Australia, New Zealand, Ireland, Italy, Czechoslovakia

Premieres:

Cortex 4/10/91, Creteil
Ch.: Maguy Marin. *M.:* Denis Mariotte. *S.:* Maguy Marin, Denis Mariotte. *C.:* Maguy Marin, Denis Mariotte. *L.:* Pierre Colomer.

Repertory:

Duo D'Eden
Ch.: Maguy Marin. *C.:* Montserrat Casanova. *L.:* Pierre Colomer.

May B
Ch.: Maguy Marin. *M.:* Schubert, Carnaval de Binche, Gavin Bryars. *C.:* Louise Marin. *L.:* Pierre Colomer.

COMPAGNIE PRELJOCAJ

52 rue Pierre-Marie Derrien
94500 Champigny-sur-Marne
Tel: 1-4886 5632/4885 4120
Fax: 1-4889 6238

Artistic dir.: Angelin Preljocaj

GROUP EMILE DUBOIS

Centre Chorégraphique National de Grenoble
4 rue Paul Claudel
BP 7040
38034 Grenoble Cedex
Tel: 76.25.70.56/76.25.05.45
Fax: 76.25.73.83

Artistic dir.: Jean-Claude Gallotta

Administrative dir.: Dominique de Baecque, Blanche Guichou

Guest teacher(s): Ruth Barnes, Norio Yoshida, Sara Sugihara, Louise Burns, Susan Alexander

Principal dancers: Mathilde Altaraz, Pascal Gravat, Robert Seyfried, Eric Alfieri

Guest dancers: Anna Ariatta, Delphine Benoi, Sandrine Chaoulli, Christine Cloux, Prisca Harsch, Natacha Mas, Geneviève Reynaud, Claire Sauvajon, Jean-Philippe Costes-Muscat, Darrell Davis, Didier Gilabert, Samuel Mathieu, Thierry Verger

No. of dancers: 8 male, 9 female

No. of performances: 80

Tours to: France, Spain, Brazil, Italy, Switzerland, UK, Belgium, Netherlands, USA

Pay rates: 15000 FF and 12000 FF

Premieres:

Ulysse 92 10/92, Grenoble
Ch.: Jean-Claude Gallotta. *M:* Henry Torgue. *D.:* Jean-Yves Langlais. *L.:* Manuel Bernard.

Docteur Labus 1/93, Grenoble
Ch.: Jean-Claude Gallotta. *M:* Henry Torgue. *D.:* Jean-Yves Langlais. *L.:* Manuel Bernard.

PARIS OPERA BALLET

Opéra de Paris Garnier
8 rue Scribe
75009 Paris
Tel: 40 17 35 35

Artistic dir.: Patrick Dupond

Germany

BALLETT DER DEUTSCHEN OPER BERLIN

Richard Wagner Strasse 10
D-1000 Berlin 10
Tel: 3438 268
Fax: 3438 232

Artistic dir.: Peter Schaufuss

Administrative dir.: Steven Scott

Principal/associate choreographer(s): Peter Schaufuss

Visiting choreographer(s): Michael Clark, Bill T. Jones, Stephen Petronio

No. of dancers: 14 male, 25 female

No. of performances: 81

Tours to: England, Scotland

Premieres:

Giselle oder die Wilis 4/5/91, Deutschen Oper Berlin
Ch.: Peter Schaufuss. *M.:* Adam. *D.:* Desmond Heeley. *L.:* Duane Schuber.

Paquita (Grand Pas) 22/6/91, Deutschen Oper Berlin
Ch.: Oleg Vinogradov. *M.:* Minkus. *C.:* Irina Press. *L.:* David Mohr.

Die Herent Drummer 28/9/91, Deutschen Oper Berlin
Ch.: Kenneth MacMillan. *M.:* Webern, Schönberg. *C.:* Yolanda Sonnabend. *L.:* David Mohr.

La Sylphide 5/11/91, Deutschen Oper Berlin
Ch.: Peter Schaufuss. *M.:* Løvenskiold. *S.,C.:* David Walker. *L.:* David Mohr.

Cinderella 20/12/91, Deutschen Oper Berlin
Ch.: Valery Panov. *M.:* Prokofiev. *S.,C.:* José Varona.

B.O.G.3.0 5/4/92, Deutschen Oper Berlin
Ch.: Michael Clark. *M.:* Bruce Gilbert. *D.:* Michael Clark. *S.:* José Varona. *L.:* Charles Atlas.

Laytext 5/4/92, Deutschen Oper Berlin
Ch.: Stephen Petronio. *M.:* Stravinsky. *S.,C.:* H. Petal. *L.:* Ken Tabachnik.

The Opening 5/4/92, Deutschen Oper Berlin
Ch.: Bill T. Jones. *M.:* John Oswald. *S.,C.:* Liz Prince. *L.:* Robert Wierzel.

Cruel Garden 21/5/92, Deutschen Oper Berlin
Ch.: Christopher Bruce. *M.:* Carlos Miranda. *S.:* Ralph Koltai. *C.:* Sandy Powell, Lindsay Kemp. *L.:* John Spradbery.

Repertory:

Agon
Ch.: Balanchine. *M.:* Stravinsky.

Apollo
Ch.: Balanchine. *M.:* Stravinsky.

Carmen
Ch.: Roland Petit. *M.:* Bizet.

The Dream is Over
Ch.: Christopher Bruce. *M.:* John Lennon.

Firebird
Ch.: Maurice Béjart. *M.:* Stravinsky.

A Folk Tale
Ch.: Peter Schaufuss. *M.:* N.W. Gade, J.P.E. Hartmann.

Les Intermittences du coeur
Ch.: Roland Petit. *M.:* Various.

Land
Ch.: Christopher Bruce. *M.:* Arne Nordheim.

Ring um den Ring
Ch.: Maurice Béjart. *M.:* Wagner. *S.,C.:* Peter Sykora.

Le Sacre du printemps
Ch.: Maurice Béjart. *M.:* Stravinsky.

Song of a Wayfarer
Ch.: Maurice Béjart. *M.:* Mahler.

Swansong
Ch.: Christopher Bruce. *M.:* Philip Chambon.

Symphony in C
Ch.: Balanchine. *M.:* Bizet.

Tchaikovsky Pas de Deux
Ch.: Balanchine. *M.:* Tchaikovsky.

Twilight
Ch.: Hans van Manen. *M.:* John Cage.

Who Cares?
Ch.: Balanchine. *M.:* Gershwin.

BALLETT FRANKFURT

Untermainanlage 11
6000 Frankfurt am Main 1
Tel: 069/212-37319
Fax: 069/212-37177

Artistic dir.: William Forythe

Administrative dir.: Dr Martin Steinhoff

Principal/associate choreographer(s):
William Forsythe, Amanda Miller

Visiting choreographer(s): Ohad Naharin,
Alonzo King

Guest teacher(s): Irena Milovan, Lynn
Seymour, Robert Sund, Simon de Mowbray

No. of dancers: 20 male, 21 female

No. of performances: 97

Tours to: France, Spain

Premieres:

Slingerland 7/4/91, Frankfurt
Ch.: William Forsythe. *M.:* Gavin Bryars,
Thom Willems. *D.:* William Forsythe. *Film,
objects:* Cara Perlman.

The Loss of Small Detail 11/5/91, Frankfurt
Ch.: William Forsythe. *M.:* Thom Willems.
D.: William Forsythe. *C.:* Issey Miyake.

No Wild Ones 11/5/91, Frankfurt
Ch.: Amanda Miller. *M.:* Peter Sherer, Arto
Lindsay. *D.:* Amanda Miller.

The Second Detail 14/7/91, Frankfurt
Ch.: William Forsythe. *M.:* Thom Willems.
D.: William Forsythe. *C.:* Issey Miyake.

Snap Woven Effort 26/10/91, Frankfurt
Ch.: William Forsythe. *M.:* Thom Willems.
D.: William Forsythe. *C.:* Gianni Versace.

Arto's Book 10/1/92, Frankfurt
Ch.: Amanda Miller. *M.:* Guss Janssen. *D.:*
Amanda Miller.

Arbos 13/6/92, Frankfurt
Ch.: Ohad Naharin. *M.:* Arvo Pärt. *D.:* Ohad
Naharin. *C.:* Rakefet Levy. *L.:* Bambi.

As a Garden in this Setting 13/6/92,
Frankfurt
Ch.: William Forsythe. *M.:* Thom Willems.
D.: William Forsythe. *C.:* Issey Miyake.

Without Wax 13/6/92, Frankfurt

Ch.: Alonzo King. *M.:* Sofia Gubaidulina,
Bohuslav Martinu. *D.:* Alonzo King. *C.:*
Sandra Woodall. *L.:* Craig Miller.

Repertory:

Artifact
Ch.: William Forsythe. *M.:* J.S. Bach, Eva
Crossman-Hecht. *D.:* William Forsythe.

Die Befragung des Robert Scott
Ch.: William Forsythe. *M.:* Thom Willems.
D.: William Forsythe.

Impressing the Czar
Ch.: William Forsythe. *M.:* Beethoven, Leslie
Stuck, Eva CrossmanHecht, Thom Willems.
D.: William Forsythe.

Isabelle's Dance (Musical)
Ch.: William Forsythe. *M.:* Eva Crossman-
Hecht. *D.:* Michael Simon. *C.:* Férial Simon.
L.: William Forsythe.

Limb's Theorem
Ch.: William Forsythe. *M.:* Thom Willems.
D.: William Forsythe.

New Sleep
Ch.: William Forsythe. *M.:* Thom Willems.
D.: William Forsythe.

Pretty Ugly
Ch.: Amanda Miller. *M.:* Arto Lindsay, Peter
Scherer. *D.:* Amanda Miller. *S.:* Amanda
Miller, Ricardo Castilla von Bennewitz.

Steptext
Ch.: William Forsythe. *M.:* J.S. Bach. *D.:*
William Forsythe.

The Vile Parody of Address
Ch.: William Forsythe. *M.:* J.S. Bach. *D.:*
William Forsythe.

BALLETT SCHINDOWSKI

Musiktheater im Revier Gelsenkirchen
Kennedy Platz
4650 Gelsenkirchen
Tel: 0209-4097138
Fax: 0209-4097250

Artistic dir.: Bernd Schindowski

Administrative dir.: Esther Nöcker. Gianni
Malfer

Principal/associate choreographer(s): Bernd
Schindowski, Rubens Reis, Eden Summers,
Sheyla Silva, Henning Paat

Principal dancers: Carmen Balochini, Rita
Barretto, Ellen Bucalo, Emma-Louise

Jordan, Schela Silva, Eden Summers, Marta Nejm, Rianna Kuipers, Tung Hon, Rubens Reis, Bernd Schindowski, Cassio Vitaliano, Neng-Sheng Yu

No. of dancers: 11 male, 12 female

No. of performances: 85

Pay rates: approx. £700 per month

Premieres:

Als hät der Himmel die Erde still geküsst 1/6/91, Musiktheater im Revier
Ch.: Rubens Reis. *S.:* Manfred Dorra. *C.:* Bennie Voorhaar. *L.:* Rubens Reis. *Text:* Jean Genet.

Bagatelle 1/6/91, Musiktheater im Revier
Ch.: Eden Summers. *M.:* Poulenc. *S.:* Manfred Dorra. *C.:* Bennie Voorhaar. *L.:* Eden Summers

Das kriminelle Kind 1/6/91, Musiktheater im Revier
Ch.: Bernd Schindowski. *S.:* Manfred Dorra. *C.:* Bennie Voorhaar. *L.:* Bernd Schindowski. *Text:* Jean Genet.

Catapapu 5/10/91, Musiktheater im Revier
Ch.: Rubens Reis. *M.:* Poulenc. *S.:* Manfred Dorra. *C.:* Bennie Voorhaar. *L.:* Rubens Reis.

Hoppla 5/10/91, Musiktheater im Revier
Ch.: Sheyla Silva. *S.:* Manfred Dorra. *C.:* Bennie Voorhaar. *L.:* Sheyla Silva.

Schudeldudel 5/10/91, Musiktheater im Revier
Ch.: Bernd Schindowski. *M.:* Collage. *S.:* Manfred Dorra. *C.:* Bennie Voorhaar. *L.:* Bernd Schindowski.

Tilim – Bom 5/10/91, Musiktheater im Revier
Ch.: Eden Summers. *M.:* Stravinsky. *S.:* Manfred Dorra. *C.:* Bennie Voorhaar. *L.:* Eden Summers.

B(r)achland 19/1/92, Musiktheater im Revier
Ch.: Henning Paar. *M.:* J.S. Bach. *S.:* Manfred Dorra. *C.:* Bennie Voorhaar. *L.:* Henning Paar.

Der erste Tag or Les IlluminationsBagatelle 19/1/92, Musiktheater im Revier
Ch.: Bernd Schindowski. *M.:* Britten. *S.:* Manfred Dorra. *C.:* Bennie Voorhaar. *L.:* Bernd Schindowski.

Sequenz 19/1/92, Musiktheater im Revier
Ch.: Bernd Schindowski. *M.:* Hildegard von Bingen. *S.:* Manfred Dorra. *C.:* Bennie Voorhaar. *L.:* Bernd Schindowski.

Repertory:

Johannespassion
Ch.: Bernd Schindowski. *M.:* J.S. Bach. *S.:* Manfred Dorra. *C.:* Bennie Voorhaar. *L.:* Bernd Schindowski.

Lied der Sonne
Ch.: Bernd Schindowski. *M.:* Steve Reich. *S.:* E.W. Zimmer. *C.:* Leonie Grimm. *L.:* Bernd Schindowski.

Kaleidoskop
Ch.: Bernd Schindowski. *M.:* Various. *S.:* Manfred Dorra. *C.:* Bennie Voorhaar. *L.:* Bernd Schindowski.

Nur wer die Sehnsucht kennt. . .
Ch.: Bernd Schindowski. *M.:* Tchaikovsky. *S.:* Manfred Dorra. *C.:* Bennie Voorhaar. *L.:* Bernd Schindowski.

Reigen/La Ronde
Ch.: Bernd Schindowski. *M.:* Françaix, Weill. *S.:* E.W. Zimmer. *C.:* Leonie Grimm. *L.:* Bernd Schindowski.

Reise nach Kythera
Ch.: Bernd Schindowski. *M.:* Debussy. *S.:* E.W. Zimmer. *C.:* Leonie Grimm. *L.:* Bernd Schindowski.

BAYERISCHES STAATSBALLET

Max-Joseph-Platz
D-8000 München 22
Tel: (089) 29 00 17 11
Fax: (089) 29 00 17 17

Artistic dir.: Konstanze Vernon

Visiting choreographer(s): Wright, Barra, Kylián, van Manen, Christe, Naharin, Preljocaj, Scholz

Guest teacher(s): David Allen, Peter Appel, Magdalena Popa, Vladimir Tsukanov, Gerard Wilk

Principal dancers: Evelyn Hart, Kiki Lammersen, Christina McDermott, Natalja Trokaj, Judith Turos, Anna Villadolid, Kirill Melnikov, Robert Underwood, Oliver Wehe

Guest dancers: Jan Broeckx, Vladimir Derevianko, Oliver Matz, Zoltan Solymosi

No. of dancers: 28 male, 32 female

No. of performances: c. 110

Tours to: Italy, Spain

Premieres:

Before Nightfall 16/5/92, National Theatre, Munich
Ch.: Nils Christe. *M.:* Martinu. *D.:* Keso Dekker. *L.:* Joop Caboort.

Svadebka 16/5/92, National Theatre, Munich
Ch.: Jirí Kylián. *M.:* Stravinsky. *D.:* John Macfarlane. *L.:* Jennifer Tipton.

Repertory:

Cinderella
Ch.: Riccardo Duse. *M.:* Prokofiev. *D.:* Andreas Herrmann.

Don Quixote
Ch.: Ray Barra. *M.:* Minkus. *D.:* Thomas Pekny. *C.:* Silvia Strahammer.

Klavierkonzer es Dur
Ch.: Uwe Scholz. *M.:* Mozart. *D.:* Rosalie.

Onegin
Ch.: John Cranko. *M.:* Tchaikovsky. *D.:* Jürgen Rose.

Les Petits riens
Ch.: Heinz Manniegel. *M.:* Mozart. *D.:* Rosalie.

Romeo and Juliet
Ch.: John Cranko. *M.:* Prokofiev. *D.:* Jürgen Rose.

Sleeping Beauty
Ch.: Peter Wright. *M.:* Tchaikovsky. *D.:* Peter Farmer.

Trois gnossiennes
Ch.: Hans van Manen. *M.:* Erik Satie.

DEUTSCHE STAATSOPER BERLIN

Unter den Linden 5-7
1086 Berlin
Tel: 02 2035 40
Fax: 20 354 206

Artistic dir.: Martin Puttke (until June 1992)

Principal/associate choreographer(s):

Visiting choreographer(s): Rudolf Nureyev, Marc Bogaerts

Guest teacher(s): Marc Bogaerts

Principal dancers: Steffi Scherzer, Bettina Thul, Uwe Arnold, Torsten Händler, Jörg Lucas, Oliver Matz, Mario Perricone, Raimondo Rebeek

Guest dancers: Rudolf Nureyev, Jutta Deutschland

No. of dancers: 30 male, 41 female

No. of performances: 60

Premieres:

5-4-3-2-Einsamkeit 13/6/91, Friedrichsafen
Ch.: Marc Bogaerts. *M.:* Brahms. *D.:* Marc Bogaerts.

Thema und Variationen 10/10/92, Deutsche Staatsoper Berlin
Ch.: Balanchine. *M.:* Tchaikovsky.

Dornröschen 29/2/92, Deutsche Staatsoper Berlin
Ch.: Nureyev. *M.:* Tchaikovsky. *D.:* Georgiadis. *L.:* Sjöquist.

HAMBURGER BALLETT

Ballettzentrum Hamburg John Neumeier
Caspar-Voght-Strasse 54
2000 Hamburg 26
Tel: (040) 21 11 88-0
Fax: (040) 21 22 88-88

Artistic dir.: John Neumeier

Administrative dir.: Ulrike Schmidt

Visiting choreographer(s): Lar Lubovitch, Maurice Béjart

Guest teacher(s): Irina Jacobson, Azzari Plissetski, Sergiu Stefanschi

Principal dancers: Stefanie Arndt, Bettina Beckmann, Anna Grabka, Gigi Hyatt, Chantal Lefèvre, Gamal Gouda, Anders Hellström, Jean Laban, Ivan Liska

Guest dancers: Annelie Alhanko, Rachel Beaujean, Marcia Haydée, Marie Lindqvist, Elisabeth Maurin, Annie Mayet, Heidi Ryom, Tamas Dietrich, Clint Farha, Manuel Legris, Jöran Svalberg

No. of dancers: 27 male, 29 female

No. of performances: 123

Tours to: Austria, Northern Ireland, Italy, France

Premieres:

Fenster zu Mozart 19/4/91, State Opera of Hamburg
Ch.: John Neumeier. *M.:* Beethoven, Mozart, Reger, Schnittke, Schweinitz. *S.:* Klaus Hellenstein. *C.,L:* John Neumeier.

Spring and Fall 28/4/91, State Opera of Hamburg
Ch.: John Neumeier. M.: Dvořák. C.,L.: John Neumeier.

Requiem (Salzburg version) 16/7/91, Salzburg, Austria
Ch.: John Neumeier. M.: Mozart, Gregorian choir. D.: John Neumeier.

On the Town 15/12/91, State Opera of Hamburg
Ch.: John Neumeier. M.: Leonard Bernstein. S.,C: Zack Brown.

Requiem (Hamburg version) 12/1/92, State Opera of Hamburg
Ch.: John Neumeier. M.: Mozart, Gregorian choir. D.: John Neumeier.

Cinderella 15/5/92, State Opera of Hamburg
Ch.: John Neumeier. M.: Prokofiev. S.,C: Jürgen Rose. L.: Max Keller.

Repertory:

Des Knaben Wunderhorn/Fünfte Sinfonie von Gustav Mahler
Ch.: John Neumeier. M.: Mahler. S.,C: John Neumeier.

Die Stühle
Ch.: Maurice Béjart. M.: Wagner. *Text:* Eugène Ionesco.

Dornröschen
Ch.: John Neumeier. M.: Tchaikovsky. S.,C: Jürgen Rose

The Leaves are Fading
Ch.: Antony Tudor. M.: Dvořák. S.: Ming Cho Lee. C.: Patricia Zipprodt.

Matthäus-Passion
Ch.: John Neumeier. M.: J.S. Bach. S.,C: John Neumeier.

Le Sacre
Ch.: John Neumeier. M.: Stravinsky.

Serenade
Ch.: Balanchine. M.: Tchaikovsky. C.: Karinska.

Ein Sommernachtstraum
Ch.: John Neumeier. M.: Mendelssohn, Ligeti. S.,C: Jürgen Rose.

HEIDELBERG BALLET

Friedrichstrasse 5
D-6900 Heidelberg
Tel: (06221) 58 35 10
Fax: (06221) 58 35 99

Artistic dir.: Liz King

Principal/associate choreographer(s): Liz King

Guest teacher(s): Judy Reyn, Frey Faust

No. of dancers: 7 male, 7 female

No. of performances: 50

Premieres:

Cindy's Lied 5/91, City Theatre of Heidelberg
Ch.: Liz King. M.: J.S. Bach. D.: Manfred Biskup.

Slash 5/91, City Theatre of Heidelberg
Ch.: Liz King. M.: J.S. Bach. D.: Manfred Biskup.

WESTWEST 1/92, City Theatre of Heidelberg
Ch.: Liz King. M.: Collage. D.: Manfred Biskup.

LEIPZIGES BALLETT

Augustusplatz 12
D-O-7010 Leipzig
Tel: 341-7168
Fax: 341-293 633

Artistic dir.: Uwe Scholz

STAATSOPER DRESDEN

Theaterplatz 2
8010 Dresden
Tel: 4842469
Fax: 4842669

Artistic dir.: Johannes Bönig

Administrative dir.: Dieter Lösche

Principal/associate choreographer(s):
Joannes Bönig, Stephan Thoß

Visiting choreographer(s): Jennifer Muller, François Klaus, Bernd Schindowski

Guest teacher(s): Lisette Aquilar

Principal dancers: Thomas Hartmann, Christophe Sem, Ralf Arndt, Reiner Feistel, Jan Hein van Tol, Hannes-Detlef Vogel, Uwe Fischer, Raymond Hilbert, Carola Schwab, Carol Meyer, Beate Magulski, Romy Liebig, Beatrix Scherz, Sabine Bohlig, Carola Tautz, Ina Meinhold, Mareen Zabei, Roberta Rigamonti

No. of dancers: 19 male, 35 female

No. of performances: 53

Pay rates: DM 2300–4500

Premieres:

Les Illuminations 14/4/91, Semperoper Dresden
Ch.: Bernd Schindowski. *M.:* Benjamin Britten. *S.:* Bernd Schindowski. *C.:* Benni Voorhaar. *L.:* Friedewalt Degen, Rainer Buder.

Inneres Kreisen 14/4/91, Semperoper Dresden
Ch.: Johannes Bönig. *M.:* Arvo Pärt. *S.:* Ger van Leeuwen, Johannes Bönig. *C.:* Maja Kuyper. *L.:* Friedewalt Degen, Rainer Buder.

Plagegeister 14/4/91, Semperoper Dresden
Ch.: François Klaus. *M.:* Benjamin Britten. *S.:* François Klaus. *C.:* Gabriele Jaenecke. *L.:* Friedewalt Degen, Rainer Buder.

Getreidegasse Nr. 9 6/6/91, Kleines Haus d. Staatsschauspiels
Ch.: Carla Börner Spiewok. *M.:* Mozart. *S.:* Michael Münch. *C.:* Susanne Goder. *L.:* Günter Hegewald.

Juidth Befreierin Bethuliens 6/6/91, Kleines Haus d. Staatsschauspiels
Ch.: Carla Börner Spiewok. *M.:* Mozart. *S.:* Juan Leon Pellegrin. *C.:* Susanne Goder. *L.:* Günter Hegewald.

Alibi-Gescelschaft 15/12/91, Semperoper Dresden
Ch.: Johannes Bönig. *M.:* Samuel Barber, Anton Bruckner. *C.:* Frauke Schernau. *L.:* Torsten Schäfer

Beltane (Le Sacre du printemps) 15/12/91, Semperoper Dresden
Ch.: Johannes Bönig. *M.:* Stravinsky. *S.:* Klaus Feustel. *C.:* Maja Kuyper. *L.:* Torsten Schäfer.

Aus wilder Wurzel 22/5/92, Kleine Szene
Ch.: Carla Börner. *M.:* Uwe Donat.

Rufende Stimmen 22/5/92, Kleine Szene
Ch.: Debra Knapp-Wrigth. *M.:* Le Mystère de voix Bulgares. *S.,C.:* Debra Knapp-Wrigth. *L.:* Olaf Brusdelyins.

Tangenten 22/5/92, Kleine Szene
Ch.: Prue Sheridan. *M.:* David Wescott. *S.,C.:* Prue Sheridan. *L.:* Olaf Brusdelyins.

Unter dem Mond am Fluß 22/5/92, Kleine Szene
Ch.: Debra Knapp-Wrigth. *M.:* Joseph Shabalala. *S.,C.:* Debra Knapp-Wrigth. *L.:* Olaf Brusdelyins.

Wispern 22/5/92, Kleine Szene
Ch.: Debra Knapp-Wrigth. *M.:* Paul Sturm. *S.,C.:* Debra Knapp-Wrigth. *L.:* Olaf Brusdelyins.

Bachianas Brasileiras 28/6/92, Semperoper Dresden
Ch.: Johannes Bönig. *M.:* Heitor Villa-Lobos. *S.:* Johannes Bönig. *C.:* Frauke Schernau. *L.:* Jan van Velden.

Erinnerung an einen Freund 28/6/92, Semperoper Dresden
Ch.: Johannes Bönig. *M.:* John Adams, John Cale. *S.,C.:* Ella Späte. *L.:* Jan van Velden.

My Way 28/6/92, Semperoper Dresden
Ch.: Stephan Thoß. *M.:* Claude François, Jacque Revaux. *C.:* Stephan Thoß. *L.:* Jan van Velden.

Pourquoi pas? 28/6/92, Semperoper Dresden
Ch.: Johannes Bönig. *M.:* Aulis Sallinen. *S.,L.:* Jan van Velden. *C.:* Barbara Keßler.

Woge auf steinigem Grund 28/6/92, Semperoper Dresden
Ch.: Stephan Thoß. *M.:* Scarlatti, J.S. Bach, Petitgand. *C.:* Stephan Thoß. *L.:* Jan van Velden.

Woman with visitors at 3 am 28/6/92, Semperoper Dresden
Ch.: Jennifer Muller. *M.:* Keith Jarrett. *S.,L.:* Stageworks. *C.:* Donna Maric Larsen.

STUTTGARTER BALLETT

Oberer Schlossgarten 6
7000 Stuttgart 1
Tel: (0711) 2032-420/235/296

Artistic dir.: Marcia Haydée, Egon Madsen (assistant)

SUSANNE LINKE

c/o Francesca Spinazzi
Milinowskistrasse 1
W-1000 Berlin 37
Tel: 30-801 5335
Fax: 30-801 6519

Artistic dir.: Susanne Linke

Administrative dir.: Francesca Spinazzi

No. of dancers: 2

TANZTHEATER DER KOMISCHEN OPER BERLIN

Behrenstrasse 55
D-O-1080 Berlin
Tel: 02 220 2761
Fax: 229 90 29

Artistic dir.: Tom Schilling

Administrative dir.: Doris Laine

Principal/associate choreographer(s): Tom Schilling

Visiting choreographer(s): Birgit Scherzer, Dietmar Seyffert, Volker Tietböhl, Emöke Pöstényi, Jan Linkens, Marc Bogaerts, Arila Siegert

Principal dancers: Hannelore Bey, Jutta Deustchland, Angela Reinhardt, Beate Vollack, Alma Munteanu, Heike Keller, Dieter Hülse, Thomas Vollmer, Gregor Seyffert, Jens-Peter Urbich

Guest dancers: Steffi Scherzer, Tatiana Marinova, Torsten Händler, Mario Perricone, Jörg Simon, Eva Evdokimova, Paul Chalmer, Arila Siegert, Irek Wisniewski, Yoko Ichino, David Nixon

No. of dancers: 25 male, 33 female

No. of performances: c. 50

Tours to: Australia, Italy, UK, Austria, Russia

Pay rates: DM3000—5000 per month

Premieres:

Frauen–Männer–Paare 5/6/91, Komische Oper
Ch.: Birgit Scherzer. *M.:* Nina Simone, Keith Jarrett.

Bolero 21/6/91, Komische Oper
Ch.: Emöke Pöstényi. *M.:* Ravel. *D.:* Nancy Torres.

Clown Gottes 21/6/91, Komische Oper
Ch.: Dietmar Seyffert. *M.:* Stravinsky. *D.:* Matthias Schmidt. *C.:* Eleonore Kleiber.

Pulcinella 21/6/91, Komische Oper
Ch.: Harald Wandtke. *M.:* Stravinsky. *D.:* Hartmut Henning. *C.:* Eleonore Kleiber.

Tango 21/6/91, Komische Oper
Ch.: Volker Tietböhl. *M.:* Astor Piazolla. *D.:* Eleonore Kleiber.

Undine 21/6/91, Komische Oper
Ch.: Arila Siegert. *M.:* Hans Werner Henze. *D.:* Johannes Conen.

Wölfe 30/4/92, Komische Oper
Ch.: Dietmar Seyffert. *M.:* Brahms. *D.:* Matthias Schmidt. *C.:* Eleonore Kleiber.

Lebensräume 31/5/92, Komische Oper
Ch.: Jan Linkens. *M.:* Hindemith. *D.:* Reinhart Zimmerman. *C.:* Eleonore Kleiber.

Vier Jahreszeiten 31/5/92, Komische Oper
Ch.: Marc Bogaerts. *M.:* Vivaldi. *D.:* Reinhart Zimmerman. *C.:* Eleonore Kleiber.

TANZTHEATER WUPPERTAL PINA BAUSCH

Spinnstrasse 4
W-5600 Wuppertal 2
Tel: 202-563 4256
Fax: 202-554 765

Artistic dir.: Pina Bausch

Administrative dir.: Matthias Schmiegelt

Hong Kong

CITY CONTEMPORARY DANCE COMPANY

110 Shatin Pass Road
Wong Tai Sin
Kowloon
Tel: 3-268597

Artistic dir.: Mr Willy Tsao

HONG KONG ACADEMY FOR THE PERFORMING ARTS

1 Gloucester Road
Wanchai
Tel: 5-823532

HONG KONG BALLET

60 Blue Pool Road
G/F Happy Valley
Tel: 5-737398

ZUNI ICOSAHEDRON

12th Floor Rhenish Centre
248-250 Hennessy Road
Wanchai
Tel: 5-8938419

Artistic dir.: Danny Yung, Vicky Leong, Gabriel Yiu

Hungary

ARTUS DANCE AND JUMP THEATRE

1113 Budapest
Kökörcsin u.9
Tel: 1667-505

Artistic dir.: Gábor Goda

Principal/associate choreographer(s): Gábor Goda

Principal dancers: Mária Balázs, Ildikó Mándym Csaba Méhes, Gábor Goda, Tamás Sólyom

BALLET SOPIANAE

National Theatre
Pécs, Pf.: 126 7601
Tel: 72-11-965

Artistic dir.: Imre Eck

BERGER DANCE COMPANY

1098 Budapest
Böszörményi u. 8

Artistic dir.: Gyula Berger

Principal/associate choreographer(s): Gyula Berger

Principal dancers: Gabriella Bánki, Ildikó Bóta, Eszter Gál, Éva Gálik, Ildikó Gelencsér, Akos Hargitay, Ferenc Kálmán, Miklós Visontai, Gyula Berger

COLLECTIVE OF NATURAL DISASTERS

1078 Budapest
Péterfy S.u. 42
Tel: 1414-080

Artistic dir.: György Arvay

Principal/associate choreographer(s): Yvette Bozsik

GYÖR BALLET

Kisfaludy Theatre
Györ
Czuczor G. u. 17 9022

Artistic dir.: Iván Markö

HUNGARIAN NATIONAL BALLET

State Opera House
Budapest, IV
Népköztársaság utja 22
Pf: 503
Tel: 1373

SAROO

1084 Budapest
Rákóczi tér 6
Tel: 1333-082

Artistic dir.: Éva Molnár

Principal/associate choreographer(s): Éva Molnár

Principal dancers: Nóra Nemes, Orsolya Nemes, Zsófia Nemes, Yvette Horváth, Éva Molnár

SZEGED BALLET

National Theatre, Szeged
Deák Ferenc u. 12
H-6720 Szeged
Tel: 62-11-211

Artistic dir.: Zoltán Imre

Principal/associate choreographer(s): Zoltán Imre

Visiting choreographer(s): Matthew Hawkins, Jorma Uotinen, Yuri Vámos, Ferenc Barbay, Katalin Lörinc, György Krámer, László Seregi, Yvette Bozsik, Bertrand d'At, Bernd Schindowski

Guest teacher(s): Karavajeva, László Péter, Edith Dévényi

Principal dancers: Gizella Zarnoóczai, Annamária Prepeliczay, András Pataki, Tamás Juronics, Hedvig Fekete, Johanna Bodor, Kata Péntek, Anita Kovács, Attila Sárközi, Attila Kalmár

No. of dancers: 9 male, 12 female

No. of performances: 40

Tours to: Iraq, Yugoslavia, Poland, Austria, Italy

Premieres:

The Four Seasons 20/12/91, National Theatre of Szeged
Ch.: Zoltán Imre. *M.:* Vivaldi. *D.:* György Csík.

The Hour of Imagination 20/12/91, Szeged
Ch.: Tamás Juronics. *M.:* Collage. *D.:* György Csík.

24 Minutes 20/12/91, Szeged
Ch.: Katalin Lörinc. *M.:* arrangement. *D.:* György Csík.

Concerto of Destiny 24/2/92, Budapest
Ch.: Tamás Juronics. *M.:* Mozart, Vivaldi. *D.:* Tamás Juronics.

Women's Closet 24/2/92, Budapest
Ch.: Yvette Bozsik. *M.,D.:* György Arvai.

Die Nacht 3/4/92, Szeged
Ch.: Bertrand d'At. *M.:* Schubert, Schumann, Brahms. *D.:* Zsuzsa Molnár.

Repertory:

Dreaming of Kafka
Ch.: Zoltán Imre. *M.:* Alban Berg. *D.:* Zsuzsa Molnár.

Firework
Ch.: Bernd Schindowski. *M.:* John Adams. *D.:* Zsuzsa Molnár.

TRANZ DANZ

1013 Budapest
Attila u. 31
Tel: 1758-253

Artistic dir.: Gerzson Kovács

Principal/associate choreographer(s): Gerzson Kovács

Principal dancers: Tibor Tokai, Richárd Tóth, Gerzson Kovács

VESZPREM DANCE WORKSHOP

Katalin Lörinc:
1132 Budapest,
Victor Hugo u.36

György Krámer:
1111 Budapest,
Bartók Béla u.64
Tel: 1311-809/1666-109

Artistic dir.: Katalin Lörinc, György Krámer

Principal/associate choreographer(s): Katalin Lörinc, György Krámer

Israel

BAT-DOR DANCE COMPANY

30 Ibn Gvirol Street
Tel Aviv 64078
Tel: 03-263175
Fax: 3-6955587

Artistic dir.: Jeanette Ordman

Administrative dir.: Kenneth Mason

Principal/associate choreographer(s): Domy Reiter-Sofer

Visiting choreographer(s): Ed Wubbe

Guest teacher(s): Richard Gibson

Principal dancers: Sergie Lukin, Patricia Aharoni, Ania Brud, Alexander Alexander, Eleanor Vlodavsky, Vladislav Manayenkov

Guest dancers: Bobby Thompson

No. of dancers: 8 male, 11 female

No. of performances: 36

Premieres:

Shirim 29/6/92, Tel Aviv
Ch.: Domy Reiter-Soffer. *M.:* Sara Levy-Tanai, Ehud Manor, Matti Caspi, Alexander Argov. *C.:* Miki Shapira. *L.:* Judy Kupferman.

Bagatellen 29/7/91, Haifa
Ch.: Ed Wubbe. *M.*: Medieval, arr. Rene
Clumenic. *D.*: Ed Wubbe. *C.*: Heidi de Raad.

Repertory:

Adieux
Ch.: Richard Levi. *M.*: Pat Metheny. *L.*: Judy
Kupferman.

Aryata
Ch.: Mauricio Wainrot. *M.*: Schubert, Michel
Hoehler, Willem Breuker. *S.*: Sean
McAllister. *C.*: Carlos Gallardo.

Cantares
Ch.: Oscar Araíz. *M.*: Ravel. *C.*: Carlos
Cytrynowsky. *L.*: Danny Redler.

In and Out
Ch.: Hans van Manen. *M.*: Laurie Anderson,
Nina Hagen. *S.,C.*: Keso Dekker. *L.*: Danny
Redler.

Libertango
Ch.: Mauricio Wainrot. *M.*: Astor Piazzola.
S., C.: Carlos Gallardo. *L.*: Sean McAllister.

Luminescences
Ch.: Nils Christe. *M.*: Poulenc. *S.,C.*: Keso
Dekker. *L.*: Danny Redler.

Night Creature
Ch.: Alvin Ailey. *M.*: Duke Ellington. *C.*:
Jane Greenwood. *L.*: Chenault Spence. *Batik:*
Moti Gazit.

Only If You Dance With Pepe
Ch.: Mark Haim. *M.*: From the Dominican
Republic. *C.*: Shmuel Wilder. *L.*: Felice Ross.

Quartet II
Ch.: Nils Christe. *M.*: Shostakovich. *S.,C.*:
Keso Dekker. *L.*: Jan Kees Tjebbes.

Schlager
Ch.: Ed Wubbe. *M.*: DAF (Deustch
Amerkanische Freundschaft). *C.*: Pamela
Homoet. *L.*: Ed Wubbe.

Spectrum
Ch.: Choo San Goh. *M.*: J.S. Bach. *S.,C.*:
Carol Vollet Garber. *L.*: Tony Tucci.

Twilight Concerto
Ch.: Matthew Diamond. *M.*: Mendelssohn.
C.: Patricia Mcgourty. *L.*: Edward
Greenberg.

La Valse
Ch.: Domy Reiter-Soffer. *M.*: Ravel. *C.*:
Domy Reiter-Soffer. *L.*: Judy Kupferman.

Whirligogs (Knots, Tangles, Confusions)
Ch.: Lar Lubovitch. *M.*: Berio. *C.*: Patricia
Mcgourty. *L.*: Edward Greenberg.

INBAL DANCE THEATRE

6 Yehieli Street
Tel Aviv 65149
Tel: 03-653711

THE ISRAEL BALLET

2 Kikar Hamedinah Hey Be'iyar
Tel Aviv 62093
Tel: 03-266610

Artistic dir.: Berta Yampolsky

JERUSALEM TAMAR DANCE COMPANY

Gruss Community Centre
5 Zichron Ya'akov Street
Romena
94421 Jerusalem
Tel: 02-372711

Artistic dir.: Amir Kolben

KIBBUTZ CONTEMPORARY DANCE COMPANY

Studio: Kibbutz Ga'aton
Ma'ale Hagalil 25130
Office: 10 Dubnov Street
Tel Aviv 61400, POB 40014
Tel: Studio: 972-4-858437.
Office: 972-3-5452688/9
Fax: 972-3-5452689/5429936

Artistic dir.: Yehudit Arnon

Administrative dir.: Dan Rudolf

Principal/associate choreographer(s): Rami
Be'er

Visiting choreographer(s): Tamara Roso,
Susanne Linke, Daniel Ezralow

Guest teacher(s): Jeanne Solan, John
Wisman, Sighilt Pahl, Ivan Kramer

Principal dancers: Einav Cohen, Angeline
Doornbos, Sivan Fastman, Jasmin
Vardiman, Niza Gambo, Liat Hyams, Keren
Levy, Idit Solange, Nima Ya'acovy, Galit
Hamami, Rami Be'er, Ari Fastman, Ziv
Frenkel, Uri Ivgi, Tamas Moricz, Igor
Vejsada, Ya'acov Shapira

No. of dancers: 7 male, 10 female

No. of performances: 98

Tours to: Enlgand, France, Belgium, Germany, Hungary, Czechoslovakia

Premieres:

Man/Woman 4/91, Tel-Aviv
Ch.: Uri Ivgy. *M.:* Mark Eishen. *S.:* Uri Ivgy. *C.:* Efrat Roded. *L.:* Nissan Gelbard.

Real Time 6/91, Karmiel
Ch.: Rami Be'er. *M.:* Alex Clod, collage. *S.:* Rami Be'er. *C.:* Ora Spengental. *L.:* Nissan Gelbard.

Shidduch 9/91, Tel-Aviv
Ch.: Tamara Roso. *M.:* Smetana. *D.:* Henk Schut.

Angeles Negros 12/91, Tel-Aviv
Ch.: Rami Be'er. *M.:* Ided Zehavi, Alex Clod, collage. *S.:* Yidal Steiner. *C.:* Efrat Roded. *L.:* Nissan Gelbard.

Wing'd Dream 2/92, Naharya
Ch.: Rami Be'er. *M.:* Samuel Barber. *S.:* Rami Be'er. *C.:* Efrat Roded. *L.:* Nissan Gelbard.

Fraters 3/92, Tel-Aviv
Ch.: Ziv Frenkel. *M.:* Arvo Pärt. *S.,C.:* Ziv Frenkel. *L.:* Nissan Gelbard.

Frauenballett 4/92, Jerusalem
Ch.: Susanne Linke. *M.:* Penderecki. *S.,C.:* Susanne Linke. *L.:* Nissan Gelbard.

Repertory:

Carnival of the Animals
Ch.: Rami Be'er. *M.:* Saint-Saëns. *S.:* Rami Be'er. *C.:* Yehudit Greenspan. *L.:* Nissan Gelbard.

Down North
Ch.: Mats Ek. *M.:* J.P. Nystrom. *S.:* Mats Ek. *C.:* Ora Spengental. *L.:* Nissan Gelbard.

Fireplace
Ch.: Mats Ek. *M.:* Glass, Dausz-Nern. *S.:* Mats Ek. *C.:* Mariko Aoyama. *L.:* Nissan Gelbard.

Peter and the Wolf
Ch.: Rami Be'er. *M.:* Prokofiev. *S.:* Moshe Hadari. *C.:* Pnina Abukasis. *L.:* Nissan Gelbard.

Rocking-Horse Michael
Ch.: Rami Be'er. *M.:* Yossi Mar-Chaim. *S.:* Moshe Hadari. *C.:* Pnina Abukasis. *L.:* Nissan Gelbard.

Stoolgame
Ch.: Jirí Kylián. *M.:* Arne Nordheim. *S.,C:* Walter Nobbe. *L.:* Joop Caboort.

Women from a Soft Rock
Ch.: Anat Assulin. *M.:* Mertens, Darling. *S.:* Anat Assulin. *C.:* Zvia Silberman. *L.:* Nissan Gelbard.

LIAT DROR—NIR BEN GAL COMPANY

11 Borochov Street
Tel Aviv 63263
Tel: 03-285957
Fax: 972-3-659634

Artistic dir.: Liat Dror, Nir Ben Gal

Administrative dir.: Hagai Shlomov

Principal dancers: Náama Gafni, Shiva Haviv, Roni Livne, Lior Levy, Assaf Levitan, Kobi Tamir, Liat Dror, Nir Ben Gal

No. of dancers: 4 male, 4 female

No. of performances: 50

Tours to: UK, Belgium, Germany, Holland, France, Switzerland

Premieres:

Circles of Lust 4/92, Tel Aviv
Ch.: Liat Dror, Nir Ben Gal. *M.:* Ori Vidislavski. *C.:* Zimra Dror. *L.:* David Ginat.

OSHRA ELKAYAM MOVEMENT THEATRE

119 Bar Kochva Street
Herzelia 46341
Tel: 052-544039

Artistic dir.: Oshra Elkayam

YARON MARGOLIN DANCE COMPANY

106/15 Derech Biet Lechem
Jerusalem 93624
Tel: 02-716197

Artistic dir.: Yaron Margolin

Italy

BALLET OF TEATRO ALLA SCALA, MILAN

Teatro alla Scala
via Filodrammatici 2
20121 Milan

Tel: 2-988791
Fax: 2-887 9331

Artistic dir.: Alberto Zedda

Japan

ASAMI MAKI BALLET

Nakano 6-27-13
Nakano-ku,Tokyo
Tel: 03-3360-8251
Fax: 03-3360-8253

Artistic dir.: Asami Maki

Principal/associate choreographer(s):
Asami Maki, Kyozo Mitani

Visiting choreographer(s): Alexander Grant, Azari Plissetski, Ib Andersen

Guest teacher(s): Boris Akimov, Asaf Messerer, Dzhigarkhanjan Gajan, Raymond Franchetti, Luc Amyot

Principal dancers: Noriko Ohara, Yuriko Kawaguchi, Tamiyo Kusakari, Sobi Sasaki, Noriko Ohata, Kyozo Mitani, Hiroaki Imamura, Naoya Kojima

Guest dancers: Andrei Fedotov, Igliz Galimoulline, Vladimir Kirillov

No. of dancers: 25 male, 60 female

No. of performances: 45

Tours to: USSR

Premieres:

La Fille mal gardée 19/10/91, Tokyo
Ch.: Frederick Ashton. *M.:* Hérold/Lanchbery. *D.:* Osbert Lancaster.

La Sylphide 5/6/92, Tokyo
Ch.: Bournonville. *M.:* Løvenskiold. *D.:* Norman McDowell.

MATSUYAMA BALLET FOUNDATION

Minamiaoyama 3-10-16
Minato-ku, Tokyo
Tel: 03-3408-6640
Fax: 03-3408-7986

Artistic dir.: Mikiko Matsuyama, Tetsutaro Shimizu

Administrative dir.: Masao Shimizu

Principal/associate choreographer(s):
Tetsutaro Shimizu

Guest teacher(s): Evgenio Valukin

Principal dancers: Yoko Morishita, Kumi Hiramoto, Hiroko Kurata, Tetsutaro Shimizu, Ms Akiko Yamakawa, Akemi Sato, Mr Kazuya Nakamura, Toshiyuki Miura, Kin Houryu (Jin Bao Long)

No. of dancers: 25 male, 50 female

No. of performances: 50-70

Tours to: USA, China

Premieres:

Swan Lake 6/4/91, Tokyo Bunka Kaikan
Ch.: Tetsutaro Shimizu. *M.:* Tchaikovsky.
D.: Naoji Kawaguchi. *S.:* Kodo Tanaka, Takayuki Sugano. *C.:* Tomoko Morita, Tetsutaro Shimizu. *L.:* Toshihiko Tonozaki.

Sleeping Beauty 3/5/91, Orchard Hall
Ch.: Rudolf Nureyev. *M.:* Tchaikovsky. *D.:* Nicholas Georgiadis. *S.:* Takayuki Sugano, Kodo Tanaka. *C.:* Nicholas Georgiadis. *L.:* Toshiyuki Tonozaki.

Don Quixote 2/6/91, Nakano Sun Plaza
Ch.: Rudolf Nureyev. *M.:* Minkus. *D.:* Nicholas Georgiadis. *S.:* Takayuki Sugano. *C.:* Nicholas Georgiadis.

Romeo and Juliet 13/7/91, Fujisawa Culture Hall
Ch.: Tetsutaro Shimizu. *M.:* Prokofiev. *D.:* Naoji Kawaguchi. *S.:* Kodo Tanaka. *C.:* Tomoko Morita, Tetsutaro Shimizu. *L.:* Toshihiko Tonokazi.

Allegro Brillante 21/9/91, Kan-i Hoken Hall
Ch.: Balanchine. *D.:* Patricia Neary. *S.:*
Takayuki Sugano. *C.:* Karinska. *L.:*
Toshiyuki Tonozaki.

Serenade 21/9/91, Kan-i Hoken Hall
Ch.: Balanchine. *M.:* Bizet. *D.:* Patricia
Neary. *S.:* Takayuki Sugano. *C.:* Jean Lurcat.
L.: Toshiyuki Tonozaki.

La Sylphide 21/9/91, Kan-i Hoken Hall
Ch.: Bournonville. *M.:* Løvenskiold. *D.:*
Naoji Kawaguchi. *S.:* Takayuki Sugano. *C.:*
Tomoko Morita, Tetsutaro Shimizu. *L.:*
Toshihiko Tonozaki.

Tchaikovsky Pas de Deux 21/9/91, Kan-i
Hoken Hall
Ch.: Balanchine. *M.:* Tchaikovsky. *D.:*
Tetsutaro Shimizu, Yoko Morishita. *S.:*
Takayuki Sugano. *C.:* Karinska. *L.:*
Toshiyuki Tonozaki.

The Blessed A 22/9/91, Kan-i Hoken Hall
Ch.: Toshiko Tanaka. *M.:* Beethoven. *S.:*
Takayuki Sugano. *C.:* Tomoko Morita. *L.:*
Toshiyuki Tonozaki.

A Kingdom of Dreams 22/9/91, Kan-i Hoken
Hall
Ch.: Tetsutaro Shimizu. *M.:* Wagner. *D.:*
Naoji Kawaguchi. *S.:* Takayuki Sugano. *C.:*
Tomoko Morita. *L.:* Toshiyuki Tonozaki.

Primavera 22/9/91, Kan-i Hoken Hall
Ch.: Yoshiaki Tonozaki. *M.:* Rossini. *D.:*
Naoji Kawaguchi. *S.:* Takayuki Sugano. *C.:*
Tomoko Morita, Tetsutaro Shimizu. *L.:*
Toshiyuki Tonozaki.

2010 KV525 22/9/91, Kan-i Hoken Hall
Ch.: Tetsutaro Shimizu. *M.:* Mozart. *S.:*
Takayuki Sugano. *C.:* Tomoko Morita,
Tetsutaro Shimizu. *L.:* Toshiyuki Tonozaki.

Four Hands 6/6/92, Nakano Sun Plaza
Ch.: Tetsutaro Shimizu. *M.:* Schubert. *D.:*
Naoji Kawaguchi. *S.:* Takayuki Sugano. *C.:*
Tomoko Morita. *L.:* Toshiyuki Tonozaki.

Rossini Divertimento 6/6/92, Nakano Sun
Plaza
Ch.: Tetsutaro Shimizu. *M.:* Rossini. *D.:*
Naoji Kawaguchi. *S.:* Takayuki Sugano. *C.:*
Tomoko Morita. *L.:* Toshiyuki Tonozaki.

TOKYO BALLET

Yakumo 5-1-20
Meguro-ku,Tokyo
Tel: 03-3725-8000
Fax: 03-3718-0858

Artistic dir.: Shiro Mizoshita

Administrative dir.: Tadatsugu Sasaki

Guest teacher(s): Viktor Rona, Marina
Semyonova, Wang Jia-hong

Principal dancers: Yukari Saito, Mayumi
Katsumata, Shiori Sano, Naoki Takagishi,
Kazuo Kimura, Masayuki Morita

Guest dancers: Sylvie Guillem, Jorge Donn,
Nina Ananiashvili, Alexei Fadeyechev

No. of dancers: 36 male, 60 female

No. of performances: 60

The Netherlands

BEPPIE BLANKERT DANCE COMPANY

Theaterbureau Berbee & Rudolphi, Korte
Leidsedwarsstraat 12
1017 RC Amsterdam
Tel: 20-627 7555/627 0455
Fax: 20-625 0616

Artistic dir.: Beppie Blankert

DANSGROEP KRISZTINA DE CHATEL

Plantage Muidergracht 155
1018 TT Amsterdam
Tel: 020-627 30 70
Fax: 020-624 97 64

Artistic dir.: Krisztina de Châtel

Administrative dir.: Kees Korsman

Guest teacher(s): Josiane Geys, Helga
Langen, Vicky Summers, Juliëtte van Ingen,
Lana Carroll, Bert Terborgh, Derrick Brown,
John Brown, Simon de Mowbray, Larry
Clark, Kevin Wynn

Principal dancers: Ann van den Broek,
Cathy Dekker, Paula Vasconcelos, Juliëtte
van Ingen (until December 1991), Pieter-
Paul Blok, Gilles den Hartog, Michael
Strecker, Paul Waarts

Guest dancers: Annemarie de Ruiter

No. of dancers: 4 male, 3 female

No. of performances: 69

Tours to: Canada, USA, Venezuela

Premieres:

Typhoon 17/9/91, Theatre Bellevue, Arnhem
Ch.: Krisztina de Châtel. *M.:* Simeon ten Holt. *S.,C.:* Peter Vermeulen. *L.:* Jilles Kongkind, Peter Vermeulen.

Change 1/11/91, De Klinker, Winschoten
Ch.: Krisztina de Châtel. *M.:* David Borden. *S.,C.:* Peter Struycken. *L.:* Nelly can de Velden.

Weep, Cry and Tangle 25/1/92, Municipal Theatre, Amsterdam
Ch.: Krisztina de Châtel. *M.:* Shostakovich. *S.:* bart Stuyf, Martin Mulder. *C.:* Rien Bekkers. *L.:* Bart Stuyf, Carlus Koopman.

DANSPRODUKTIE

Plantage Kerklaan 61
1018 CX Amsterdam
Tel: 020-6242166/6253863
Fax: 020-6259329

Artistic dir.: Bianca van Dillen

Administrative dir.: Paul Toebes

Principal/associate choreographer(s): Bianca van Dillen, Guido Severien

Visiting choreographer(s): Matthew Hawkins

Guest teacher(s): Eef de Kievit, Juliette van Ingen, Pink Niessen, Guido Severien, John Taylor, Angela Linssen

Principal dancers: Guido Severien, Pink Niessen, Patricia van Nugteren, Phill Hill, Chrisopher Steel, Clive Crawford, Ilse van Dijk, Lisette Verkaik, Esmeralda Koopman

Guest dancers: Anne Affourtit, Mischa van Dullemen, Monica van Leeuwen, Jorge Miranda Filio

No. of dancers: 3 male, 3 female

No. of performances: 60

Tours to: England, France

Premieres:

De Trap 23/4/91, Amsterdam
Ch.: Bianca van Dillen. *M.:* Louis Andriessen. *S.,C.:* Keso Dekker. *L.:* Mike v.d. Lagemaat.

Five Games Without Losers 23/4/91, Amsterdam
Ch.: Matthew Hawkins. *M.:* Roel von Oosten. *D.:* Keso Dekker. *L.:* Mike v.d. Lagemaat.

Color 18/10/91, Amsterdam
Ch.: Bianca van Dillen. *M.:* Bartók. *S.:* Bianca van Dillen. *C.:* Joke v.d. Berg. *L.:* Marc van Gelder.

Space 18/10/91, Amsterdam
Ch.: Guido Severien. *M.:* Henk van der Meulen. *S.:* Guido Severien. *C.:* Joke v.d. Berg. *L.:* Marc van Gelder.

Stamina 16/5/92, Amsterdam
Ch.: Bianca van Dillen. *M.:* Michael Nyman, Henk van der Meulen. *C.:* Joke v.d. Berg. *L.:* Marc van Gelder.

DUTCH NATIONAL BALLET

PO Box 16486
1001 RN Amsterdam
Tel: (31.20)-551 89 11
Fax: (31.20)-551 80 70

Artistic dir.: Wayne Eagling

Administrative dir.: Dick Hendriks

Principal/associate choreographer(s): Rudi van Dantzig, Toer van Schayk

Visiting choreographer(s): Ted Brandsen, William Forsythe, Ashley Page, Hans van Manen

Guest teacher(s): Olga Evreinoff, Boris Akimov

Principal dancers: Nathalie Caris, Coleen Davis, Caroline Sayo Iura, Jane Lord, Karin Schnabel, Valerie Valentine, Jeanette Vondersaar, Fred Berlips, Wim Broeckx, Clint Farha, Alan Land

Guest dancers: Evelyn Hart, Rex Harrington

No. of dancers: 37 male, 43 female

No. of performances: 131

Tours to: UK, Italy, Luxembourg, Germany

Premieres:

Artifact II 27/6/91, Het Muziektheater, Amsterdam
Ch.: William Forsythe. *M.:* J.S. Bach. *S.:* William Forsythe. *L.:* William Forsythe.

Le Noces 27/6/91, Het Muziektheater, Amsterdam
Ch.: Bronislava Nijinska. *M.:* Stravinsky. *D.:* Natalia Goncharova *L.:* Jan Hofstra.

Pyrrhische Dansen IV 27/6/91, Het Muziektheater, Amsterdam
Ch.: Toer van Schayk. *M.:* Beat Furrer, Burno Liberda. *S.,C.:* Toer van Schayk. *L.:* Toer van Schayk, Jan Hofstra.

Four Sections 11/10/91, Het Muziektheater, Amsterdam
Ch.: Ted Brandsen. *M.:* Steve Reich. *S.:* Ted Brandsen. *C.:* François-Noël Cherpin. *L.:* Jos Janssen.

Stilleven wit plein 21/3/92, Het Muziektheater, Amsterdam
Ch.: Toer van Schayk. *M.:* Schönberg. *S.:* Leoni Molenaar. *C.:* Toer van Schayk. *L.:* Jan Hofstra.

Touch your coolness to my fevered brow 21/3/92, Het Muziektheater, Amsterdam
Ch.: Ashley Page. *M.:* Orlando Gough. *S.:* Antony McDonald. *C.:* Antony McDonald, Jon Morrell. *L.:* Jos Jonssen.

HET FOLKORISTISCH DANSTHEATER

Postbus 16885
1001 RJ Amsterdam
Kloveniersburgwal 87-89
Tel: 020-6239112
Fax: 020-6235359

Artistic dir.: Ferdinand van Altena

Administrative dir.: Willy Rückert

Principal dancers: Ine van Alebeek, Geka Bleker, Saskia Franke, Claudia Hartman, Marloes Hof, Ingrid Jansen, Miriam Kleppe, Martine Klein, Thérèse Laurant, Monique Le Belle, Marjan Mieremet, Daisy Rebel, Armin Dorn, Peter Jakab, André de Jong, Hans Minnaert, Jenö Molnar, Junior van Rijn, Mihaly Szabo, Istvan Tanacs, Tadeusz Zdybal

No. of dancers: 9 male, 12 female

No. of performances: 120

Tours to: Belgium, Germany

Repertory:

Dance 4 Ever
Ch.: Various. *M.:* Theo van Tol and others. *D.:* Maurits van Geel, Martien van Stiphout. *C.:* Patricia Henry, Herbert Wardenaar. *L.:* Martien van Stiphout.

Dansend langs de Zijde Route
Ch.: Various. *M.:* Theo van Tol. *C.:* Herbert Wardenaar. *L.:* Martien van Stiphout.

Van de Madonna tot Madonna
Ch.: Various. *M.:* Floor Minaert, Theo van Tol. *S.:* Martien van Stiphout. *C.:* Herbert Wardenaar. *L.:* Reinier Tweebeehe.

INTRODANS

Vijfzinnenstraat 80-82
6811 LN Arnhem
Tel: 085-512111
Fax: 085-515647

Artistic dir.: Ton Wiggers

Administrative dir.: Hans Focking

Visiting choreographer(s): Graham Lustig, Norbert Taatgen, Mark Bruce, John Wisman, Jean-Christophe Maillot, Gian Franco Paoluzi, Tamara Roso, Mirjam Diedrich, Philip Taylor

Guest teacher(s): Glenn Eddy, Simon de Mowbray, Karl Toth

Guest dancers: Carola van Rijn

No. of dancers: 8 male, 9 female

No. of performances: c.90

Tours to: France

Pay rates: c.5000 DFL

Premieres:

Elysios 26/4/91, Arnhem
Ch.: Gian Franco Paoluzi. *M.:* Gianandrea Gazolla. *C.:* Quirino Conti. *L.:* Gian Franco Paoluzi.

Garcin, Inès en Estelle 26/4/91, Arnhem
Ch.: Norbert Taatgen. *M.:* Angelo Badalamenti, Nino Rota. *S.:* Willem Wits. *C.:* Pamela Homoet. *L.:* Berry Claassen.

Green Fields of America 26/4/91, Arnhem
Ch.: Mark Bruce. *M.:* Martin Simpson. *C.:* Sarah Deane. *L.:* Nico van der Krogt.

Lueur d'amour 26/9/91, Arnhem
Ch.: Jean-Christophe Maillot. *M.:* Marin Marais, Paolo Conte. *D.:* Dominique Drillot. *C.:* Heidi de Raad. *L.:* Henk van der Geest, Dominique Drillot.

Souvenir de Florence 26/9/91, Arnhem
Ch.: John Wisman. *M.:* Tchaikovsky. *S.,C.:* Henk Schut. *L.:* Dominique Drillot, Henk Schut.

U.L. Unidentified Light 26/9/91, Arnhem
Ch.: Mirjam Diedrich. *M.:* Jerry Goldsmith.
C.: Heidi de Raad. *L.:* Berry Claassen,
Mirjam Diedrich.

White Streams 26/9/91, Arnhem
Ch.: Ed Wubbe. *M.:* Arvo Pärt. *C.:* Heidi de
Raad. *L.:* Henk van der Geest, Dominique
Drillot.

Haunted Passages 26/12/91, Arnhem
Ch.: Philip Taylor. *M.:* Britten. *S.:* Philip
Taylor. *C.:* Heidi de Raad. *L.:* Nico van der
Krogt, Philip Taylor.

When She Is Asleep 26/12/91, Arnhem
Ch.: Tamara Roso. *M.:* Louis Andressen.
S.,C.: Henk Schut. *L.:* Nico van der Krogt,
Henk Schut.

George's Day Out 4/3/92, Arnhem
Ch.: Graham Lustig. *M.:* Willem Jeths. *S.,C.:*
Mirja Grote Gansey. *L.:* Nico van der Krogt,
Mirja Grote Gansey, Graham Lustig.

The Dream King 16/4/92, Zwolle
Ch.: Ton Wiggers. *M.:* Collage. *S.:* Hans
Focking, Ton Wiggers. *C.:* Pamela Homoet.
L.: Nico van der Krogt.

NEDERLANDS DANS THEATER 1

Box 333
2501 CH The Hague
Tel: 070-609931
Fax: 070-3617156

Artistic dir.: Jirí Kylián

Administrative dir.: Michael de Roo

Principal/associate choreographer(s): Jirí
Kylián, Hans van Manen

Visiting choreographer(s): Mats Ek, Nacho
Duato, David Parsons, Ohad Naharin,
William Forsythe

Guest teacher(s): Jan Nuyts, Benjamin
Harkarvey, Kathy Bennetts, Olga Evreinoff,
Marian Sarstadt, Christine Anthony, Sighilt
Pahl, Irene Milovan

No. of dancers: 15 male, 14 female

No. of performances: 182

Tours to: Germany, France, Czechoslovakia,
Portugal, Italy, Spain, Greece, Austria

Pay rates: 4100 Guilders per month

Premieres:

Sinking of the Titanic 18/4/91, The Hague
Ch.: Ohad Naharin. *M.:* Gavin Bryars. *C.:*
Ohad Naharin. *L.:* Bambi.

Ljusvarelser (Light Creatures) 17/10/91, The
Hague
Ch.: Mats Ek. *M.:* Collage. *S.,C.:* Peder Freiij.
L.: András Balogh.

Duende 21/11/91, The Hague
Ch.: Nacho Duato. *M.:* Debussy. *S.:* Walter
Nobbe. *C.:* Susan Unger. *L.:* Joop Caboort.

The Envelope 16/1/92, The Hague
Ch.: David Parsons. *M.:* Rossini. *C.:* Judy
Wirkula.

Black Milk 27/2/92, The Hague
Ch.: Ohad Naharin. *M.:* Paul Smadbeck. *C.:*
Rakefet Levy. *L.:* Bambi.

Kyr 27/2/92, The Hague
Ch.: Ohad Naharin. *M.:* Ohad Naharin. *C.:*
Rakefet Levy. *L.:* Bambi.

As If Never Been 16/4/92, The Hague
Ch.: Jirí Kylián. *M.:* Lukas Foss. *C.:* Joke
Visser. *L.:* Joop Caboort.

On the Move 1/6/92, The Hague
Ch.: Hans van Manen. *M.:* Prokofiev. *S.,C.:*
Keso Dekker. *L.:* Joop Caboort.

Petite Mort 12/9/92, The Hague
Ch.: Jirí Kylián. *M.:* Mozart. *C.:* Joke Visser.
L.: Joop Caboort.

Repertory:

Andante
Ch.: Hans van Manen. *M.:* Mozart. *S.,C.:*
Keso Dekker. *L.:* Joop Caboort.

Un Ballo
Ch.: Jirí Kylián. *M.:* Ravel.

Black Cake
Ch.: Hans van Manen. *M.:* Stravinsky,
Massenet, Mascagni, Janacek, Tchaikovsky.
S.,C.: Keso Dekker. *L.:* Joop Caboort.

L'Enfant et les sortilèges
Ch.: Jirí Kylián. *M.:* Ravel.

Falling Angels
Ch.: Jirí Kylián. *M.:* Steve Reich. *C.:* Jirí
Kylián. *L.:* Joop Caboort.

Forgotten Land
Ch.: Jirí Kylián. *M.:* Britten. *S.,C.:* John
Macfarlane. *L.:* Joop Caboort.

293

Gamla Barn (Old Children)
Ch.: Mats Ek. M.: Saint-Saëns, Massenet, Uuno Klami, Gunnar de Frumerie. S.,C.: Karin Ek. L.: Dick Lindström.

Kagayahime
Ch.: Jirí Kylián. M.: Maki Ishii.

Lieder eines fahrende Gesellen
Ch.: Jirí Kylián. M.: Mahler. S.,C.: John Macfarlane. L.: Jennifer Tipton.

No More Play
Ch.: Jirí Kylián. M.: Webern. S.,C.: Jirí Kylián. L.: Joop Caboort.

Overgorwn Path
Ch.: Jirí Kylián. M.: Janácek.

Passomezzo
Ch.: Ohad Naharin. M.: Anonymous. C.: Ohad Naharin. L.: Joop Caboort.

Raptus
Ch.: Nacho Duato. M.: Wagner. Dec.: Walter Nobbe. C.: Nacho Duato. L.: Joop Caboort.

Sarabande
Ch.: Jirí Kylián. M.: J.S. Bach. C.: Joke Visser. L.: Joop Caboort.

Sechs Tänze
Ch.: Jirí Kylián. M.: Mozart. L.: Joop Caboort.

Silent Cries
Ch.: Jirí Kylián. M.: Debussy.

Sinfonietta
Ch.: Jirí Kylián. M.: Janácek. L.: Joop Caboort.

Soldatenmis
Ch.: Jirí Kylián. M.: Martinu. S.,C.: Kylián. L.: Joop Caboort.

Stamping Ground
Ch.: Jirí Kylián. M.: Carlos Chávez.

Steptext
Ch.: William Forsythe. M.: J.S. Bach. D.: William Forsythe.

Stoolgame
Ch.: Jirí Kylián. M.: Arne Nordheim.

Sweet Dreams
Ch.: Jirí Kylián. M.: Webern. C.: Joke Visser. L.: Joop Caboort.

Symphony of Psalms
Ch.: Jirí Kylián. M.: Stravinsky. S.: William Katz. C.: Joop Stokvis. L.: Joop Caboort.

Svadebka
Ch.: Jirí Kylián. M.: Stravinsky.

Synaphai
Ch.: Nacho Duato. M.: Xenakis, Vangelis. S.,C.: Walter Nobbe. L.: Joop Caboort.

Tabula Rasa
Ch.: Ohad Naharin. M.: Arvo Pärt. L.: Joop Caboort.

Two
Ch.: Hans van Manen. M.: Busoni. S.,C.: Keso Dekker. L.: Joop Caboort.

Verklärte Nacht
Ch.: Jirí Kylián. M.: Schönberg.

Visions Fugitives
Ch.: Hans van Manen. M.: Prokofiev. S.,C.: Keso Dekker. L.: Joop Caboort.

NEDERLANDS DANS THEATER 2

Box 333
2501 CH The Hague
Tel: 070-609931
Fax: 070-3617156

Artistic dir.: Jirí Kylián

Administrative dir.: Michael de Roo

Principal/associate choreographer(s): Jirí Kylián, Hans van Manen

Visiting choreographer(s): Amanda Miller, Patrizia Tuerlings, Lionel Hoche, Martin Müller

Guest teacher(s): Jan Nuyts, Benjamin Harkarvey, Kathy Bennetts, Olga Evreinoff, Marian Sarstädt, Christine Anthony, Sighilt Pahl, Irena Milovan

No. of dancers: 7 male, 7 female

No. of performances: 92

Tours to: Spain, Switzerland, Germany, Yugoslavia, Greece, Antilles, New Zealand, Canary Islands, Austria, Arabia

Pay rates: 2400 Guilders per month

Premieres:

Arto's Books 14/11/91, The Hague
Ch.: Amanda Miller. M.: Guus Janssen. D.: Amanda Miller.

Ravel Without a Pause 14/11/91, The Hague
Ch.: Amanda Miller. M.: Ravel. D.: Amanda Miller. *Backdrop:* Ricardo Castillo von Benninwitz.

Blancs d'y voir 20/2/92, The Hague
Ch.: Lionel Hoche. *M.:* Collage. *S.:* Lionel
Hoche. *C.:* Sylvie Skinazi. *L.:* Joop Caboort,
Lionel Hoche.

Port Bou 20/2/92, The Hague
Ch.: Patrizia Tuerlings. *M.:* Jean-Marc
Zelwer, Jan Schouten. *S.:* Boes Diertens. *C.:*
Henk Knaap. *L.:* Joop Caboort.

Who's Watching Who 20/2/92, The Hague
Ch.: Martin Müller. *M.:* Paul Winter, Paul
Halley, Jan Schouten. *S.:* Martin Müller. *C.:*
Martin Müller, Asalia Khadjé. *L.:* Joop
Caboort. *Costume colouring:* Marlies Kwade.

Repertory:

Un Ballo
Ch.: Jirí Kylián. *M.:* Ravel. *S.:* Jirí Kylián. *C.:*
Joke Visser. *L.:* Joop Caboort.

Grosse Fuge
Ch.: Hans van Manen. *M.:* Beethoven. *S.:*
Jean-Paul Vroom. *C.:* Hans van Manen. *L.:*
Joop Caboort.

In and Out
Ch.: Hans van Manen. *M.:* Laurie Andernon,
Nina Hagen. *S.:* Keso Dekker. *C.:* Keso
Dekker. *L.:* Jan Hofstra.

Squares
Ch.: Hans van Manen. *M.:* Erik Satie. *D.:*
Bonies.

NEDERLANDS DANS THEATER 3

PO Box 333
2501 CH The Hague
Tel: 070-609931
Fax: 070-3617156

Artistic dir.: Jirí Kylián

Administrative dir.: Michael de Roo

Principal/associate choreographer(s): Jirí
Kylián, Hans van Manen, Mats Ek, William
Forsythe

No. of dancers: 4

No. of performances: 30

Tours to: Germany, Belgium, France, Spain

Premieres:

Evergreens 8/11/91, The Hague
Ch.: Hans van Manen. *M.:* Saint-Saëns,
Peyronnnin, Villa-Lobos. *C.:* Keso Dekker.
L.: Joop Caboort.

Journey 8/11/91, The Hague
Ch.: Mats Ek. *M.:* Steve Reich. *S.,C.:* Peder
Freij. *L.:* Joop Caboort.

Marion/Marion 8/11/91, The Hague
Ch.: William Forsythe. *M.:* Bernhard
Hermann. *S.,L.:* William Forsythe. *C.:*
Gianni Versace.

Obscure Temptations 8/11/91, The Hague
Ch.: Jirí Kylián. *M.:* John Cage. *S.:* Jirí
Kylián. *C.:* Joke Visser. *L.:* Joop Caboort.

REFLEX DANCE COMPANY

Moesstraat 7
9717 JT Groningen
Tel: 050-719888
Fax: 050-735117

Artistic dir.: Patrizia Tuerlings

Administrative dir.: Charles Rÿsbosch

Visiting choreographer(s): Michelle Noiret,
Dries van der Post, Charles Corneille, Itzik
Galili, Marcelo Evelin, Glenn van der Hoff,
Lionel Hoche, Thomas Lankau

Guest teacher(s): Norio Mamiya

Principal dancers: Patrizia Tuerlings, Diane
Elshout, Marjolein Elsink, Neel Verdoorn,
Josje Manuputty, Klaus Jürgens, Dietmar
Janech, Tim Galvin

Guest dancers: Janine Dijkmeijer

No. of dancers: 4 male, 5 female

No. of performances: 75

Tours to: Germany

Premieres:

Le Sacre du Printemps 28/4/91,
Academietheater Utrecht
Ch.: Hans Tuerlings. *M.:* Stravinsky. *D.,L.:*
Jan van Velden. *S.:* Ghieslaine van de
Kamp. *C.:* Jacqueline Mayen.

Een dag te veel 13/6/91, Stadsschouwburg
Amsterdam
Ch.: Patrizia Tuerlings. *M.:* Scelsi. *S.:* Boes
Diertens. *C.:* Liesbeth Zuidema. *L.:* Jan van
Velden.

Comment séduire en cas d'incendie 12/10/91,
De Kolk, Assen
Ch.: Lionel Hoche. *M.:* Collage. *S.:* Boes
Diertens. *C.:* Lionel Hoche. *L.:* Nico van der
Klugt.

Head over Heels 12/10/91, De Kolk, Assen
Ch.: Charles Corneille. *M.*: Walter Hus. *S.*:
Boes Diertens. *C.*: Jacqueline Mayen. *L.*:
Nico van der Klugt.

Negen min één 12/10/91, De Kolk, Assen
Ch.: Glen van der Hoff. *M.*: Yens & Yens,
Bob Dylan. *S.*: Boes Diertens. *C.*: Jacqeline
Mayen. *L.*: Nico van der Klugt.

Klytämnästra's Muttertag 12/10/91, De Kolk,
Assen
Ch.: Thomas Lankau. *M.*: Lindsay Cooper.
S.: Boes Diertens. *C.*: Jacqeline Mayen. *L.*:
Nico van der Klugt.

Tran Chan 12/10/91, De Kolk, Assen
Ch.: Marcelo Evelin. *M.*: Caetano Veloso. *S.*:
Boes Diertens. *C.*: Jacqueline Mayen. *L.*: Nico
van der Klugt.

Trekidos 12/10/91, De Kolk, Assen
Ch.: Itzik Galili. *M.*: Yens & Yens. *S.*: Boes
Diertens. *C.*: Jacqueline Mayen. *L.*: Nico van
der Klugt.

Bubamxicoi 1/2/92, Stadsschouwburg,
Groningen
Ch.: Joaquin Sabaté. *M.*: Axel Schultz. *S.*:
Joaquin Sabaté. *C.*: Joaquin Sabaté,
Annemiek Langen. *L.*: Jan van Velden.

Old Cartoon 1/2/92, Stadsschouwburg,
Groningen
Ch.: Itzik Galili. *M.*: Sharon Faber. *C.*:
Annemiek Langen. *L.*: Nico van der Klugt.

Meetings in Time 1/2/92, Stadsschouwburg,
Groningen
Ch.: Dries van der Post. *M.*: Guus Janssen.
C.: Dries van der Post. *L.*: Kiek Groendijk.

Tottu Liscio 1/2/92, Stadsschouwburg,
Groningen
Ch.: Hans Tuerlings. *M.*: Bernard van
Beurden. *S.*: Tom Schenk. *L.*: Joop Caboort,
Kiek Groendijk.

Triomf of dood 1/2/92, Stadsschouwburg,
Groningen
Ch.: Marc Vanrunxt. *M.*: Mozart. *S.*: Marc
Vanrunxt, Boes Diertens. *C.*: Marc
Vanrunxt, Annemiek Langen. *L.*: Marc
Vanrunxt, Kiek Groendijk.

Poussière d'ocre 12/4/92, Stadsschouwburg,
Groningen
Ch.: Michèle Noiret. *M.*: Ingram Marshall,
Billie Holiday, Dominique Lawarlee, David
Lynx. *S.*: Michèle Noiret, Boes Diertens. *C.*:
Michèle Noiret, Annemiek Langen. *L.*:
Xavier Lauwers.

Repertory:

A Noeud Coulant!
Ch.: Hans Tuerlings. *M.*: Bert Kliejn, Jan
Kuiper. *S.*,*C.*: Henk Kraayenzank. *L.*:
Roderick van Gelder.

BRMS
Ch.: Patrizia Tuerlings. *M.*: John Adams. *S.*:
Wim de Vries. *C.*: Aafje Horst. *L.*: Jan van
Velden.

Hymne an die kleinen Freuden
Ch.: Patrizia Tuerlings. *M.*: Collage. *S.*: Boes
Diertens. *C.*: Claudia Berbée. *L.*: Jan van
Velden.

I Am a Hotel
Ch.: Hans Tuerlings. *M.*: Bert Kleijn, Jan
Kuioer. *S.*,*C.*: Hans Kraayenzank. *L.*: Jan van
Velden.

SCAPINO BALLET ROTTERDAM

Luchtvaartstraat 2
1059 CA Amsterdam
Tel: 020-153916
Fax: 020-6179206

Artistic dir.: Nils Christe

Administrative dir.: Jan Schretzmeijer

Principal/associate choreographer(s): Nils
Christe, Armando Navarro, Ed Wubbe

Visiting choreographer(s): Daniel Ezralow,
Mats Ek, Keso Dekker, Hans van Manen

Guest teacher(s): Simom Mottram, Ivan
Kramar, Benjamin Harkarvey

Principal dancers: Charlotte Baines, Olivier
Deguine, Fátima Brito, Matthias Eidmann,
Kirsten Debrock, Miquel de Jong, Anik
Dorion-Coupal, Andreas Jüstrich, Victoria
Edgar, Håakan Larsson, Sandra Klijn, Lior
Lev, Valerie Lecocq, Waldo Oliveira, Ija
Louwen, Keith-Derrick Randolph, Talia
Paz, Eytan Sivak, Mariëtte Redel, Rinus
Sprong, Esperanza Aparicio-Romero,
Thomas Stuart, Sacha Steenks, Michiel
Verkoren, Samantha Stegeman, Brent
Williamson, Margaret Tappan, Robin
Woolmer, Katherine Thompson, Maren
Timm, Paula Vink

Guest dancers: Valerie Valentine, Kriysztof
Pastor

No. of dancers: 14 male, 16 female

Tours to: Germany, France, USA

Premieres:

Chanson Russe 11/4/91, Rotterdam
Ch.: Nils Christe. *M.*: Stravinsky. *D.*: Keso
Dekker. *L.*: Kees Tjebbes.

På Norrbotten 11/4/91, Rotterdam
Ch.: Mats Ek. *M.*: Trad. folk music. *D.*: Karin
Ek. *L.*: Göran Westrup.

Parts 11/4/91, Rotterdam
Ch.: Ed Wubbe. *M.*: J.S. Bach. *D.*: Pamela
Homoet. *L.*: Kees Tjebbes.

Before Nightfall 10/10/91, Rotterdam
Ch.: Nils Christe. *M.*: Martinu. *D.*: Keso
Dekker. *L.*: Joop Caboort.

Cages 10/10/91, Rotterdam
Ch.: Kirsten Debrock. *M.*: Shostakovich. *D.*:
Judith v.d. Kwast. *L.*: Kees Tjebbes.

I Wrapped My Head in Yellow Paper 22/2/92,
Rotterdam
Ch.: Nils Christe. *M.*: Leoni Jansen. *D.*: Paula
Vink. *S.*: Nils Christe. *L.*: Kees Tjebbes.

Perfect Skin Parts I & II   22/2/92,
Rotterdam

Ch.: Ed Wubbe. *M.*: J.S. Bach. *D.*: Hans Wap.
C.: Pamela Homoet. *L.*: Kees Tjebbes.

Perfect Skin Part III   14/4/92, Rotterdam
Ch.: Ed Wubbe. *M.*: J.S. Bach. *D.*: Hans Wap.
C.: Pamela Homoet. *L.*: Kees Tjebbes.

Scapino Meets Dap 14/4/92, Rotterdam
Ch.: Daniel Ezralow. *M.*: Thom Willems. *D.*:
Hans Wap. *S.*: Daniel Ezralow. *C.*: Anita
Eveneport. *L.*: Daniel Ezralow.

Repertory:

Next
Ch.: Keso Dekker. *M.*: Collage. *D.*: Keso
Dekker. *L.*: Kees Tjebbes.

Nutcracker
Ch.: Armando Navarra. *M.*: Tchaikovsky.
D.: Willem Bijmoer. *L.*: Bob Pellemans.

Pulcinella
Ch.: Nils Christe. *M.*: Stravinsky. *D.*: Tom
Schenk. *L.*: Bob Pellemans.

Rameau
Ch.: Ed Wubbe. *M.*: Rameau. *D.*: Pamela
Homoet. *L.*: Kees Tjebbes.

New Zealand

COMMOTION DANCE COMPANY

PO Box 9296
Wellington
Tel: (644) 3842006

Artistic dir.: Michael Parmenter

DOUGLAS WRIGHT DANCE COMPANY

PO Box 68533
47 Clyde Street
Island Bay, Auckland
Tel: (64.9) 3765.792

Artistic dir.: Douglas Wright

Administrative dir.: Carla van Zon

Principal/associate choreographer(s):
Douglas Wright, Shona McCullagh
(associate)

FOOTNOTE DANCE COMPANY

PO Box 3387
Wellington
Tel: (644) 3849285

JENDEN & SOLINO

42 Hollis Road
Paraparaumu Beach
Wellington
Tel: (644) 3837801

Artistic dir.: Paul Jenden

JORDAN & PRESENT COMPANY

PO Box 9653
Wellington
Tel: (04) 382-9112

Artistic dir.: Susan Jordan

Administrative dir.: Fenn Gordon

Principal/associate choreographer(s): Susan Jordan

No. of performances: 31

Pay rates: NZ$450 per week

Premieres:

Still 4/9/91, Taki Rua Theatre
Ch.: Susan Jordan. *M.:* Sue Alexander. *D.:* Susan Jordan. *C.:* Paul Jenden. *L.:* Kim Hunter.

Repertory:

Carillon Dance
Ch.: Susan Jordan. *M.:* Timothy Hurd. *D.:* Susan Jordan. *C.:* Holly Cooper.

Stone the Crow
Ch.: Susan Jordan. *M.:* Various. *D.:* Susan Jordan. *C.:* Paul Jenden. *L.:* Kim Hunter.

THE ROYAL NEW ZEALAND BALLET

2nd Floor, 29 Brandon Street
PO Box 10-786
Wellington 6036
Tel: 64-4-499-1107
Fax: 64-4-499-0773

Artistic dir.: Harry Haythorne (until 31.5.92); Ashley Killar (from 1.6.92)

Administrative dir.: Mark Keyworth

Visiting choreographer(s): Grey Veredon, Jack Carter, Patricia Rianne, Shona McCullagh, Timothy Gordon, Garth Welch (AM), Douglas Wright, Rudi van Dantzig

Guest teacher(s): Viktor Rona, Florin Brindusa, Micaela Kirkaldie, Garth Welch (AM)

Principal dancers: Kerry-Anne Gilberd, Karin Wakefield, Lee Patrice, Ann Anderson, Eric Languet, Brando Miranda, Kilian O'Callaghan, Ou Lu (resident guest principal)

Guest dancers: Philip Markham

No. of dancers: 13 male, 13 female

No. of performances: 159

Tours to: New Zealand, USA

Pay rates: Per week – NZ$414 (corps 1) – NZ$533 (first prinicpal)

Premieres:

Cinderella 6/8/91, Wellington
Ch.: Jack Carter. *M.:* Prokofiev. *D.:* Kristian Fredrikson. *L.:* Ian Nicholls.

Petits riens 8/10/91, Paraparaumu
Ch.: Patricia Rianne. *M.:* Mozart. *L.:* Ian Perkins.

Artemis 31/10/91, Wellington
Ch.: Shona McCullagh. *M.:* Traditional. *L.:* Ian Perkins.

The Empty Fortress 31/10/91, Wellington
Ch.: Eric Languet. *M.:* Bernstein. *C.:* Gayle Wilson. *L.:* Ian Perkins.

Les Galanteries 31/10/91, Wellington
Ch.: Timothy Gordon. *M.:* J.S. Bach. *L.:* Ian Perkins.

The Season of Sorrow 31/10/91, Wellington
Ch.: Garth Welch (AM). *M.:* Larry Sitsky. *L.:* Ian Perkins.

The Decay of Lying 28/2/92, Wellington
Ch.: Douglas Wright. *M.:* Jean Baptiste Lully. *D.:* Michael Pearce. *L.:* Allan McShane.

Example # 22 31/10/92
Ch.: Kim Broad. *M.:* Laurie Anderson.

Ch.: Jason Carnachan. *M.:* Enigma.

Repertory:

Fantasie
Ch.: Peter Boyes. *M.:* Schubert.

Faust Divertiseement
Ch.: André Prokovsky, Galina Samsova. *M.:* Gounod. *D.:* Peter Farmer.

Four Last Songs
Ch.: Rudi van Dantzig. *M.:* Richard Strauss. *D.:* Toer van Schayk. *L.:* Jan Hofstra.

Love Sonnet
Ch.: Garth Welch (AM). *M.:* Fauré. *D.:* Janet Williamson.

La Malinche
Ch.: José Limón. *M.:* Norman Lloyd. *C.:* Pauline Lawrence.

No Exit
Ch.: Ashley Killar. *M.:* Shostakovich. *D.:* Peter Cazalet.

The Nutcracker
Ch.: Patirica Rianne (Grand Pas De Deux Act II: Petipa/Ivanov). *M.:* Tchaikovsky. *D.:* Robert Ryan. *L.:* Paul Craven.

Orpheus
Ch.: Graeme Murphy (AM). *M.:* Stravinsky. *D.:* Kristian Fredrikson. *L.:* Chris J. Mangin.

Ramifications
Ch.: Peter Boyes. *M.:* Ligeti.

Square within a Circle
Ch.: Eugene Polyakov. *M.:* Chevalier de Saint-Georges. *D.:* Eugene Polyakov.

Tell Me a Tale
Ch.: Gray Veredon. *M.:* Matthew Fisher. *D.:* Kristian Fredrikson.

Wintergarden of Love
Ch.: Arthur Turnbull. *M.:* David Farquhar. *D.:* Kristian Fredrikson.

Wolfgang Amadeus
Ch.: Gray Veredon. *M.:* Mozart. *D.:* Erik Ulfers. *L.:* Allan McShane.

TAIAO

PO Box 5857
Wellesley Street
Auckland
Tel: 0 9 765792

Artistic dir.: Stephen Bradshaw

Norway

BLACK BOX THEATRE

Stranden 3
Aker Brygge
0250 Oslo
Tel: 2-836171/833900

Artistic dir.: Inger Burøysund

Administrative dir.: Cathleen Marchant

COLLAGE DANCE COMPANY

Drammensveien 130
0277 Oslo 2
Tel: 02-443450/443240

Artistic dir.: Lise Nordal

Administrative dir.: Gabriella Grossmann

Principal/associate choreographer(s): Lise Nordal, Kristin Gjems, Sølvi Edvardsen

Principal dancers: Aase With, Mona Walderhaug, Cathrine Smith, Kristin Gjems, Gry Kipperberg, Odd Johan Fritzøe

Guest dancers: Nina Lill Svendsen, Gina Hjort-Larsen, Viktor Trutt

No. of dancers: 2 male, 8 female

No. of performances: c. 20

Tours to: Finland, Faroe Islands

Pay rates: NKr 8000/month

Premieres:

Foreign Traces 13/4/91, Collage Studio
Ch.: Sølvi Edvardsen, Kristin Gjems. *M.:* Astor Piazzolla, Ondekoza, Zakir Hussain, Guo. *D.:* Gitte Dæhlin. *C.:* Taran Sæther. *L.:* Bent Roenlien.

Untitles Songs 28/6/92, Norwegian Music Festival
Ch.: Kristin Gjems. *M.:* Agnes Buen Garnås, Jan Garbarek. *D.:* Henk Jansen. *C.:* Taran Sæther. *L.:* Hank Jansen.

Repertory:

Tide
Ch.: Lise Nordal. *M.:* Kjell Samkopf. *D.,L.:* Henning Winger. *C.:* Svein Ove Kirkhorn.

DANS DESIGN

Reichweinsgate 1
0254 Oslo 1
Tel: 2-551 945
Fax: 2-551 945

Artistic dir.: Leif Hernes, Anne Grete Eriksen

NORWEGIAN NATIONAL BALLET

Den Norske Operas Ballett
Storgaten 23c
0184 Oslo 1
Tel: 2-44 34 50

Artistic dir.: Dinna Bjørn

NYE CARTE BLANCHE

Sigurdsgt. 6
5015 Bergen
Tel: (05) 321710
Fax: (05) 960484

Artistic dir.: Fredrik Rütter

Visiting choreographer(s): Robert Cohan, Darshan Singh Bhuller, Sølvi Edvardsen, Raza Hammadi, Toni Herlofson, Michel Rahn, Robert North, Jessica Iwanson, Arne Fagerholt, Ina Christel Johannessen, Tere O'Connor

No. of dancers: 6 male, 6 female

No. of performances: 64

Tours to: Denmark

Pay rates: Corps: NKR 174000 + 400 per performance

Premieres:

Fluesmekkeren 25/10/91, Bergen
Ch.: Kenneth Kreutzmann. *M.:* Ole Højer Jansen. *C.:* Iver Villefrance. *L.:* Erik Wiedersheim-Paul.

Killing Fantasies 25/10/91, Bergen
Ch.: Tommy Håkansson. *M.:* Angelo Badalamenti. *S.:* Tommy Håkansson. *C.:* Indrani Balgobin. *L.:* Erik Wiedersheim-Paul.

Med Ryggen Mot Veggen 25/10/91, Bergen
Ch.: Joel Schnee. *M.:* Joel Schnee, Mike Oldfield, Det Wiene. *S.:* Joel Schnee. *L.:* Erik Wiedersheim-Paul.

Skagen 25/10/91, Bergen
Ch.: Jessica Iwanson. *M.:* Steve Reich. *S.:* Svein Lund-Roland. *C.:* Sabine Atzberger. *L.:* Erik Wiedersheim-Paul.

Nighthawks 13/12/91, Bergen
Ch.: Jessica Iwanson. *M.:* Harald Weiss. *S.:* Svein Lund-Roland. *C.:* Indrani Balgobin. *L.:* Erik Wiedersheim-Paul.

Beast 19/3/92, Bergen
Ch.: Tere O'Connor. *M.:* James Baker. *C.:* Tere O'Connor. *L.:* Erik Wiedersheim-Paul.

Déjà Vu 19/3/92, Bergen
Ch.: Arne Fagerholt. *M.:* Gluck. *C.:* Arne Fagerholt. *L.:* Erik Wiedersheim-Paul.

Repertory:

Interlock
Ch.: Darshan Singh Bhuller. *M.:* Clem Alford.

Sleep Studies
Ch.: David Parsons. *M.:* Flim and the BB's. *C.:* Mona Vikøren. *L.:* Howell Binkley.

The Philippines

BALLET PHILIPPINES I/BALLET PHILIPPINES II

Cultural Center of the Philippines
Roxas Boulevard Manila
Tel: 832-3688

Artistic dir.: Denisa Reyes, Cecile Sicangco (associate) (BPI); Agnes Locsin (BPII)

BAYANIHAN PHILIPPINE DANCE COMPANY

Unlad Building
Taft Avenue Manila
Tel: 583-187

RAMON OBUSAN FOLKLORIC GROUP

4 Chapel Road
MIA Housing Area
Pasay City
Tel: 831-0894

Russia

BOLSHOI BALLET

Theatre Square 2
Moscow
Tel: 292-9986

Principal/associate choreographer(s): Yuri Grigorovich

Principal dancers: Nina Ananiashvili, Natalia Arkhipova, Yelena Akhulkova, Natalia Bessmertnova, Yelena Bobrova, Maria Bylova, Elvira Drozdova, Maria Filippova, Svetlana Filippova, Nadezhda Gracheva, Yulia Levina, Erika Luzina, Natalia Malandina, Yulia Malkhasiantz, Alla Mikhalchenko, Irina Nesterova, Larissa Okhotnikova, Nadezhda Pavlova, Elena Palshina, Inna Petrova, Irina Piatkina, Nina Semizorova, Olessia Shulzhitskaya, Nina Speranskaya, Galina Stepanenko, Yulia Volodina, Irina Zibrova, Oxana Zvetnitskaya, Valery Anissimov, Andrei Buzavtsev, Vadim Bubnov, Sergei Bobrov, Nikolai Dorokhov, Alexei Fadeyechev, Sergei Filin, Sergei Gromov, Yuri Klevtsov, Andrei Korolkov, Alexei Lazarev, Andrei Melanin, Vladimir Moiseyev, Andrei Nikonov, Leonid Nikonov, Mark Peretokin, Yuri Posokhov, Alexander Petukhov, Ruslan Pronin, Andrei Shakhlin, Mikhail Sharkov, Andrei Smirnov, Gediminas Taranda, Alexander Valuyev, Yuri Vasuchenko, Alexander Vetrov, Yuri Vetrov, Viacheslav Yelaguin, Igor Zakharin

Premieres:

La Bayadère 17/11/91
Ch.: Petipa/Grigorovich. M.: Minkus. D.: Valery Löventhal.

Le Corsaire 11/3/92
Ch.: Petipa/Sergeyev. M.: Adam, Pugni. D.: Irina Tebilova.

Repertory:

Aniuta
Ch.: Vasiliev. M.: Gavrilin.

Cippolino
Ch.: Mayorov. M.: Karen Khachaturian.

Conservatoriet
Ch.: Bournonville. M.: Paulli.

Giselle
Ch.: Perrot/Petipa/Grigorovich. M.: Adam.

Goleizovsky Programme
Ch.: Goleizovsky. M.: Various.

Ivan the Terrible
Ch.: Grigorovich. M.: Prokofiev.

Legend of Love
Ch.: Grigorovich. M.: Melikov.

Love for Love
Ch.: Boccadoro. M.: Khrennikov.

Nutcracker
Ch.: Grigorovich. M.: Tchaikovsky.

Petrushka
Ch.: Fokine. M.: Stravinsky.

Romeo and Juliet
Ch.:Grigorovich. M.: Prokofiev.

Spartacus
Ch.: Grigorovich. M.: Khatchaturian.

Stone Flower
Ch.: Grigorovich. M.: Prokofiev.

Swan Lake
Ch.: Petipa/Ivanov/Gorsky/Grigorovich. M.: Tchaikovsky.

Les Sylphides (Chopiniana)
Ch.: Fokine. M.: Chopin.

ST PETERSBURG MARYINSKY BALLET

Theatre Square 1
St Petersburg 190000
Tel: (812) 114-59-24; 114-84-01

Artistic dir.: Oleg Vinogradov

Principal/associate choreographer(s): Oleg Vinogradov

Principal dancers: Altynai Asylmuratova, Janna Ahupova, Tatiana Berezhnaya (Terekhova), Elena Evteeva, Svetlana Efremova, Annelina Kashirina, Margarita Kullik, Lubov Kunakova, Olga Likhovskaya, Julia Makhalina, Natalia Pavlova, Irina Sitnikova, Olga Chenchikova, Irina Chistiakova, Elena Sherstneva, Veronica Ivanova, Larisa Lezhnina, Galina Zakrutkina, Eldar Aliev, Victor Baranov, Sergei Bereznoi, Ravil Bagautdinov, Mahar Vaziev, Sergei Viharev, Andrei Garbuz,

Alexander Gulyaev, Marat Daukaev,
Konstantin Zaklinsky, Nikolai Kovmir,
Vladimir Kolesnikov, Alexander Kurkov,
Evgeny Neff, Vitali Tsvetkov, Farukh
Ruzimatov, Igor Zelensky, Vladimir Kim

No. of dancers: 76 male, 99 female

No. of performances: 102

Premieres:

Harlequinade 22/9/91
Ch.: Trad., revived Piotr Gousev. *M.:* Drigo.
D.: Semion Pastookh. *C.:* Galina Solovieva.

Apollo 26/1/92
Ch.: Balanchine. *M.:* Stravinsky.

The Leaves Are Fading 26/1/92
Ch.: Antony Tudor. *M.:* Dvorák.

Lilac Garden 26/1/92
Ch.: Antony Tudor. *M.:* Chausson.

Coppélia 18/3/92
Ch.: Oleg Vinogradov. *M.:* Delibes.

Les Noces 18/3/92
Ch.: Jerome Robbins. *M.:* Stravinsky.

Repertory:

La Bayadère
Ch.: trad., revived Vladimir Ponomarev,
Vakhtang Chabukiany. *M.:* Minkus.

Le Corsaire
Ch.: trad. revived Peter Gusev. *M.:* Adam.

Don Quixote
Ch.: trad., revived Vladimir Ponomarev. *M.:*
Minkus.

The Fairy of Puppets
Ch.: Nikolai Legat, rev. Konstantin
Sergeyev. *M.:* I. Bayer.

The Fountain of Bakhchisarai
Ch.: Rostislav Sakharov. *M.:* Boris Asafiev.

The Nutcracker
Ch.: Vasiliy Vainonen. *M.:* Tchaikovsky.

Romeo and Juliet
Ch.: Lavrovsky. *M.:* Prokofiev.

The Sleeping Beauty
Ch.: trad., revived Konstantin Sergeyev. *M.:*
Tchaikovsky.

The Stone Flower
Ch.: Yuri Grigorovich. *M.:* Prokofiev.

Swan Lake
Ch.: trad., revived Konstantin Sergeyev. *M.:*
Tchaikovsky.

La Sylphide
Ch.: Bournonville, Elsa Marianne von
Rosen. *M.:* Løvenskiold.

Les Sylphides (Chopiniana)
Ch.: trad., revived Agrippina Vaganova. *M.:*
Chopin.

ST PETERSBURG MARYINSKY MALY BALLET

Ploschad Iskusstva 1
St Petersburg 191011
Tel: (812)-314-72-84; 219-19-86; 219-11-10
Fax: (812)-314-36-53

Principal/associate choreographer(s):
Nikolai Boyarchikov

Principal dancers: Regina Kuzmicheva,
Natalia Kirichek, Anna Linnik, Natalia
Chapurskaya, Anjella Kondrasheva, Elena
Malisheva, Tatiana Eremicheva, Ludmila
Polonskaya, Mikhail Zavialov, Yuri
Petukhov, Pavel Romanuk, Vladimir
Adjamov, Kirill Miasnikov, Konstantin
Novoselov, Gennadi Sudakov

No. of dancers: 45 male, 65 female

No. of performances: 170

Repertory:

And Quiet Flows the Don
Ch.: Nikolai Boyarchikov. *M.:* Leonid
Klinichev.

Coppélia
Ch.: Oleg Vinogradov. *M.:* Delibes.

The Crane Fly
Ch.: Yuri Petukhov. *M.:* Vladislav Uspenski.

La Esmeralda
Ch.: Trad., revived Nikolai Boyarchikov. *M.:*
Pugni.

Fadette
Ch.: Nikolai Boyarchikov. *M.:* Delibes.

Gayané
Ch.: Boris Eifman. *M.:* Khachaturian.

Giselle
Ch.: trad., revived Nikita Dolgushin. *M.:*
Adam.

The Humpbacked Horse
Ch.: Igor Belski. *M.:* Rodion Schredin.

Macbeth
Ch.: Nikolai Boyarchikov. *M.:* Shandor
Kallosh.

The Nutcracker
Ch.: Igor Belski. *M.:* Tchaikovsky.

Petrouchka
Ch.: trad., revived Konstantin Boyarski. *M.:* Stravinsky.

The Rest of Cavalry
Ch.: trad., revived Peter Cusev. *M.:* Ivan Armsgeimer.

The Rite of Spring
Ch.: Vladimir Vasiliev, Natali Kasatkina. *M.:* Stravinsky.

The Robbers
Ch.: Nikolai Boyarchikov. *M.:* Minkov.

Romeo and Juliet
Ch.: Nikolai Boyarchikov. *M.:* Prokofiev.

Swan Lake
Ch.: Trad., revived Nikolai Boyarchikov. *M.:* Tchaikovsky.

La Sylphide
Ch.: August Bournonville, revived by Elsa Marianne von Rosen. *M.:* Løvenskiold.

There is a Time for All Things
Ch.: José Limón. *M.:* Norman dello Joio. Pauline Laurence.

The Tsar Boris
Ch.: Nikolai Boyarchikov. *M.:* Prokofiev.

The Ugly Duckling
Ch.: Leonid Lebedev. *M.:* Olga Petrova, Ira Tsesloukevich, Andrei Mikita.

STANISLAVSKI AND NEMIROVICH-DANCHENKO MUSIC THEATRE BALLET (STANISLAVSKY BALLET)

Pushkin Street 17
Moscow
Tel: Moscow 229-28-35

Singapore

SINGAPORE DANCE THEATRE

Fort Canning Centre, 2nd Storey
Cox Terrace
Singapore 0617
Tel: 223-1511 3380 611
Fax: 3389 748

Artistic dir.: Goh Soo Khim, Anthony Then

Administrative dir.: Hew Yee Min

Principal/associate choreographer(s): Dmitri Briantzev

Visiting choreographer(s): Helen Lai, Timothy Gordon, Ying E Ding

Guest teacher(s): Lin Yang Yang, Timothy Gordon

No. of dancers: 10 male, 8 female

No. of performances: 16

Tours to: China

Premieres:

Ballade 1/7/91, Singapore
Ch.: Choo-San Goh. *M.:* Fauré. *C.:* Goh Soo Khim, Paul Tan. *L.:* Colin Ho.

The Breath of Time 29/11/91, Singapore
Ch.: Timothy Gordon. *M.:* Sirocco. *S.,C.:* Timothy Gordon. *L.:* Colin Ho.

Moon Flight 29/11/91, Singapore
Ch.: Ying E Ding. *M.:* Ravel. *S.,C.:* Tan Swie Hian. *L.:* Colin Ho.

Melodious Accents 2/6/92, Singapore
Ch.: Timothy Gordon. *M.:* Jiang Jian Hua. *C.:* Timothy Gordon. *L.:* Colin Ho.

Momentum 2/6/92, Singapore
Ch.: Choo-San Goh. *M.:* Prokofiev. *C.:* Carol Vollet Kingston. *L.:* Beth Newbold.

Repertory:

Gemini
Ch.: Vicente Nebrada. *M.:* Mahler. *C.:* Vicente Nebrada. *L.:* Colin Ho.

Jack and the Beanstalk
Ch.: Ricardo Culalic. *M.:* Collage. *S.,C.:* Ricardo Culalic. *L.:* Colin Ho.

Princess Alitaptap
Ch.: Jamaludin Jalil. *M.:* Jamaludin Jalil, Karen D'Conceicao, Linda D'Mello. *D.:* Jamaludin Jalil. *L.:* Colin Ho.

303

Rainbow River
Ch.: Timothy Gordon. *M.:* Riuichi Sakamoto. *C.:* Goh Soo Khim, Anthony Then. *L.:* Colin Ho.

Secuencias Electricas (Pas de Deux)
Ch.: Vicente Nebrada. *M.:* Gershwin. *C.;* Vicente Nebrada. *L.:* Colin Ho.

South Africa

CAPAB BALLET

Nico Malan Theatre Centre
PO Box 4107
Cape Town 8000
Tel: (021) 6894346

Artistic dir.: Veronica Paeper

Administrative dir.: Janet le Sueur

Principal dancers: Leigh Anderson, Sean Bovin, Philip Boyd, Candice Brathwaite, Erica Brumage, Stanislav Chalov, Debra Earle, Hubert Essakow, Karen Freeman, Antoinette Haupt, Tertia Hinrichsen, Farouk Irving, Lisa Itzikovitz, Mzonke Jama, Geneviève Jooste, Johan Jooste, François Joubert, Carol Kinsey, Anton Labuschagne, Linda Lee, Janet Lindup, Paul Lloyd, Nicolette Loxton, Leigh McFayden, Brendan McLaren, Stephen Nicholenas, Hisham Omardien, Sharon Paulsen, Daniel Rajna, Simon Rowe, Desiré Samaai, John Simons, Bruce Spilsbury, Denise Stephani, Mandy Stober, Penny Swain, Deon Swanepoel, Caroline Thomas, Christal Turner, Nicholas van der Merwe, Bernice van Eck, Leanne Voysey, Andrew Warth, Amanda Whittle, Mervyn Willaims, Michelle Witten, Colleen Woolf, Juanita Yazbek

NAPAC DANCE COMPANY

The Play House
PO Box 5353
Durban 4000
Tel: (031) 304-3631

Artistic dir.: Garry Trinder

Administrative dir.: Beverley Stewart

Principal dancers: Clinton Brown, Mary-Ann de Wet, Celeste Dovale, Dina Erasmus, Elaine Fletcher, Nigel Galliene, Amancio Gonzalez, Selva Hannam, Vincent Hantam, Daniel Havas, Mark Hawkins, Judy Holme, Irene Hogarth, Tracy Li, Llewelyn Malan, Wendy Mason, Rene Oliver, Quinton Ribbonaar, Maria Roselli, Janice Russell, Gerard Samuel, Helen Thomas, Rupert Turner, Shireene Vande, Alida van Staden, Ayako Yoshikawa

PACT BALLET

The State Theatre
PO Box 566
Pretoria 0001
Tel: (021) 3221665

Artistic dir.: Dawn Weller-Raistrick

Administrative dir.: Martin Raistrick

Principal dancers: Johnny Bovang, Jeremy Coles, Dianne Finch, Tanja Graafland, Daniel Gwatkin, Nigel Hannah, Jeremy Hodges, Marion Lindsay, Odette Millner, Christopher Montague, David Palmer, Simon Crowther, Ashley Durrant, Allison Foat, Dianne Harris, Andrew Lyons, Manuel Noram, Brent Rokos, Siegfried Roth, Nadine Sacker, Craig Hedderwick, Karen Henning, Sharon Jones, Cheryl Mirtle, Leticia Müller, Ann Wixley

South Korea

CHANG MU DANCE COMPANY

GPO Box 9511
Seoul
Tel: (02) 739 3577

Artistic dir.: Prof. Kim MaeJa

UNIVERSAL BALLET COMPANY

25 Neung-Dong Sung
Dong-ku
Seoul 133-180
Tel: 82-2-452-1392
Fax: 82-2-452-7391

Artistic dir.: Roy Tobias, Julia H. Moon (assistant)

Administrative dir.: Moon Kyung Lee

Principal/associate choreographer(s): Roy Tobias, Adrienne Dellas (associate)

Principal dancers: Julia H. Moon, In-Hee Kim, Jae-Hong Park

Guest dancers: Fernando Bujones, Marin Boieru, Ross Stretton, Kevin Mckenzie, Richard Marsden, Simon Dow, George Bodnarciuc

No. of dancers: 21 male, 31 female

No. of performances: 100

Tours to: Japan, Korea

Premieres:

Reflections 29/7/91, Moonye Theatre
Ch.: James Jeon. *M.:* J.S. Bach. *C.:* Choong-Yul Bolton. *L.:* Chun Heung Ahn.

Festival Variations 24/8/91, Sejong Cultural Center
Ch.: Roy Tobias. *M.:* Brahms. *C.:* Sylvia Taalsohn. *L.:* Chun Heung Ahn.

Paquita 24/8/91, Sejong Cultural Center
Ch.: Natalia Makarova. *M.:* Minkus, Drigo. *S.,C.:* José Verona. *L.:* Chun Heung Ahn.

La Sonnambula 24/8/91, Sejong Cultural Center
Ch.: Balanchine. *M.:* Rieti. *S.,C.:* Rouben Ter-Arutunian. *L.:* Chun Heung Ahn.

Songs of Olympia 3/11/91, Moonye Theatre
Ch.: Roy Tobias. *M.:* Edith Piaf. *D.:* Roy Tobias. *L.:* Chun Heung Ahn.

Three Moments 3/11/91, Moonye Theatre
Ch.: James Jeon. *M.:* Handel. *C.:* James Jeon. *L.:* Chun Heung Ahn.

The Creatures of Prometheus 26/3/92, Litte Angels Performing Arts Centre
Ch.: Roy Tobias. *M.:* Beethoven. *S.:* Dong Hwa Yoo. *C.:* Sylvia Taalsohn. *L.:* Song Keun Kim.

Carnival of the Animals 1/5/92, LAPAC
Ch.: Roy Tobias. *M.:* Saint-Saëns. *S.,C.:* José Varona. *L.:* Chun Heung Ahn.

Repertory:

Coppélia
Ch.: Roy Tobias. *M.:* Delibes. *S.:* Kyung-Mo Yoon. *C.:* Adrienne Dellas, Sylvia Taalsohn. *L.:* Chun Heung Ahn.

La Fille mal gardée
Ch.: Roy Tobias. *M.:* Hertel. *S.,C.:* David Guthrie. *L.:* Chun Heung Ahn.

Giselle
Ch.: Coralli, Perrot. *M.:* Adam. *S.:* Campbell Baird. *C.:* Sylvia Taalsohn, Campbell Baird. *L.:* Chun Heung Ahn.

The Lady of the Camellias
Ch.: William Dollar. *M.:* Verdi. *S.:* Rouben Ter-Arutunian. *C.:* Choong-Yul Bolton. *L.:* Chun Heung Ahn.

The Nutcracker
Ch.: Roy Tobias, Adrienne Dellas. *M.:* Tchaikovsky. *C.:* Campbell Baird, Choong-Yul Bolton. *L.:* Chun Heung Ahn.

Pulcinella
Ch.: Roy Tobias. *M.:* Stravinsky. *S.:* Campbell Baird. *C.:* Sylvia Taalsohn. *L.:* Chun Heung Ahn.

Serenade
Ch.: Balanchine. *M.:* Tchaikovsky. *C.:* Jean Lurcat. *L.:* Ronald Bates.

Spain

ANANDA DANZA

Padre Rico 8 B Izq.
46008 Valencia
Tel: 6 384 2222

ANGELS MARGARIT/COMPAÑIA MUDANCES

Morales 21-27
08029 Barcelona
Tel: 3 430 8763

Artistic dir.: Angels Margarit

ANTONIA ANDREU Y BAILARINES

Marqués de Pontejos, 1
28012 Madrid
Tel: 34 1 521-9183

Artistic dir.: Antonia Andreu

Principal/associate choreographer(s):
Antonia Andreu

Principal dancers: Inma Vicente, Mila Martinez, Diana Morilla

No. of dancers: 5 female

No. of performances: 15

Tours to: France, Spain, Italy

Premieres:

Locos Solos 5/2/92, Teatro Pradillo, Madrid
Ch.: Antonia Andreu. M.: Various. D.: Antonio Alvarado. L.: Freddie Gerlache.

BALLET CLASICA DE ZARAGOZA

Centro Cultural 'Palafox'
Domingo Miral s/n
50009 Zaragoza
Tel: 76 56 64 11

BALLET CONTEMPORANI DE BARCELONA

Guitard 41 Bajos
08014 Barcelona
Tel: 3 490 8896

Fax: 3 490 8896

Artistic dir.: Amèlia Boluda

Administrative dir.: Joaquim Ramírez

Principal/associate choreographer(s):
Bebeto Cidra

Guest teacher(s): Enric Castan

Principal dancers: Bebeto Cidra, Martina Burlet, Amèlia Boluda, Carlos Ovares, Bibiana Calvitti

No. of dancers: 2 male, 3 female

No. of performances: 40

Tours to: Mexico, Spain, Italy, Germany

Pay rates: The company has a quota of $6000 per year

Premieres:

Fetitxe 11/91, Universidad de Málaga
Ch.: Amèlia Boluda. M.: Xavier Maristany.
D.: Xavier Maristany, Amèlia Boluda. C.: Mercè Bertrán, Maite Ferrer. L.: Eduard Inglés, Pere Anglada.

Repertory:

Quomix
Ch.: Amèlia Boluda, Blanca Calvo, Oscar Molina. M.: Xavier Maristany, Pau Riba, Joan Saura. C.: Cristina Armengol, Mercè Bertrán, Teresa Ferrer. L.: Luis Mella, Constancio Simarro.

BALLET CRISTINA HOYOS

Danzarte Bailén 1, 1o A
41001 Sevilla
Tel: 95 456 0705/0576
Fax: 95 456 08 44

Artistic dir.: Cristina Hoyos

Administrative dir.: Tina Panadero

Principal/associate choreographer(s):
Cristina Hoyos

Visiting choreographer(s): Manolo Marin

Principal dancers: Cristina Hoyos

No. of dancers: 4 male, 6 female

Tours to: France, Turkey, Italy, Scotland, Finland, Bulgaria, Germany, Switzerland, Belgium, Sweden, Greece, Israel, Venezuela, Japan, Denmark

Premieres:

Lo Flamenco 17/3/92, Champs Elysées, Paris
Ch.: Cristina Hoyos, Manolo Marin. *M.:*
Paco Arriaga. *D.:* Cristina Hoyos. *S.,C.:*
Danzarte. *L.:* Paco Dóniz.

Yerma 17/3/92, Champs Elysées, Paris
Ch.: Cristina Hoyos, Manolo Marin. *M.:*
Paco Arriaga. *D.:* Cristina Hoyos. *S.:*
Gerardo Vera. *C.:* Franca Squarciapino. *L.:*
Freddy Gerlache.

Repertory:

Sueños Flamencos
Ch.: Cristina Hoyos, Manolo Marin. *M.:*
Arriaga, Freire, Hoyos. *D.:* Cristina Hoyos.
S.: Danzarte. *L.:* Paco Dóniz.

BALLET DE ESPAÑA DE PACO ROMERO

Gutierrez de Cetina 16
28017 Madrid
Tel: 1 407 5791

Artistic dir.: Paco Romero

BALLET DE EUSKADI

Ribera de Deusto 65 B
48014 Bilbao
Tel: 4 476 22 34

BALLET ESPAÑOL DE MARIA ROSA

Ayala 43
28001 Madrid
Tel: 1 576 7238

BALLET LIRICO NACIONAL

Soria 2
28005 Madrid
Tel: (34 1) 468 08 44
Fax: (34 1) 468 09 32

Artistic dir.: Nacho Duato

Administrative dir.: José Antonio Muñoz

Principal/associate choreographer(s):
Nacho Duato

Visiting choreographer(s): Jirí Kylián, Hans
van Manen, Olga Roriz

Guest teacher(s): Irena Milovan, Benjamin
Harkarvey, Jan Nuyts, Jeannie Solan, Jorge
Salavisa, Peter Stam

No. of dancers: 23 male, 31 female

No. of performances: approx. 75

Tours to: Mexico, Italy, Venezuela

Premieres:

Empty 5/4/91, Albéniz Thearte, Madrid
Ch.: Nacho Duato. *M.:* Izumi Kobayashi,
Philip Glass, Jimi Hendrix, Peter
Sculthorpe, Ravi Shankar, Istvan Marta,
Camille Saint-Saëns. *S.,C.:* Nacho Duato. *L.:*
Edward Effron.

Return to the Strange Land 5/4/91, Albéniz
Theatre, Madrid
Ch.: Jirí Kylián. *M.:* Janácek. *L.:* Joop
Caboort.

Bits and Pieces 12/12/91, Teatro Lírico
Nacional de Zarzuela, Madrid
Ch.: Hans van Manen. *M.:* David Byrne,
Brian Eno, Felix Mendelssohn. *S.,C.:* Keso
Dekker. *L.:* Jan Hofstra.

Rassemblement 13/12/91, Teatro Lírico
Nacional de Zarzuela, Madrid
Ch.: Nacho Duato. *M.:* Toto Bissainthe. *S.:*
Walter Nobbe. *C.:* Nacho Duato. *L.:* Nicolás
Fischtei, after Dick Lindström.

Coming Together 23/12/91, Teatro Lírico
Nacional de Zarzuela, Madrid
Ch.: Nacho Duato. *M.:* Frederic Rzewski. *C.:*
Nacho Duato. *L.:* Nicolás Fischtei.

Stamping Ground 23/12/91, Teatro Lírico
Nacional de Zarzuela, Madrid
Ch.: Jirí Kylián. *M.:* Carlos Chávez. *S.:* Jirí
Kylián. *C.:* Heidi de Raad. *L.:* Joop Caboort.

Jardi Tancat 3/4/92, Albéniz Theatre,
Madrid
Ch.: Nacho Duato. *M.:* Maria del Mar Bonet.
S.,C.: Nacho Duato. *L.:* Nicolás Fischtei,
after Joop Caboort.

Thirteen Gestures of a Body 3/4/92, Albéniz
Theatre, Madrid
Ch.: Olga Roriz. *M.:* António Emiliano. *S.,C.:*
Nuno Carinhas. *L.:* Orlando Worm.

BALLET NACIONAL DE ESPAÑA

Isaac Peral 14
28015 Madrid
Tel: 1-5448596
Fax: 1-5449159

Artistic dir.: José Antonio Ruiz de la Cruz

Administrative dir.: Luis Roberto Zafra

Visiting choreographer(s): José Granero,
José Antonio, Felipe Sanchez, Rafael
Aguilar

Principal dancers: Antonio Alonso, Antonio Garcia, Santillana, Concepción Cerezo Rubio, Isabel Gallardo Gomez, Aida Gomez Agudo, Ana Gonzalez Aranda, Juan Manuel Mata Ortega, Adelaida Calvín Hernandez, Montserrat Marin Lacueva, Adoración Casas Carpio, Guadalupe Gomez de Miguel, Jesus Florencio Aragon, Guerrero Serrano

Guest dancers: Dolores Greco Arroyo

No. of dancers: 30 male, 30 female

BALLET REGION DE MURCIA

Gran Via Salzillo 42 Esc. 3, 4o
30005 Murcia
Tel: 68 214 832/214 884

BALLET VICTOR ULLATE

Dr Castelo 7
28009 Madrid
Tel: 1 275 03 85

Artistic dir.: Victor Ullate

BLANCA CALVO COMPANY OF CONTEMPORARY DANCE

Julio Danvila 12
28033 Madrid
Tel: 1 3020615
Fax: 1 5931026

Artistic dir.: Blanca Calvo

Administrative dir.: Gloria Tous

Principal/associate choreographer(s): Blanca Calvo

Principal dancers: Juan Dominguez, Iñaki Azpillaga, Susana Casenave, Gerson Alexandre, Blanca Calvo

No. of dancers: 3 male, 2 female

No. of performances: 17

Tours to: Spain, Italy, Portugal France

Premieres:

Detras del Viento 10/91, Madrid
Ch.: Blanca Calvo. *M.:* Javier López de Guereña. *S.:* Carmen Cantero. *C.:* Blanca Calvo. *L.:* Tano Astiaso.

Los Juancaballos 5/92. Madrid
Ch.: Blanca Calvo, Juan Dominguez. *M.:* A. Calero, F. Anguita. *S.:* Carmen Cantero. *C.:*

Blanca Calvo, Juan Dominguez. *L.:* Anibal Corrado.

Repertory:

Las Cosas Perdidas
Ch.: Blanca Calvo. *M.:* Javier López de Guereña. *S.:* Carmen Cantero. *C.:* Alfredo Mas. *L.:* Tano Astiaso.

CARMEN SENRA

Apolonio Morales 3
28036 Madrid
Tel: 34 1 359 16 47

COMPAÑIA BLANCA DEL REY

San Nicolás No. 5
28013 Madrid
Tel: 34-1-5421655
Fax: 34-1-5420533

Artistic dir.: Blanca del Rey

Administrative dir.: Juan Manuel Avila

Principal/associate choreographer(s): Blanca del Rey, Ciro (associate)

Principal dancers: Joaquin Ruiz, Mariano Torres, Gabriel Heredia, Juan Fernandez, Blanca del Rey, Inmaculada Aguilar, Marta Sol, Sole Payo, Carmen Torres

No. of dancers: 4 male, 4 female

No. of performances: 66

Tours to: Italy, Germany, Japan, Brazil, Greece, Taiwan, France

Premieres:

Pasión Flamenca 17/6/91, Tenerife
Ch.: Blanca del Rey. *M.:* Felipe Maya. *D.:* Blanca del Rey. *S.:* J. Avila. *C.:* Keiko. *L.:* Gerlache-Canales.

COMPAÑIA DE BAILE MANOLO MARIN

Apdo. Correoa 905
41080 Sevilla
Tel: 5 424 38022

COMPANIA DE DANZA CONTEMPORANEA AVELINA ARGÜELLES

Benet Mateu 60 entlos.
08034 Barcelona
Tel: 3 455 1952

Artistic dir.: Avelina Argüelles

Visiting choreographer(s): Martin Kravitz, Joe Alegado, Marcia Plevin, Alicia Condodina

Guest teacher(s): Martin Kravitz, Joe Alegado, Rick Merrill

Principal dancers: Avelina Argüelles, Toni Gomez, Emilio Gutierrez, Maria Roca, Lucia Sanchez, Miguel Vazquez

Guest dancers: Martin Kravitz, Joe Alegado, Rick Merrill

No. of dancers: 3 male, 3 female

No. of performances: 24

Tours to: Spain, Italy, France

Repertory:

Ahora me toca bailar con le mas fea
Ch.: Avelina Argüelles. *M.:* Gabriel Banci, E. Schwarz. *L.:* Keith Yelton.

Parfums
Ch.: Avelina Argüelles.

COMPAÑIA DE DANZA DE MARIO MAYA

Centro de Actividades Flamencas
Pasaje Mayol 20
41003 Gevilla
Tel: 5 441 5209

CUMBRE FLAMENCA

Corredera Baja de San Pablo 19
28004 Madrid
Tel: 1 531 6870/522 4973

Artistic dir.: Francisco Sanchez

DANAT DANZA

Apdo. Correoa 9388
08080 Barcelona
Tel: 3 442 1757
Fax: 3 443 2556

Artistic dir.: Sabine Dahrendorf, Alfonso Ordóñez

Principal dancers: Amalia Cabeza, Susana Castro, Sabine Dahrendorf, Beatriz Fernandez, Alfonso Ordóñez, Iosu Lezameta

No. of dancers: 2 male, 4 female

Tours to: France, Spain, Germany, Austria, EEUU, Australia

Premieres:

Y Quedare Delante de los Muros Inmenos . . A Kaspar 11/5/92, Sevilla
Ch.: Sabine Dahrdendorff, Alfonso Ordóñez. *M.:* Juanjo Ezquerra. *D.:* José Menchero. *C.:* Antonio Belart. *L.:* Evaristo Valera.

Repertory:

El Cielo esta Enladrillado
Ch.: Sabine Dahrdendorff, Alfonso Ordóñez. *M.:* Jean-Luc Plouvier, Bernard Plouvier. *D.:* José Menchero. *C.:* Nathalie Trouve, Maribel Salvans.

Una Cierta Mirada
Ch.: Sabine Dahrdendorff, Alfonso Ordóñez. *M.:* Albert Garcia. *D.:* José Menchero. *C.:* Danat Danza, Maribel Salvans. *L.:* Sabine Dahrendorff, Evaristo Valera.

DART COMPAÑIA DE DANSA

Casp 108. 6 C
08010 Barcelona
Tel: 3 246 5962

FLAMENCO FUSION

Corredera Baja de San Pablo 19
28004 Madrid
Tel: 1 531 6870/522 4973

Artistic dir.: Francisco Sanchez

GELABERT–AZZOPARDI COMPANYIA DE DANSA

Torrent de l'Olla 146 etr. 3er.
08012 Barcelona
Tel: (3) 416 00 68
Fax: (3) 237 12 43

Artistic dir.: Cesc Gelabert, Lydia Azzopardi

Principal/associate choreographer(s): Cesc Gelabert, Lydia Azzopardi

No. of dancers: 5 male, 6 female

No. of performances: 40

Tours to: italy, Germany, France, Spain

Premieres:

El Seuño de Artemis 24/5/91, Bayonne, France
Ch.: Cesc Gelabert, Lydia Azzopardi. *M.:* Javier Navarrete, Mauricio Villavecchia. *S.:* Thomas Pupkiewicz. *C.:* Leslie Languish. *L.:* Cesc Gelabert.

Repertory:

Solos - Cesc Gelabert
Ch.: Cesc Gelabert. *M.:* Javier Navarrete, Mauricio Villavecchia, A. Lewin-Richter, Calres Santos. *C.:* Lydia Azzopardi. *L.:* Cesc Gelabert.

HIDRA DANZA

Luis Montono 147 3o D
41007 Sevilla
Tel: 95 457 91 45

LA TATI

Del Prado 7
28014 Madrid
Tel: 1 429 3454/462 9665

LANONIMA IMPERIAL

Calle Morales 21-27
08029 Barcelona
Tel: 34 3 439 11 91
Fax: 34 3 405 05 56

Artistic dir.: Juan Carlos Garcia

Administrative dir.: Dietrich Grosse

LUISILLO TEATRO DE DANZA ESPAÑOLA

Felipe III 4, 1° Izq.
28012 Madrid
Tel: (34-1) 265 8404
Fax: (34-1) 364 0018

Artistic dir.: Luisillo

Administrative dir.: Luis P. Vivó

Principal/associate choreographer(s): Luisillo

Principal dancers: Maria Vivó, Adrian, Joaquín Grilo

No. of dancers: 8 male, 9 female

No. of performances: 80

Tours to: Spain, Italy, Greece, France

MAL PELO

Aribau 45 atico
08011 Barcelona
Tel: 3-454 90 89
Fax: 3-454 90 89

Artistic dir.: Maria Muñoz, Pep Ramis

Administrative dir.: Cuqui/Montse Garcia

Principal/associate choreographer(s): Maria Muñoz, Pep Ramis

Principal dancers: Maria Muñoz, Pep Ramis

Guest dancers: Jordi Casanovas

No. of dancers: 2 male, 1 female

No. of performances: 19

Tours to: USA, Canada, Spain, Croatia

MALAGA DANZA TEATRO

Huerta 3
29014 Malaga
Tel: 52 26 55 89

MARIA ANTONIA OLIVER

Carrer del Carme 30-32
08001 Barcelona
Tel: 3 302 5490

MARIA JOSÉ RIBOT COMPAÑIA DE DANZA

Nicolas Usera 64
28026 Madrid
Tel: 1 475 4922

METROS

Apertat 213
08292 Esparrageura (Barcelona)
Tel: 34 3 458 08 16
Fax: 34 3 207 79 79

MONICA VALENCIANO

Zurita 20 3o Pta. 2
28012 Madrid
Tel: 1 230 4027

PABLO VENTURA DANZA CONTEMPORANEA

Conde Duque 24 3o
28015 Madrid
Tel: 341 541 3858
Fax: 34 1 541 3858

Artistic dir.: Pablo Ventura

Administrative dir.: Elena Fontana

Principal/associate choreographer(s): Pablo Ventura

Principal dancers: Arlette Kunz, John Leathart, Pablo Ventura, Beatriz Villar, Sue Hawksley, Raquel Lamadrid

No. of dancers: 2 male, 4 female

No. of performances: 12

Premieres:

Julieta 12/91, Madrid
Ch.: Pablo Ventura. *M.:* José Luis Carles. *D.:* José Luis Raymond, Pedro Moreno. *S.:* José Luis Raymond. *L.:* Freddy Gerlache.

RAYO MALAYO DANZA

Calle Marqués de Santa Ana 5 4º A
28004 Madrid
Tel: 34 1 523 05 47

TRANSIT

Carrer San Bru 9
08301 Mataro, Barcelona
Tel: 3 379 4031

VIANANTS DANZA

Calle Calamocha 3 24 A
46018 Valencia
Tel: 34 6 380 1358
Fax: 34 6 380 0609

Artistic dir.: Gracel Meneu

Principal dancers: Antonio Aparisi, Maite Bacete, Gracel Meneu

No. of dancers: 1 male, 2 female

No. of performances: 21

Tours to: Spain, Italy, France, Germany

Premieres:

π 28/11/91, Bancaja, Valencia
Ch.: Gracel Meneu, Antonio Aparisi. *M.:* Carles Santos. *D.:* Rafa Ganarra. *C.:* Marisa Chisbert. *L.:* Miguel Blasco.

YAUZKARI DANZA CONTEMPORANEA

Urzainki 7
31013 Pamplona
Navarra
Tel: 48 12 87 33

10 Y 10 DANZA

Arturo Soria 241
28033 Madrid
Tel: 1 475 7222

Sweden

THE CULLBERG BALLET

Riksteatern 145
83 Norsborg
Tel: 46 8-531 99 157
Fax: 46 8-531 99 159

Artistic dir.: Mats Ek

Administrative dir.: Marian Laurell

Principal dancers: Yvan Auzely, Philippe Blanchard, Bernard Cauchard, Boaz Cohen, Anna Diehl, George Elkin, Gunilla Hammar, Antii Honkanen, Marc Hwang, Ana Laguna, Rami Levi, Vanessa de Lignière, Joke Martin, Gaétan Massé, Vanessa McIntosh, Monica Mengarelli, Veli-Pekka Peltokallio, Pompea Santoro, Anu Sistonen, Allyson Way

No. of dancers: 10 male, 10 female

No. of performances: 78

Tours to: Mexico, Italy, France, Hong Kong, Switzerland, Austria, Germany

Premieres:

Stamping Ground 14/1/92, Dansens Hus, Stockholm
Ch.: Jirí Kylián. *M.:* Carlos Chávez. *D.:* Jirí Kylián. *C.:* Heidi de Raad.

Carmen 13/5/92, Dansens Hus, Stockholm
Ch.: Mats Ek. *M.:* Bizet, Shedrin. *D.:* Marie-Louise Ekman.

Repertory:

Bernada
Ch.: Mats Ek. *M.:* Spanish guitar music, J.S. Bach. *D.:* Marie-Louise Ekman, Kristina Elander.

Down North
Ch.: Mats Ek. *M.:* J.P. Nyström. *D.:* Karin Ek.

Giselle
Ch.: Mats Ek. M.: Adolphe Adam. D.: Marie-Louise Ekman.

Grass
Ch.: Mats Ek. M.: Rachmaninov. D.: Karin Ek.

Light Beings
Ch.: Mats Ek. M.: Collage. D.: Peder Freiij.

Old Children
Ch.: Mats Ek. M.: Collage. D.: Karin Ek.

Overgrown Path
Ch.: Jirí Kylián. M.: Janácek. D.: Walter Nobbe.

Rassemblement
Ch.: Nacho Duato. M.: Toto Bissainthe, Walter Kallup. D.: Walter Nobbe.

Swan Lake
Ch.: Mats Ek. M.: Tchaikovsky. D.: Marie-Louise Ekman, Peder Freiij.

Transfigured Night
Ch.: Jirí Kylián. M.: Schönberg. C.: Joop Stokvis.

DANSENS HUS (THE HOUSE OF DANCE)

Wallingatan 21
111 24 Stockholm
Tel: 8-7964940 (admin)/8-7964910 (box office)
Fax: 8-7967040

EFVA LILJA DANCEPRODUCTION

Festsalen
16104 Bromma
Tel: 46 8 87 87 20
Fax: 46 8 87 87 20

Artistic dir.: Efva Lilja

Administrative dir.: Barbro Gramén

Principal/associate choreographer(s): Efva Lilja

Principal dancers: Denise Hartman, Efva Lilja, Urban Skoglund, Jan Abramson, Jesper Krosness

Guest dancers: Isabel Gustafson, Paul Johnson, Gerd Anderson, Ingvar Boman, Peter Amoghli, Per Inge Janérus, Hervor Sjöstrand, Maria Villa-Lobos

No. of performances: 129

Tours to: Sweden, Yugoslavia, Denmark

Pay rates: 10000 SKR

Premieres:

Respass 27/4/91, Jönköping
Ch.: Efva Lilja. M.: Tommy Zwedberg. L.: Bengt Larsson.

Fara 13/8/91, Stockholms Ström
Ch.: Efva Lilja. S.: Bengt Larsson.

Värnamodansen 6/2/92, Värnamo
Ch.: Efva Lilja. M.: Chubby Checker.

Brunnen 19/3/92, Kulterhuset, Stockholm
Ch.: Efva Lilja. M.: Bo Rydberg. S.: Bengt Larsson. C.: Anna Persson. L.: Mats Andreasson.

Fukt 6/6/92, Stockholm
Ch.: Efva Lilja. M.: Tommy Adolfsson, Lars Almkvist.

Repertory:

Ana Rage
Ch.: Efva Lilja. S.,C.: Efva Lilja.

Blåst
Ch.: Efva Lilja. S.,L.: Bengt Larsson. C.: Anna Persson.

Dans och Poesi
Ch.: Efva Lilja. C.: Anne Goodrich.

...eho...
Ch.: Efva Lilja.

Ensamma Duon
Ch.: Efva Lilja. M.: Tommy Zwedberg.

Fast
Ch.: Efva Lilja.

Orda
Ch.: Efva Lilja. M.: Tommy Zwedberg. S.: Bengt Larsson. C.: Lena Lucki. L.: Bengt Larsson.

Vana Språng
Ch.: Efva Lilja. M.: Tommy Zwedberg. S.: Hjördis Tegsell. C.: Efva Lilja.

Volt
Ch.: Efva Lilja.

GOTHENBURG BALLET

Stora Teaterns Balett
Stora Teatern
Parkgatan 2
41138 Gothenburg
Tel: 031-17 47 45

Artistic dir.: Robert North

MALMÖ BALLET

Malmö Stadtteatern
PO Box 17520
Malmö
Tel: 040 100220

Artistic dir.: Jonas Kåge

MODERNA DANSTEATERN

Skeppsholmen, Hus 103
111 49 Stockholm
Tel: 08-611 14 56

Artistic dir.: Margaretha Åsberg

ÖSTGÖTABALETTEN

Östgötatheater
Box 3114
600 03 Norrköping
Tel: 011-10 62 80
Fax: 011-19 97 52

Artistic dir.: Lena Stranger-Weinar

Principal/associate choreographer(s): Vlado Juras

Visiting choreographer(s): Mats Ek, Birgit Cullberg, Jirí Kylián

Guest teacher(s): Aurora Musatescu, Konstantin Damianov, Victor Valcu, Norio Yoshida, Allyson Way

Principal dancers: Anne Charlotte Bengtsson, Ann-Louise Moberg, Joacim Keusch, Berit Tancred (actress), Johanna Bergfeldt, Annika Sohlman, Julia S. Pasic, Conny Jansson, Ingvar Jönsson, Josef Tran, Kertsiu Abrahamsson, Morten Junstrand

No. of dancers: 5 male, 6 female

No. of performances: c. 90

Tours to: Denmark

Premieres:

På Norrbotten 4/4/91
Ch.: Mats Ek. *M.:* J.P. Nyströms. *D.,C.:* Karin Ek. *L.:* Mats Ek, Monica Sykersen.

Primadonnor 5/4/91, Motata
Ch.: Vlado Juras. *M.:* Goerge Pommer, Puccini, Berio, Mozart, Verdi. *D.,C.:* Örjan Säll. *L.:* Dick Lindström.

Stoolgame 5/4/91, Motata
Ch.: Jirí Kylián. *M.:* Arne Nordheim. *D.:* Jirí Kylián. *L.:* Joop Caboort.

Eldfågeln (Firebird) 12/11/91, Linköping
Ch.: Vlado Juras. *M.:* Stravinsky. *D.,C.:* Örjan Säll. *L.:* Dick Lindström. *Masks:* Robin Karlsson.

ROYAL SWEDISH BALLET

Kungliga Teatern
PO 160 94
103 22 Stockholm
Tel: 08-791 43 00
Fax: 08-10 79 45

Artistic dir.: Nils-Åke Häggbom

Guest teacher(s): Simon Mottram, Olga Evreinoff, Nicholas Johnson, Alexander Chmelnitski

Principal dancers: Anneli Alhanko, Johanna Björnson, Pär Isberg, Margareta Lidström, Hans Nilsson, Madeleine Onne, Per Arthur Segerström, Göran Svalberg, Mats Wegmann

Guest dancers: Phillip Broomhead

No. of dancers: 32 male, 47 female

No. of performances: 69

Tours to: Finland, Norway, Czechoslovakia

Premieres:

Cinderella 20/4/91, Royal Opera
Ch.: Frederick Ashton. *M.:* Prokofiev. *D.:* David Walker. *L.:* H-Å Sjoquist.

Elvira Madigan 8/2/92, Royal Opera
Ch.: Regina Beck-Friis. *M.:* Mahler. *D.:* David Walker.

Organ Concerto 8/2/92, Royal Opera
Ch.: Nils Christe. *M.:* Poulenc. *D.:* Keso Dekker. *L.:* Kees Tjebbe.

Figaro 22/5/92, Drottningholm Court Theatre
Ch.: Ivo Cramér. *M.:* Anon, 18th-century.

Repertory:

The Kingdom of the Shades (La Bayadère Act 2)
Ch.: Petipa/Makarova. *M.:* Minkus. *S.:* P. Samaritani. *C.:* Theoni V. Aldredge.

A Midsummer Night's Dream
Ch.: John Neumeier. *M.:* Mendelssohn, Ligeti. *D.:* Jürgen Rose.

Miss Julie
Ch.: Birgit Cullberg. *M.:* Ture Rangström. *D.:* Sven Ericson.

Romeo and Juliet
Ch.: Kenneth MacMillan. *M.:* Prokofiev. *D.:*
Nicholas Georgiadis.

Le Sacre du printemps
Ch.: Maurice Béjart. *M.:* Stravinsky. *D.:* John
van der Heyden.

Swan Lake
Ch.: Natalia Conus, after Petipa. *M.:*
Tchaikovsky. *D.:* Henry Bardon. *C.:* David
Walker.

RUBICON

Övre Husargaten 1
411 22 Göteborg
Tel: 031-11 82 00

Artistic dir.: *Gun Lund, Gunilla Witt, Eva*
Ingemarsson

Switzerland

BALLET OF THE ZÜRICH OPERA
HOUSE

Schillerstrasse 1
8001 Zürich
Tel: (01) 251 69 20

BASLER BALLETT

Basel Theatre
4010 Basel
Tel: (061) 22 11 30
Fax: (061) 295 15 95

Artistic dir.: Youri Vàmos

Administrative dir.: P. Marschel

Principal/associate choreographer(s): Joyce
Cuoco

Visiting choreographer(s): Judith Jamison

Guest teacher(s): Niels Kehlet

Principal dancers: Joyce Cuoco, Paul Boyd

No. of dancers: 18 male, 19 female

No. of performances: 65

Pay rates: SFr. 3800

Premieres:

Spartacus 12/10/91, Basel
Ch.: Yuri Vàmos. *M.:* Khatchaturian. *D.:*
Michael Scott. *L.:* H. Münzer.

Vathek 20/11/91, Basel
Ch.: Yuri Vàmos. *M.:* Shostakovich. *D.:*
Michael Scott. *L.:* H. Münzer.

Tease/Forgotten Time/Divining 28/1/92, Basel
Ch.: Judith Jamison. *M.:* Collage/Le Mystère
des Voix Bulgares/Dinizulu. *D.:* Allen,
Miller, Jamison, Mahlke, Kaye. *S.:* Heinz
Berner. *L.:* Timothy Hunter.

Lucidor 10/5/92, Basel
Ch.: Yuri Vàmos. *M.:* Glazunov. *D.:* Michael
Scott. *L.:* H. Münzer.

BÉJART BALLET LAUSANNE

Palais de Beaulieu
Avenue des Bergiers
CH-1000 Lausanne 22
Tel: (21) 452400

COMPAGNIE PHILIPPE SAIRE

PO Box 422
CH-1110 Morges
Tel: 41-21-803 08 50
Fax: 41-21-803 06 62

Artistic dir.: Philippe Saire

Principal/associate choreographer(s):
Philippe Saire

Principal dancers: Julie Salgues, Rahel
Vonmoos, Marc Berthon, Charles Linehan,
Philippe Saire

Repertory:

Ah! Finir
Ch.: Philippe Saire.

Don Quixote
Ch.: Philippe Saire. *M.:* Martin Chabloz. *S.:*
Jean-Marie Bosshard, Thierry Baechtold,
Antoine Delarue. *C.:* Jocelyne Pache. *L.:*
Christian Yerly.

L'Ombre du doute
Ch.: Philippe Saire.

Vie et moers de cameleon nocturne
Ch.: Philippe Saire. *M.:* Ravel. *S.:* Jean-Marie
Bosshard. *C.:* Nadia Cuénoud. *L.:* Christian
Yerly.

STADTTHEATER BERN BALLET COMPANY

Nägeligasse 1
3000 Bern 7
Tel: (031) 21 17 11
Fax: 031) 22 39 47

Artistic dir.: François Klaus

Administrative dir.: Ernst Gosteli

Principal/associate choreographer(s): François Klaus

Principal dancers: Paul De Masson, Martin Schläpfer

Guest dancers: Rebecca Yates

No. of dancers: 10 male, 11 female

No. of performances: 46

Premieres:

L'Heure de la Danse 29/9/91, Stadttheater Bern

Ch.: Michel Fokine, François Klaus, John Neumeier, Marius Petipa. *M.:* Saint-Saëns, D. Scarlatti, Tchaikovsky, Elgar, Stravinsky, Weber. *D.:* François Klaus. *S.:* Gino Fornasa. *C.:* Inge Borisch, Gabriele Jaenecke. *L.:* Jacques Battocletti.

Juans Traum 13/12/91, Stadttheater Bern
Ch.: François Klaus. *M.:* Boris Blacher, Charles Ives, Edward Elgar, Jehan Alain, Samuel Barber. *D.:* François Klaus. *S.,C.:* Wilhelmine Bauer. *L.:* Otto Kucis.

La Petite Sirène 15/2/92, Stadttheater Bern
Ch.: François Klaus. *M.:* Poulenc, Fauré. *D.:* François Klaus. *S.:* Thomas Ziegler. *C.:* Thomas Ziegler, Dagmar Schlenzka. *L.:* Otto Kucis.

Hamamelis Coxinus, Zauberer 18/3/92, Theater am Käfigturm, Bern
Ch.: François Klaus. *M.:* Mozart, Paganini, Rochberg, Dvořák. *D.:* François Klaus. *S.:* Natascha von Steiger. *C.:* Dagmar Schlenzka. *L.:* Hanspeter Liechti.

United Kingdom

ADVENTURES IN MOTION PICTURES

Sadler's Wells Theatre
Rosebery Avenue
London WC1H 9AB
Tel: 071-380 1268
Fax: 071-713 6040

Artistic dir.: Matthew Bourne

Administrative dir.: Katharine Doré

Principal dancers: Matthew Bourne, Scott Ambler, Andrew George, Simon Murphy, Ally Fitzpatrick, Etto Murfitt

No. of dancers: 4 male, 2 female

No. of performances: c. 50

Tours to: Hong Kong

Premieres:

Deadly Serious 3/92, Arnolfini, Bristol
Ch.: Matthew Bourne. *M.:* Various. *D.:* David Manners. *L.:* Rick Fisher.

THE BIRMINGHAM ROYAL BALLET

Birmingham Hippodrome
Thorp Street
Birmingham B5 4AV
Tel: 21-622 2555
Fax: 21-622 5038

Artistic dir.: Peter Wright

THE CHOLMONDELEYS

The Place
17 Dukes Road
London WC1H 9AB
Tel: 071-383 3231
Fax: 071 383 4851

Artistic dir.: Lea Anderson

Administrative dir.: Rosalind Powell

Principal/associate choreographer(s): Lea Anderson

No. of dancers: 6 female

No. of performances: 53

Tours to: France, Ireland

315

Pay rates: £230 per week

Premieres:

Birthday
Ch.: Lea Anderson. *M.:* Steve Blake. *C.:*
Sandy Powell. *L.:* Francis Stevenson.

Opera Sportif
Ch.: Lea Anderson. *M.:* Steve Blake. *D.:*
Central School of Art students. *L.:* Francis
Stevenson.

Repertory:

Cold Sweat
Ch.: Lea Anderson. *M.:* Drostan Madden,
Steve Blake. *DeC.:* Sandy Powell. *L.:* Chris
Nash.

Flesh and Blood
Ch.: Lea Anderseon. *M.:* Steve Blake. *C.:*
Sandy Powell. *L.:* Mark Parry.

DV8 PHYSICAL THEATRE

Artsadmin
295 Kentish Town Road
London NW5 2TJ
Tel: 071-482 3841

Artistic dir.: Lloyd Newson

ENGLISH NATIONAL BALLET

Markova House
39 Jay Mews
London SW7 2ES
Tel: 071-581 1245

Artistic dir.: Ivan Nagy

Administrative dir.: Carole McPhee

Principal/associate choreographer(s):
Christoper Bruce (associate, until August
1991)

Principal dancers: Carlos Acosta (from 9/
91), Tim Almaas, Maurizio Bellezza, Renata
Calderini, José Manuel Carreno, Paul
Chalmer (to 8/91), Angela DeMello (to 8/
91), Thomas Edur, Alexander Grant (to 8/
91), Ana Lobe (to 8/91), Laurent Novis (to
8/91), Lourdes Novoa (from 9/91), Agnes
Oaks, Koen Onzia (to 8/91), Oskana
Panchenko (to 8/91), Maria Teresa del Real,
Pablo Savoye (to 8/91), Ludmila Semeniaka
(from 12/91)

Guest dancers: Daniela Angelini, Marcello
Angelini, Nicholas Beriosoff, Lynne Charles
(resident guest), Richard Cragun, Eva
Evdokimova, Marcia Haydée, Benito

Marcelino, Laurie Miller (resident guest),
Yelena Pankova (resident guest), Matz
Skoog, Elizabeth Toohey (resident guest),
Trinidad Vives

No. of performances: 271

Tours to: Germany, Italy, Hungary

Premieres:

The Taming of the Shrew 16/4/91, Mayflower
Theatre, Southampton
Ch.: John Cranko. *M.:* Kurt-Heinz Stolze,
after Domenico Scarlatti. *D.:* Elisabeth
Dalton.

Anne Frank 28/6/91, London Coliseum
Ch.: Mauricio Wainrot. *M.:* Bartók. *D.:*
Carlos Gallardo.

The Nutcracker 28/11/91, Palace Theatre,
Manchester
Ch.: Ben Stevenson. *M.:* Tchaikovsky. *D.:*
Desmond Heeley.

Apollo 18/2/92, Arts Theatre, Cambridge
Ch.: Balanchine. *M.:* Stravinsky.

A Stranger I Came 18/2/92, Arts Theatre,
Cambridge
Ch.: Robert North. *M.:* Schubert. *D.:* Andrew
Storer.

Cinderella 29/4/92, Mayflower Theatre,
Southampton
Ch.: Ben Stevenson. *M.:* Prokofiev. *D.:* David
Walker.

The Envelope 19/6/92, Connaught Theatre,
Worthing
Ch.: David Parsons. *M.:* Rossini, arr. Charles
Gouse. *D.:* Judy Wirkula.

Sleep Study 19/6/92, Connaught Theatre,
Worthing
Ch.: David Parsons. *M.:* Flim the the BBs. *D.:*
David Soar.

L 23/6/92, London Colisuem
Ch.: Ben Stevenson. *M.:* Don Dawson. *D.:*
David Soar.

White Nights 23/6/92, London Coliseum
Ch.: Kim Brandstrup. *M.:* Gerald McBurney,
after Mussorgsky. *D.:* F. Dimov.

Repertory:

Aureole
Ch.: Paul Taylor. *M.:* Handel. *D.:* Tacit.

Black Swan Pas de Deux
Ch.: Petipa. *M.:* Tchaikovsky. *D.:* Carl Toms.

Coppélia
Ch.: Ronald Hynd. M.: Delibes. D.:
Desmond Heeley.

The Dance of the Bungaloo
Ch.: Janet Smith. M.: Christopher Benstead.
D.: Nick Somerville.

Don Quixote Pas de Deux
Ch.: Petipa. M.: Minkus.

The Dying Swan
Ch.: Fokine. M.: Saint-Saëns. D.: after Bakst.

Etudes
Ch.: Harald Lander. M.: Riisager, after
Czerny.

Flower Festival in Genzano Pas de Deux
Ch.: Bournonville. M.: Paulli. D.: David
Walker.

Four Last Songs
Ch.: Ben Stevenson. M.: Richard Strauss. D.:
Matthew Jacobs.

Giselle
Ch.: Mary Skeaping after Perrot/Coralli/
Petipa. M.: Adam. D.: David Walker.

Graduation Ball
Ch.: David Lichine. M.: Anatol Dorati after
Johann Strauss. D.: Alexandre Benois.

Kingdom of the Shades from La Bayadère
Ch.: Makarova, after Petipa. M.: Minkus.

Onegin
Ch.: John Cranko. M.: Tchaikovsky, arr.
Stolze. D.: Jürgen Rose.

Our Walztes
Ch.: Vicente Nebrada. M.: Teresa Carreno.
D.: Maria Puig.

Polovtsian Dances from Prince Igor
Ch.: Fokine. M.: Borodin. D.: Roerich.

The Sanguine Fan
Ch.: Ronald Hynd. M.: Elgar. D.: Peter
Docherty.

Schéhérazade
Ch.: Fokine. M.: Rimsky-Korsakov. D.: after
Bakst.

Le Spectre de la rose
Ch.: Fokine. M.: von Weber. D.: Geoffrey
Guy, after Bakst.

Swansong
Ch.: Christopher Bruce. M.: Philip
Chambon.

Les Sylphides
Ch.: Fokine. M.: Chopin. D.: Geoffrey Guy,
arfer Corot.

Three Preludes
Ch.: Ben Stevenson. M.: Rachmaninov. D.:
Peter Farmer.

THE FEATHERSTONEHAUGHS

The Place
17 Dukes Road
London WC1H 9AB
Tel: 071-383 3231
Fax: 071 383 4851

Artistic dir.: Lea Anderson

Administrative dir.: Rosalind Powell

Principal/associate choreographer(s): Lea
Anderson

No. of dancers: 6 male

No. of performances: 78

Tours to: Ireland, France, Austria, Belgium

Pay rates: £230 per week

Repertory:

Big Feature
Ch.: Lea Anderson. M.: Various. L.: Mark
Parry.

Birthday
Ch.: Lea Anderson. M.: Steve Blake. C.:
Sandy Powell. L.: Francis Stevenson.

LONDON CITY BALLET

London Studio Centre
42-50 York Way
London N1 9AB
Tel: 071-837 3133
Fax: 071-713 6072

Artistic dir.: Harold King

Administrative dir.: Heather Knight

Visiting choreographer(s): Ben Stevenson

Guest teacher(s): Elizabeth Anderton,
Margaret Barbieri, Brenda Last, Woyteck
Lowski, Petal Miller, Katia Svelebilova

Principal dancers: Victor Barykin, Bryony
Brind*, Beverly Jane Fry, Kirill Melnikov*,
Kim Miller, Yelena Pankova*, Jane Sanig,
Stanislav Tchassov*, Paul Thrussell, Jack
Wyngaard
Resident guest artists

Guest dancers: Eva Evdokimova, Miximiliano Guerra, Koen Onzia

No. of dancers: 16 male, 20 female

No. of performances: 261

Tours to: UK and overseas

Premieres:

Romeo and Juliet 4/9/91, Gordon Craig Theatre, Stevenage
Ch.: Ben Stevenson. *M.:* Prokofiev, arr. Chris Nicholls. *D.:* David Walker. *L.:* John B. Read.

Nutcracker Suite 16/9/91, Theatre Royal, Windsor
Ch.: Harold King. *M.:* Tchaikovsky. *D.:* Peter Farmer.

Donizetti Variations 26/5/92, King's Theatre, Edinburgh
Ch.: Balanchine. *M.:* Donizetti. *D.:* Karinska.

Les Patineurs 26/5/92, King's Theatre, Edinburgh
Ch.: Ashton. *M.:* Meyerbeer, arr. Lambert. *D.:* William Chappell.

Repertory:

Cinderella
Ch.: William Morgan. *M.:* Rossini, arr. Bramwell Tovey. *D.:* Johan Engels. *L.:* John B. Read.

Le Corsaire Pas de Deux
Ch.: after Petipa. *M.:* Drigo.

Dances from Napoli
Ch.: Bournonville. *M.:* Helsted.

Don Quixote Pas de Deux
Ch.: after Petipa. *M.:* Minkus.

Giacosa Variations
Ch.: Istvan Herczog. *M.:* Martinu. *D.:* Istvan Herczog.

Giselle Pas de Deux
Ch.: Coralli/Perrot. *M.:* Adam.

Graduation Ball
Ch.: Lichine. *M.:* Johann Strauss, arranged Antal Dorati. *D.:* Peter Farmer after Benois.

Laurencia Pas de Six
Ch.: Chabukiani, produced by Galina Samsova. *M.:* Minkus. *D.:* Elisabeth Dalton.

Othello
Ch.: Peter Darrell. *M.:* Liszt. *D.:* Peter Farmer.

Pie Jesu Pas de Deux
Ch.: Garry Trinder. *M.:* Fauré.

Prince Igor
Ch.: Harold King, Michael Beare. *M.:* Borodin. *D.:* Johan Engels.

Swan Lake
Ch.: Bourmeister/Ivanov. *M.:* Tchaikovsky. *D.:* Peter Cazalet. *L.:* John B. Read.

Transfigured Night
Ch.: Frank Staff. *M.:* Schönberg. *D.:* Peter Farmer.

Walpurgis Night Pas de Deux
Ch.: recreated by Galina Samsova. *M.:* Gounod.

LONDON CONTEMPORARY DANCE THEATRE

The Place
17 Dukes Road
London WC1H 9AB
Tel: 071-387 0161
Fax: 071-383 4851

Artistic dir.: Nancy Duncan

Administrative dir.: Janet Eager MBE

Principal/associate choreographer(s): Jane Dudley, Jonathan Lunn, Dan Wagoner, Darshan Singh Bhuller

Visiting choreographer(s): Nina Wiener, Bill T. Jones, Lloyd Newson, Simon de Mowbray, Margaret Foyer, Janet Smith, Terry Etheridge, Mary Evelyn, Mark Morris

Guest teacher(s): Lloyd Newson, Gill Clarke, Gwyneth Jones, Jean Françoise Durore

Principal dancers: Darshan Singh Bhuller, Kate Coyne, Peter Dunleavy, Elizabeth Fancourt, Tracey Fitzgerald, David Hughes, Bernadette Iglich, Isabel Mortimer, Leesa Phillips, Andrew Robinson, Isabel Tamen, Kenneth Tharp, Tom Ward, Sheron Wray, Benjamin Wright

No. of dancers: 7 male, 9 female

Tours to: Denmark, Italy, Czechoslovakia

Pay rates: As equity agreement

Premieres:

Rikud 5/4/91, The Place Theatre, London
Ch.: Liat Dror, Nir Ben Gal. *M.:* Shostakovich. *C.:* Liat Dor, Nir Ben Gal. *L.:* Tina MacHugh.

In Dream I Dream a Dream 9/4/91, The Place Theatre, London
Ch.: Kim Branstrup. *M.*: John Lunn. *D.*: Fotini Dimou. *L.*: Tina McHugh.

Wind Devil 15/10/91, Arts Centre, University of Warwick
Ch.: Nina Wiener. *M.*: Sergio Cervetti. *C.*: Jenny Henry. *L.*: Tina MacHugh.

Freedom of Information 20/10/91, Hippodrome, Bristol
Ch.: Arnie Zane. *M.*: David Cunningham. *D.*: Gretchen Bender. *L.*: Robert Wierzel.

Repertory:

Flee as a Bird
Ch.: Dan Wagoner. *M.*: Cole Porter, Art Hodes & Milt Hinton, Chris Barber, Walter Melrose. *C.*: Candice Donnelly. *L.*: Jennifer Tipton.

Forest
Ch.: Robert Cohan. *M.*: Brian Hodgson. *D.*: Norberto Chiesa. *L.*: Robert Cohan.

Hang Up
Ch.: Jonathan Lunn. *L.*: Tim Johnson.

Harmonica Breakdown
Ch.: Jane Dudley. *M.*: Sonny Terry, Oh Red. *C.*: Jane Dudley. *L.*: Tom Johnson.

Orfeo
Ch.: Kim Brandstrup. *M.*: Ian Dearden. *D.*: Craig Givens.

Something to Tell
Ch.: Richard Alston. Text: Getrude Stein.

Tango
Ch.: Yael Flexer. *M.*: Karni Postel. *C.*: Nicki Gibbs. *L.*: Ross Cameron.

White Heat
Ch.: Dan Wagoner. *M.*: Bartók. *D.*: William Ivey Long. *L.*: Jennifer Tipton.

MICHAEL CLARK & COMPANY

Allarts
387B King Street
London W6 9NJ

Artistic dir.: Michael Clark

NORTHERN BALLET THEATRE

Spring Hall
Huddersfield Road
Halifax HX3 0AQ
Tel: 0422 380531

Artistic dir.: Christopher Gable, Elaine McDonald (associate)

PHOENIX DANCE COMPANY

3 St Peter's Buildings
St Peter's Square
Leeds
West Yorkshire LS9 8AH
Tel: 0532-423486
Fax: 0532-444736

Artistic dir.: Margaret Morris

Administrative dir.: Liza Stevens

Visiting choreographer(s): Philip Taylor, Tom Jobe, Darshan Singh Bhuller, Danial Shapiro, Joanie Smith, Neville Campbell

Principal dancers: Clare Connor, Stephen Derrick, Dawn Donaldson, Chantal Donaldson, Donald Edwards, Ricardo Goodison, Pamela Johnson, Booker T. Louis, Martin Robinson, Seline Thomas

No. of dancers: 5 male, 5 female

No. of performances: 75

Tours to: Austria, Jamaica, USA

Pay rates: Dancer - £10700 pa; Senior dancer - £11000 pa

Premieres:

Heavy Metal 7/91, Sheffield Festival
Ch.: Neville Campbell. *M.*: Malcolm Swann. *D.*: Neville Campbell, Carole Waller. *S.*: Carole Waller. *C.*: Carole Waller. *L.*: Jim Simmons.

Even Cowgirls Get The Blues 9/91, Theatre Royal and Opera House, Wakefield
Ch.: Tom Jobe. *M.*: kd lang. *D.*: Peter Docherty, Tom Jobe.

Interlock 9/91, Theatre Royal and Opera House, Wakefield
Ch.: Darshan Singh Bhuller. *M.*: Clem Alford. *D.*: Darshan Singh Bhuller.

Sacred Space 9/91, Sadler's Wells Theatre, London
Ch.: Philip Taylor. *M.*: Arvo Pärt. *C.*: Heidi de Raad. *L.*: Philip Taylor, Norman Perryman, Mark Smith.

Subject of the City 9/91, Theatre Royal and Opera House, Wakefield
Ch.: Pamela Johnson. *M.*: Malcolm Swann, Penguin Café Orchestra. *D.*: Pamela Johnson. *L.*: Mark Smith.

Family 6/92, Greenwich Festival
Ch.: Danial Shapiro, Joanie Smith. *M.*: Kamikaze Ground Crew, Astor Piazzola, Scott Killian. *D.*: Joanie Smith. *L.*: Mark Smith.

Repertory:

Gang of Five
Ch.: Aletta Collins. *M.*: 'B' Word, John Matsuura. *D.*: Andy Papas. *L.*: Mark Smith.

Haunted Passages
Ch.: Philip Taylor. *M.*: Britten. *D.,C.*: Heidi de Raad. *S.*: Philip Taylor. *L.*: Mark Smith.

Rights
Ch.: Michael Clark. *M.*: Big Hard Excellent Fish. *D.*: Michael Clark. *L.*: Mark Smith.

Shock Absorber
Ch.: Darshan Singh Bhuller. *M.*: Ry Cooder, John Martyn. *S.*: Darshan Singh Bhuller. *C.*: Sonja Kirkham. *L.*: Mark Ridler.

Solo
Ch.: Neville Campbell. *M.*: Density. *S.*: Neville Campbell. *C.*: Emma Tregidden. *L.*: Mark Ridler.

Tainted Love
Ch.: Tom Jobe, Anita Griffin (assistant). *M.*: Stephen Smith. *D.*: Paul Dart. *L.*: Mark Ridler.

RAMBERT DANCE COMPANY

94 Chiswick High Road
London W4 1SH
Tel: 081-995 4246

Artistic dir.: Richard Alston

Principal dancers: Shelley Baker, Mark Baldwin, Lee Boggess, Steven Brett, Amanda Britton, Alexandra Dyer, Sue Hawksley (guest), Jeremy James (to April 1992), Jacqueline Jones (apprentice from November 1991), John Kilroy, Gary Lambert, Gabrielle McNaughton, Sara Matthews, Mihalis Nalbantis (to August 1991), Elizabeth Old (to April 1992), Paul Old, Colin Poole, Cathrine Price (from June 1992), Sarah Warsop, Glenn Wilkinson, Yolande Yorke-Edgell (from September 1991)

No. of performances: 100

Tours to: Italy, USA, France, Austria

Premieres:

Slippage 23/4/91, Riverside Studios, London
Ch.: William Tuckett. *M.*: Dan Jones. *D.*: Candida Cook.

La Chambre des trois paravents (Hiding-Game) 19/7/91, Complexe sportif de Val de l'Arc, Aix, France
Ch.: Hervé Robbe. *M.*: Kaspar T. Toeplitz. *S.*: Robin Brown. *C.*: Allison Amin.

Completely Birdland 11/10/91, Haymarket, Leicester
Ch.: Laurie Booth. *M.*: Hans Peter Kuhn. *S.*: Graham Snow. *C.*: Jeann Spaziani.

Island to Island 22/11/91, Apollo Theatre, Oxford
Ch.: Mark Baldwin. *M.*: Ben Craft.

Winnsboro Cotton Mill Blues 13/3/92, Theatre Clwyd, Mold
Ch.: Siobhan Davies. *M.*: Frederic Rzewski, Mark Underwood, Roger Heaton. *D.*: Peter Mumford.

Still Dance 16/4/92, Northcott Theatre, Exeter
Ch.: Paul Old.

Cat's Eye 12/6/92, Old Vic, Bristol
Ch.: Richard Alston. *M.*: David Sawer. *D.*: Paul Huxley.

Touchbase 20/6/92, Royalty Theatre, London
Ch.: Merce Cunningham. *M.*: Micheal Pugliese. *D.*: Mark Lancaster.

Phillidor's Defence 26/6/92, Royalty Theatre, London
Ch.: Guido Severien. *M.*: Glyn Perrin. *D.*: Carolien Scholtes.

Plain Song 12/4/91 Mayflower Theatre, Southampton
Ch.: Siobhan Davies. *M.*: Satie. *D.*: David Buckland.

Repertory:

Dealing with Shadows
Ch.: Richard Alston. *M.*: Mozart. *D.*: English Eccentrics.

Doubles
Ch.: Merce Cunningham. *M.*: Takehisa Kosugi. *D.*: Mark Lancaster.

Embarque
Ch.: Siobhan Davies. M.: Steve Reich. C.:
David Buckland.

Four Elements
Ch.: Lucinda Childs. M.: Gavin Bryars. D.:
Jennifer Bartlett.

Opal Loop
Ch.: Trisha Brown. D.: Judith Shea.

Roughcut
Ch.: Richard Alston. M.: Steve Reich. D.:
Tim Hatley.

Septet
Ch.: Merce Cunningham. M.: Erik Satie. D.:
Remy Charlip.

Signature
Ch.: Siobhan Davies. M.: Kevin Volans. D.:
Kate Whiteford.

Soda Lake
Ch.: Richard Alston. D.: Nigel Hall.

Sounding
Ch.: Soibhan Davies. M.: Giacinto Scelsi. D.:
Peter Mumford.

Wildlife
Ch.: Richard Alston. M.: Nigel Osborne. D.:
Richard Smith.

RICOCHET

Flat 4
84 Englefield Road
London N1 3LG
Tel: 071-226 7433

Artistic dir.: Kate Gowar, Karin Potisk

Administrative dir.: Carolyn Naish

Principal/associate choreographer(s): Ben
Craft

Visiting choreographer(s): Gill Clarke,
Russell Maliphant

Guest dancers: Ikky Maas, Christopher
Carney, Ben Craft, Anna Williams, Sarah
Barron

No. of dancers: 3 male, 4 female

No. of performances: c.30

Tours to: Germany, France, Austria,
Czechoslovakia, Holland, Israel

Pay rates: c. £200-300 per week

Premieres:

Trism 1/6/91, Alternative Arts Festival,
London
Ch.: Ben Craft. M.: Joy Division, Ben Craft.
C.: Ricochet. L.: Mark Galione.

Effeuillage 18/10/91, Théâtre Chatillon,
Paris
Ch.: Jean-Christophe Boclé. M.: M. Boclé. L.:
Jean-Christophe Boclé.

Imagine 7/11/91, Bloomsbury Theatre,
London
Ch.: Ben Craft. M.: Ben Craft. C.: Craig
Morrison, Tomoko. L.: Mark Galione.

Avatara 24/3/92, The Place Theatre, London
Ch.: Ron Howell. M.: Raga Malkoums,
Sultan Khan. D.: Alan Watkins. L.: Mark
Galione.

For Christ's Sake 24/3/92, The Place Theatre,
London
Ch.: Gill Clarke. M.: John Adams. D.: Gill
Clarke. S.: Julie McCluskey. C.: Kate Gowar.
L.: Mark Galione.

Morality ♀ 20/4/92, Suzanne Dellal Theatre,
Tel Aviv, Israel
Ch.: Ben Craft. M.: Karin Potisk. D.:
Ricochet. L.: Mark Galione.

Repertory:

Love
Ch.: Ben Craft. M.: Andrew MacKay. D.:
Mehdi Norowzian. C.: Kate Gowar. L.: Mark
Galione.

ROSEMARY BUTCHER DANCE
COMPANY

Independent Arts Administration
3 Gasholder Place
London SE11 5QR
Tel: 071 793 7090
Fax: 071 793 7373

Artistic dir.: Rosemary Butcher

Administrative dir.: Sarah Trist

Guest dancers: Michael Popper, Fin Walker,
Desirée Chemington, Sally Owen, Lizie
Saunderson, Marcus Grolle

No. of performances: 5

Pay rates: £194 per week

Premieres:

Of Shadows and Walls 10/91, Riverside
Studios, London
Ch.: Rosemary Butcher. *M.:* Jim Fulkerson.
L.: John Mark. *Film:* Nicola Baldwin.

THE ROYAL BALLET

Royal Opera House
Covent Garden
London WC2E 9DD
Tel: 071-240 1200
Fax: 071-497 9220

Artistic dir.: Anthony Dowell

Administrative dir.: Anthony Russell-
Roberts

Principal/associate choreographer(s): Sir
Kenneth MacMillan, David Bintley
(resident)

Principal dancers: Darcey Bussell, Fiona
Chadwick, Lesley Collier, Viviana Durante,
Sylvie Guillem (principal guest artist),
Karen Paisey, Stuart Cassidy, Robert Hill,
Stephen Jeffereis, Irek Mukhamedov,
Ashley Page, Errol Pickford, Bruce Sansom,
Mark Silver, Zoltan Solymosi

Guest dancers: Nina Ananiashvili, Altynai
Asylmuratova, Stephen Galloway, Laurent
Hilaire, Virginia Johnson, Kevin O'Hare,
Eddie J. Shellman, Judy Tyrus, Donald
Williams, Miyako Yoshida

No. of performances: 153

Tours to: Japan

Premieres:

In the middle, somewhat elevated
Ch.: William Forsythe. *M.:* Thom Willems.
D.: William Forsythe.

The Judas Tree
Ch.: Kenneth MacMillan. *M.:* Brian Elias. *D.:*
Jock McFayden.

La Luna
Ch.: Maurice Béjart. *M.:* Bach.

Present Histories
Ch.: William Tuckett. *M.:* Schubert. *S.:* Andy
Klunder. *C.:* Lucy Bevan.

Stoics
Ch.: Jonathan Burrows. *M.:* Mendelssohn.
D.: Craig Givens.

Stravinsky Violin Concerto
Ch.: Balanchine. *M.:* Stravinsky. *L.:* Ronald
Bates.

Symphony in C
Ch.: Balanchine. *M.:* Bizet. *C.:* Anthony
Dowell.

Repertory:

Agon
Ch.: Balanchine. *M.:* Stravinsky. *L.:* John B.
Read.

La Bayadère
Ch.: Natalia Makarova, after Petipa. *M.:*
Minkus, arr. Lanchbery. *S.:* Pier Luigi
Samaritani. *C.:* Yolanda Sonnabend.

Cyrano
Ch.: David Bintley. *M.:* Wilfred Josephs. *D.:*
Hayden Griffin. *L.:* John B. Read.

Elite Syncopations
Ch.: Kenneth MacMillan. *M.:* Scott Joplin
and others. *D.:* Ian Spurling.

La Fille mal gardée
Ch.: Ashton. *M.:* Hérold, arr. Lanchbery. *D.:*
Osbert Lancaster.

Giselle
Ch.: Petipa after Coralli/Perrot. *M.:* Adam.
D.: John MacFarlane.

Manon
Ch.: Kenneth MacMillan. *M.:* Massenet. *D.:*
Nicholas Georgiadis. *L.:* John B. Read.

Monotones II
Ch.: Ashton. *M.:* Erik Satie. *D.:* Ashton. *L.:*
William Bundy.

A Month in the Country
Ch.: Ashton. *M.:* Chopin, arr. Lanchbery. *D.:*
Julia Trevelyan Oman.

The Nutcracker
Ch.: Petipa/Ivanov. *M.:* Tchaikovsky. *L.:*
John B. Read.

Romeo and Juliet
Ch.: Kenneth MacMillan. *M.:* Prokofiev. *D.:*
Nicholas Georgiadis.

Scènes de ballet
Ch.: Ashton. *M.:* Stravinsky. *D.:* André
Beaurepaire.

Les Sylphides
Ch.: Fokine. *M.:* Chopin. *D.:* Benois.

Tchaikovsky Pas de Deux
Ch.: Balanchine. *M.:* Tchaikovsky. *D.:*
Anthony Dowell.

Thais Pas de Deux
Ch.: Ashton. *M.:* Massenet. *D.:* Anthony
Dowell.

Winter Dreams
Ch.: Kenneth MacMillan. *M.:* Tchaikovsky,
arr. Philip Gammon. *D.:* Peter Farmer. *L.:*
John B. Read.

SCOTTISH BALLET

261 West Princes Street
Glasgow G4 9EE
Tel: 041-331 2931
Fax: 041-331 2629

Artistic dir.: Galina Samsova

Administrative dir.: Peter Kyle

Principal/associate choreographer(s):
Robert North

Visiting choreographer(s): Jirí Kylián,
Amanda Miller, André Prokovsky

Guest teacher(s): Sulamit Messerer

Principal dancers: Galina Mezentseva,
Noriko Ohara, Linda Packer, Robert
Hampton, Vincent Hantam

No. of dancers: 22 male, 25 female

No. of performances: 311

Tours to: Russia, Ukraine

Premieres:

That Certain Feeling 25/1/92, Robin
Anderson Theatre, Glasgow
Ch.: André Prokovsky. *M.:* George
Gershwin. *D.:* Scottish Ballet.

Macbeth 28/5/92, Perth Theatre
Ch.: André Prokovsky. *M.:* David Earle. *D.:*
Robin Don. *L.:* George Thomson.

Wildlife One 28/5/92, Perth Theatre
Ch.: Neville Campbell. *M.:* Rhythm Street.
D.: Neville Campbell. *L.:* George Thomson.

Repertory:

Brief
Ch.: Amanda Miller. *M.:* J.S. Bach. *D.:*
Amanda Miller.

Cinderella
Ch.: Peter Darrell. *M.:* Rossini. *D.:* John
Fraser. *L.:* John B. Read.

Concerto Barocco
Ch.: Balanchine. *M.:* J.S. Bach.

Coppélia
Ch.: after Cechetti, Petipa. *M.:* Delibes. *D.:*
Peter Snow. *L.:* John Hall.

Esprit
Ch.: Paulo Lopes. *M.:* Edward McGuire. *D.:*
B.J. Ryan. *L.:* Grahame Gardner.

Five Brahms Waltzes in the Manner of Isadora
Duncan
Ch.: Frederick Ashton. *M.:* Brahms. *D.:*
David Dean. *L.:* John B. Read.

Forgotten Land
Ch.: Jirí Kylián. *M.:* Britten. *D.:* John
Macfarlane. *C.:* . *L.:* Joop Caboort.

Giselle
Ch.: Coralli/Perrot. *M.:* Adam. *D.:* Peter
Cazalet. *L.:* John B. Read.

Grad Pas
Ch.: Tiit Harm. *M.:* Massenet. *D.:* Tiit Harm.
L.: Colin Wolstencroft.

Jeux
Ch.: Peter Darrell. *M.:* Debussy. *D.:* Harry
Waistnage. *L.:* Ian Irving, Peter Darrell.

Laurencia
Ch.: Chabukiani/Galina Samsova. *M.:*
Alexander Krein, Ludwig Minkus. *D.:*
Norman McDowell.

Monotones
Ch.: Frederick Ashton. *M.:* Erik Satie. *D.:*
Frederick Ashton. *L.:* John B. Read.

Napoli Act III
Ch.: Bournonville. *M.:* Gade/Helsted/
Paulli/Lumbye. *L.:* John B. Read.

Nutcracker Acts II & III
Ch.: Ivanov/Darrell. *M.:* Tchaikovsky. *D.:*
Philip Prowse. *L.:* John B. Read.

Othello
Ch.: Peter Darrell. *M.:* Liszt. *D.:* Peter
Farmer.

Scarlatti and Friends
Ch.: André Prokovsky. *M.:* Alessandro and
Domenico Scarlatti, Nicolai Fiorenza. *D.:*
André Prokovsky.

Sea of Troubles
Ch.: Kenneth MacMillan. *M.:* Webern,
Martinu. *D.:* Deborah MacMillan. *L.:*
Richard Caswell.

Swan Lake
Ch.: Petipa/Ivanov/Darrell. *M.:*
Tchaikovsky. *D.:* Peter Cazalet. *L.:* John B.
Read.

Les Sylphides
Ch.: Fokine. *M.*: Chopin. *D.*: Peter Cazalet.
C.: Jane Etta Roberts.

Symphony in D
Ch.: Jirí Kylián. *M.*: Haydn. *D.*: Tom Schenk.
L.: Joop Caboort.

Troy Game
Ch.: Robert North. *M.*: Batucada/Bob
Downes. *D.*: Peter Farmer.

Vespri
Ch.: André Prokovsky. *M.*: Verdi. *D.*:
Norman McDowell. *L.*: Peter Searle.

Who Cares?
Ch.: Balanchine. *M.*: Gershwin. *D.*: Chas
Haines. *L.*: Grahame Gardner.

SECOND STRIDE

Sadler's Wells
Rosebery Avenue
London EC1R 4TN
Tel: 071-278 2917/6589
Fax: 071-278 5927

Artistic dir.: Ian Spink

Administrative dir.: Lucy Mason

Pay rates: c. £230 per week

Premieres:

4 Marys 12/2/92, Arnolfini, Bristol
Ch.: Ian Spink. *M.*: Peter Salen. *D.*: Neil
Irish. *L.*: John MacKinnon.

SHOBANA JEYASINGH DANCE COMPANY

The Place
17 Dukes Road
London WC1H 9AB
Tel: (071)-383 3252
Fax: (071)-383 4851

Artistic dir.: Shobana Jeyasingh

Administrative dir.: Penny Andrews

Visiting choreographer(s): Chandralekha

Principal dancers: Mira Balchandran-
Gokul, Kumari Nina, Vinata Godbole,
Monisha Patil-Bharadwaj, Vidya
Thirunarayan

No. of dancers: 5 female

No. of performances: 30

Tours to: Belgium, Holland

Pay rates: £216 per week

Premieres:

Byzantium 2/10/92, Bury St Edmunds
Ch.: Shobana Jeyasingh. *M.*: Christos Hatzis.
D.: Iona McLeish. *L.*: Mike Segnior.

Late 2/10/92, Bury St Edmunds
Ch.: Shobana Jeyasingh. *M.*: Orlando
Gough. *D.*: Iona McLeish. *L.*: Mike Segnior.

Speaking of Sakti 2/10/92, Bury St Edmunds
Ch.: Chandralekha. *M.*: Prof V.V.
Subrahmanyam. *C.*: Chandralekha. *L.*: Mike
Segnior.

SIOBHAN DAVIES DANCE COMPANY

190 Upper Street
London N1 1RQ
Tel: 071-226 6006
Fax: 071-359 5773

Artistic dir.: Siobhan Davies

Administrative dir.: Elizabeth Anderson

Principal/associate choreographer(s):
Siobhan Davies

Guest teacher(s): Jeremy Nelson, Scott Clark

Principal dancers: Gill Clarke, Paul
Douglas, Sean Feldman, Jeremy James,
Elizabeth Old, Deborah Saxon

No. of dancers: 3 male, 3 female

No. of performances: 8

Pay rates: £275 per week

Premieres:

White Bird Featherless 11/6/92, Theatr
Clwyd, Mold
Ch.: Siobhan Davies. *M.*: Gerald Barry. *S.*:
David Buckland. *C.*: Antony McDonald. *L.*:
Peter Mumford.

Repertory:

Wyoming
Ch.: Siobhan Davies. *M.*: John Marc
Gowans. *D.*: David Buckland. *L.*: Peter
Mumford.

YOLANDE SNAITH & DANCE QUORUM

49 de Montfort Road
Brighton BN2 3AW

Artistic dir.: Yolande Snaith

USA

AMERICAN BALLET THEATRE

890 Broadway
New York
NY 10003
Tel: (212) 477 3030
Fax: (212) 254 5938

Artistic dir.: Jane Hermann, Oliver Smith

Principal dancers: Victor Barbee, Julio Bocca, Gil Boggs, Leslie Browne, Fernando Bujones, Wes Chapman, Jeremy Collins, Christine Dunham, Guillaume Graffin, Cynthia Harvey, Susan Jaffe, Amanda McKerrow, Kathleen Moore, Michael Owen, Danilo Radojevic, Johan Renvall, Marianna Tcherkassky, Cheryl Yeager

Guest dancers: Steven Heathcote, Laurent Hilaire

No. of dancers: 76

Tours to: Greece, Denmark, Mexico

Premieres:

Grass 28/5/92, Metropolitan Opera House, New York
Ch.: Mats Ek. *M.:* Rachmaninov. *S.,C.:* Karin Ek. *L.:* Goran Westrup.

Jack and Jill 27/5/92, Metropolitan Opera House, New York
Ch.: John Selya. *M.:* Edwin Robertson, Charles Knox.

Moondance 30/1/92, Wiltern Theater, Los Angeles
Ch.: John Selya. *M.:* Moondog. *C.:* Gary Lisz. *L.:* Todd Elmer.

Peter and the Wolf 18/1/92, War Memorial Opera House, San Francisco
Ch.: Michael Smuin. *M.:* Prokofiev. *S.:* Tony Walton. *C.:* Willa Kim. *L.:* Natasha Katz. *Libretto:* Larry Gelbart.

Serious Pleasures 24/3/92 Civic Opera House, Chicago
Ch.: Ulysses Dove. *M.:* Robert Ruggieri. *S.,C.:* Jorge Gallardo. *L.:* William H. Grant III.

Symphonic Variations 20/3/92 Civic Opera House, Chicago
Ch.: Ashton. *M.:* Franck. *S.,C.:* Sophie Fedorovitch. *L.:* Michael Somes.

Repertory:

La Bayadère
Ch.: Natalia Makarova, after Petipa. *M.:* Minkus, arr. Lanchbery. *S.:* Pier Luigi Samaritani. *C.:* Theoni V. Aldredge. *L.:* Toshiro Ogawa.

Bruch Violin Concerto No. 1
Ch.: Clark Tippet. *M.:* Max Bruch. *C.:* Dain Marcus. *L.:* Jennifer Tipton

Fall River Legend
Ch.: Agnes de Mille. *M.:* Morton Gould. *S.:* Oliver Smith. *C.:* Miles White. *L.:* Thomas Skelton.

The Firebird
Ch.: after Fokine. *M.:* Stravinsky. *S.,C.:* Gontcharova. *L.:* Thomas Skelton

Giselle
Ch.: after Coralli/Perrot/Petipa. *M.:* Adam. *S.:* Gianni Quaranta. *C.:* Anna Anni. *L.:* Jennifer Tipton.

Other Dances
Ch.: Jerome Robbins. *M.:* Chopin. *C.:* Santo Loquasto. *L.:* Nananne Porcher.

Raymonda
Ch.: Fernando Bujones after Petipa. *M.:* Glazunov. *L.:* Todd Elmer.

Sinfonietta
Ch.: Jirí Kylián. *M.:* Janácek. *S.,C.:* Walter Nobbe. *L.:* Joop Caboort.

Swan Lake
Ch.: David Blair, after Ivanov. *M.:* Tchaikovsky. *S.:* Oliver Smith. *L.:* Jean Rosenthal.

Theme and Variations
Ch.: Balanchine. *M.:* Tchaikovsky. *C.:* Theoni V. Aldredge. *L.:* David K.H. Elliott.

Undertow
Ch.: Antony Tudor. *M.:* William Schuman. *S.,C.:* Raymond Breinin. *L.:* Jean Rosenthal.

BALLET CHICAGO

222 S. Riverside
Plaza #865
Chicago, IL 60606
Tel: 312/993 7575

Artistic dir.: Daniel Duell, Patricia Blair (assistant)

BOSTON BALLET

42 Vernon Street
Newton MA 02158
Tel: (617) 964-4070

Artistic dir.: Bruce Marks

DANCE THEATRE OF HARLEM

466 West 152nd Street
New York
NY 10031

Artistic dir.: Arthur Mitchell

GARTH FAGAN DANCE

50 Chestnut Street
Rochester
NY 14606
Tel: (716) 454-3260
Fax: (716) 454-6191

Artistic dir.: Garth Fagan

Administrative dir.: Cynthia Wassell

Principal/associate choreographer(s): Garth Fagan

Principal dancers: Steve Humphrey, Norwood Pennewell, Bit Knighton, Valentina Alexander, Natalie Rogers, Rebecca Gose, Chris Morrison, Sharon Skepple, Bill Ferguson, Lavert Benefield, Joel Valentin, Jeffrey Cox, Micha Willis, Danny Gwirtzman, Lazette Rayford

No. of dancers: 8 male, 7 female

No. of performances: 61

Tours to: Europe, Asia, Africa, South America, Australia

Premieres:

Repertory:

From Before
Ch.: Garth Fagan.

Griot New York
Ch.: Garth Fagan.

Landscape for 10
Ch.: Garth Fagan.

Mask Mix Masque
Ch.: Garth Fagan. *M.:* Grace Jones, Trevor Horn.

Mozhaps Mall
Ch.: Garth Fagan.

Never Top 40 (Juke Box)
Ch.: Garth Fagan.

Oakta Trail
Ch.: Garth Fagan. *M.:* Dvorák. *L.:* C.T. Oakes.

Passion Distanced
Ch.: Garth Fagan. *M.:* Arvo Pärt.

Sojourn
Ch.: Garth Fagan.

Sonata and the Afternoon
Ch.: Garth Fagan. *M.:* Brahms.

Telling a Story
Ch.: Garth Fagan. *M.:* Miles Davis.

Time After Before Place
Ch.: Garth Fagan. *M.:* Art Ensemble of Chicago.

Touring Jubilee 1924 (Professional)
Ch.: Garth Fagan. *M.:* Preservation Hall Jazz Band.

Traipsing Through the May
Ch.: Garth Fagan. *M.:* Vivaldi.

Until, By & If
Ch.: Garth Fagan.

JAN ERKERT AND DANCERS

2121 W Webster
Chicago, IL 60647
Tel: 312/252 60647

JOFFREY BALLET

130 West 56th Street
New York
NY 10019
Tel: (212) 265-7300

Artistic dir.: Gerald Arpino, Scott Bernard (assistant)

JOSEPH HOLMES CHICAGO DANCE THEATRE

1935 S Halstead
Chicago, IL
Tel: 312/942 0065

Artistic dir.: Randy Duncan

MARGARET JENKINS DANCE COMPANY

1182 Market Street, Suite 418
San Francisco
CA 94102

MARTHA GRAHAM DANCE COMPANY

316 East 63rd Street
New York, NY 1002
Tel: (212) 832-9166

MERCE CUNNINGHAM DANCE COMPANY

463 West Street
New York
NY 10014
Tel: (212) 255 8240

Artistic dir.: Merce Cunningham

MIAMI CITY BALLET

905 Lincoln Road
Miami Beach
FL 33139
Tel: (305) 532 4880

Artistic dir.: Edward Villella

MORDINE & COMPANY

Dance Centre of Columbia College
4730 N Sheridan
Chicago IL 60640
Tel: 312/271 7804

Artistic dir.: Shirley Mordine

Administrative dir.: Michael McStraw

MUNTU DANCE THEATRE

6800 S. Wentworth
Rm 3E96
Chicago IL 60621
Tel: 312/602 1135

Artistic dir.: Amaniyea Payne

Administrative dir.: Joan Gray

NEW YORK CITY BALLET

New York State Theatre
Lincoln Centre Plaza
New York
NY 10023
Tel: (212) 870 5500

Artistic dir.: Peter Martins

OAKLAND BALLET

Paramount Theatre
2025 Broadway
Oakland, CA 94612
Tel: 510/452-9288
Fax: 510/452-9557

Artistic dir.: Ronn Guido

Administrative dir.: Laird Rodet

Visiting choreographer(s): Frederic Franklin, David McNaughton, Sallie Wilson, Lyn Vella-Gatt, Viveka Ljung, Val Caniparoli, Tomm Ruud, Margaret Jenkins, Ellie Klopp, Betsy Erickson

No. of dancers: 18 male, 19 female

No. of performances: 68

Premieres:

Sightings 5/10/91, Paramount Theater, Oakland
Ch.: Margaret Jenkins, Ellie Klopp. *M.:* Peter Sculthorpe. *C.:* Sandra Woodall. *L.:* Jack Carpenter.

Echoing of Trumpets 25/10/91, Zellenbach Hall, Berkeley
Ch.: Antony Tudor. *M.:* Martinu. *D.:* Birger Bergling. *L.:* Robert Klemm.

PACIFIC NORTHWEST BALLET

4649 Sunnyside Avnue North
Seattle, WA 98103

Artistic dir.: Kent Stowell, Francia Russell

PAUL TAYLOR DANCE COMPANY

552 Broadway
New York, NY 0012

Artistic dir.: Paul Taylor

REMY CHARLIP

60 East 7th Street
New York, NY 10003
SAN FRANCISCO BALLET

455 Franklin Street
San Francisco
CA 94102
Tel: (415) 861 5600

Artistic dir.: Helgi Tomasson

No. of dancers: 25 male, 43 female

Premieres:

Aurora Polaris 16/4/91, San Francisco
Ch.: Helgi Tomasson. *M.:* J.S. Bach. *D.:* Santo Loquasto. *L.:* David Finn.

Bugaku 18/4/91, San Francisco
Ch.: Balanchine. *M.:* Mayuzumi. *S.:* David Hays. *C.:* Karinska. *L.:* Ronald Bates.

'Haffner' Symphony 25/6/91, San Francsico
Ch.: Helgi Tomasson. *M.:* Mozart. *S.,C.:*
Santo Loquasto. *L.:* Thomas R. Skelton.

Meistens Mozart 25/6/91, San Francisco
Ch.: Helgi Tomassson. *M.:* Mozart, Haibl,
Flies, von Dittersdorf. *L.:* Thomas R.
Skelton.

Tryst 25/6/91, San Francisco
Ch.: Val Caniparoli. *M.:* Mozart. *S.:* Sandra
Woodall. *L.:* Lisa Pinkham.

Forever More 5/2/92, San Francisco
Ch.: Helgi Tomasson. *M.:* Dvorák. *C.:*
Michael Casey. *L.:* Lisa J. Pinkham.

Two Plus Two 5/2/92, San Francisco
Ch.: Helgi Tomasson. *M.:* Rossini. *C.:*
Barbara Matera. *L.:* Lisa J. Pinkham.

Le Quattro Satgioni (The Four Seasons)
13/2/92, San Francisco
Ch.: Helgi Tomasson. *M.:* Vivalid. *S.,C.:*
Santo Loquasto. *L.:* Jennifer Tipton.

Who Cares? 18/2/92, San Francisco
Ch.: Balanchine. *M.:* Gershwin. *C.:* after
Karinska. *L.:* Ronald Bates.

Beads of Memory 17/3/92, San Francisco
Ch.: Helgi Tomasson. *M.:* Tchaikovsky.

Job 17/3/92, San Francisco
Ch.: David Bintley. *M.:* Vaughan Williams.
S.,C.: Hayden Griffin. *L.:* Andy Phillips.

The End 14/4/92, San Francisco
Ch.: James Kudelka. *M.:* Brahms. *S.,C.:* Santo
Loquasto. *L.:* Nicholas Cernovitch.

Repertory:

Agon
Ch.: Balanchine. *M.:* Stravinsky.

Air de Ballet
Ch.: Lew Christensen. *M.:* Andrée Gretry.
C.: Robert O'Hearn. *L.:* Sara Linnie Slocum.

Ballo della Regina
Ch.: Balanchine. *M.:* Verdi. *C.:* Ben Benson.
L.: Ronald Bates.

The Comfort Zone
Ch.: James Kudelka. *M.:* Beethoven. *C.:*
Santo Loquasto. *L.:* Nicholas Cernovitch.

Connotations
Ch.: Val Caniparoli. *M.:* Britten. *C.:* Sandra
Woodall. *L.:* Sara Linnie Slocum.

Dark Elegies
Ch.: Antony Tudor. *M.:* Mahler. *D.:* after
Nadia Benois.

La Fille mal gardée
Ch.: Frederick Ashton. *M.:* Herold. *D.:*
Osbert Lancaster. *L.:* David K.H. Elliott.

Flower Festival in Genzano
Ch.: Bournonville. *M.:* Paulli, Helsted.

Harvest Moon
Ch.: Lisa de Ribere. *M.:* Big Band Sounds. *S.:*
Robin Wagner. *C.:* Theoni V. Aldredge. *L.:*
Nicholas Cernovitch.

Napoli - Divertissments
Ch.: Bournonville. *M.:* Paulli, Helsted.

New Sleep
Ch.: William Forsythe. *M.:* Thom Willems.
S.,L.: William Forsythe.

Nutcracker
Ch.: Helgi Tomasson, Lew Christensen. *M.:*
Tchaikovsky. *S.,C.:* José Varona. *L.:* David
K.H. Elliott.

Pulcinella
Ch.: Val Caniparoli. *M.:* Stravinsky. *S.,C.:*
Nadine Baylis. *L.:* Sara Linnie Slocum.

Rubies
Ch.: Balanchine. *M.:* Stravinsky. *S.:* Peter
Harvey. *C.:* Karinska. *L.:* Ronald Bates.

Serenade
Ch.: Balanchine. *M.:* Tchaikovsky. *C.:* after
Karinska. *L.:* Ronald Bates.

The Sleeping Beauty (Act III)
Ch.: Helgi Tomasson, after Petipa. *M.:*
Tchaikovsky. *S.,C.:* Jens-Jacob Worsaae. *L.:*
Craig Miller.

The Sons of Horus
Ch.: David Bintley. *M.:* Peter McGowan.
S.,C.: Terry Bartlett. *L.:* John B. Read.

Swan Lake
Ch.: Tomasson, after Petipa/Ivanov. *M.:*
Tchaikovsky. *S.,C.:* Jens-Jacob Worsaae. *L.:*
David K.H. Elliott.

Theme and Vatiations
Ch.: Balanchine. *M.:* Tchaikovsky. *C.:* Nicola
Benois. *L.:* Daivd K.H. Elliott.

Valses Poeticos
Ch.: Helgi Tomasson. *M.:* Granados. *C.:*
Theoni V. Aldredge. *L.:* Nicholas
Cernovitch.

SARASOTA BALLET

PO Box 49094
Sarasota
FL 34230
Tel: 813 954 7171
Fax: 813 951 0047

Artistic dir.: Eddy Toussaint

Repertory:

Alexis le Trotteur
Ch.: Eddy Toussaint. M.: Dominique Tremblay. C.: Sylvain Labelle. L.: Peter Giorgiev.

All Chers Couples
Ch.: Eddy Toussaint. M.: Frederic Methe. C.: Sylvain Labelle. L.: Marty Petlock.

Bonjour Brel
Ch.: Eddy Toussaint. M.: Jacques Brel. S.,L.: Peter Giorgiev. C.: Sylvain Labelle.

Cantates
Ch.: Eddy Toussaint. M.: J.S. Bach. C.: Sylvain Labelle. L.: Peter Giorgiev.

Concerto pour Sophie
Ch.: Eddy Toussaint. M.: Max Bruch. C.: Sylvain Labelle. L.: Peter Giorgiev.

Florida Suite
Ch.: Eddy Toussaint. M.: Delius. C.: Dixie Rick. L.: Marty Petlock.

Luna Zao
Ch.: Eddy Toussaint. M.: Haitian folk music. C.: Sylvain Labelle. L.: Marty Petlock.

Miraculous Mandarin
Ch.: Jean Garcia. M.: Bartók. C.: Sylvain Labelle. L.: Marty Petlock.

TRISHA BROWN COMPANY

225 Lafayette Street
Suite 807
New York, NY 10012

Tel: 212-334-9374
Fax: 212-334-9438

Artistic dir.: Trisha Brown

Administrative dir.: Susan Fait-Meyers

Principal/associate choreographer(s):
Trisha Brown

Principal dancers: Trisha Brown, Nicole Juralewicz, Kevin Kortan, Gregory Lara, Carolyn Lucas, Diane Madden, Kelly McDonald, Trish Oesterling, Wil Swanson, David H. Thompson

No. of dancers: 4 male, 6 female

No. of performances: 39

Premieres:

For M.G The Movie 8/11/91, Douai, France
Ch.: Trisha Brown. M.: Alvin Curran. L.: Spencer Brown.

One Story as in Falling 25/6/92, Montpellier
Ch.: Trisha Brown. M.: Alvin Curran. D.: Roland Aeschlimann. L.: Spencer Brown.

TULSA BALLET THEATRE

4512 S. Peoria
Tulsa, OK 74105-4563
Tel: (918) 749-6030
Fax: (918) 749-0532

Artistic dir.: Moscelyne Larkin

Administrative dir.: Connie Conley

Visiting choreographer(s): Anne-Marie Holmes, Alun Jones

Guest teachers: Frederic Franklin, Irina Nijinska, Howard Sayette, Larry Long

Principal dancers: Kimberly Smiley

Guest dancers: Aleksandr Lunev

No. of dancers: 12 male, 18 female

No. of performances: 100